Santería, Vodou and Resistance in Caribbean Literature
Daughters of the Spirits

LEGENDA

LEGENDA is the Modern Humanities Research Association's book imprint for new research in the Humanities. Founded in 1995 by Malcolm Bowie and others within the University of Oxford, Legenda has always been a collaborative publishing enterprise, directly governed by scholars. The Modern Humanities Research Association (MHRA) joined this collaboration in 1998, became half-owner in 2004, in partnership with Maney Publishing and then Routledge, and has since 2016 been sole owner. Titles range from medieval texts to contemporary cinema and form a widely comparative view of the modern humanities, including works on Arabic, Catalan, English, French, German, Greek, Italian, Portuguese, Russian, Spanish, and Yiddish literature. Editorial boards and committees of more than 60 leading academic specialists work in collaboration with bodies such as the Society for French Studies, the British Comparative Literature Association and the Association of Hispanists of Great Britain & Ireland.

The MHRA encourages and promotes advanced study and research in the field of the modern humanities, especially modern European languages and literature, including English, and also cinema. It aims to break down the barriers between scholars working in different disciplines and to maintain the unity of humanistic scholarship. The Association fulfils this purpose through the publication of journals, bibliographies, monographs, critical editions, and the MHRA Style Guide, and by making grants in support of research. Membership is open to all who work in the Humanities, whether independent or in a University post, and the participation of younger colleagues entering the field is especially welcomed.

ALSO PUBLISHED BY THE ASSOCIATION

Critical Texts
Tudor and Stuart Translations • *New Translations* • *European Translations*
MHRA Library of Medieval Welsh Literature

MHRA Bibliographies
Publications of the Modern Humanities Research Association

The Annual Bibliography of English Language & Literature
Austrian Studies
Modern Language Review
Portuguese Studies
The Slavonic and East European Review
Working Papers in the Humanities
The Yearbook of English Studies

www.mhra.org.uk
www.legendabooks.com

STUDIES IN HISPANIC AND LUSOPHONE CULTURES

Studies in Hispanic and Lusophone Cultures are selected and edited by the Association of Hispanists of Great Britain & Ireland. The series seeks to publish the best new research in all areas of the literature, thought, history, culture, film, and languages of Spain, Spanish America, and the Portuguese-speaking world.

The Association of Hispanists of Great Britain & Ireland is a professional association which represents a very diverse discipline, in terms of both geographical coverage and objects of study. Its website showcases new work by members, and publicises jobs, conferences and grants in the field.

www.legendabooks.com/series/shlc

STUDIES IN HISPANIC AND LUSOPHONE CULTURES

1. *Unamuno's Theory of the Novel*, by C. A. Longhurst
2. *Pessoa's Geometry of the Abyss: Modernity and the* Book of Disquiet, by Paulo de Medeiros
3. *Artifice and Invention in the Spanish Golden Age*, edited by Stephen Boyd and Terence O'Reilly
4. *The Latin American Short Story at its Limits: Fragmentation, Hybridity and Intermediality*, by Lucy Bell
5. *Spanish New York Narratives 1898–1936: Modernisation, Otherness and Nation*, by David Miranda-Barreiro
6. *The Art of Ana Clavel: Ghosts, Urinals, Dolls, Shadows and Outlaw Desires*, by Jane Elizabeth Lavery
7. *Alejo Carpentier and the Musical Text*, by Katia Chornik
8. *Britain, Spain and the Treaty of Utrecht 1713-2013*, edited by Trevor J. Dadson and J. H. Elliott
9. *Books and Periodicals in Brazil 1768-1930: A Transatlantic Perspective*, edited by Ana Cláudia Suriani da Silva and Sandra Guardini Vasconcelos
10. *Lisbon Revisited: Urban Masculinities in Twentieth-Century Portuguese Fiction*, by Rhian Atkin
11. *Urban Space, Identity and Postmodernity in 1980s Spain: Rethinking the Movida*, by Maite Usoz de la Fuente
12. *Santería, Vodou and Resistance in Caribbean Literature: Daughters of the Spirits*, by Paul Humphrey
13. *Reprojecting the City: Urban Space and Dissident Sexualities in Recent Latin American Cinema*, by Benedict Hoff
14. *Rethinking Juan Rulfo's Creative World: Prose, Photography, Film*, edited by Dylan Brennan and Nuala Finnegan
15. *The Last Days of Humanism: A Reappraisal of Quevedo's Thought*, by Alfonso Rey
16. *Catalan Narrative 1875-2015*, edited by Jordi Larios and Montserrat Lunati
17. *Islamic Culture in Spain to 1614: Essays and Studies*, by L. P. Harvey
18. *Film Festivals: Cinema and Cultural Exchange*, by Mar Diestro-Dópido
19. *St Teresa of Avila: Her Writings and Life*, edited by Terence O'Reilly, Colin Thompson and Lesley Twomey
20. *(Un)veiling Bodies: A Trajectory of Chilean Post-Dictatorship Documentary*, by Elizabeth Ramírez Soto

Santería, Vodou and Resistance in Caribbean Literature

Daughters of the Spirits

PAUL HUMPHREY

LEGENDA

Studies in Hispanic and Lusophone Cultures 12
Modern Humanities Research Association
2019

Published by Legenda
an imprint of the Modern Humanities Research Association
Salisbury House, Station Road, Cambridge CB1 2LA

ISBN 978-1-78188-702-8

First published 2019

Copy-Editor: Charlotte Brown

CONTENTS

	Acknowledgements	ix
	Note on Translations and Spelling	x
	Introduction	1
1	Intersections of Religion, Resistance and Gender in Caribbean Narratives	11
2	Staging Subversion: Santería, Performance and Corporeality	43
3	Women, Haitian Vodou and Reconstitution of the Self	76
4	Destructive Masculinity, Vodou and the State	105
5	Until Death...: Sexuality, Death and the Sacred	141
	Conclusion	159
	Bibliography	171
	Index	189

ACKNOWLEDGEMENTS

This book is based on my doctoral thesis completed at the University of Birmingham, for which I was awarded one of the Association of Hispanists of Great Britain and Ireland (AHGBI)-Spanish Embassy Postgraduate Publication Prizes in 2013. I would like to thank the AHGBI, the Embassy of Spain in London and the editorial board at Legenda for their support of this award. I would also like to thank my viva examiners, Professor Lizabeth Paravisini-Gebert and Dr Stewart Brown, who supported my candidacy and offered their guidance.

This project could not have been completed without the generosity of people and institutions both in the UK and abroad. The Sir Henry Thomas Junior Fellowship, awarded by the Department of Modern Languages at the University of Birmingham, enabled me to begin my doctoral studies, followed by the College of Arts and Law Scholarship and Student Development Scholarships also from the University of Birmingham, which provided me with the means to complete them. A special thanks to my supervisor, Dr Conrad James, for his unwavering support and encouragement throughout the different stages of the process, and to colleagues at Colgate, Syracuse and Monmouth Universities for their assistance and advice as this manuscript took its final shape.

In Cuba, thanks go to: Magaly Hernández, the late Lalita Martiatu, Roberto Zurbano, Arsenio Castillo, Tato Quiñones, Lázara Menéndez, Tomás Fernández Robaina and América Centeno Tamayo Omoyemayá — you all took me under your wing and pointed me in many new directions. In Haiti, Manbo Mireille Aïn, Italy, Pascale Jaunay and Viviane Nicolas, for your generous hospitality and invaluable insight; the late Max Beauvoir, for your words of encouragement; Manbo Yaya and family, for opening your doors to me and introducing me to Vodou practice in the North. I would also like to thank Manbo Maude Evans and family in Boston for welcoming me into your home, leading to so many fruitful conversations and exchanges between the many of us who cross your threshold; Manbo Jacqueline Épingle in Montreal, for your time and generosity; and the librarians at the Montreal-based Centre International de Documentation et d'Information Haïtienne, Caribéenne et Afro-canadienne, for your patience and kind assistance.

Finally, I would like to thank my family, especially my parents, who encouraged me to begin this journey, and Danny, who has been a great support throughout. An earlier version of Chapter 4 was published as 'Of Sound, Mind and Body: Female Sexuality and Vodou in Kettly Mars' *Fado*', *International Journal of Francophone Studies*, 17.2 (2014): 137–57. I am grateful to Intellect for their permission to include this material.

P.H., December 2018

NOTE ON TRANSLATIONS AND SPELLING

Unless otherwise indicated (such as when a published translation exists), all translations into English are my own. The spelling of terms in Haitian Kreyòl conforms to official established norms, unless an accepted alternative spelling of a key term exists which is more commonly used in studies of Haiti and Haitian culture. Notable examples in this manuscript are: *Macoutes* (official spelling, *Makout*), the name given to François Duvalier's militia; and Baron Samedi (official spelling, *Bawon Samdi*), one of the Vodou Gede spirits. Similarly, for ease of comprehension by the reader, place names in Haiti will be rendered in their French spelling — the form in which they are more widely known outside Haiti — rather than in Kreyòl (for example, Port-au-Prince instead of Pòtoprens and Bois Caïman instead of Bwa Kayiman).

INTRODUCTION

Dominican author Rita Indiana opens her 2015 novel, *La mucama de Omicunlé* [Omicunlé's Servant], with a series of references to the sea.[1] Citing as her epigraph the second stanza of Ariel's song from Shakespeare's *The Tempest* — 'Full fathom five thy father lies, Of his bones are coral made' — Indiana signals the destruction that has been wrought and introduces the 'sea-nymphs' who will carry out the necessary 'sea-change' her novel depicts. Turning the page, the title to her first chapter, 'Olokun', invokes one of the Santería *orisha* (spirits) of the sea, a powerful androgynous spirit, part woman/man, part fish, thus a 'sea-nymph' to employ the Shakespearian term.[2] The reader is then invited into the text via a doorbell programmed to sound like a wave, abruptly arriving in the technologically advanced future where images from security cameras are beamed directly into the observers' eyes and those Haitians escaping the quarantine on the western side of the island of Hispaniola are scanned for the 'virus' and, if carriers, killed on the spot by an automatic jet of lethal gas. As these opening lines suggest, Indiana's novel then proceeds to challenge many of the divisions — religious, epistemological, gender-based and racial, to name but a few — that have characterized Caribbean societies.

Situating her narrative in a space the islands of the Antilles share, that of the sea, the novelist recognizes from the outset the multiple meanings carried by these bodies of water, not least their importance within African-derived religions in the Caribbean. As the means by which Santería and Vodou spirits travelled to the Caribbean and the residence of particular *orisha* such as Olokún and Yemayá, or in Vodou the *lwa* Ezili Dantò and Lasirèn, the 'tibio mar de las Antillas' [warm sea of the Antilles] (to use Arcadio Díaz-Quiñones's words) is also the tomb of those who perished in the Atlantic slave trade, and continues to claim more victims from among those who have come to be known by the disparaging term boat people.[3] In her anthology of the same name, Puerto Rican author Mayra Santos-Febres encapsulates the polysemy of the dangerous yet welcoming space of the sea in her poem 'aqui al fondo danzan concejales' [here at the bottom councillors dance]. She writes:

> aqui al fondo danzan concejales —
> ahogados todos del Caribe
> emisarios
> de las naciones del pasaje intermedio:
> delegados de Costa de Marfil,
> ciboneyes todavía suicidándose en rituales de mar
> disidentes de Trujillo, de Batista, Duvalier (Santos-Febres 2005: 47)

> [here at the bottom councillors dance —
> all drowned, all from the Caribbean
> emissaries
> from the nations of the middle passage:
> delegates from the Ivory Coast,
> ciboneys still committing suicide in sea rituals
> dissidents from Trujillo, from Batista, Duvalier]

The sea is a site for 'coumbites' (cooperative work teams in rural Haiti), for sirens — and the *orisha* or *lwa* they embody — who entreat those on the surface to join them in the depths; and, by extension of Santos-Febres's use of the term *concejal*, it is the home of the Vodou spirits of the dead, the Gede, with their governmental structure (see Chapter 4 for further discussion).[4] Returning to *La mucama de Omicunlé*, the framework that Indiana constructs from aspects of Santería, Vodou, Gagá and other Caribbean religious practices offers her protagonist the opportunity to traverse divisions both in time and within the politics of gender, sexual and national identities in an attempt to avoid the destruction of the marine environment in the narrative present. Framing her novel thus, it is only by recognizing the region's diversity, religious and otherwise, contained in and represented by its waters that the future environmental disaster will ultimately be averted.

As an integral part of Caribbean culture and society, African-derived religious practices are expressed in numerous ways in everyday life, both in public and private. This book explores their presence in a number of Caribbean literary and theatrical texts, examining the participation in religious, social and political life of *santeros* and *vodouyizan* (practitioners of Santería and Vodou respectively), as well as adherents of associated religious traditions such as Cuban Abakuá, Sino-Cuban Sanfancón and Dominican Gagá. As I have demonstrated elsewhere in reference to four of Cuban-Puerto Rican author Mayra Montero's novels, *La trenza de la hermosa luna* (1987) [The Braid of the Beautiful Moon], *Del rojo de su sombra* (1992) (*The Red of His Shadow*, 2002), *Tú, la oscuridad* (1995) (*You, Darkness*, 1997) and *Como un mensajero tuyo* (1998) (*The Messenger*, 2000), African-derived religions that are practised across the Caribbean constitute a framework which can be used to draw together dynamic and unique cultural contexts from across the region, transcending to a certain extent the linguistic and political divisions that have been forced upon it.[5] Set for the most part in Haiti, the Dominican Republic and Cuba, on the one hand these novels echo postcolonial theorists such as Frantz Fanon, Édouard Glissant and Antonio Benítez Rojo who have sought to emphasize ties across the region; on the other, they contribute to the discourse of 'unity in diversity', engendered through recognizing difference rather than attempting to remove it.[6] Like Indiana, Montero situates her narrative within the context of African-derived religions, forging connections across borders and between islands without negating difference or reducing the various rites and practices into a single, homogeneous whole.

Santería and Vodou are arguably among the most widely known African-derived religions practised in the Caribbean, not only for the number of practitioners in Cuba, Haiti, the wider Caribbean and their diasporas, but also due to the way in which they have been depicted in overwhelmingly disparaging and stereotypical terms through film and print media. This has particularly been the case for Haitian Vodou, which became distorted as a long-standing trope in Hollywood films, comic books and fiction that saw 'Voodoo' doctors fashion dolls to inflict pain, turn unsuspecting bystanders into zombies and strike fear into the hearts of viewers and readers alike.[7] Such reductive descriptions of Santería and Vodou have not been the sole preserve of European and North American outlets, however: in Cuba and Haiti, terms such as witchcraft or pagan superstition, animism and simply folklore have often been used to denigrate these religions and their practitioners. Yet, as explored in Chapter 1 and throughout this book, for *santeros*, *vodouyizan* and many scholars of these religions, Santería and Vodou are living systems in which the realities of the transatlantic slave trade and colonialism, creolization in its numerous forms, hybridity and associated identity politics, and the circumstances and complexities of the postcolonial Caribbean all intersect.

As products of the various processes of creolization in the region, these religions comprise elements from a range of religious traditions and worldviews, including but not limited to indigenous rites and practices, rituals and spiritual entities that travelled with enslaved peoples transported from Africa to the Caribbean, and Catholic and Protestant practices and traditions. Indeed, the term Santería — used to denote the religion of Regla de Ocha — highlights just one aspect of this religious system: the historical association between the *orisha* and certain Catholic saints, and thus the popular use in some circumstances of the word *santos* to refer to both the *orisha* and their Catholic counterparts.[8] Vodou, for its part, saw the association between *lwa* and Catholic saints too, although the use of Catholic iconography such as chromolithographs or similar depictions of the saints to represent the *lwa*, while extant, is less prevalent in contemporary practice. As Marguerite Fernández Olmos and Lizabeth Paravisini-Gebert outline in the introduction to *Creole Religions of the Caribbean*, there exist a number of similarities between African-derived religions practised in the region and its diasporas, not least that at their core 'is a belief in a unique Supreme Being — creator of the universe', complemented by the pantheon of spirits 'who are emanations of the Creator and who serve as intermediaries between mankind and the supreme god'.[9] These *orisha* and *lwa*, in the cases of Santería and Vodou, manifest themselves through a number of practices and rituals, which include divination, spiritual possession, sacrifice and healing, while ceremonies strengthen 'the conscious sense of community' among practitioners through these practices, music and dance.[10] Necessarily 'creole' in their development, Santería and Vodou are religious systems that are not just the sum of the parts from which they derive, but rather the products of a unique set of historical, political and cultural processes in Cuba, Haiti and the other places in which they are practised.[11] Moreover, they are dynamic systems that continue to develop and respond to the circumstances of the postcolonial Caribbean. As such, in this book they serve as sites of inquiry that permit the exploration of such overlapping notions as religious practice, gender, sexual and identity politics in both sacred and secular contexts and the representation of postcolonial realities of the Caribbean through embodied ritual performance. In this vein, given the links that exist between these African-derived religions due to the manner in which they have developed and their migration with practitioners, they serve as interwoven frameworks through which to view the larger region.

To this end, recognizing the close connections that exist across the region and through its diasporas while resisting the negation of difference has been a concern of authors and scholars working throughout the Caribbean, particularly so in reference to notions of creolization, *mestizaje* and *métissage*, hybridity and postcolonial identities. Puerto Rican author Ana Lydia Vega's short story 'Encancaranublado' (1982) ('Cloud Cover Caribbean', 1990) serves as a pithy reminder of the complexity of the Caribbean when viewed from within, as temporary alliances and conflicts surface between a Haitian, a Dominican and a Cuban — each fiercely proud of their individuality — in their quest to reach Miami in a small boat. Any notions the three men entertain of individual pride based on national origin or a hierarchy among their respective countries are nullified in one fell swoop when, having capsized and been rescued during a storm by a passing American ship, the captain, 'Aryan and Apollo-like' (Vega 1990: 110), instructs his crew, '*Get those niggers down there and let the spiks take care of 'em*' (Vega 1982: 17). Taken down to the ship's hold, the refugees are, in Elizabeth DeLoughrey's words, 'interpellat[ed] into the colonial hierarchies of race ("niggers") and language ("spiks")' by the captain, who 'homogenizes these diverse Caribbean migrants under the rubric of exploited labor'.[12] The result is that, from the captain's perspective, the Haitian, Dominican and Cuban form a single, undifferentiated group, which is then subsumed by his larger, equally 'homogeneous' crew, at least one of whom is Puerto Rican.

As her short story develops, Vega highlights the diverse religious beliefs held by her three protagonists. The Haitian describes the rocking boat with an image from a Vodou ceremony, 'el bote se remeneaba más que caderas de mambó en servicio a Dambalá' (16) [the boat was rocking more than a *manbo*'s (female Vodou priest's) hips in a Dambala ceremony], invoking the wise serpent *lwa* of Haitian Vodou. Later, the narrator ascribes the trio's rescue to 'un milagro conjunto de la Altagracia, la Caridad del Cobre y las Siete Ponencias Africanas' [a joint miracle of the Virgin Mary of Altagracia, Our Lady of Charity of El Cobre and the Seven African Powers], drawing together the protective Virgins of the Dominican Republic and Cuba respectively, along with a grouping of *orisha* in recognition of the African-derived religious traditions of the Caribbean. Indeed, 'Encancaranublado' is a modern-day, Antillean rendering of the myth of Caridad del Cobre's appearance in the waters surrounding Cuba, in which, as the story goes, the Virgin — herself associated with the *orisha* Ochún — appears to three men in a boat who represent the indigenous, black and creole peoples of colonial Cuba. Vega's reference to these *orisha* and *lwa* alongside the named Catholic Virgins underlines the diverse religious heritage of the region, contrasting the African-derived spirits with the captain's 'Aryan' features. In spite of the latter's imposition of a fixed white-black racial binary, thus differentiating solely along the lines of self and other, the invocation of the rescued trio's multiple religious patrons serves to resist this attempt at homogenization.

Such an account of practitioners of African-derived religions in the Caribbean calling on Catholic figures of protection and mercy not only underscores the diversity of religious practice, but also the notion that, for many *santeros* and *vodouyizan*, these religions and Catholicism are perceived as mutually dependent rather than necessarily contradictory religious systems. For many adherents, practising Santería or Vodou does not preclude participation in or espousal of other religious practices, be they Christian or other African-derived traditions such as Cuban Abakuá or Palo Monte.[13] Such a worldview serves to strengthen the complex framework of religious belief and practice that connects the Caribbean region, while the reiteration of plurality within an interconnected network of religious practices and ritual performance also allows for the celebration of difference rather than the negation of this very concept. As religions of resistance, Santería, Vodou and associated traditions have a long history of acting on the margins of society. This has been the case during periods of prohibition that forced practitioners further into the periphery, or indeed of appropriation and/or secularization by the state, which saw practices folklorized or their ritual meaning co-opted in order to present a mediated version of African-descended identity that supported a state-sanctioned national discourse. In spite of such attempts at marginalization and circumscription, Santería and Vodou remained a repository for African-derived and -oriented religious worldviews that continued the culture of resistance they exemplified during periods of colonial oppression, revolution and economic and cultural isolation. As often occurs, such events occasioned the movement of people across the region and in the diaspora, thus seeing the geographical reach of the interconnected network of African-derived religions in the Caribbean increase. This in turn provided new spaces for resistance outside the physical boundaries of the region as well as opportunities for co-existence or indeed interaction between them. It is this established notion that Santería, Vodou and associated African-derived practices constitute interconnected sites of resistance that this book employs as its premise, to then explore this theme alongside the key concepts of gender and female participation, sexuality, patriarchy and power in the texts examined over the course of the following chapters.

In Chapter 1, I set out the theoretical framework for the subsequent literary analysis and examine the intersections of religion, resistance and gender in Caribbean scholarship and fiction. The chapter explores in greater detail the designation of Santería and Vodou as religions of resistance, and briefly considers the manner in which these and associated religious traditions developed, as well as their roles in Cuban and Haitian society. Throughout, I use Montero's above-cited novels as key texts in which to situate the discussion, introducing the key *orisha* and *lwa* that are central to the discussion in the chapters that follow and identifying the numerous ways in which Montero's protagonists embody and represent their associated spirits. Further, with regard to ritual and performance, the analysis brings together scholarship on the process of spirit possession and gender performance, before examining the position of women within Santería and Vodou, together with the possibilities for participation and potential for agency they offer. Finally, in weaving these elements together, it explores how Montero challenges gender and racial hierarchies in the Caribbean, as well as her process of rewriting in order to undermine the hegemonic practices of historiography that accompany these systems.

Within this framework, Chapter 2 turns to Cuban theatre and Eugenio Hernández Espinosa's seminal work, *María Antonia*. Written in 1964 and first performed in 1967, the play has been staged numerous times in Cuba and abroad, with Hernández Espinosa returning to direct this his most famous work in April 2011 at the Teatro Mella in Havana. *María Antonia* sees its eponymous protagonist — daughter of Ochún — tell her story at the point at which she has been claimed by Ikú (death), and depicts her problematic relationships with both Santería and the religious community that practises it. Drawing on the *pataki* (myths recounting the relationships between the *orisha*) that describe the interactions between Ochún, Yemayá and Changó, the play shows María Antonia's violent rejection of societal and religious impositions placed on her — exemplified by her murder of Julián, the lover who has rejected her — and culminates in María Antonia's own death at the hands of Carlos, a lover she has herself spurned. The reading outlined focuses on the subversion of patriarchal frameworks both in Santería and in wider Cuban society, and explores the representation of these constructs in the play and the complexities inherent in María Antonia and her *madrina*'s negotiation of them.[14] By employing theoretical frameworks proposed by scholars such as Catherine Bell, Richard Schechner and Judith Butler with regard to ritual performance, spirit possession and gender performance, the analysis demonstrates the protagonist's limited success in her destabilization of male-oriented societal norms. Namely, although María Antonia's death indicates the punitive nature of Santería in this context and the violent masculinities to which she is subjected in the play, the corporeal and often gendered nature of ritual performance in Santería enables her to, in some respects, maintain a position of resistance, while her actions in both religious and secular contexts permit María Antonia to a gain a certain amount of agency therein. Importantly, the continued relevance of *María Antonia* is a key aspect of the resistance communicated through the work, not least in reference to a Cuban cultural context in which restrictive notions regarding specific gender roles remain prevalent. In this vein, the chapter intercalates into the analysis Georgina Herrera's epilogue to the play, 'Conversación con María Antonia (cuarenta años después)' (2004) [Conversation with María Antonia (Forty Years Later)], which both points to María Antonia as the first of many María Antonias who enact the role on Havana's streets and further exemplifies the manner in which the protagonist both suffers and subverts patriarchal frameworks through death and sacrifice.

Chapter 3 continues the examination of the patriarchal framework surrounding female sexuality reinforced and destabilized in *María Antonia* and explores how it is further undermined and subverted in Kettly Mars's novel *Fado* (2008). Set in Port-au-Prince in a hybrid context of Haitian Vodou interwoven with Portuguese fado, the body of the female protagonist is inhabited by two discrete subjectivities, Anaïse and Frida, the former a *bourgeoise* who works in advertising and whose husband has left her for his pregnant mistress, the latter a prostitute at a brothel in the city slum. Having been raped as a teenager and forced to have two botched abortions,

Anaïse/Frida traverses the discrete spaces of uptown Pétionville and the 'bas-ville' [lower town] in a quest to reconstitute her sense of self by conflating, in the context of Vodou spirituality, the dualities she embodies: the spurned wife and the whore, the bourgeois professional and the denizen of the city slum. Combining multiple female identities and bridging divisions in space, the protagonist challenges the restrictive binaries that have defined her in such a fashion, continually interacting with the multiple subjectivities she comprises made possible through her association with Ezili and the tripartite twin *lwa*, the *marasa twa*. Within this context, the chapter examines Mars's exploration of both restrictive and liberating notions of womanhood, most notably with regard to sexual identities and motherhood, and the extent to which male-dominated frameworks of womanhood examined by scholars such as Julia Kristeva, Trinh T. Minh-ha and literary critic Jean Franco are undermined in this and other related texts. To this end, the wider context of Vodou spirituality that Mars presents in her work permits the interrogation, by means of the female body, of the intersecting socio-political, geographic, spiritual and psychological spaces of Port-au-Prince and the wider Caribbean, and thus the exploration of the multifaceted nature of womanhood and female sexuality depicted therein.

In counterpoint to the themes examined in the preceding chapters of resistance through African-derived religious practices and the deconstruction of patriarchal frameworks by female protagonists, Chapter 4 explores the alignment of Vodou and other religions with destructive masculinity and the state in Duvalierist Haiti. It focuses on three main fictional portrayals of François Duvalier's 1957–71 dictatorial regime, during which he conflated nation, state and Vodou into a single entity that he embodied himself.[15] Firstly, Marie Vieux-Chauvet's *Folie* (1968) [Madness], the third novella in her trilogy *Amour, Colère et Folie* (*Love, Anger, Madness*, 2009), follows the story of René, a young poet trapped by the Macoutes in a small shack, who, by virtue of his profession and training, is considered subversive and thus positioned in opposition to the state apparatus of control. The second work, *Général Baron-la-Croix ou Le Silence masqué* [General Baron-la-Croix or The Masked Silence], written by Franck Fouché (1974) shortly after his exile to Canada, draws on the incorporation of Vodou and Haitian folklore into the playwright's earlier works and depicts the installation of le Chef's dictatorial regime by means of the help he receives from the Gede spirit, Baron-la-Croix. In contrast to this direct parody of François Duvalier and his policies, Kettly Mars's novel *Saisons sauvages* (2010a) (*Savage Seasons*, 2015) focuses on the experiences of Nirvah Leroy as she petitions Raoul Vincent, the head of the Macoutes, for the release of her husband in the period around the 1964 massacre of political opponents and their families in Jérémie, south-western Haiti. Subjected to sexual and psychological violence at the hands of this representative of the Duvalierist state, Nirvah sees both her position and agency eroded in the face of the destructive power of the regime. Through its analysis of these three texts and others, the chapter examines the gendered dichotomy imposed by the Duvaliers on Haitian society and focuses on two main consequences they depict: the physical, sexual and psychological violence suffered by women; and the negation of the possibility of resistance through religions such as Vodou in this context. To this end, I use Hannah Arendt's work with regard to power and violence in conjunction with formulations of masculinity and violence to underscore the gendered hierarchy of power upon which the notion of destructive masculinity is predicated. Consequently, the male-oriented dichotomy thus constructed genders those who participate in the Duvalierist state apparatus as masculine and places those who do not in a position of opposition, rendering them feminine. In this construct, male individuals who are placed in opposition are also emasculated, as the protagonists René, le Chef and Raoul Vincent all exemplify, while destructive masculinity in a framework of state terror not only subjects those designated feminine to physical and sexual violence, but also sees the agents of terror themselves destroyed.

Finally, Chapter 5 examines the intersections of death and sexuality in the texts previously analyzed in relation to their conceptualization within Santería and Vodou. Placing these into conversation with theorizations of death and sexuality by scholars such as Georges Bataille, Jean Baudrillard and Julia Kristeva, it focuses on the themes of prostitution, motherhood, rape and sacrifice as four contexts in which the gender-based conflict running through each of the chapters is centred. In so doing, the chapter underscores not only the complex manner in which these notions are formulated within African-derived religious traditions, but also the ways in which the protagonists in these Caribbean texts resist hegemonic structures that seek to circumscribe and oppress women and others who have been gendered feminine within a male-female dichotomy. As the analysis proposes, the interactions between death and the concepts of prostitution, motherhood, sex and sacrifice within the frameworks of Santería and Vodou in these works illustrate that, in spite of the imposition of physical death on the protagonists, their intertwined nature indicates possibility for women rather than complete annihilation on both the physical and spiritual planes. Following this, the conclusion looks to contemporary narratives that have appeared in the aftermath of the 2010 earthquake that had such a devastating effect on Haiti and saw varying short- and long-term responses from national and international entities in the region and beyond. Drawing on fiction, oral testimony and other artistic interventions, this final section explores some of the ways in which issues pertaining to gender, sexuality and resistance intersect in these contemporary texts, and exemplifies the use of Santería and Vodou as spaces in which the complexities of these notions continue to be examined.

In his analysis of the development of Vodou and its relationship with politics in Haiti, Michel Laguerre writes that, for the enslaved population of colonial Saint-Domingue, Vodou was 'a way of expressing and of resisting their cultural and religious assimilation', a repository for 'collective memory'.[16] As the chapters that follow demonstrate, this has not ceased to be the case, with African-derived religions and practices continuing to serve as sites of resistance to cultural, social and political hegemony. In the texts analyzed, Santería, Vodou and associated traditions constitute a complex framework that draws the Caribbean together without negating difference, while providing a space in which the voices of those marginalized and on the periphery come to the fore. However, Santería and Vodou are not presented as a panacea through which to resolve all political and social issues the texts depict, for that would belie the complexities inherent in the region and undermine the narratives they recount. Rather, just as the *orisha* and *lwa* are complicated entities that comprise the wide range of possible spiritual and human experiences, emotions and conditions, so too the novels, plays and short stories examined here interrogate the political and social realities of the Caribbean within the context of an interconnected African-derived religious framework. In so doing, they invite the reader to consider such notions as national and regional identity, the politics of gender and sexuality, the intersections and ramifications of political and sexual violence, and the possibilities offered for peripheral voices to be heard, all through the lens of an inherently Caribbean and heterogeneous worldview.

Notes to the Introduction

1. This novel was published in English as *Tentacle* in 2018, translated by Achy Obejas.
2. The *orisha* are not gods or deities as understood in Western terms, but rather spiritual 'archetypes' or 'personified natural forces' who interact with adherents (*orisha* are also referred to as *santos* in Cuba due to their association with the Catholic saints) (Matibag 1996: 46; Fernández Olmos & Paravisini-Gebert 2011: 42). A similar description can be made of the *lwa*, the spirits that form the Vodou pantheon. It should be noted that the spelling and pluralization of *orisha* is not fixed in scholarship discussing the religion; it is sometimes spelt *oricha* and also often pluralized with an 's' (*orishas/orichas*). In the interest of uniformity, *orisha* will be used throughout for both the singular and plural, thus remaining consistent with the Haitian Kreyòl *lwa* (the standard Kreyòl spelling of their equivalent in Haitian Vodou) which is not pluralized in this fashion.
3. Díaz-Quiñones 1993: 166.
4. 'Coumbite' is the spelling Santos-Febres uses, which can be seen in earlier Haitian texts such as Jacques Roumain's widely read *Gouverneurs de la rosée* [Masters of the Dew]. The standard Kreyòl spelling is now *konbit*, often also seen as *koumbit* and *kounbit*.
5. Humphrey 2012. All quotations in English from the latter three novels are taken from these published translations.
6. Hennessy 1992; Stuart Hall in Grossberg 1986: 53.
7. One effect of this has been the negative connotations ascribed to the religion, especially when spelt in English as 'Voodoo'. In an attempt to reject the pejorative and colonial overtones associated with the term, the spelling used in contemporary scholarship is 'Vodou', which has been accepted into use by the US Library of Congress. For further information regarding these efforts, see contributions by Ramsey (2012), Desmangles (2012) and Bellegarde-Smith & Ramsey (2012) to volume 18(2) of the *Journal of Haitian Studies*.
8. Fernández Olmos & Paravisini-Gebert (2011: 33) translate Regla de Ocha as 'the rule or religion of the orisha', observing in a note that, '*Regla* translates as religion, order or rule, based on the *reglamientos* or regulations of Afro-Cuban religious life after independence in 1898. In Cuba, *regla* is used to describe the various African-based religions, sects, and practices' (264).
9. Fernández Olmos & Paravisini-Gebert 2011: 12.
10. Ibid.: 12–13.
11. See Chapter 1 for an overview of the different terms used to describe the ways in which these religions developed and the polemics surrounding such terminology as syncretism, creolization and transculturation.
12. DeLoughrey 2007: 39–40.
13. To this end, the late Cuban scholar Inés María Martiatu described this idea in a 2009 interview with me in terms of the absence of the notion of 'apostasy' within Afro-Cuban religious traditions, a term she employed elsewhere (see Martiatu Terry 1992: 99). The concept of simultaneously belonging to different religions and religious traditions in Cuba and Haiti

(except Protestantism) has also been noted in numerous scholarly works, albeit without using the word 'apostasy'; see, among others, Ayorinde (2004), Fernández Robaina (2008), Miller (2000) and Michel (2006). Likewise, informal interviews conducted at the same period with practitioners and practitioner-scholars communicated similar findings.

14. An individual who practises Santería as part of an *ilé* has a spiritual godparent or godparents, who lead the *ilé*. A godmother is a *madrina* and a godfather, a *padrino*.

15. It should be noted that upon François Duvalier's death in 1971, his son was installed as his successor in accordance with the late dictator's wishes. Jean-Claude Duvalier continued his father's dictatorship until his overthrow and exile in 1986.

16. Laguerre 1989: 70.

CHAPTER 1

Intersections of Religion, Resistance and Gender in Caribbean Narratives

As seen in the Introduction, literary texts such as Ana Lydia Vega's 'Encancaranublado' and Rita Indiana's *La mucama de Omicunlé* exemplify the importance of African-derived religions and religious traditions in the Caribbean as sources of knowledge and identity that traverse the region. These practices and their adherents have long been marginalized in political and social settings, with rites and religious ceremonies variously restricted, discouraged and/or outlawed at different points in colonial and postcolonial Caribbean history. In this context, religions such as Santería and Vodou — the two traditions on which this book focuses — have served as sites of resistance, be it against cultural and linguistic hegemony, the colonial systems of slavery and the politics of oppression, male-oriented hierarchical frameworks or the many constraints and characterizations that have been imposed on practitioners and their belief systems from the colonial period to the present day. In preparation for the literary analyses that follow, this chapter will explore the notion that Santería and Vodou are religions of resistance, examining their historical contexts and religious frameworks, as well as the importance of women's participation in these religious spaces. Furthermore, through the analysis of a number of literary texts alongside the myths surrounding the *orisha* and *lwa*, it will consider the concept of hybridity in relation to these religions and delineate some key intersections between Santería and Vodou, resistance and gender in narratives that themselves draw the Caribbean region together via the religious frameworks they explore.

Santería and Vodou: Religions of Resistance

In reference to the manner in which African-derived religions in the Caribbean have been characterized, religions like Santería and Vodou have been variously described in terms such as *brujería* (witchcraft) or pagan superstition, collections of animistic beliefs, folklore and symbioses or syncretic religions based on folk Catholicism, West African beliefs and other cultural influences each rendered in their respective historical and political contexts.[1] *Santeros* and *vodouyizan*, while rejecting such loaded and pejorative terms as witchcraft and superstition, do not subscribe to a single definition of their religious traditions; they remain highly personal belief systems, the purpose and value of which differ among adherents. As George Brandon and

Claudine Michel, among others, have observed in relation to these two religious traditions, they comprise basic attitudes towards life which are expressed in various ways and contexts through each aspect of a person's daily existence, and are reflections of the distinct Afro-Cuban and Afro-Haitian contexts in which these expressions of belief, doctrine and ritual take place.[2] Through interaction with the *orisha* or *lwa* and the spirits of ancestors, devotees seek to facilitate their negotiation of everyday life, at times petitioning for help in overcoming specific obstacles, for example, and at others propitiating the *orisha* and *lwa* for feast days or to keep a promise made.[3] 'The goal of religious work is health, wealth, and love', Ayorinde has noted in reference to Santería, this her translation into English of the phrase often repeated among *santeros* — *salud, amor, dinero* — which pithily encapsulates the everyday needs of adherents.[4] A similar understanding exists among *vodouyizan*, who also seek to maintain or better their situation through their interactions with the *lwa*. In short, a close relationship is formed between *santeros/vodouyizan* and the *orisha/lwa*, one which is integral to practitioners' daily lives.

The development of Santería and Vodou has been much researched and theorized by scholars who have drawn on polemical concepts such as syncretism, creolization, *mestizaje/métissage* and Fernando Ortiz's (1963) theory of transculturation, concepts which have been variously critiqued as conveying notions of Eurocentric hierarchy, of tainting and/or whitening, and as suggesting unequal binarial relationships between the component elements of the Santería or Vodou framework.[5] An in-depth analysis of the animated discussions in this regard is beyond the scope of this book, although reference will be made later in this chapter to the debates in postcolonial studies about the terms *mestizaje*, creolization and hybridity. Despite the polemics surrounding the term creolization, it does recognize the necessary 'creole' nature of Santería and Vodou, that they are not just the sum of the parts from which they derive but the product of a unique set of historical, political and cultural processes within Cuba and Haiti. One important aspect of these processes is the association of the *orisha* and *lwa* with particular Catholic saints, an example of which is shown above when Vega invokes Ochún in 'Encancaranublado' as a component part of what the Virgin of 'la Caridad del Cobre' represents in Cuba, and as one of the 'Siete Ponencias Africanas'.

The designation of Santería and Vodou as 'religions of resistance' by scholars such as Andrew Apter, Mercedes Cros Sandoval, George Brandon and Laënnec Hurbon, among others, is therefore drawn from much more than the description of these religions as witchcraft or paganism;[6] the creolized renderings of the Catholic saints as *orisha* and *lwa* are a further example of this resistance, a product of what Leslie Desmangles has referred to as 'symbiosis by identity', though debate remains regarding the exact processes by which such associations occurred.[7] Some posit that these affiliations are the result of a desire to mask African deities with Catholic saints thus permitting their continued worship, while others have suggested that the Church permitted similarities to be drawn as a step in the process of proselytization.[8] Moreover, still others point to a process likened to religious acculturation whereby saints known to devotees were incorporated into the pantheon and/or assigned as creole avatars (*caminos* in Santería) of the *orisha* or *lwa*; in short, a revision and transformation of 'the religion of the masters'.[9] The points of convergence between the *orisha/lwa* and saints indicate that such associations foreground specific attributes of the manner in which the saint is represented that 'correspond to the age, functions, or symbols' of their counterparts.[10] As these critics demonstrate, Santería and Vodou developed in contexts both of tolerance and disparagement of African-derived beliefs and practices and of the imposition of the Catholic faith by colonial powers. Placed in positions outside those occupied by the dominant culture, these traditions have remained to a greater or lesser degree on the margins, and from this position constitute a locus of strength for their participants.[11]

Speaking from the margins in order to reject totalizing notions of homogeneity is a common tool used by Caribbean authors, as Myrna García-Calderón notes in 'La imaginación insubordinada: el Caribe y la cultura marginal' [The Insubordinate Imagination: the Caribbean and Marginal Culture]. In particular reference to Mayra Santos-Febres as one of these authors, García-Calderón highlights that 'consciente de la falta de poder a cualquier nivel, no es sorprendente que [...] desafíe y desmitifique en su obra cualquier sistema de explicación total y recurra a lo marginal como su lugar de enunciación' [conscious of the lack of power at all levels, it is not surprising that in her work she distrusts and demythifies any system of all-encompassing explanation and turns to the margins as a site from which to speak].[12] Indeed, as Dawn Stinchcomb underlines, Santos-Febres opens her novel *Sirena Selena vestida de pena* [Sirena Selena Dressed in Sorrow] with a *divinación de cocos* [coconut shell divination], which also invokes the *orisha* of the sea as well as the protagonist himself, the eponymous gay male drag artist Sirena Selena.[13] Speaking from the margins of Puerto Rican and Dominican society, Sirena Selena channels several of the Seven African Powers of Santería through various aspects of his character and physique, embodying the sensual temptress Ochún, the headstrong *orisha* of the sea Yemayá and the sexual ambiguity of Obatalá and Eleggua.[14]

As African-derived religions such as Santería and Vodou developed, they did so on the margins of society and served as sources of strength for practitioners and as sites of resistance. Much has been written regarding the origins of Vodou in the plantation and maroon communities of Saint-Domingue prior to the Haitian Revolution. Rémy Bastien, Laguerre and Desmangles, for example, have all indicated that religious systems based on the African gods, rites and rituals which survived the Middle Passage developed in these communities and that, over time, they incorporated elements of Catholicism to become a multifaceted belief system that sustains its devotees in their earthly life and beyond.[15] In addition to the continued practice of African rites and rituals by slaves and maroons in various 'cults', described by Laguerre as a 'politics of survival', the notion of Vodou as a religion of resistance is exemplified by the figures of Makandal before the Revolution and Boukman as part of it.[16] These two figures, both Vodou priests, have been credited in popular belief and elsewhere with sowing the seeds of revolution. With regard to Makandal, whether a pre-revolutionary maroon leader as popularly described or merely a man bestowed with these qualities after his death, as Geggus contends,

Vodou was and still is believed to have been central to the uprising he is purported to have been planning to lead.[17] Boukman, for his part, is repeatedly cited as having led the Bois Caïman ceremony in August 1791 on the eve of the initial uprising that is regarded as having ultimately led to independence in 1804.[18] Although Geggus once again questions the veracity of these events,[19] what is important to note is that, in popular belief, Boukman is credited with officiating a Vodou ceremony at this point and that Vodou then 'bound the members of the conspiracy and [...] served as a catalyst when the time for action came'.[20] In the context of literature, Cuban author Alejo Carpentier draws on the centrality of Makandal, Boukman and Vodou in accounts of the Haitian Revolution in his novel *El reino de este mundo* (1969) [The Kingdom of This World], the seminal text with which he exemplified his concept of *lo real maravilloso* [the marvellous real] as part of his narrative of Saint-Domingue's anticolonial struggle and victory in gaining independence. As Joseph Murphy notes, the Haitian Revolution continues to be an integral part of Vodou ceremony and symbolism, and the role of Vodou in the revolutionary struggle remains an important example of its status as a site of resistance.[21]

A brief examination of relations between Afro-Cuban and Afro-Haitian religious practices and the state exemplifies further the trend of these practices both being placed in a position of resistance and enabling resistance. While the *cabildos* (brotherhoods) — made up of slaves and freedmen in Cuba and from which the various Afro-Cuban religious traditions developed — were tolerated by the Church as part of its project of proselytization, the African-derived religious practices associated with them were forced underground towards the end of the nineteenth century.[22] Following independence from Spanish rule in 1898, there was a period of Europeanization in a bid to 'de-Africanize Cuban culture', against which there was a counter effort by the literary and cultural *movimiento afrocubano* [Afro-Cuban movement] from the late 1920s through to 1940, developing from the political ambition enshrined in the Partido Independiente de Color [Independent Party of Colour].[23] This had limited success from the standpoint of the visibility of Santería in cultural production and, in spite of its documented shortcomings, Ortiz's *afrocubanismo* at least allowed Santería to be legitimated in cultural production and express true 'cubanidad', or 'Cubanness'.[24] Politically, however, Afro-Cuban practices and the black population continued to be marginalized Initially, the populist revolution of 1959 saw those associated with these religious traditions stand to benefit from the social programmes put in place and to a certain extent Afro-Cuban culture and religious traditions were espoused by the state.[25] However, following the regime's declaration of support for Marxist-Leninism, Afro-Cuban religious traditions were once again subjected to restrictions, deemed counterrevolutionary — initiated members of any religious tradition were barred from the Cuban Communist Party and the Union of Communist Youth — and only officially sanctioned as secularized folkloric performances illustrating Cuba's creole culture. Reinforcing the notion of African-derived religious traditions as sites of resistance, those adherents now considered as outside the dominant culture due to its prohibition of their religious practices increased in number despite the restrictions imposed, as a 1991 study by the governmental Departamento de Estudios Sociorreligiosos [Department of Socio-Religious Studies] concluded.[26] Furthermore, in light of these policies which served to 'exclude blacks from positions of authority, to silence discussions on racism and to acknowledge only the process of assimilation', Santería and other Afro-Cuban traditions remained a repository for these African-derived practices, thus continuing their culture of resistance.[27]

The relationship of Vodou with the Haitian state has also been one characterized by long-term marginalization through the nineteenth and the first part of the twentieth centuries, before being appropriated by the state under François Duvalier. In spite of the central role Vodou was considered to have played in the Haitian Revolution, upon independence Catholicism was declared the official religion. Although it must be recognized that there existed a significant threat of recolonization and/or economic isolation provoked by a European backlash should Vodou be declared the state religion of the world's first independent black republic, the act of declaring Haiti a Catholic state placed Vodou once again outside the state apparatus and therefore in a position of resistance.[28] Indeed, Kate Ramsey argues that Vodou's placement outside the law was in part due to its role in empowering the slaves during the Revolution and that it then offered an alternative power hierarchy which threatened social — and later political — cohesion.[29] It should be noted that the Catholic Church refused to recognize Haiti as a Catholic nation until 1860; however, the 1860 Concordat reinstalled Catholic hegemony and attempts were made to continue the work of Haiti's first three black presidents in suppressing the increasingly established practice of Vodou.[30] Remaining marginalized, if tolerated at times, the election of François Duvalier as president in 1957 and the subsequent installation of his dictatorial regime saw Vodou subsumed by the state, thus negating any possibility of resistance. Although Papa Doc never elevated the legal status of Vodou, he was an *oungan* (male Vodou priest) and cultivated the image that he 'was one with, was possessed by, was Baron Samedi', thereby incorporating Vodou into the Haitian state that he also personified.[31] As the networks of *ounfò* (Vodou temples) were absorbed into the state apparatus to impose Duvalier's rule, Vodou priests became members of his nationwide militia, officially known as the Volontaires de la Sécurité Nationale [National Security Volunteers] but more commonly referred to as the *Tonton Macoutes*, often shortened to *Macoutes*.[32] Upon his death in 1971 François Duvalier's regime was continued by his nineteen-year-old son Jean-Claude, appointed by his father, who was regarded by Papa Doc's ministers as a playboy lacking the necessary experience to continue his father's project. Although Baby Doc seemed less fervent in his belief and practice of Vodou, its alignment with the state through the Macoutes and the performance of rituals by and for the Duvalier family continued nonetheless.[33] It was not until after the fall of the regime in February 1986 with the Duvaliers' exile to France that Vodou was accorded legal recognition as an official religion alongside Catholicism in the Haitian constitution of 1987. This followed a period of *dechoukaj* [lit. uprooting] during which Vodou priests and temples were attacked due to their association with the state, provoking the foundation of the Bodè Nasyonal by the late *oungan* Max Beauvoir to counter the effects on Vodou of the Duvalier regimes. Despite now being legally recognized, Vodou continues to be marginalized in spite of adherents having been accorded the right to practice, and as such it remains in a position of resistance on the periphery of society, with *vodouyizan* struggling for legitimacy in the face of the increased influence of Protestantism alongside Catholicism on many aspects of official and cultural life.[34] Moreover, Santería and Vodou also constitute a space from and in which to resist and subvert the dominant gender-based hierarchies that continue to exist in Cuban and Haitian society.

The *orisha* and *lwa* in Santería and Vodou

In Santería and Vodou, the *orisha* and *lwa* are spiritual archetypes that have been associated with Catholic saints through a process of creolization. Both religious traditions function on a basis of reciprocal personal and communal relationships between practitioners and the *orisha* and *lwa*: devotees offer sacrifices to the spirits to propitiate them and give them sustenance, and some practitioners are 'horses' who can be 'mounted' by their *orisha de cabecera* or *mèt tèt* (the primary *orisha* or *lwa* with whom they are associated), enabling the latter to manifest itself during ceremonies. As a result, the *orisha* and *lwa* may offer advice and help solve problems through manipulation of the coexistent physical and spiritual planes to provide knowledge and favour practitioners' well-being.

In addition to spirit possession, divination by means of initiation, sacrifice and the interpretation of the will of the *orisha* and *lwa* is central to these traditions. In Santería, the will of the *orisha* is determined using three main processes of divination, the first of which is exemplified in the opening of Santos-Febres's novel *Sirena Selena vestida de pena*. *Obi* or *biagué* is divination with four coconut shells, *dilogún*, with sixteen cowry shells, and *Ifá*, the expression of the voice of Olodumare through Orula, conducted using divining chains or palm nuts and a *tablero de Ifá* (divining board). *Ifá*, the most complex, can only be performed by a *babalao* (male priest) or, more controversially, an *iyanifá* (female priest), though it must be noted that the initiation of *iyanifá* is rejected by a large proportion of the Cuban Santería community.[35] This 'communal ethic', as Murphy terms it, of both religious traditions is a key part of the ritual they comprise; not only is spirit possession the embodiment of an *orisha* or *lwa* by a devotee which then must be witnessed and interpreted by the community for it to be of benefit, the rituals and practices that form part of initiation and ceremony in Santería and Vodou require the involvement of members of the *ilé* or *ounfò* (the religious communities centred on a specific temple, headed by a *padrino* and/or *madrina*, or an *oungan* and/or *manbo* respectively) and at times the wider religious community, as both active participants and witnesses.[36]

Turning to Mayra Montero's novels mentioned in the Introduction, these texts serve as a useful context in which to both introduce and situate some of the *orisha* and *lwa* key to the analysis in the chapters that follow. In the fourth of these novels,

Como un mensajero tuyo, Montero rewrites and reinterprets the brief disappearance of Italian opera singer Enrico Caruso in Havana in 1920. The text revises the account printed in the contemporary press to situate it within a narrative that reinterprets both the story of Radames and Aïda in Verdi's opera *Aïda* (the work Caruso was performing in Havana) and several Santería *patakí* that focus on Yemayá, Ochún and Changó. Transcribed by protagonist Aída's daughter, Enriqueta, prior to her mother's death, the novel recounts Aída's relationship with Caruso, which began in the aftermath of the bomb that exploded during the performance on 13 June 1920. Jorge Marbán (2005) has appraised the different accounts of the event, but Montero's narrative rewrites the report published the following day in the *New York Times*, contradicting the latter's contention that Caruso was rushed 'to the Hotel Sevilla in Mme. Navarrete's automobile' ('Bomb Explodes at Caruso Performance'). Instead, in the novel — itself comprising twelve chapters whose Italian titles are taken from the libretto of the opera — Aída recounts that he ran into the kitchen of the Hotel Inglaterra, chanced upon her there, and so began their romance.[37]

Beginning with Yemayá, the *orisha* propitiated alongside Olokún in Indiana's *La mucama de Omicunlé*, she is associated with the Virgin of Regla and is the *orisha* of motherhood, the sea and salt water. In Lucumí tradition she is said to have helped her sister, Ochún, cross the ocean from Africa and is considered to be the mother figure of all the *orisha*.[38] Yemayá's colours are navy blue and white, as are the vestments of her Catholic counterpart, a black Virgin (her sister, Ochún, and associated Virgin of Caridad del Cobre are *mulata*). Yemayá has numerous *caminos*, at times she is calm and sensual, at others angry and vengeful, and she raises her children 'with absolute motherly rigor'.[39] In *Como un mensajero tuyo*, while Aída, Caruso and her *padrino*, the *babalao* Calazán, are staying in Matanzas, the characters indicate that the love story in Verdi's opera, the romance between Aída and Caruso, and the *patakí* which involve Yemayá, Changó and Ochún are all reflections of each other. Here, one of Calazán assistants, 'la conga Mariate', an *iyalocha* (fully initiated female priest), describes the love between Changó and Yemayá as follows: 'Changó no sabía que su verdadera madre era Yemayá. Sin saber que era su madre, quiso que fuera su mujer. "Omó mi," dijo Changó, y Yemayá le ofreció el pecho, donde Changó, reconociéndola, se echó a llorar' (Montero 1998: 99) ('Changó didn't know his real mother was Yemayá. He didn't know she was his mother, he wanted her to be his wife. "Omó mi," said Changó, and Yemayá offered him her breast, then Changó recognized her and began to cry', Montero 2000: 75). There are various *patakí* that describe this interaction, some sources recounting that Yemayá had an incestuous relationship with Changó fully aware that he was her son, and others describing her simply as Changó's wife.[40] Yemayá is Aída's *orisha de cabecera* and at different points in the narrative she mounts Aída. In these instances, Yemayá acts through Aída: on one occasion she prevents Caruso from drowning, acting out of her love for Changó, and on another she saves Aída's unborn daughter when the protagonist has been kidnapped, beaten and left in a cave to die. In this latter instance, the association of Yemayá with motherhood comes to the fore, and Aída asserts that it was either Yemayá Asesú or Yemayá Achabá — two different *caminos* of the same *orisha* — that kept her and her daughter alive. Respectively 'mensajera de Olokún y [...] secretaria de Olofi' ('messenger of Olokún and [...] minister of Olofi'), Aída recalls, 'No sé cual de las dos fue la que se quedó conmigo, batallando con todo lo que había a mi alrededor [...]. Todavía me pregunto cómo no me comieron y cómo no entraron en mi vientre para comerte a ti' (235) ('I don't know which one stayed with me, fighting everything that was around me [...]. I still ask myself why they didn't eat me, why they didn't come into my belly and eat you', 191). The invocation of these two *caminos* of Yemayá is significant: Yemayá Achabá would seek to protect Aída and Caruso's child since she was Changó's lover, while also being gifted in divination as the wife of Orula and therefore able to interpret the future importance of Enriqueta as the scribe of this alternative narrative; Yemayá Asesú resides in turbid and dirty water, and would therefore serve as a protector in the dark and dank environment in which Aída was abandoned.[41]

Changó, in addition to being Yemayá's son and/or lover, is a warrior *orisha* who is master of fire, thunder, lightning and the sacred *batá* drums, and as such is considered to represent Afro-Cuban male virility.[42] However, Changó's status as the epitome of the virile man might seem to be undermined by his most common association with Santa Bárbara since, on the surface, being identified with a chaste female Catholic martyr might dilute Changó's macho image and nature. In other *caminos*, Changó's Catholic counterparts are Saint Patrick, Saint Mark and Saint George, as Fernández Olmos and Paravisini-Gebert indicate.[43] In his research, William Bascom underlined a disparity that he observed in the way in which *santeros* regard Changó's male and female manifestations, but one should bear in mind that at least one of the *pataki* describes Changó as disguising himself as a woman to escape Ogún.[44] Notwithstanding, there are many similarities between the symbols and attributes of Changó and Santa Bárbara: they are both crowned and associated with conflict, fire and the colour red. Whether or not the identification with Santa Bárbara undermines Changó's virility, this association emphasizes an important characteristic of the *orisha* and of the *lwa*, that 'far from being incompatible categories, life and death, maleness and femaleness, illness and its cure ultimately meet and feed upon each other'.[45] The different elements that make up these archetypes come together to form a complex, interdependent whole, the constituents of which cannot be viewed in isolation.

Indeed, when Calazán foresees the arrival of Caruso in *Como un mensajero tuyo*, the singer is described in terms that reflect attributes associated with Changó: a crown, thunder and lightning and a bomb. During a divination ceremony in January 1920, 'Dice Ifá que va a venir un hombre [...]. Viene a coronarte, a decirte que eres la reina de su pensamiento. Antes de eso escucharás el trueno, se derrumbarán las paredes, habrá polvo y fuego' (28) ('Ifá says a man will come [...]. He will come to crown you and tell you that you are the queen of his thoughts. Before that you will hear the thunder, the walls will fall down, there will be dust and fire', 11). The following May was punctuated by frequent storms, heralding the arrival of Caruso in Havana and causing Aída's mother to not only consult Calazán again, but also turn to Yuan Pei Fu, priest of Sanfancón and Aída's godfather, who warns of Caruso and Aída's imminent meeting.[46] In origin, Sanfancón is a Chinese spirit known as Guan Gong and is venerated by an all-male society. Importantly, however, he has also been associated with Changó within the framework of Afro-Cuban religious traditions and so too with Santa Bárbara.[47] Representative of Changó in various forms, therefore, Caruso's numerous love affairs add to his identification with the *orisha* of macho virility; similarly, his relationship with Aída/Yemayá, tainted with death and thus unnatural from the outset, was doomed just as the *patakí* had foretold.

A further *patakí* describes the unrequited love held for Changó by Ochún, the *orisha* of fresh water, love, female sensuality and sexuality whom both Vega and Santos-Febres invoke in the examples cited above. Ochún is associated with Cuba's patron saint, the Virgin of Caridad del Cobre, who appears in folk tradition to save 'los tres Juanes' — variously described as one *mestizo*, one black slave and one Native American, or two Native Americans and a Cuban-born black man — from drowning, each of whom worked in the copper mine of El Cobre whence she derives her name.[48] In addition to representing the 'Cuban everyman' by appearing to the three ethnic groupings of the day, la Caridad del Cobre herself is depicted as *mulata*, thus representing 'something of the racial and class dynamics of Cuban society'.[49] Within this context, Ochún displays in her different *caminos* a variety of characteristics that may be viewed as desirable: she is flirtatious and coquettish, beautiful, sensuous and industrious. As Ochún Ololodí, she has a serious nature and is known for her gift at divination (thereby associated with the *babalao*), although this is a skill she no longer uses,[50] whereas in her *camino* as Panchágara she is a capricious seductress who seeks to 'wrest men away from all women'.[51] Her colour is yellow, like the vestments of la Caridad del Cobre, and in her dances she requests 'oñí' [honey], symbolic of her sweetness and of love. The *patakí* tell of Ochún's turbulent love affair with Changó, during which he repeatedly humiliated her, and when he moved away, she renounced her possessions to follow him; in spite of this, it is said that Changó never really loved Ochún.[52] In these terms, then, Ochún has been described as one of the most venerated of the Cuban *orisha*, not only due to her identification with Cuba's patron saint and therefore her symbolic alignment with the Cuban nation, but also for her 'sensual grace and Creole mischievousness'.[53]

In *Como un mensajero tuyo*, la conga Mariate follows her summary of Yemayá and Changó's complicated relationship with an explanation for Ochún's unrequited love: 'Oshún tampoco sabía que Changó era su sobrino — susurró [...]. No lo sabía y quiso ser su mujer, por eso terminó tan mal, llorando también sobre una piedra' (100) ('Oshún didn't know that Changó was her nephew, [...] [she] whispered [...]. She didn't know and wanted to be his wife, that's why she came to such a bad end. She cried over a stone too', 75). This *patakí* is central to the narrative in the key text analyzed in Chapter 2, Eugenio Hernández Espinosa's *María Antonia*, in which the playwright underlines the coexistence between the *orisha* and *santeros/as*, using the story of Ochún and Changó to explore the interactions between protagonist María Antonia and her lover Julián. The latter, an archetypal macho figure who is a boxer, treats María Antonia in the same way as Changó does Ochún, allowing her to go to prison for a crime he commits but adamant that he cannot be restricted by entering into a monogamous relationship with her. Drawing on elements of Ochún's character expressed in her other *caminos* such as her associations with death and her vengeful nature, Hernández Espinosa writes an alternative *pataquí*, using his work as a creative space in which to construct alternative stories to those recounted by practitioners, a project that can be compared to Excilia Saldaña's collection of short stories *Kele Kele* (1987) and Montero's rewriting of historical accounts in her novels.[54] In so doing, the playwright changes the Ochún depicted in the *pataquí* from a solely submissive individual and sees María Antonia destabilize the patriarchal construct that requires her to act in the manner in which Julián and the wider Santería community attempt to dictate.

As *orisha* who in their different *caminos* interact with each other as family members, lovers and, at points, adversaries, the relationships between Ochún, Yemayá and Changó enable a multifaceted discourse to be delineated regarding womanhood and women's participation in society when transposed to fictional works. By situating their narratives in the spiritual world, which draws together concepts such as sexuality, sensuality, death, vengefulness and motherhood, authors can then tackle machismo — a central concern in these *pataquí* in the form of Changó — in a way that recognizes the complexities involved in these interactions in both religious and secular contexts.

Ochún's and Yemayá's respective counterparts in Haitian Vodou are two distinct avatars of the *lwa* Ezili: Ezili Freda and Ezili Dantò. Like Ochún, Ezili Freda is a beautiful *mulata* of light complexion who is the *lwa* of love and sexuality, while Ezili Dantò, the second most popular manifestation of this *lwa*, is identified with motherhood, is black, a warrior and fighter and, some say, a lesbian.[55] A third manifestation of Ezili, Ezili Je Wouj (Ezili Red Eyes), is Ezili Dantò's knife-wielding alter ego, 'a dangerous and offensive spirit who can cause harm to recalcitrant devotees'.[56] Regarding their Catholic counterparts, Ezili Freda is associated with Our Lady of Sorrows, dressed in light blue with heart-shaped pendants surrounding her and a dagger in her hands. The knife is an important accoutrement of the Ezilis as a whole and appears in both Ezili Freda's and Ezili Dantò's *vèvè* (ritual drawings), while the heart is the other main component and represents the womb.[57] Ezili Dantò is associated with a particular manifestation of Mater Salvatoris, a black Virgin known as Our Lady of Czestochowa, and is said to be a single mother and a 'warrior for the poor and the oppressed who fought [...] during the Haitian Revolution'.[58] Her status as a woman who is central to Vodou spirituality has seen scholars underline the fact that Vodou 'speaks to the issue of women's equality and inequality', an observation based on the fact that women who are often placed in a subaltern position are represented positively in this religious tradition, itself often regarded as inferior.[59] The child Ezili Dantò is depicted as carrying in the chromolithographs of her as a black virgin is her daughter Anaïs or Anaïse, while the scars on her cheek are most often described as wounds sustained in battle during the Haitian Revolution, although alternatively it is sometimes said they are the result of a fight with Ezili Freda over a lover or with Ezili Mapiang who wanted to take Anaïs.[60]

The different Ezilis are embodied by, and their myths retold through, the protagonist of Montero's *Del rojo de su sombra*, Zulé. This novel takes place over the course of Holy Week celebrations among the Haitian and Haitian-descended cane cutter communities (*bateyes*) of the Dominican Republic, specifically in La Romana. Montero's characters are practitioners of Gagá, a socioreligious practice that developed from Haitian *rará* in the often cramped and unsanitary *bateyes*.[61] Organized in a similar way to the *sosyete* in Haitian Vodou (communities affiliated with an *ounfò* and which Montero spells 'societé'), the hierarchy of the *gagá* offers the practitioners an opportunity to occupy a position of prestige and provides them with a social identity, both of which are denied them as *braceros* at the lowest level of Dominican society.[62] Characteristic of her *mèt tèt*, Zulé — whose name also resembles Ezili in sound and form — is described in *Del rojo de su sombra* as 'llorosa y puta como la metresa Freda, sumisa y grande como la Virgen de Erzulie' (Montero 1992: 96) ('weeping and whorish like Metresa Freda, submissive and great like the Virgin of Erzulie', Montero 2002: 78). Here, 'la metresa Freda' corresponds to Ezili Freda and 'la Virgen de Erzulie' to Ezili Dantò of the Petwo rite. Like Zulé, Metresilí, synonymous with Montero's 'metresa Freda', is a passionate *lwa* of much renown in the Dominican Republic, whose 'mayor defecto consiste en coquetear con los hombres' [greatest flaw lies in her flirting with men].[63] A more in-depth discussion of the relationship between Ezili Freda and Ezili Dantò, and its importance in Haitian novelist Kettly Mars's *Fado* (2008), is found in Chapter 3.

The relationship between Ezili and Ogou Feray is also important for its similarities to that which Zulé has with her *gagá*. Married to Ezili, Ogou Feray is one of the three *lwa* propitiated during Holy Week, along with Ti Jean Petró and Erzulie Zeux Rouges (Ezili Je Wouj).[64] Their presence in the physical world over this period is represented by the *bukán*, a metal stake that serves as a ceremonial fire fed with rum and gasoline, described in *Del rojo de su sombra* as 'la verga de Ogún Ferraille' (54) ('Ogún Ferraille's prick', 38). This relationship is therefore reflected in the spiritual marriage that exists between Zulé as *dueña* (leader) and her *gagá*, and also symbolically within the text as the *bukán* has to be 'extinguished' once the *gagá* returns on Easter Sunday, the day on which Zulé is killed (176). In addition to this, not only are Zulé and her lover and rival Similá depicted as physical representations of the *lwa* they serve throughout the narrative, but their interactions also reflect those of Ezili and Toro Belecou. Alfred Métraux writes that Toro Belecou belongs to a family of *lwa* called the 'loa-taureaux' (bull *lwa*), which includes Taureau-trois-graines (Bull with three testicles) and Ezili-taureau; the latter is an avatar of Ezili, which for Fernández Olmos reinforces the fitting nature of Zulé as a counterpart to Similá.[65] Montero combines the other two *lwa* mentioned by Métraux in Similá however, depicting him as a physical representation of Toro Belecou: having been cured of his savannah sores by Zulé's poultices and ardent passion, Similá leaves Colonia Engracia with his face adorned by the cottony tufts from the pods of the nearby ceiba that had been pulled apart by the parrots nesting in it, thus transforming his countenance into 'la cara exacta del misterio más temido y rencoroso del Panteón: [...] la misma cara de Toro Belecou' (95) ('[the mirror image of] the most feared and rancorous mystery in the Pantheon: [...] the face of Bull Belecou', 77). The fact it is a ceiba reinforces the presence of the *lwa* here, since this tree serves as a conduit between the physical and spiritual worlds. Seeing himself in the mirror, Similá intones the song Métraux has transcribed as the one used to greet Taureau-trois-graines when he mounts his initiates, thereby juxtaposing the two within the body of Similá.[66] This is further reinforced by the anatomical singularity of having three testicles that the latter and Taureau-trois-graines share.

However, as Alicia Vadillo underlines, in *Del rojo de su sombra* Montero rewrites the myth surrounding Ezili, Toro Belecou and Belié Belcán, in which Ezili had propitiated Belié Belcán in order to kill Toro Belecou, or at least bring her his blood.[67] In the novel, Belié Belcán is transformed into Carfú (representative of the crossroads and the link between the physical and spiritual planes) who, instead of killing Toro Belecou as in the myth, murders Ezili. Vadillo suggests that, in so doing, Jérémie Candé/Carfú simultaneously closes the path for Zulé/Ezili and opens it for her *gagá*, preventing the possible alliance that he fears will be agreed between the *dueña* and her rival, against which the *sosyete*'s previous *dueño* — Zulé's husband and Jérémie Candé's father — had warned. This closing of Zulé's path has been described by Fernández Olmos as the *manbo*'s liberation, allowing her to serve as the conduit 'through which man ascends and gods descend', with the same result of ensuring the continued existence and independence of her *sosyete*.[68] Montero's rewriting of the myth must also be considered in light of the relationship between Ezili and Ogou Feray, with whom Belié Belcán is affiliated as they are both avatars of Ogou.[69] Mounted by Carfú, Jérémie Candé begins to threaten Similá, whom the latter dismisses and orders Zulé to remove from the battlefield. Refusing at first, she tells Similá, 'Jérémie es mi Primer Mayor. No lo puedo sacar de aquí' (168) ('Jérémie is my First Elder. I can't take him out of here', 146). Naming him as her 'First Elder' in the hierarchy of the *gagá* is significant since this rank is associated with Ogou Feray, a link that is reinforced by Jérémie Candé's subsequent murder of Zulé since Ogou Feray is also angered by Ezili when she gives her lover preference over him. Furthermore, Ogou Feray fulfils the role of uncompromising general among the group of warrior *lwa* who fought in the Haitian Revolution against the oppression of the French.[70] When seen in such terms, Jérémie Candé/Ogou Feray, although angered by Zulé/Ezili's rejection of him, is also acting in the interests of the *gagá* in order to prevent the *sosyete*'s subjugation by Similá.

Turning to Changó, his counterpart in Vodou is the *lwa* Ogou Chango, an avatar of Ogou since the distinction still extant between the Yoruba Shango and Ogun — and therefore the Lucumí Changó and Ogún — has disappeared in Haiti.[71] Ogou Chango is associated with the political arm of the military, though is much less commonly venerated in Haiti than the abovementioned Ogou Feray, a warrior *lwa* considered a national hero.[72] Similar to the amorous relationships between Changó and both Ochún and Yemayá, Ogou is married to Ezili Freda and is Ezili Dantò's lover.[73] Moreover, Ogou's qualities as a warrior, coupled with his infidelity and drunkenness, illustrate his status as the archetypal male. However, as Karen McCarthy Brown observes, the prime example of such male sexual prowess and lewdness is embodied by the group of spirits known as the Gede.[74]

The Gede, the last group of Vodou spirits to be examined here, are structured in a manner that ties in with the organization of Gagá *sosyete*. They are described as a *fanmi* (family) of spirits who reside in the world of the dead.[75] Keepers of the cemetery with Baron Samedi at their head, the Gede stand at the crossroads between the living and the dead and draw together the notions of sex, death and humour. In addition to the cross, they are symbolized by a large wooden phallus, both in religious ceremony and in wider art (for example, the Atis Rezistans sculptors on Grand Rue in Port-au-Prince depict their Gede sculptures, made from used car parts and other discarded items, with large wooden penises; the collective and their work are discussed in detail in Donald Cosentino's *Sacred Arts of Haitian Vodou* (1995), Leah Gordon's documentary *Atis Rezistans: Sculptors of the Grand Rue* (2008) and Katherine Smith's 'Atis Rezistans: Gede and the Art of Vagabondaj' (2012)). The Gede are also often portrayed wearing sunglasses, an important symbol when considering the association between them and the Macoutes, who were issued sunglasses as part of their uniform. Although the moniker 'Tonton Macoute' is taken from Haitian folklore, referring to the bogeymen who kidnapped naughty children at night and carried them away in their *makout* (straw satchels), the militia are symbolically linked to both Zaka (a peasant *lwa* dressed in denim) and the Gede, the latter due to their status as the omnipresent agents of the Duvalierist state, carrying out the orders of François Duvalier (Baron Samedi). Derived from Papa Doc's embodiment of the Baron, further symbolism between those participating in the Duvalier regime and the Gede can be seen in the similar way in which the two are organized: the Gede form a government comprising several ministers and numerous spirits, the latter of whom serve both the ministers and Baron Samedi.[76] This is reflected in the hierarchy within the *gagá*, where the *dueño/a* who leads the *gagá* is affiliated with Gede Nibo, and under his/her authority there are a variety of roles fulfilled by the members of the *sosyete*, such as president, head of the armed forces, various ministers, elders, queens and a female chorus.[77] Furthermore, the inherent patriarchy of the Duvalierist state embodied by Papa Doc finds reflection in Baron Samedi also: as head of the *fanmi*, epitome of masculinity through his sexual prowess and the power he wields, the Baron's wife, Grann Brijit, is subordinate to him. For the Baron and Gede, Brown suggests, fixed gender roles are fundamental and his 'domination of the realm of the dead reflects a time when male ancestors, as well as living males, held all the power in Haitian families'.[78]

This link between the Duvalierist Macoutes and the Gede spirits can be seen in *Del rojo de su sombra* through the character of Similá. Although the novel is set just after the end of the Baby Doc regime, it suggests that this character, a long-serving member of the Macoutes who is also linked to the trafficking of Haitian *braceros*, was involved with the regime of Papa Doc as well as that of his son. The passage of time in this novel is inexact when the number of years is tallied with regard to the necessary periods of initiation and the relative age of the characters. However, the textual references that are present and the assertion that Similá has always been involved with the Macoutes, as well as the fact that his son Tarzán Similá is depicted as continuing his legacy just as Baby Doc did that of his father, would suggest a link, if only symbolic, between Similá and both the François and Jean-Claude Duvalier regimes.

In short, as intimately connected *lwa* who represent various forms of sexuality, motherhood and death, the popular Ezilis serve as a counterpart in the spiritual realm of the multiple forms of womanhood that are explored in the texts examined in this chapter and beyond. As complementary yet at times conflicting entities who are fiercely independent, they allow a wider view of female participation and agency in society to be represented and counter restrictive frameworks that seek to circumscribe the roles women fulfil, rendering them subordinate to men. The Gede also conflate sex and death, though at the same time embodying patriarchal authority, closely associated notions that are examined further in Chapters 4 and 5.

Women Practitioners, Spirit Possession and Hybridity

Intrinsic to the idea that Santería and Vodou are loci of resistance is the notion that both are sites of increased participation for women. In reference to Vodou, Michel writes that women are considered to be on an equal footing with men as female priests, *lwa* and *vodouyizan* who participate fully in the religious community.[79] This constitutes an example of gender equality in a society to which the full extent of women's contributions have not been recognized, as Marie-José N'Zengou-Tayo (1998) and the directors of *Poto Mitan: Haitian Women, Pillars of the Global Economy* Renée Bergan and Mark Schuller (2009) have noted. A further example of this cited by Joan Dayan is that of Cécile Fatiman, the *manbo* who assisted Boukman at the Bois Caïman ceremony but who is not mentioned in standard histories.[80] In contrast, in his novel *El reino de este mundo*, Carpentier (1969) writes that Makandal was trained in Vodou practice by a *manbo*, and so recognizes in a literary context — albeit briefly — the important position female *vodouyizan* held as part of the revolutionary struggle for which the praise is often reserved for men; this in turn serves as a step towards beginning to rectify, in part at least, the deletion of women's participation from historical accounts. The recognition that Vodou offers a relative 'place of security for women' has been underlined in the interviews Claudine Michel, Patrick Bellegarde-Smith and Marlène Racine-Toussaint conducted with ten *manbo*, one of whom, Margaret Armand, described the religious tradition as 'provid[ing] women with that extra edge for overcoming obstacles' in a 'world [that] is a man's world'. She continued, 'the outside world looks more at the *houngan* because he is a man, though on the inside, in Vodun, there is no special or different training that distinguish men from women, though women may be more intuitive'. Acknowledging these possible influences from outside the religious context, Michel, Bellegarde-Smith and Racine-Toussaint's interviews also point to class as a contributing factor, observing that the '*bourgeoises* were the ones who resisted public identification as *manbo*, unable or unwilling to take the risk'.[81]

The context of Santería is a little thornier when it comes to evaluating equality between male and female practitioners, however. While the historically marginalized sectors of society, including women, have a greater opportunity for participation in Santería, there are particular practices and rituals from which *santeras* are traditionally excluded, notably playing the sacred *batá* drums, sacrificing four-legged animals and being initiated into *Ifá*. Despite this traditional prohibition, there are a small but increasing number of women being initiated as *iyanifá*, which, as noted above, has split the Santería community, the majority of whom condemn it.[82] In her study *Where Men Are Wives and Women Rule*, Mary Ann Clark (2005) explores the gender implications in Santería ritual practices, concluding that while divination through *Ifá* often forms an important part of Santería practice in Cuba, as a tradition it is distinct from what she terms 'Santería proper' — that is, based on *oriaté* who conduct divination using the *dilogún* — which does not require *Ifá* in order for a practitioner to undergo *orisha* initiation. A different perspective regarding this issue has been expressed in interviews Lázara Menéndez conducted with a number of *santeras*, who articulated an understanding of power as drawn from both knowledge and a close interaction with the *orisha* rather than an overtly visible equitable position with male practitioners and *babalao*.[83] In response to Menéndez's questions about *iyanifá*, one interviewee declared that, by being initiated alongside the *babalao*, she would 'perder poder' [lose power], being unable to dance for her *orisha* and be mounted, since *babalao* (and by extension *iyanifá*), once initiated into *Ifá*, cannot be mounted as Orula only expresses himself through *Ifá* divination rather than in spirit possession. This sentiment was echoed by another *santera*, who stated that being mounted by her *santo de cabecera* was the key to her spiritual experience of Santería. Menéndez therefore concluded that these notions of power and freedom of participation are based on the manner in which an individual conceptualizes these ideas and that, while for some the traditional prohibition of women being initiated into *Ifá* was an example of the patriarchy inherent in the framework of Santería, for others this allowed them to maintain a closer personal relationship with the *orisha* unfettered by the constraints placed on the *babalao* and *iyanifá*.

In her in-depth analysis, *Spirit Possession in French, Haitian, and Vodou Thought: An Intellectual History*, Alessandra Benedicty-Kokken writes that possession, 'that is, the ability to find equilibrium within the most unstable of situations, becomes a philosophy and a practice, an essential way of being in the world'.[84] Adeptly engaging with and critiquing scholarship on possession from the beginning of the twentieth century to the early twenty-first, Benedicty-Kokken examines the notions of possession, dispossession and self-possession to demonstrate, in lived practice and in literature, 'how possession cultivates the experience of the body in negotiating human experience' and that 'possession is an expression of embodied knowledge'.[85] In light of her work, the brief discussion here will serve as an introduction to the performative and gendered nature of spirit possession, which will then be applied to Hernández Espinosa's *María Antonia* in the chapter that follows.

The corporeal process of spirit possession is a bi-directional process in which both the practitioner and the *orisha* or *lwa* actively participate. Inherently performative, it constitutes a bodily performance whereby the spiritual elements that inhabit the initiate's body are displaced by the spirit possessing it, passing from the physical plane to the spiritual plane as the *orisha* or *lwa* passes from the spiritual into the physical body of the practitioner. In Vodou, the human is conceived as tripartite, comprising the *kò kadav* (the body itself), the *gwobonanj* and the *tibonanj*, of which the latter two have a complex relationship and have been described as forming what can be described as the notion of 'soul' (for a discussion of the *gwobonanj* and *tibonanj* and how they have been characterized in scholarship, see Strongman (2013)). In reference to the *kò kadav*, Benedicty points to the performance of spirit possession, writing that 'in a sense, the *kò kadav* becomes a proscenium, a canvas, across which varied voices — *ti-bon-anj, gwo-bon-anj, lwa* — leave their imprint'.[86] Indeed, Brown uses the term 'possession performance' in her analysis of the phenomenon, noting its theatrical quality while underscoring that her use of the term does not 'indicate that there is anything false or contrived about these visits from the spirits'.[87] On the stage that is the body, it is important to underline that the participant entities never become — in Mary Ann Clark's words — the 'self-same subject' and neither is the *orisha* or *lwa* merely represented.[88] When analyzing performance, Schechner has described the position of a performer as one of 'not me, not not me'; here, spirit possession constitutes a performance centred on the body during which the spirit is not the initiate, but not not the initiate, while in turn, within this performative framework, the initiate is not the spirit, but not not the spirit.[89] The performativity inherent in possession therefore underlines the necessary reciprocal nature of the relationship between the *orisha* or *lwa* and the initiate, a power hierarchy that Margaret Thompson Drewal, in her studies of possession in Yoruba ritual, has likened to that which exists between a mother and child.[90] Drawing these notions of agency and performativity in ritual together with that of possession as a source of empowerment for those mounted, the body then becomes invested with power as the nodal point between the physical and spiritual from which both domains can be influenced.

In an analysis of possession by the *orisha* and *lwa* and the manner in which physical possession is described, it is also important to consider the intersecting frameworks of gender and performance. Butler (1988; 1993), among others, has theorized in detail the notion that gender is performed, a process in which norms of behaviour are created by embodying certain ideals of femininity and masculinity, and subversion and resistance of these norms through performance enable resistance and the corollary non-relinquishment of power. This fluidity of gender is seen both in the fact that many *orisha* and *lwa* have male and female avatars or are considered androgynous (such as Changó in the former instance and Olokún in the latter), and that the assigned sex of the *orisha* or *lwa* that mounts an adherent during spirit possession may or may not correlate with that of its 'horse'. In this not uncommon instance, the gender performed is that aligned with the embodied spirit, not of the initiate. In Santería, although the 'cultural genitals' that the embodied *orisha* are accorded may alter in light of whether the *caballo* is male or female, such as male priests mounted by female *orisha* being dressed in trousers rather than a skirt, for example, these point to the influence of societal norms upon concepts of gender and its performance.[91] As Gabriela Castellanos Llanos has observed, 'en la cosmovisión de la santería no encontramos la división tajante e inescapable entre los dos sexos a la que estamos acostumbrados en la tradición judeo-cristiana' [the categorical and absolute division between the two sexes to which we are accustomed in the Judeo–Christian tradition is not found in the cosmovision of Santería], an observation echoed by Conner (2005) with respect to Vodou.[92]

Turning to literary works, Rita De Maeseneer examines gender performance and the embodiment of both male and female *orisha* by Santos-Febres's protagonist in *Sirena Selena vestida de pena*, a drag *bolerista* who demonstrates the fluidity of notions of masculinity and femininity in his professional and personal lives.[93] Rita Indiana takes this a step further in *La mucama de Omicunlé*, as her female protagonist Acilde undergoes a futuristic process of gender reassignment using the drug 'Rainbow Bright' in conjunction with her initiation as a devotee of Yemayá and Olokún. Reborn in the past through an indigenous ritual which involves an anemone, both as Giorgio, an ostensibly Italian-Swiss conservationist in the 1990s, and as Roque, a seventeenth-century buccaneer, Acilde conflates the past, present, and future in an attempt to avert the destruction of the marine environment in the Caribbean Sea, which is also the space in which Yemayá and Olokún reside. As part of this process, Acilde not only embodies the androgynous Olokún — part woman/man, part fish — but also Yemayá, who, in one of her *caminos*, has been described by Solimar Otero as a *marimacho* (tomboy or masculine woman) who 'perform[s] her own queerness' and 'dresses like a man'.[94] In reference to Lydia Cabrera's *Yemayá y Ochún*, Otero foregrounds the 'crossing [of] boundaries and borderlands' between fixed notions of gender and sexuality that these *orisha* display, such as 'Yemayá's affinity for friendship for and infatuation with queerly gendered and sexualized spiritual beings'.[95] More than Acilde's mere association with Yemayá in this manner, the reader also observes how the protagonist outwardly demonstrates — both through physical bodily attributes and performed actions — the premise of spirit possession and a practitioner's identification with one or more *orisha* or *lwa*, that 'one's body can inhabit several selves that are constructed in a broad range of ways in terms of gender, race, culture, and even time period'.[96]

Otero's conclusion regarding spirit possession in Santería underlines another area of rich discussion in Caribbean colonial and postcolonial studies, that of creolization, *mestizaje/métissage* and hybridity. In her study *Coloniality of Diasporas: Rethinking Intra-Colonial Migrations in a Pan-Caribbean Context*, Yolanda Martínez-San Miguel (2014) examines the use of these interwoven terms, foregrounding the ways in which they have been employed and critiqued as unsatisfactory in both insular and wider regional, translinguistic contexts. As Silvio Torres-Saillant has argued, this is due in part to the inability of any of these terms to capture fully the specificity of both the Caribbean as a whole and its constituent elements.[97] Guillermina De Ferrari underscores this in her observation that:

> The master tropes of the predominant theories, mestizaje, métissage, creolization transculturación, and créolité, are both surprisingly similar to each other and yet operate as if they had been formulated in complete isolation, each maintaining what seems like a parallel trajectory to the others.[98]

Explaining that this is due in part to a lack of cross-linguistic dialogue in the Caribbean, De Ferrari also points to the exportation of these theories to non-

Caribbean settings as a contributing factor. As concepts that continue to be debated, these scholars and others have demonstrated that their application has not been uniform: at times these notions are employed as synonyms while at others there is repeated conflict over which is the most suitable.

Importantly, in her study *The Caribbean Postcolonial: Social Equality, Post-Nationalism, and Cultural Hybridity*, Shalini Puri (2004) examines this debate in considerable detail, to then both include and critique the term hybridity as part of this conversation. Drawing on works from across the region and beyond, Puri demonstrates that, while terms such as *mestizaje*, creolization and transculturation allow for cultural and historical specificity, the various binary frameworks inherent within them also limit their use as means through which to theorize the Caribbean. Hybridity, she illustrates, goes beyond these restrictions and recognizes the increased racial, cultural and linguistic heterogeneity evident both within constituent elements of and across the region. Yet, hybridity does not offer a singular term by which to describe Caribbean reality, as both Puri and Lourdes Martínez-Echazábal (1997) have underlined. Using Derek Walcott's metaphor of the 'vase shattered and reassembled', Puri argues that such an image presents 'the national vision of hybridity [as] a more traditional composite' and 'posits in advance a unity and equality that has yet to be achieved'.[99] Therefore, although hybridity permits a move beyond the restrictive binaries or presumed resultant homogeneity of previous theorizations, it does not offer a catchall framework with which to discuss Caribbean societies. In reference to Puri's observation, it should be acknowledged that a hybrid society does not require that each constituent element be equally influential upon the whole, or indeed that each element exert an influence on every other. Moreover, as she writes in her introduction, 'with its array of conflicting discourses of hybridity, the Caribbean example suggests we should be wary of any generalization about cultural hybridity' but rather be cognizant of the 'immense diversity of [...] hybridities' evident there.[100] With this in mind, it is intended that the use of terms such as creolization, *mestizaje* and hybridity in the following analyses be viewed in light of these discussions, which seek to recognize the cultural complexity of the region.

Across the four of her novels cited here, Montero synthesizes a variety of sources and discourses in her presentation of an overarching narrative, a narrative that illustrates this 'diversity of hybridities' in the Caribbean to which Puri refers. Prior to exploring the complexities inherent in such an analysis, it is important to note that, in reference to the binary frameworks outlined above, one could trace within Montero's texts a narrative based on a female/male dichotomy, as simplified a construct as this might seem. In *Como un mensajero tuyo*, Caruso, as Lucía Anglade de Aguerrevere correctly observes, represents 'la cultura europea, lo viejo, lo caduco y lo decadente' [European culture, that which is old, outdated and decadent], as opposed to Aída, 'la nueva, la mestiza, la que sobrevivirá el paso del tiempo' [what is new, mixed, that will survive the passage of time].[101] Meanwhile, Similá Bolosse, embodiment of the destructive nature of the Duvalier dictatorships in *Del rojo de su sombra* by dint of being a Tonton Macoute, is counterpointed with Zulé, *manbo* who works for the good of her *gagá* and dies to save it. In *La trenza de la hermosa luna*, this counterpoint is slightly more nuanced though still present: the accounts of Papá Rigaud and Papá Marcel, who serve as local counterparts of François and Jean-Claude Duvalier respectively, are placed in opposition to Choucoune's narrative, all which are then mediated by the male narrator Jean Leroy. However, in each of the novels it is clear that these seemingly exclusive and oppositional groupings are rendered more complex: the testimonies which complement Aída's in *Como un mensajero tuyo* are provided by men and women alike; Zulé's male *sèvitè* [servitor] and oldest initiate, Jérémie Candé, is integral to her narrative in *Del rojo de su sombra*; and also in *Del rojo de su sombra*, Galeona, 'vieja mambo vengativa' (98) ('vengeful, hard-hearted old mambo', 80) who works *con las dos manos* (with both hands), is allied with Similá and his narrative that is representative of the oppression of the patriarchal dictatorship.[102] For his part, Papá Marcel in *La trenza de la hermosa luna*, while representative of Baby Doc, does not blindly continue the work of his father but seeks to better the community and resist 'el mandamás de Port au Prince' [the big boss in Port-au-Prince] and the Macoutes, in spite of his links to the dictatorial regime (Montero 1987: 73, 120, 167, 188).[103]

When considered in the order in which they were published, Montero's four texts depict increasingly complex racial and cultural hybridities in the Caribbean, a process that culminates with the narrator of *Como un mensajero tuyo*, Enriqueta Cheng. Beginning with Choucoune in *La trenza de la hermosa luna*, her namesake is the *marabout* of nineteenth-century Haitian poet and politician Oswald Durand's *Choucoune*. Representative of *mestizaje* as a woman of European and African descent, she is 'a dark skin mulatto woman with straight hair, considered the perfect mix of African and European beauty'.[104] The Choucoune of Montero's text is regarded in much the same light by its narrator Jean Leroy, who after twenty years of absence is still enraptured by her beauty and recognizes the power she holds over him. As an adolescent, she enthralled the boys of the neighbourhood, and later, the relationships maintained with her now dead husband Hubert Gourgue, Papá Marcel, Jean Leroy and the old second-hand clothing salesman were based on their perception of her as the epitome of beauty by virtue of being mulatta. In addition, the presence and influence of the Dominican Republic in Haiti is embodied by Papá Marcel's live-in companion and assistant, Nicolasina Tiburcio, who then becomes Jean Leroy's companion when he replaces Papá Marcel as the *oungan* of Gonaïves at the novel's close.

Del rojo de su sombra moves beyond the synthesis inherent in *mestizaje* to illustrate creolization in the Caribbean, with a greater focus on the interaction of different cultural influences in a specific locale. In Coridón's — which later becomes Zulé's — *sosyete*, Anacaona, a Dominican woman who moves to the *batey* upon marrying Zulé's uncle and whose name comes from the last chief of the Tainos on Hispaniola, represents both the Dominican Republic and the Taino past of the island. Again through her name, María Caracoles — *oungan* Coridón's lover — directly ties Gagá together with both Catholicism ('María') and other African-derived belief systems that use cowrie shells ('caracoles') in the process of divination through *Ifá*, such as Santería and Candomblé. The important presence and influence of the Chinese in the Caribbean is indicated by Jérémie Candé, son of Coridón and a Chinese ship's maid. Though these different influences evident in the practice of Gagá could be interpreted in light of the notion of *mestizaje* or 'hybridity as symbiosis', as Martínez-Echazábal terms it, the interactions and tensions that exist between each of these elements within Gagá point to a process of continued cultural creolization exemplified by Montero's rewriting of the myth surrounding Ezili, Toro Belecou and Belié Belcán.[105] This cultural creolization is further demonstrated by Ganesha, the Indo-Guadeloupean partner of American herpetologist Jasper Wilbur in *Tú, la oscuridad*, whose prayers to the Hindu deity Mariamman are integrated into Thierry's prayers to Agwé Tarayo as the ship sinks, returning the *grenouille du sang* (a blood-red frog, identified as *Eleutherodactylus sanguineus*) to the depths (Montero 1995: 119, 239).

These influences come together in the mother and daughter in *Como un mensajero tuyo*, Aída and Enriqueta. Aída is a 'chinita amulatada' (209) ('Chinese mulatta', 170) of Lucumí, Spanish and Chinese descent on the part of her mother, representing a racial hybridity that is further nuanced in her daughter by virtue of Enriqueta's Italian father, Caruso. In spite of their hybrid ethnicity, both Aída and Enriqueta state that 'lo chino era lo primero que veían las personas' (30) ('my Chinese part was the first things that people saw', 16). Evelyn Hu-DeHart outlines the ambiguous position the Chinese occupied in the construction of race in nineteenth-century Cuba, where they had the legal status of 'white' but were often considered to be 'of colour'.[106] Aída and Enriqueta both note this ambiguity, as their almond eyes and straight hair coupled with the body of a *mulata* was considered attractive by many (174–75). Aída interacts with the Chinese community in Havana, regularly visiting her Chinese *padrino* Yuan Pei Fu, devotee of Sanfancón. Though Aída and her mother turn to Yuan Pei Fu for help and guidance at times, they are more intimately involved with Santería. Aída has Yemayá as her *orisha de cabecera* and, as has been outlined above, a close interaction exists between the *patakí* regarding Yemayá and Changó and the development of Aída's relationship with Enrico Caruso. Furthermore, she regularly visits her *padrino* Calazán, who intervenes and propitiates the *orisha* on her behalf to prevent her death and that of her lover. In the process of collating the interviews that are interspersed within her mother's testimony, Enriqueta also interacts with these different communities, visiting the house where the *paisanos* (the term used to refer to the members of the Sanfancón community in Havana) live many years after her grandfather's death and others who knew Aída around the time of the bomb. Some were close friends who often visited Aída and her mother, like María Vigil and Amable Casanova, others were professionals whom she met on her travels to Matanzas and Santa Clara with Caruso, such as Dr Benito Terry. Enriqueta also interviews one of the suspects of the bombing, a pharmacist from El Cerro. The narrative that results is a written account of these meetings and interactions which draws together a series of communities — religious, ethnic, professional, personal.[107]

Returning to Jérémie Candé in *Del rojo de su sombra*, he represents what at first glance might seem to be an unusual case for the Chinese in the Dominican Republic.

Edith Wen-Chu Chen's study of Chinese Dominicans echoes that of Hu-DeHart's in Cuba, whereby Chinese 'have been included in contemporary notions of *la raza blanca*'.[108] On the one hand, if considered from a merely phenotypical point of view, it might be possible that Jérémie Candé occupy a more privileged position in Dominican society than the other members of the *batey* by virtue of his being perceived as 'whiter' than the necessarily 'black' Haitians and Dominicans of Haitian descent in this community. However, Chen concludes that 'Chinese Dominicans may be able to contest traditional racial notions of Dominicanness through culture, language, and citizenship', and it is in these areas that any privilege would be negated.[109] Rejected by his Chinese mother, not only does Jérémie Candé have a black Haitian-Dominican father, he is raised in the cane-cutting community and the Gagá tradition, thus his acceptance as a Dominican would be precluded since from a social, economic and cultural position, he occupies a space reserved for *haitianos*.[110] Yet, Jérémie Candé is also considered as 'other' within the *sosyete*, never really gaining acceptance despite participating in the community, cutting cane and fulfilling his socioreligious role. He is neither Dominican nor Haitian, and although Zulé encourages his actions and sexual fantasies, she terms them 'cosas de chino' (108) ('things Chinamen do', 90) in disgust and flatly refuses the formal relationship with him proposed by her husband and his father, Coridón, as a last wish before the *oungan* died. As such, though Anacaona, as a Dominican and therefore notionally linked to whiteness, manages to become accepted in the *sosyete*, Jérémie Candé continues to occupy a liminal space as continually 'other', not fully accepted by any community.

Drawing women practitioners, spirit possession and hybridity together, the narrative that Montero writes across these novels simultaneously challenges the gendered division between public and private and the imposition of official histories and processes of historiography. Religions such as Santería and Vodou have long been placed conceptually within the private sphere in the Caribbean due to their proscription and marginalization, considered in opposition to Catholicism or Protestantism as official religions which are therefore denoted as 'public'. The classification of certain religious traditions as 'private' in a wider patriarchal construct that associates the public with masculinity and the private with femininity has conceptually gendered Afro-Cuban and Afro-Haitian traditions as feminine. As such, despite Santería and Vodou constituting loci of feminine strength in comparison to wider society, due to the historical marginalization of the religious traditions within state hegemony, female practitioners are conceptually further marginalized when viewed within a conflation of the male-dominated binary and the public/private dichotomy since they are both women and *santeras/vodouyizan*. As noted above, this hierarchy is reinforced within Santería, for example, which traditionally precludes women from participation in certain roles, as well as in other Afro-Cuban religious traditions like the all-male Sociedad Abakuá, the latter completely excluding women from its membership and enshrining misogyny within its foundational myth of Sikán. However, the movement of Santería and Vodou between private and public spaces by means of the female body in literature focusing on Cuba and Haiti, such as Montero's novels, has challenged this dichotomy. Moreover, by coupling this challenge with the depiction of these religious traditions as sites in which women can indeed gain agency through the female body, other patriarchal notions extant in Cuban and Haitian society regarding historiography and female sexuality and agency — each incorporating a male-dominated power hierarchy within it — are also destabilized and/or deconstructed. In this context, therefore, a complex framework is constructed from the following intersecting notions: the concept of power; the plurality inherent within Santería and Vodou with regard to gender and sexuality; the position of the religious traditions as neither wholly public or private since they participate and are represented in both spheres; the ability of the body to move between spaces within the traditions; and the fact that women are able to destabilize hierarchies that seek to restrict them in these same areas. This then places practitioners in a position from which subversion and resistance are possible.

Focused on the body as the site of interaction between the physical and spiritual, spirit possession is an important aspect of religious practice that Montero foregrounds as an example of initiates challenging the gendered public/private dichotomy. One such example in *Como un mensajero tuyo* occurs during the ceremony performed at a lagoon in order to cleanse Caruso and attempt to prevent his impending death. Mounted by Yemayá several times, here Aída's body functions in both the public and private spheres. In the public sphere, her being ridden by the *orisha* serves the community itself, allowing Yemayá's devotees to greet her and permitting this visible relationship between Yemayá and the Santería community. Necessarily a public action, as Murphy underlines, this interaction is only made possible '*by* the actions of the community and *in* the actions of the community'.[111] However, as the reader observes, Yemayá also acts in the interests of her love for Changó, mounting Aída and giving her the strength to run into the lagoon and stop Caruso from drowning. For Aída, this then functions in her private sphere, prolonging the amount of time she can maintain her relationship with her lover. Later, kidnapped and left in a cave to die, Aída is once again mounted by Yemayá, and the *orisha* protects Aída/Yemayá's and Caruso/Changó's unborn child. As an adult, their daughter Enriqueta would go on to transcribe her mother's testimony and is the old lady in the narrative present who exchanges the manuscript for fifty-two photographs of her father. As a published novel, this offers an alternative public account of Caruso's documented disappearance in Havana, situated squarely within the context of these simultaneously public and private religious traditions. A further example of this examined above is that of Zulé in *Del rojo de su sombra*, whose body traverses to a greater or lesser degree the divisions between spiritual and physical, public and private, female and male. As a *manbo* who dies in a battle with Similá, himself representative of the state and patriarchal authority, Zulé's physical demise sees her rise to be with her *mèt tèt* Ezili and ensure the integrity — spiritual and physical — of her *sosyete*. As *dueña* she is also aligned with the male Gede Nibo, and her death is juxtaposed with the moment at which the *bukán*, or 'Ogún Ferraille's prick', is extinguished.

Del rojo de su sombra also exemplifies the challenge Montero mounts across all four of the novels to the male-oriented processes of official historiography. As in *Como un mensajero tuyo*, in which she refutes the *New York Times*, Montero rewrites another official account — this time a Dominican police report — in order to narrate 'los hechos verídicos ocurridos hace pocos años en algún punto de La Romana' (10) ('real events that occurred a few years ago in La Romana', xiii) and criticize the police's reduction of this event to a single sentence, 'un simple "crimen pasional"' (10) ('a simple "crime of passion"', xiv). Rejecting these accepted versions of history, Montero incorporates a plurality of voices in her narratives — those of *orisha/lwa* and *santeros/vodouyizan* alike — 'engendering history', to use Patricia Mohammed's term, through inclusion of traditionally non-historical considerations such as family relations and sexuality, while using oral testimony in its various forms as legitimate historical sources and accounts.[112] This act of resistance not only places oral testimony at the centre of this challenge to official history and historiography, it also echoes Rogelio Rodríguez Coronel's statement in reference to the legends, *pataki* and songs that comprise the body of oral texts in Santería that 'quien tiene la memoria, tiene el poder' [the person able to remember retains the upper hand].[113] Montero, by centring on African-derived religious traditions and the myths, songs and prayers they comprise — that is, on the orality inherent within them — , directly challenges the hegemonic discourse embodied by the accepted written reports. She therefore mounts her own battle, reminiscent of that between Zulé and Similá, whereby her narrative rises up against and supplants official historical account.

As part of this critique of the processes of historiography, Montero's incorporation of oral testimony into the narratives challenges the precedence of patriarchal notions of history. The link between women, the transmission of oral history and 'oraliterature' has been investigated and theorized by numerous scholars of the Caribbean from a range of disciplines.[114] Carolyn Cooper's *Noises in the Blood* examines gender in what she terms 'oral and oral/scribal texts' that comprise Jamaican popular culture, underlining the 'hierarchical gender relations between (white) men and (black) women [which] are reproduced in the patriarchal discourse of master texts conspiring to exclude secondaried female "minor" forms from the (scribal) literary canon'.[115] In her analysis of women's writing in the Caribbean, Susanne Mühleisen points to women's 'strong ties in oral culture as preservers and perpetuators of indigenous traditions' and 'the traditional exclusion of women from the domains of public power', but then concludes that Caribbean women have challenged the resultant 'oral-literate divide' by writing oral culture into their work.[116] Montero's texts present the same challenge, moving away from these patriarchal lines by placing the focus on writing oral culture. In addition to Zulé's and Aída's personal accounts, Choucoune's story in *La trenza de la hermosa luna*, though mediated by Jean Leroy, rewrites that depicted in Durand's poem to give her the voice she was denied in the poet's text to recount it herself. It is important to note, however, that the accounts transcribed are not solely those of women, and that to do so would serve as mere counterpoint to these patriarchal notions instead of an active, direct challenge. One example is that of *Tú, la oscuridad*, which provides an alternative to the news clippings through the eyes of Thierry Adrien, Haitian guide to Victor Griggs, who himself is the American herpetologist searching for the *grenouille du sang*. Notwithstanding, Montero's critique of notions of historiography really comes to the fore in *Como un mensajero tuyo*: the entire novel comprises the account of Aída Petrirena Cheng as transcribed by her daughter, intercalated with other oral testimonies from witnesses — both men and women — which corroborate and complement Aída's story. This methodological approach emphasizes the importance Montero places on the process of recording history. Yet, rather than conceptually locating the narrative back inside patriarchal notions of historiography, its content and oral nature, as well as the context within which it takes place, further underline that Caribbean women will be situated in history through a recognition of heterogeneity, not the creation of a binary where notionally gendered narratives are placed in counterpoint to each other.

Montero's challenge as a novelist to the processes of historiography in the Caribbean fits with the work of previous authors, not least that of Glissant who repeatedly emphasized the conceptual link between 'history' and 'story', perhaps most concisely in the title of his essay 'Histoire, Histoires'.[117] Indeed, the more cumbersome English translation offered by J. Michael Dash, 'History-Histories-Stories', serves to further accentuate their interrelatedness.[118] In her analysis of fiction by Glissant, Carpentier and Wilson Harris, Barbara Webb examines the close connection that these and other Caribbean writers demonstrate between myth and history, whereby myth both preserves and produces history. She summarizes the disruptive act of their writing that draws on the close relationship between myth, history and story as 'a dual process of naming and unnaming; the first by laying claim to their own past and their own traditions, and the latter by dismantling the hidden mechanisms of political and cultural domination'.[119] In the same vein, Montero not only transcribes the oral testimonies of her protagonists and their communities, and so allows them to lay claim to their pasts and traditions, she also incorporates and (re)writes the myths of Changó, Yemayá and Ochún or of Ezili and Toro Belecou, as intrinsic elements of these histories. It should be noted that through the use of *libretas* and *manuales*, the scribal has long formed a part of Afro-Cuban religious practice — at the very least informally — in spite of the tradition that the *pataki*, rites and methods of divination have traditionally been passed down orally from *padrino/madrina* to initiate. As Erwin Dianteill and Martha Swearingen observe, such written texts have informed scholarly works such as Lydia Cabrera's *El monte* (1954), while practitioners have cited use of written materials during *consultas*.[120] With this in mind, Montero's novels participate in this oral-scribal tradition, but importantly challenge the aforementioned processes of historiography that have devalued the importance of African-derived religious traditions in Caribbean society and relegated them to the private sphere. Instead, she offers those positioned on the margins of society the voice that they warrant in historical discourse.

As part of her rewritings, Montero also critiques the existence of patriarchal frameworks within the religious traditions themselves. In her discussion of *Tú, la oscuridad*, Vadillo analyzes Montero's reorganization and combination of the different versions of the myth of Sikán and the foundation of the Sociedad Abakuá.[121] Enrique Sosa Rodríguez has transcribed the three main versions of the myth, correspondent with the three warring nations of *Efor*, *Efik* and *Oru*.[122] Though certain details change between them, in each one the fish that embodies the voice of Tanze — the supreme being — is captured in the gourd of river water that Sikán has collected. When the fish dies, the voice of Tanze is therefore lost and the male leaders declare that Sikán must be sacrificed, either in order for the voice to be recovered or as punishment for having exposed its secret, depending on the version of the myth. In spite of Sikán's death, the voice of Tanze does not return until she is replaced by a goat, which then gives Ekué (the sacred drum) its voice. In contrast to each of these versions, Montero does not substitute Sikán with the goat in her writing of the myth but rather Sikán fulfils this role herself. In altering it thus, as Vadillo observes, Montero reorients the myth to foreground Sikán's role in allowing the Tanze to be heard and peace to be declared between the three nations, thereby tempering the victim's negative characteristics as a traitor who broke her vow not to repeat the secret of Tanze. On the one hand, Montero's rewriting therefore 'propone que el signo femenino cese de ser juzgado desde una visión totalmente destructora y machista' [suggests that the sign of femininity cease to be considered from a solely destructive and *machista* point of view].[123] On the other hand, although Montero reformulates the myth and so removes the entirely negative image of women portrayed therein, the inferior status of women and their preclusion from membership continues, with Thierry explicitly stating in *Tú, la oscuridad* that women who discover the secret must die as Sikán did (170). The inferiority of women and their association with emasculation and death is further exemplified when Thierry recalls an instance of an important *ñáñigo* (member of the Sociedad Abakuá) who was 'killed' by being 'turned into a woman' (Montero 1997: 179). Cabrera explains that the brotherhood excommunicates members who are *rayado* (marked) on their backs with a piece of chalk held between the toes of their assailant since, now emasculated and thus perceived as a woman, this renders the *ñáñigo* dead. Such an event, Cabrera writes, is 'la mayor desgracia, lo más trágico que puede ocurrirle a un abakuá' [the worst disgrace, the most tragic thing that can happen to an *abakuá*].[124] Charged with avenging this 'murder' as the rules of the brotherhood dictate, Thierry uses similar terminology and states that the assailant 'cogió una tiza [...] con los dedos de los pies [...] y allí mismo le rayó la espalda. La espalda de un Ireme es sagrada y él lo destruyó, lo hizo muerto, lo convirtió en mujer' (237) ('he took a piece of chalk in his toes [...] and drew a line on his back. The back of an Ireme is sacred, and he destroyed him, killed him, turned him into a woman', 179). As such, although Montero rewrites the founding myth of the Abakuá, she does not shy away from exemplifying the misogynistic framework within which the brotherhood functions.

Finally, travel and displacement are central to the ways in which African-derived religious traditions are presented in each of the literary texts discussed in the Introduction and this chapter, as individuals and communities move between different physical, spiritual and conceptual spaces. Caren Kaplan argues that the notions of travel and displacement are juxtaposed, one informing the other, the first broadly defined as 'commercial and leisure movement' and the latter as the 'mass migrations that modernity has engendered'.[125] In this vein, each of Montero's novels involves a long journey of sorts. Protagonist of *La trenza de la hermosa luna* Jean Leroy has travelled around the Caribbean for twenty years working on a schooner, in direct contact with the ocean and thus the *lwa* who reside in it. This serves as preparation for the journey that constitutes his initiation into Vodou that he makes upon his return to Haiti. Mirroring the physical trials of Papá Marcel's own initiation, the journey Jean Leroy undertakes permits him to spend time in isolation and pass the necessary tests to cement his relationship with the *lwa*. For him, this takes place during the fall of the Baby Doc regime and the *dechoukaj* which saw many Vodou priests killed and their temples ransacked due to the links between Vodou and the Duvalierist state, as the closing pages of this novel and the character of Similá Bolosse in *Del rojo de su sombra* both demonstrate. In spite of the attempts Papá Marcel made to distance himself from the policies of Jean-Claude Duvalier, the crowd still perceives him as a participant in the state apparatus and calls for Jean Leroy to relinquish him. Papá Marcel dies soon after Baby Doc fled, and Jean Leroy's initiation into Vodou allows him to make the conceptual journey from the old Haiti of the dictatorship to the new Haiti (with which the writing of Montero's novel between San Juan and Port-au-Prince in 1986 and its publication in March 1987 are contemporary). The physical space does not change: Choucoune maintains her relationship with the second-hand clothing salesman, the *ounfò* and sea blue house are still the same, Nicolasina Tiburcio continues to be called 'mujer' [wife] as she was by Papá Marcel. However, having travelled between different communities by means of Vodou, Jean Leroy can conceptually make the transition from the Haiti of Baby Doc to the post-Duvalier period.

In *Del rojo de su sombra*, the movement of the community from one space to another is a necessary element both of Gagá and of Zulé's role as *manbo* and *dueña de la societé*. Zulé's earliest journey, at the age of twelve, is crossing the border with her father from Haiti to the Dominican Republic in an attempt to escape the *amarre* (curse) in the water that had led to numerous deaths in her immediate family. Moving to Colonia Azote to be educated in the ways of Gagá, she has her eyes worked to descend to the world of the dead and visits different communities in her role as a powerful *manbo* in the region. As an adult and *dueña* of her own *gagá*, Zulé leads her community in the collective journey they make during Holy Week, visiting different *bateyes* in order to reaffirm friendships and reiterate ongoing conflicts between the *sosyete* they visit. The final step of this procession on Easter Sunday is the culmination of Zulé's physical and spiritual journey, bringing the novel full circle as she is subjected to the same *amarre* she sought to escape. Sacrificed in the water of a storm, she becomes the conduit through which the *lwa* and her *sosyete* can interact, which then conflates the myths of Ezili, Toro Belecou and Belié Belcán with the lives of Zulé, Similá and Jérémie Candé, while closing the path for Ezili/Zulé and opening it for her *gagá*.

The protagonists make similar journeys in *Tú, la oscuridad* and *Como un mensajero tuyo*, as does Sirena Selena, while Vega's Antenor, Diógenes and Carmelo in

'Encancaranublado' and Santos-Febres's *boat people* are also displaced northwards from the Greater Antilles. For Indiana's Acilde in *La mucama de Omicunlé*, the sea and its resident *orisha* are the means by which she can journey in time, transported from 2027 to the late twentieth and the seventeenth centuries through a process that sees her undergo simultaneous ritual initiation and the physical female to male transformation she sought. The heterogeneous religious landscape that has influenced the Dominican Republic which Indiana depicts across the three time periods — Catholicism, indigenous practices, Cuban Santería, Dominican Vodou and Gagá — brings these traditions together in one locale, while in Montero's work, the interconnected web of religious traditions she delineates stretches to locations across the Caribbean. In addition to the various African-derived and associated practices on the island of Cuba, there is a branch of the Sociedad Abakuá in Port-au-Prince, a reference to *Ifá* in the Dominican Republic and a Mayombe (also known as Palo or Palo Monte) community in Saint Croix. There are also Vodou communities in Saint Croix and Cuba, Zulé officiates in both the Gagá and Vodou traditions either side of the Massacre River, and in *Tú, la oscuridad* Ganesha brings her Indo-Guadeloupean practices with her when she moves to Haiti with Papá Crapaud.

In her discussion of the notion of 'archipelago' in the context of the Caribbean, Martínez-San Miguel seeks to focus attention back on the sea rather than on the group of islands that have been 'conceived and articulated as a single unit from the imperial perspective'.[126] She notes that the sea as a 'signifying unit' is central to Glissant's work, as it is in more contemporary work on the region by scholars such as Elizabeth DeLoughrey (2007). As this theoretical discussion and literary analysis has shown, the conversations in the Caribbean regarding creolization and hybridity, gender, sexual and cultural identities, participation in multiple public and private spheres and the articulation of marginalized voices are animated, complex and often difficult to negotiate. The context of African-derived religions such as Santería and Vodou in fiction from across the region is one space in which these conversations have come together. This has facilitated — and continues to facilitate — the exploration of the 'diversity of hybridities' present in the region while simultaneously challenging and resisting fixed notions of political and linguistic borders, gendered dichotomies and male-oriented frameworks of power.

Notes to Chapter 1

1. For further discussion see, for example: Brandon 1993: 1–8, 79–98; Fernández Olmos & Paravisini-Gebert 2011: 13–17; Desmangles 1992: 1–15; Bellegarde-Smith & Michel 2006: xvii–xxvii.
2. Brandon 1993: 11; Michel 2006: 33.
3. Feast days for the *orisha* and *lwa* usually coincide with those of their Catholic counterparts. On these days offerings are made to the *orisha* or *lwa* associated with a particular temple or community, or those with whom an adherent is associated. In this way, *santeros* and *vodouyizan* celebrate the birthdays of their most important spirits as they would a member of their family's or one of their friends'. Offerings may also be given to particular *orisha* or *lwa* on their feast days as thanks for service rendered or in order to propitiate for services to be petitioned.
4. Ayorinde 2004: 14.

5. See, for example, Droogers (1989), Brandon (1993), Shaw & Stewart (1994), Barnet (1996), Martínez-San Miguel (2014), as well as the introduction to Fernández Olmos & Paravisini-Gebert's *Creole Religions of the Caribbean* (2011: 1–19). It should be noted that, although references are taken from the 1963 version of Ortiz's *Contrapunteo cubano del tabaco y el azúcar*, it was originally published in 1940. It is translated into English as *Cuban Counterpoint: Tobacco and Sugar* (1947).

6. Apter 1991; Cros Sandoval 2006: 309–11; Brandon 1993: 88–92; Hurbon 1987: 158–59.

7. Desmangles 1992: 10–11.

8. Brandon 1993: 69.

9. Apter 1991: 254. In addition to Apter, Desmangles and Brandon, for further discussion of these processes in reference to Santería, see, for example, Murphy (2001), Ayorinde (2004) and Cros Sandoval (2006), and with regard to Vodou, Price-Mars (1928), Métraux (1958), Bastide (1971) and Laguerre (1989).

10. Bastien 1966: 65; see also Desmangles (1992).

11. Burton (1997: 6–8) has argued that 'Afro-Creole cultures', by virtue of their reproduction of the dominant system if only in their underlying structures, 'tend to be much more *cultures of opposition* than *cultures of resistance*'. In spite of this, it must be recognized that, although these traditions may be challenging the dominant culture on its own ground (to use Burton's terminology) when viewed from a wider perspective, when considered on a smaller scale such as that of the community or individual, Santería and Vodou are sites which enable resistance by employing notions which do not form part of the dominant culture and, in certain historical or political contexts, are also forced to occupy a position outside that culture. That said, one example of the negation of such a possibility of resistance is the context of the father-son Duvalier dictatorship in Haiti (1957–86), which is analyzed in Chapter 4.

12. García-Calderón 2004: 160.

13. The English translation of this novel is published as *Sirena Selena* (2000).

14. Stinchcomb 2013: 10.

15. Bastien (1966), Laguerre (1989), Desmangles (1992). It should be noted that historian David Geggus has questioned whether Vodou as such had indeed developed at this time (2002). However, whether or not it was recognizable as Vodou per se does not alter the fact that, over time, the rites and rituals practised during slavery became the religious tradition that is now referred to as Haitian Vodou.

16. Laguerre 1989: 25.

17. Geggus 2002: 75.

18. As Elizabeth McAlister writes, the Bois Caïman ceremony 'has been written about, painted, dramatized and rendered in poetry countless times' (2012: 189). The ceremony itself is said to have been 'a nighttime gathering at a place called Bois Caïman (Alligator Woods) in the north of colonial Saint-Domingue on 14 August 1791', where 'several hundred slaves from different ethnic groups united under a leader named Boukman and vowed to fight the French who ruled the colony and used forced labor to fuel the sugar industry' (189). For further details, see McAlister's article in which she explores many of the representations and analyses of this event.

19. Geggus 2002: 82.

20. Bastien 1966: 42.

21. Murphy 1994: 12.

22. Brandon 1993: 82–83.

23. Ibid.: 85.

24. See Matibag 1996: 87–93, and Ayorinde 2004: 49–52. Instructive in this regard are analyses of the presentation of Afro-Cubans in theatre, such as Turner's book chapter, 'El negro en el teatro cubano' (1994) [The Black Man in Cuban Theatre], and Inés María Martiatu's edited volume on *teatro bufo*, *Bufo y nación: interpelaciones desde el presente* (2009) [Bufo and Nation: Interpellations from the Present].

25. Ayorinde 2004: 104–07.

26. Ibid.: 123.

27. Matibag 1996: 230.

28. Laguerre 1989: 19; Bellegarde-Smith 2005a: 54.

29. Ramsey 2011: 51–52; for further discussion see Chapter 2 of Ramsey (2011).

30. Bellegarde-Smith 2005a: 55; Desmangles 1992: 43–45. It should also be noted that Vodou was recognized by the state at times during this period, most notably between 1847 and 1858 under President Faustin Soulouque.

31. Johnson 2006: 438.

32. For a detailed exposition of the Duvaliers' use of the networks provided by the *ounfò*, see Laguerre 1989: 103–20.

33. Abbott 2011: 195–96. Speaking to Riccardo Orizio in 2001, Jean-Claude Duvalier reaffirmed the importance of Vodou during the Haitian Revolution. He also stated that he believed in Vodou, as well as the values of harmony and solidarity it espouses (Orizio 2007: 148–49).

34. See Richman (2012) for an examination of the influence of Protestantism in Haiti. In May 2012, former President Michel Martelly undertook to 'remettre "Haïti à Jésus de Nazareth"' [rededicate Haiti to Jesus of Nazareth] at a Protestant conference in Delmas, Port-au-Prince. While no specific threat to the legal status of Vodou had been articulated by the President's office, the language of some of those pastors quoted in *Le Nouvelliste*'s article 'Le secteur protestant prend le président Martelly au mot' [The Protestant community takes President Martelly at his word] on 6 August 2012 — a desire to 'changer la mentalité des Haïtiens' and 'mettre un terme au règne des ténèbres, celui des démons' [change the Haitian mentality and end the reign of darkness, that of the devils] (Cincir 2012) — is reminiscent of that used by American televangelist Pat Robertson on his television channel The Christian Broadcasting Network after the 2010 earthquake when he spoke of Haiti having 'swor[n] a pact to the devil' and that they needed to 'turn to God'. See McAlister's 'From Slave Revolt to a Blood Pact with Satan: The Evangelical Rewriting of Haitian History' (2012) for an analysis of this depiction of the Bois Caïman ceremony as 'blood pact with Satan'.

35. Interview conducted by the author with Tato Quiñones — *babalao*, scholar of Afro-Cuban religious traditions and filmmaker — in Miramar, Havana (June 2009).

36. Murphy 1994: 12.

37. Paravisini-Gebert 2008: 150.

38. Barnet 1997: 92–93. 'Lucumí' refers to traditions of Yoruba origin in Cuba and is used as a name for the ritual language often employed in Santería rituals and ceremonies. It was also used as a term to describe enslaved people of Yoruba origin.

39. Barnet 1997: 92.

40. See Lachatañeré 1992: 37–38; Barnet 1997: 93.

41. Cabrera 1980: 29–30.

42. Bolívar Aróstegui 1990: 108; Cros Sandoval 2006: 235–36.

43. Fernández Olmos & Paravisini-Gebert 2011: 51.

44. Bascom 1972: 13–14. For further discussion, see Cros Sandoval 2006: 223–36.

45. Castellanos 2001: 43.

46. The reader learns later in the novel that in fact Yuan Pei Fu was Aída's father instead of Noro Cheng — her mother's husband — whom Aída had believed was her father when she was a child.

47. Pérez Fernández & Rodríguez González 2008: 143; Scherer 2001: 164.

48. Matibag 1996: 27; Murphy 2001: 88; Cabrera 1980: 56.

49. Murphy 2001: 88.

50. Castellanos 2001: 35.

51. Barnet 1997: 95.

52. Lachatañeré 1992: 50–52.

53. Barnet 1997: 95.

54. In this regard, Hernández Espinosa discusses his approach and the reception his work has received within the Santería community in an interview with Christilla Vasserot (1998).

55. Michel, Bellegarde-Smith & Racine-Toussaint 2006: 70; Conner 2005: 146–47.

56. Desmangles 1992: 95.

57. Ibid.: 143–44.

58. Conner 2005: 146.
59. Michel, Bellegarde-Smith & Racine-Toussaint 2006: 71.
60. Brown 2010: 246, 256; Déita 1993: 272–74.
61. Rosenberg 1979: 23, 35.
62. Fernández Olmos 1997: 275; Rosenberg 1979: 203. In the episode that focuses on Haiti and the Dominican Republic in his mini-series *Redemption Song: History of the Caribbean*, filmed for the BBC, sociologist and cultural theorist Stuart Hall observes that the communities founded around the sugar cane industry that subscribe to this cult have been divorced from their historical and physical environments: they do not belong to the Haitian community, neither physically nor spiritually, while at the same time they are rejected from Dominican society, 'where the poorest citizen wouldn't be seen dead cutting cane with a machete' (1991).
63. Deive 1988: 185.
64. Montero follows the spelling used by Rosenberg for the names of these *lwa*. Following current spelling norms in Kreyòl, Ti Jean Petró is Ti Jan Petwo, Erzulie Zeux Rouges is Ezili Je Wouj and Ogún Ferraille is Ogou Feray.
65. Métraux 1958: 105; 1959: 118–19; Fernández Olmos 1997: 279.
66. Métraux 1958: 105; 1959: 119.
67. Vadillo 2002: 97–98.
68. Fernández Olmos 1997: 280.
69. Alegría Pons 1993: 118; Deive 1988: 238.
70. Rosenberg 1979: 76; Brown 2010: 114, 95–96.
71. Brown 1997: 78.
72. Brown 1997: 71; Déita 1993: 175–76; Desmangles 1992: 148.
73. Brown 2010: 248, 235.
74. Ibid.: 379–80.
75. Brown 1997: 84–85.
76. Déita 1990: 195.
77. Rosenberg 1979: 69.
78. Brown 2010: 380.
79. Michel 2006: 38.
80. Dayan 1995: 47. Joan Dayan has subsequently published as Colin Dayan; all the works listed under Dayan in the Bibliography were written by her.
81. Michel, Bellegarde-Smith & Racine-Toussaint 2006: 74–76.
82. For an in-depth discussion of this debate, see Beliso-De Jesús 2015: 183–211.
83. Interview conducted by the author with Lázara Menéndez at the University of Havana (July 2009).
84. Benedicty-Kokken 2015a: 19.
85. Ibid.: 19, 24.
86. Benedicty 2012: 299.
87. Brown 2006: 13.
88. Clark 2004: 7.
89. Schechner 1985: 110.
90. Drewal 1992: 182.
91. Clark 2005: 101. This, Clark posits, is due to the 'Western abhorrence of male-to-female cross-dressing', and so 'the priest may be constructed as female both in terms of the possession event itself and in respect to the Orisha that has possessed him, but the appropriation of female clothing by male priests presents this situation in perhaps too strong and open a manner'. Further to this, though Clark asserts that, in her experience, possession of a male priest by a female *orisha* does not put into question his sexual identity, interviews conducted in Cuba (in particular with Babalao Tato Quiñones and Tomás Fernández Robaina) suggest that while this may be the case from a theological perspective, in practice few, if any, heterosexual men are mounted by female *orisha*. This suggestion has been reiterated in print by Palmié (2002) and Fernández Robaina (2008), though both recognize the absence of empirical evidence to this end. Hagedorn (2010: 147), for her part, asserts that most *orisha* possessions are 'same-sex', since 'the

majority of female practitioners have female-associated head-ruling *orichas*, and the majority of male practitioners have male-associated head-ruling *orichas*'. Cabranes-Grant (2010: 127) has also indicated that possession of male adherents by female *orisha* is less common than the reverse. With regard to Vodou, Jacqueline Épingle, *manbo* in Montreal, has indicated that, anecdotally, it seems that fewer men are mounted by female *lwa* than women by male *lwa* and that this is perhaps due to the questions some male *vodouyizan* think might be posed regarding their sexual identity if they were to be mounted by a female *lwa* (personal conversation with the author, July 2010).

92. Castellanos Llanos 2006: 17.
93. De Maeseneer 2004: 130–35.
94. Otero 2013: 98.
95. Ibid.: 86, 98.
96. Ibid.: 96.
97. Torres-Saillant 2006: 42–44, 238–41.
98. De Ferrari 2007: 16.
99. Puri 2004: 69.
100. Ibid.: 3.
101. Anglade de Aguerrevere 2005: 77.
102. An *oungan* or *manbo* who works 'with both hands' is one that uses Vodou for both positive outcomes (the right hand) and malevolent purposes (the left hand).
103. Notably, the term 'mandamás' is also used in *Del rojo de su sombra* (125).
104. N'Zengou-Tayo 1998: 133.
105. Martínez-Echazábal 1997: 117–18.
106. Hu-DeHart 1999: 108–10.
107. As I have argued elsewhere, the resultant account of the interactions between these communities can be viewed in Benedict Anderson's terms as that of a nation (Humphrey 2012).
108. Chen 2008: 30.
109. Ibid.: 31.
110. It should be noted that the term *haitiano* (Haitian) as employed here often designates a much larger group than just those of Haitian nationality. Citizenship rights and the associated issue of racial profiling continue to cause problems for Haitians and Dominicans of Haitian descent resident in the Dominican Republic, exemplified not least by the 2013 ruling by the Constitutional Court of the Dominican Republic that stripped Dominican citizenship rights from the latter of these two groups.
111. Murphy 1994: 110.
112. Mohammed 2003: 120.
113. Rodríguez Coronel 1997: 204.
114. See, for example, the works and edited volumes of Bridget Brereton, Eudine Barriteau and Patricia Mohammed. Importantly, the Havana-based publication, *Oralidad: anuario para el rescate de la tradición oral en América Latina y el Caribe* (published by UNESCO La Habana), has brought together scholarship focusing on orality from across the region since 1988. Discussions of orality, oral literature and the scribal tradition have variously coined terms such as 'orature' and 'oraliterature' to underline the dual heritage and process of interaction between the oral and scribal that have informed works in this genre, a necessary shift in terminology as Walter Ong has exemplified. For further discussion see: Ong (1982), Wilentz (1992), Arndt (1998) and Anim-Addo (1996).
115. Cooper 1993: 7–9.
116. Mühleisen 1996: 170.
117. Glissant 1997: 221–79.
118. Glissant 1989: 61.
119. Webb 1992: 7.
120. Dianteill & Swearingen 2003: 280–87; interview conducted by the author with Babalao Tato Quiñones in June 2009.
121. Vadillo 2002: 165–68.

122. Sosa Rodríguez 1982: 191–215; see also Quiñones 1994: 25–31.
123. Vadillo 2002: 166.
124. Cabrera 1970a: 205.
125. Kaplan 1996: 3.
126. Martínez-San Miguel 2014: 40.

CHAPTER 2

Staging Subversion:
Santería, Performance and Corporeality

As demonstrated in Chapter 1, the process of writing and rewriting oral texts and myths within the context of Santería and Vodou is a central component of the way in which Mayra Montero and others examine the theme of resistance. Indeed, the rewriting of the *pataki* in *Como un mensajero tuyo* saw Montero's mother and daughter protagonists, Aída and Enriqueta, challenge the published account of Enrico Caruso's disappearance and subsequent death, and render visible Aída's relationship with the singer. In addition, as the chapter details, Montero's and other authors' reconfigurations of these myths in Santería, Vodou and other religious practices fulfil the important role of recounting and adapting oral texts for audiences old and new alike, a necessary process for their transmission to — and continued relevance for — subsequent generations of participants and storytellers.

In this chapter, the analysis will focus on one particular Cuban text, Eugenio Hernández Espinosa's 1964 play *María Antonia*, which in the more than fifty years since its premiere has enjoyed numerous performances and stagings, been rewritten by the playwright and appended by others, and been adapted for the silver screen by Cuban-American director Sergio Giral. Hernández Espinosa has described his work as one of a creative artist for whom Afro-Cuban spirituality provides the freedom to invent *pataki* and construct alternative stories to those recounted by practitioners (see Vasserot 1998). The two examples he gives are *Odebí el cazador* [Odebí the Hunter], an invented story, and *Obá y Shangó* [Obá and Shangó], in which he draws on what he terms the fundamental characteristics of these two *orisha*. Further, he notes in an anecdote that his incorporation of Santería into *María Antonia* led to at least one *santera* describing him as 'un descarado, un atrevido' [shameless, impudent].[1] A two-volume collection of his works published in 2010 under the title *Quiquiribú Mandinga* (the name of another of his plays) sees editor Alberto Curbelo Mezquida assemble numerous of Hernández Espinosa's works that display this characteristic creative process, such as *Ochún y las cotorras* [Ochún and the Parrots] and *Oyá Ayawá*, in addition to the aforementioned *Odebí el cazador*. While this chapter focuses on Hernández Espinosa and *María Antonia* in particular, his work fits into a larger framework in which this process of writing and rewriting of *pataki* occurs. Pertinent examples include author Excilia Saldaña's collection of short stories *Kele Kele* [Softly, Softly] (1987), which retells five *pataki* that focus on the theme of love, and many of Nancy Morejón's poems, fictional narratives and scholarly works, which consistently engage with the themes of Afro-Cuban religious and social life. In the field of theatre, playwright and scholar Gerardo Fulleda points to numerous plays that focus on Santería, from Carlos Felipe's *Réquiem por Yarini* [Requiem for Yarini] (1960) and José Ramón Brene's *Santa Camila de La Habana Vieja* [Saint Camila of Old Havana] (1962), to Elaine Centeno's *La piedra de Elliot* [Elliot's Stone] (1993) and his own *Chago de Guisa* [Chago of Guisa] (1989).[2] Throughout the last of these, Chago de Guisa interacts with various *orisha* as well as his ancestors, a process that invites the audience to draw on their knowledge of the *pataki* in order to interpret the scenes and constituent interactions performed on stage. In this vein, as Martiatu has demonstrated on numerous occasions, it should be noted that the performance of myths and rituals of Santería and other African-derived religious practices is longstanding in Cuba, even more so in informal and/or religious contexts.[3] Their translation to the stage in a non-reductive, non-essentializing manner, however, is thanks in great part to the work of Hernández Espinosa, beginning with *María Antonia*.

The playwright's rewriting of the *pataki* that focus Ochún, Changó and Yemayá in *María Antonia* sees his eponymous protagonist attempt to reject, challenge and subvert the established patriarchal norms within Santería and popular Cuban society. The analysis that follows explores the manner in which the male-oriented frameworks present in Cuban Santería (as scholars like Beliso-De Jesús (2015) and Clark (2005) have exemplified) and other Afro-Cuban religious traditions such as the Sociedad Abakuá are both reinforced and subverted in the play. By engaging with the theories of ritual performance and bodily performance of gender examined in Chapter 1, it interrogates the actions of both female and male characters, and outlines the restrictive social context with regard to female agency and possibility for autonomy found within the religious and social frameworks in which the play takes place. As such, it offers a reading which, while recognizing the inescapable patriarchal nature of many aspects of Santería as performed in the play, illustrates that the protagonist's actions in its overlapping religious and secular contexts subvert this very framework and enable her to gain agency therein.

First performed in 1967, *María Antonia* has been described as the first play in Cuba to move beyond the reductive manner in which black Cubans were presented in *teatro bufo* and *teatro vernáculo* in the nineteenth and twentieth centuries, instead representing both 'la realidad del negro, del pobre y marginado' [the everyday reality for the black man, for the poor and marginalized man] and Afro-Cuban religious traditions in a more complex fashion.[4] The relevance of the play to Cubans from the Batista period during which it was set through to the present day is clear and warrants brief consideration. Numerous scholars have analyzed the criticisms *María Antonia* makes of pre-revolutionary and specifically Batista-era Cuba, such as Martiatu (1992; 2000; 2004a; 2004b), Flora González (1998; and González Mandri 2006), Catherine Davies (1993) and Graziella Pogolotti (2004), among others. Post-1959, Leo Cabranes-Grant warns that the text should not be read 'as though it were an allegory for the Cuban Revolution' as 'this would be too easy and perhaps untrue'.[5] However, while that might be the case, the work's relevance as a critique of the period in which it was penned is notable, as Rufo Caballero rightly indicates:

> *María Antonia* podía referirse al propio año 1964. Si todavía hoy la promiscuidad de los solares constituye un estamento social inocultable, si hoy la marginalidad ha ocupado el *centro* que parece entonces todo el tiempo *margen*, cómo no iba a ser verosímil el drama de *María Antonia* en los conflictivos años 60, plenos de colisiones y enfrentamientos.[6]

> [*María Antonia* could refer to 1964 itself. If today the promiscuity in the tenements is still indicative of an unconcealable social class, if marginality has now occupied the *centre* that seemingly remains the *margin*, how was the drama of *María Antonia* not going to seem realistic in the unsettled and troubled period of the 60s, during which conflicts and clashes were so common.]

The play's continued relevance is further indicated by its return to theatres on several occasions: Roberto Blanco, the original director in 1967, reprised the piece in 1968 and again on its twentieth anniversary in 1984, whereas the playwright himself directed *María Antonia*'s return in April 2011 to the site of its original premiere, the Teatro Mella in Havana. On this occasion, Hernández Espinosa spoke with Kathi Kaity as part of her project documenting the return of *María Antonia* to the Teatro Mella, one part of which she included in a short documentary video, *Seguimos: retorno de 'María Antonia'* [We Will Continue: Return of *María Antonia*]. In it he remarked:

> Yo siempre veo que María Antonia está en la calle. En la calle con sus pasiones, con sus frustraciones, con su ansia de cambiar códigos también. Poner una conducta con el machismo, siempre con el machismo [...]. Pero está, está. Y la gente se siente identificada.

> [I always see that María Antonia is in the street. In the street with her passions, with her frustrations, anxious to change social norms, too. To take up against machismo, always against machismo [...]. But she's there, she's there. And people identify with her.]

In addition to staged performances of *María Antonia*, the play was adapted for film in 1990, a version in which critiques of post-revolutionary and special period Cuba are clear.[7] Hernández Espinosa also edited and rewrote sections of his original play to serve as stand-alone pieces: one was a short monologue by María Antonia's lover and murderer, Carlos, *El masigüere* [The Madman] (1987), and another, a much abbreviated and pared-down version of the play, titled *María de los cuchillos* [María, Our Lady of Daggers] (1994). Taking its title from a line used to describe the protagonist in the original, *María de los cuchillos* focuses more closely on María Antonia and her interactions with the world of Santería, and any actions by her lovers Julián and Carlos or her *madrina* are conveyed through reported speech. Finally, Georgina Herrera's 'Conversación con María Antonia (cuarenta años después)' (2004), which serves as a form of epilogue to the various iterations of the play, constitutes a further articulation of *María Antonia*'s pertinence to contemporary Cuban, and more specifically Havanan, society. Recounting an interaction with María Antonia in terms similar to communicating with the dead in the context of

Santería, Herrera reminds the reader in the protagonist's words, 'Es una historia que viene desde lo más remoto de todos los tiempos, y con las variantes de cada época, se repite' [It's a story that comes from the remotest point of all time, and with the variations of each age, it repeats itself].[8] As the following analysis will explore, it is in María Antonia's performance and the repetition of her actions that the narratives of both subversion and defiance come to the fore.

Performance and Corporeality

As demonstrated in Chapter 1, in Santería, Vodou and related religious traditions, the body serves as the conduit through which the spiritual and physical planes intersect, and the site in which the reciprocal relationship between *santero/a* and *orisha* or *vodouyizan* and *lwa* is expressed. In her analysis of the African presence in Cuban theatre, Cariad Astles explains the importance of corporeality in this context in terms of 'the body as primary focus of expression through the embodiment of ritual and the dances of the *orichas*'.[9] Possession is a somatic experience, and the process through which a practitioner is *montado* and an *orisha* is manifested in order to interact with the Santería community centres on the body. Similar to Benedicty's discussion of the body as a 'proscenium' in the context of spirit possession in Vodou, Roberto Strongman points to the 'transcorporeal conceptualization of the self', whereby various 'subjectivities rest upon a concave corporeal surface', as a way to understand the process of spirit possession in these African-derived religious traditions.[10] Importantly, to reiterate from Chapter 1, possession is inherently visceral and performative in nature; it is not merely representation but rather 'provoca [...] una verdadera catarsis donde el hombre sale *renacido*' [engenders [...] a real catharsis from which man emerges *reborn*].[11]

Furthermore, embodiment of the *orisha* through possession is not the only corporeal element of Santería. As Bárbara Balbuena Gutiérrez writes: 'En el contexto de las rituales de la santería [...] la danza constituye [...] el medio más propicio y orgánico para establecer los nexos de significación y comunicación con las divinidades' [In the context of Santería rituals [...] dance constitutes [...] the most propitious and organic medium in order to establish connections with the divinities through which to communicate and transmit meaning].[12] Although the principal aim of Santería ceremonies is the manifestation of the *orisha* through possession, not every dancer will be mounted by the *orisha* invoked; the dance performed by numerous participants is itself an important element of the process of propitiation. This necessary communal and somatic aspect of the *toque de santo* (ritual ceremony using consecrated drums, in honour of one or more *orisha*) is seen on both occasions that it is performed in *María Antonia*, most extensively during the ceremony to celebrate Ochún's *día de santo* (saint's day) in the third *cuadro* (scene) of the play (Hernández Espinosa 1992: 975–91).[13] La Madrina, the *iyalochas*, *iyawó* and men carrying the image of Caridad del Cobre/Ochún process down to the river, singing and dancing, where they are joined by María Antonia.[14] Although there are numerous *santeros/as* involved in the ceremony, only one *iyalocha* is mounted while the others and María Antonia continue to sing and dance in order to both propitiate and interact with Ochún. With this in mind, it should be noted that as the ceremony progresses and María Antonia feels that she too will be mounted by Ochún, she refuses to continue to participate and breaks the circle of dancers, an event considered in further detail later in this chapter. Divination through consultation of *Ifá*, coconut shells or the *dilogún* is a further example of the corporeal and communal aspects of Santería rituals outside the context of the *toque de santo*. Each of these is open to male and female initiates, to a greater or lesser degree and with certain caveats particularly in the case of *Ifá* (see Chapter 1, as well as Clark (2005) and Beliso-De Jesús (2015), among others). In reference to the bodily performance of divination, the human body is a vehicle for the *orisha* to speak, as the practitioner performs the gestures of divination and serves 'as a receptacle for collective memory in earthly and cosmic space'.[15] As such, whether it be through spirit possession, dancing and/or drumming to invoke the *orisha* or the various forms of divination, the body remains the central point of interaction between the spiritual and physical in the context of Santería ritual.

The link between Santería and healing is the final point to be discussed here regarding corporeality and the visceral nature of Santería. Whether it be in anecdotal accounts of the circumstances that led *santeros/as* to practise the religion or in one of the numerous scholarly studies of the theme such as Johan Wedel's *Santería Healing* (2004), it is common to hear that the path to initiation for a practitioner was entwined with a desire to overcome a physical, mental or emotional affliction by means of serving the *orisha*. Indeed, María Antonia suffers (or, at least, is perceived to suffer) in all three of these categories, the reason for which La Madrina brings her to the *babalao* Batabio. As her spiritual and earthly guardian, La Madrina implores Batabio to seek a way in his consultations with *Ifá* for María Antonia to be cleansed and born anew. The protagonist's death is inescapable, however, and her demise ensured even if she were to follow the *babalao*'s advice and submit to what he terms 'la ley con que tiene que vivir aquí' [the rules by which one must live here] (949).

One of the characteristics of performance and performativity, as Diana Taylor observes, is 'the possibility of anti-hegemonic agency' that they offer, which in turn points to the liminality inherent within performance itself.[16] The performer and the performed, Schechner writes, are 'not me, not not me', which in the context of Santería and Vodou become the practitioner and the *orisha* or *lwa*.[17] 'Betwixt and between', to use Victor Turner's terminology,[18] both the performer and performance inhabit a liminal space, be it the theatre itself as a 'space that by means of performing could become anywhere', or the stage and the performances that take place upon it, which link the audience with that which is being performed.[19] In keeping with Taylor, therefore, as a liminal entity the performer embodies the potential for agency, both to define one's own being and to mediate the simultaneous experiences of the performed and the observer.

In order to discuss the performance of Santería on stage, and in particular reference to *María Antonia*, the conceptual link between ritual and performance must also be examined. Bell explores this relationship in her influential work, *Ritual Theory,*

Ritual Practice, in which she underlines that ritual had, for many years, 'consistently [been] depicted as a mechanistically discrete and paradigmatic means of social integration, appropriation, or transformation'.[20] The performance of ritual had therefore been considered as a way to formalize groups and communities. However, as she demonstrates, ritualization is tied to the construction and reinforcement of power relationships and the performance of ritual is centred on the body. Basing her concept of power on the Foucauldian notion that power and freedom go hand in hand, and that power is not synonymous with the forces of violence or coercion, Bell concludes that the possibility for creation and individual appropriation must therefore be inherent within ritualization.[21] This in turn offers a space in which personal agency is necessary in order that the social hierarchy reinforced through ritual be maintained, and since ritual is performed, then such agency is effectuated through the body.

Bell's conclusion regarding ritual and ritualization is demonstrated in the reciprocal nature of the relationship between *santero/a* and *orisha* in the performance of spirit possession. Although possession requires a practitioner to temporarily relinquish control of their body — which, as noted above, María Antonia finds problematic — the embodiment of the *orisha* constitutes a source of empowerment, investing the body with power as the performing entity in this liminal position.[22] As Beatriz Rizk observes, 'cuando se habla de la "posesión", [...] se está hablando de jerarquías, de poder, de *status* social dentro de una comunidad' [when speaking of 'possession', [...] one is talking about hierarchies, about power, about social *status* within a community].[23] Moreover, Bell underscores that ritualization (and thus ritual performance) is a source of social interaction which empowers its agents, albeit within a hierarchical setting, and that the possibility of resistance is an integral element of this performance.[24] In reference to Santería, the body is the receptacle of this power, constituting the nodal point between the spiritual and physical in which the force of both the *orisha* and the subject come together. Inserted into a hierarchy within the Santería community, the body is thus the site from which the spiritual and physical domains can be influenced, and as such, the space in and through which the norms involved in ritual performance can be reinforced and/ or subverted. In this regard, it is notable that during Hernández Espinosa's play only women are mounted: La Madrina by Yemayá, and both an *iyalocha* and María Antonia by Ochún. Though Batabio speaks for Orula through *Ifá*, which is a bodily performance through the gestures performed, it is only the women who embody the *orisha* by means of a process of penetration. Indeed, as Beliso-De Jesús and others have observed, if a male initiate is penetrated by the *orisha*, this precludes him from receiving *Ifá* and becoming a *babalao*.[25] Drawing these ideas together with the notion of spirit possession as a gendered performance, *orisha* possession in *María Antonia* is thus a gendered performance played out by the female body, this a liminal entity that through the performance of ritual and gender occupies a position of power with the potential for both reinforcement and subversion of social and ritualized norms. Furthermore, in both ritual and gender performance, the agents exerting influence over the body can be internal — the self-same human subject — and external. As the following analysis demonstrates, it is this mediatory position with regard to ritual and gender performance that María Antonia occupies; moreover, this same position, coupled with the primacy of, and negotiation between, the internal and external forces influencing her, accords the protagonist the power and agency to subvert the constraining and destructive patriarchal constructs present in the overlapping secular and religious domains of the play.

Violent Masculinities

The restrictions that the social and religious frameworks presented in *María Antonia* place on the protagonist, and the consequent harmful effects they impose on her, are clear from the beginning of the play. In spite of Hernández Espinosa's decision to describe his opening section as the 'prologue', for Martiatu it is the subsequent first *cuadro* that serves this purpose, during which the spectator views a series of thirteen *imágenes* followed by a market scene.[26] Indeed, these tableaux provide the background to the characters' lives in the *barrio* [neighbourhood] in which the play is set, an area of Havana that Curbelo names as the playwright's native El Cerro.[27] This community, comprising several *barrios*, exemplifies the divisions in Cuban society that had existed under the Republic: the former bourgeoisie were familiar with the large houses and gardens typical of the area, while the majority of its dense population was black and *mulato*, and practitioners of Afro-Cuban religions.[28] In such an environment, associated with decay and ruination in the post-revolutionary Cuba during which the play has been performed and its filmic version set, the characters depicted in the *imágenes* are stricken by poverty, forced by circumstance to seize every opportunity, however slight or temporary, for brief respite from their desperate situation.[29]

The violence suffered by these characters driven to their wits' end, to use Curbelo's term, is not only inflicted on numerous levels — physical, emotional, structural and situational — but is also of an inherently patriarchal nature.[30] For example, the ninth 'image' portrays a father giving a knife to his son, a gift that is accompanied by the exhortation, 'Pa'que te defiendas. [...] Los hombres no lloran. Antes se sacan los ojos' [So you can defend yourself. [...] Men don't cry. It'd be better to gouge out your eyes] (954). After two further tableaux which depict the poverty and the desire for a fleeting escape through drunkenness and popular music that characterize the community, 'image' twelve shows two boys fighting, one strangling the other until the latter submits and answers the repeated question '¿Quién es el más hombre?' [Who's more of a man?] with the desired response of 'Tú' [You]. Upon releasing the second boy, the winner reiterates what he perceives to be his own manliness, and thus the loser's exclusion from this category, with the warning, 'Eso para que aprendas a jugar con los hombres' [That'll teach you to play with men] (955). Further to these two examples involving male characters, a number of women are also portrayed as espousing violence of the same nature. 'Image' two sees a mother beat her son for not answering her when summoned and simultaneously warn him, 'No llores. Los hombres no lloran. No quiero mariquitas en la familia. ¡Yo parí un hombre!' [Don't cry. Men don't cry. I'm not having sissies in my family. I gave birth to a man!] (952). Moreover, Carlos recollects in his later soliloquy a scene similar to 'image' nine cited above, in which he is instructed to defend himself against a regular bully in the neighbourhood. In this instance, it is his mother rather than his father who gives him the knife, and after Carlos kicks it away in the middle of an argument, he recalls, 'Mi madre salió a fajarse. A sacar la cara por mí' [My mother went out into the street to fight. To stand up for me] (1000). He then continues to recount that it was upon killing the leader of the local gang after the bullying had escalated to death threats that he earned the congratulations of his father and was finally considered a man, being taken to a brothel in order to celebrate. As Ian Lumsden notes in reference to the period prior to the Revolution, women as well as men expected the latter to assert their machismo, and that this 'same brand of stifling paternalism' continues in post-revolutionary Cuba, in spite of legislation and claims to the contrary.[31] Importantly, this is not to say that the characters in the examples cited necessarily have an alternative option to perpetuating these social norms; as Martiatu emphasizes, 'La sociedad los acorrala, los obliga y luego los rechaza en el colmo de la violencia' [Society rounds them up, binds them, and then forces them back into the den of violence].[32]

Returning to Hernández Espinosa's 'prologue', this is a scene taken from the final *cuadro*, at which point Batabio foretells through *Ifá* María Antonia's imminent death. Considering the opening alongside the series of *imágenes* that follow it, the playwright thus introduces the work as one framed — figuratively as well as literally — by the patriarchal restrictions and violence of the inextricably entwined religious and secular contexts he presents in the play. To this end, Martiatu points to an acceptance in Santería 'del predominio de un sexo sobre el otro' [of the predominance of one sex over the other], explaining this further as 'la dominación masculina que se expresa en patakines, prohibiciones, advertencias y aun en el sentir popular entre santeros' [the male domination that is expressed in *patakí*, prohibitions, warnings and even in popular viewpoints among *santeros*].[33] Martiatu's observation is important in that it underscores male dominance as an element of Santería tradition and practice independent of the way Hernández Espinosa presents the religion in *María Antonia*. When read in conjunction with Mary Ann Clark's work, the reader can see that, although Clark is critical of the way in which Santería is perceived as male-oriented since, to her mind, it is in fact a female-normative religion, she recognizes that what she terms the 'story of babalawo primacy' is a widely accepted attribute of the religion.[34]

In the opening scene, then, this structure is made clear. Conrad James has indicated that from Batabio's first word, '¡Lárgate!' [Get out!], the desire of the 'patriarchal domain to maintain control' is manifest, a position reinforced by the 'condemnation of woman' contained in the *babalao*'s subsequent line, '¿Con qué derecho vienes a perturbar la tranquilidad de este lugar? Esto no es el mundo donde el hombre revienta todo. ¡Quítate los zapatos y limpia tus pensamientos!' [What gives you the right to come and disrupt the tranquillity of this place? This isn't the world in which man can destroy what he likes. Take off your shoes and clean your thoughts!] (946).[35] In comparison, the formality with which Batabio speaks when interpreting *Ifá* is in stark contrast to the manner in which he addresses María Antonia directly. Following his first throw of the *ekuele*, Batabio reads, 'si usted no sabe la ley con que vivir aquí, lo aprenderá en otro mundo' [if you don't know the rules by which you must live here, you will learn them in another world] (949), a form he continues to use when asking questions to facilitate the consultation, such as '¿Usted es hija de Oshún, no?' [You are an *hija de Ochún*, aren't you?] (950). *Ifá* also condemns María Antonia, as demonstrated by the *babalao*'s final pronouncement in the prologue, at which point he repeats in Lucumí the phrase 'Cuando la luna sale, mija, no hay quien la apague' [When the moon comes out, my child, no one is able to extinguish it], an utterance accompanied by the stage directions '*Como si repitiera una sentencia*' [*As if he were once again passing sentence*] (950). Batabio's statement regarding the moon can be read as a link to one of the *pataki* regarding a dispute between the son of a *babalao* and the son of Ikú. As Cros Sandoval recounts, the two sons were arguing over the rising of the moon, and the former claimed it would not rise for three days, with both pledging their lives that they were right.[36] Concerned that Ikú (death) would come for his son, the *babalao* made a sacrifice to Orula in order to help his son win the argument and thus cheat death, and the moon indeed did not appear for three days. In this *pataki* the moon and Ikú are both controlled together, a link reinforced near the play's close when Cumachela, embodiment of Ikú in *María Antonia*, exclaims, '¡Esta noche, antes de que la luna se pierda, bailaré contigo!' [Tonight, before the moon sets, I will dance with you!] (1034). Batabio's pronouncement therefore not only refers to the unavoidable nature of the events to follow, but also to María Antonia's death itself. However, the difference in tone between the *babalao*'s voicing of *Ifá* and his condemnation when speaking on his own behalf is stark, with the latter being formulated in a much more authoritarian and paternalistic manner.

In contrast, it could be concluded that Batabio's manner of speaking is proportionate when considered within the context of Santería. Conrad James suggests in reference to the *babalao*'s opening words, 'Not only has [María Antonia] been taken to Batabio [...] because of a physical illness but she is also seen as a contaminatory force'.[37] In this regard, as becomes apparent with the progression of the play, the characters of Cumachela (Ikú) and María Antonia are inseparable, both physically and conceptually. Upon her entrance into Batabio's house, María Antonia has Cumachela on her shoulders, and at this point they are one entity who speaks as such. Indeed, as the embodiment of Ikú, Cumachela is, as Davies observes, 'el lado oscuro de la heroína, su ser mortal' [the dark side of the heroine, her mortal being].[38] For his part, Sergio Giral (2013) describes Cumachela as 'la una vez María Antonia convertida en agorera borracha y pordiosera' [the erstwhile María Antonia now become drunken doomsayer and beggar], while in the play both are called prostitutes as well as 'la mujer más linda de San Isidro' [the prettiest woman of San Isidro] (1018). Cumachela is therefore both Ikú and the woman María Antonia would have become had she lived, and here at the outset, the single entity of the two perceived as one — an errant woman who both embodies and is marked by death — is contaminatory in itself. So, in addition James's conclusion that Batabio's response to their entry is 'the condemnation of woman, the declaration of her as a figure of corruption', the fact that La Madrina perceives the presence of another influence at this point must also be considered, demonstrated by her plea that the *babalao* 'Aleje de su cabeza la sombra del muerto' [Remove the dead man's shadow from her head] and her question, '¿qué cuelga de ese cuerpo?' [what's hanging from that body?] (947).[39] Once again, the scenes presented in the prologue occur chronologically in the final *cuadro* of the play, following María Antonia's murder of her lover, Julián. The lack of distinction between body and mind, self and others in Santería, as Wedel observes and Chapter 1 has demonstrated, might then suggest that the lingering presences of Julián — 'la sombra del muerto' — and Ikú in María Antonia's mind are those which must be cleansed when she is told to do so by Batabio.[40] Equally, is it the presence of death within her body that the *babalao* classifies as contaminatory upon its entry into his house and so instructs her to leave? As Fernández Robaina writes, one of the *pataki* indicates that a pact was forged between Orula and Ikú whereby the latter may not take anyone without having informed Orula and, if the individual is initiated into *Ifá*, Orula must also give his consent.[41] Anecdotally, Migene González-Wippler quotes a *babalao* whom he consults as asserting that this pact also prevents anyone from dying in a room in which someone is wearing the *idé* (the green and yellow beaded bracelet worn by devotees of Orula).[42] Therefore, while Batabio's manner of speech is directed at María Antonia and her 'female defiance', to use James's words, her coexistence with Ikú and thus the presence of death at the *tablero de Ifá* would both provoke the ire of the *babalao* and of Orula.[43] This is further reinforced by Batabio's final command in the last *cuadro* when, upon seeing María Antonia's death confirmed in the *ekuele*, he demands, '¡Sal de esta casa con tu muerte!' [Get out of this house and take your death with you!] (1036).

Finally with regard to this particular series of interactions, the deference with which La Madrina speaks to Batabio in comparison to the manner in which he addresses her — similar to his mode of speaking to María Antonia — reinforces the *babalao*'s perception of La Madrina as occupying a position subordinate to his.[44] Though she supplicates Orula directly prior to her arrival at Batabio's house with María Antonia, once inside La Madrina directs her petitions to the *babalao*. She speaks in a respectful way, a quality related to her being an *hija de Yemayá*, which, Natalia Bolívar Aróstegui writes, connotes an innate respect for and understanding of social and religious hierarchies.[45] Batabio, however, continues to address her using 'tú', thereby reinforcing the primacy of the male position over that of the female in this context. In addition, the staging of this scene further exemplifies the hierarchical structure it communicates. The *iyalochas*, by definition, are all female, while the *akpwón*, though gendered masculine in the script as 'el Akpwón', is a role that could be fulfilled by a male or female singer, as Katherine Hagedorn describes and Hernández Espinosa's 2011 production of the play demonstrated.[46] Importantly, however, upon La Madrina and María Antonia's arrival, the *iyalochas* lead them both to the *babalao* in a reverential manner, and the latter appears as follows: '*En el fondo, centro, aparece sentado en el suelo, [...] frente al tablero de Ifá, Batabio el babalao'* [*Upstage, centre, Batabio el babalao appears, sitting on the floor [...] in front of the* tablero de Ifá] (946). Following these directions, Batabio is positioned as the most important entity present after the divination board. Furthermore, he does not enter but appears already seated at the back of the stage, and the other characters move towards him. Having physically established the *babalao* as both superior and worthy of deference, his position is further reinforced by the necessary translation of Lucumí that is provided. Even when Batabio himself translates rather than the *iyalochas*, the fact that he is able to converse directly with the *orisha* while others require translation into Spanish in order to understand emphasizes his privileged status. The image set on stage here is one of male supremacy and a patriarchal hierarchy, which then illustrates and impresses on the audience from the outset the construct with which María Antonia will clash throughout the play.

María Antonia: 'hembrista, retadora y transgresora'

In her discussion of María Antonia, Martiatu writes that she is 'hembrista, retadora y transgresora' [*hembrista*, a challenger and a transgressor].[47] *Hembrismo*, from which *hembrista* derives, can be described as the oppositional counterpart of machismo, that is, the rejection of *machista* values and behaviours, and the reconfiguration of such principles to centre on women rather than men. The discussion of María Antonia's conflict with machismo is clear throughout the play and has been explored by numerous critics in addition to those most cited above.[48] For her part, Martiatu describes the 'gender conflict' in terms of a polarized antagonistic opposition of *hembrismo* and machismo, embodied by María Antonia and Julián respectively and which culminates in their deaths.[49] This conflict is a result of the orientation of the religious and secular contexts along patriarchal lines and the acceptance of the primacy of men over women throughout.

To begin with Julián, his attitude and actions towards his various lovers demonstrate that, to all intents and purposes, he considers their primary role to be his personal gratification. Notably, his first appearance on stage is in the company of an unnamed woman, whom he has taken to a small storage area that, since boyhood, he has used initially to hide from the police, then later as a place to sleep and a private spot for sexual encounters. Julián is disinterested in her from the beginning, but after having brought the woman to his hideaway for company, he rebuffs her when he hears María Antonia approach, threatening her with '¡Y como vuelvas a mirarme la cara, te rajo en dos!' [And if you look me in the face again, I'll slice you in two!] (968). This capricious treatment of female acquaintances is repeated upon his next appearance in the sixth *cuadro*, as he flits between the owner of the bar he frequents, Nena, and two prostitutes, one of whom is his prize for having just won a boxing match and signed a contract with his new manager (1003–11).

Julián's machismo is equally evident and further developed in his relationship with María Antonia. Refusing to visit her for ten days while she languished in her room, ill and alone, the interactions between the two are marked by violence and conflict, not least in the manner in which Julián continues to restate his claim over María Antonia, despite having repeatedly abandoned her. For example, during their first depicted intimate encounter, he asserts, 'Julián no ha abandonado nunca a María Antonia. Soy tu dueño y tuyo' [Julián has never abandoned María Antonia. I'm your master and yours] (969), then, in the second of these — which culminates in his murder — he shouts, '*(Agarrándola)* Yo soy tu macho, ¿oíste? Eres mía y te tengo cuando me dé la gana' [*(Grabbing her)* I'm your man, do you hear me? You're mine and I'll have you when I feel like it] (1024). Julián acts in the manner expected of him by his friends and those in the community, displaying what he and those around him perceive to be the qualities of the quintessential Cuban macho encapsulated in their notion of what it means to be 'un hombre': physically strong, seemingly fearless womanizers who are flirtatious yet uncompromising, especially with regard to issues of sex and gender roles. By means of illustration, when Julián makes the first of the above claims, he suggests that María Antonia also has an influence over him in spite of the higher hierarchical position he holds as a man. However, when he perceives his authority to have been undermined, he asserts his privileged position through the violence of his speech, thereby reinforcing it:

> JULIÁN   [...] Cuando nos conocimos, [...] quedamos en que yo por mi lado y tú por el tuyo; que siempre habría un momento para nosotros.
> MARÍA ANTONIA   Yo no soy ninguna puta de San Isidro.
> JULIÁN   ¿Y qué quieres? ¿Que me case contigo? ¿Encaramarte arriba de mí? Yo soy hombre, no el pelele ese que estaba contigo. (1025–26)

> [JULIÁN   [...] When we met, [...] we agreed that I'd do my thing and you'd do yours; that there'd always be a moment for the both of us.
> MARÍA ANTONIA   I'm not one of those whores from San Isidro.
> JULIÁN   So what do you want? For me to marry you? To climb up and rise above me? I'm a man, not that wimp that was with you.]

To his mind, Julián's machismo is further justified by his *orisha de cabecera*, Changó, and his membership of the all-male Sociedad Abakuá. Bolívar Aróstegui notes that *hijos de Changó* are 'pendencieros, fiesteros y libertinos, [...] verdaderos espejos de machismo' [argumentative, partygoers and lacking restraint, [...] true mirror images of machismo], qualities reiterated by Davies and Martiatu, though the latter uses terms like 'virilidad' [virility] and 'voluptuosidad masculina' [male voluptuousness].[50] The misogyny inherent in the myth of Sikán upon which the Sociedad Abakuá is founded and its preclusion of women as members is equally relevant here. Additionally, within this context it is important to note that when a rite of passage is celebrated, the sacrifice of Sikán — representative of women in this context — is symbolically re-enacted, which would have therefore occurred when both Julián and his friend Tino were initiated prior to the narrative present of the play.[51] Indeed, Cabrera situates the misogyny of Ekué within the framework of the Sociedad, contending that, 'Fuera del Fambá — el cuarto de los Misterios — los *obonekues [moninas, o hermanos abakuá]* no son misóginos como su numen' [Outside the Fambá — the house of mysteries — the *obonekues [moninas or abakuá brothers]* are not misogynous like their forefathers].[52] Further to this, the relationship between

Julián and María Antonia must be viewed in light of the previous discussion of the *pataki* that involve Changó and Ochún. While lovers, the relationship between the two *orisha* is difficult and characterized by abandonment, unrequited love and jealousy. It is for this reason that Martiatu underscores the traditional proscription within Santería of allowing the union of an *hija de Ochún* and an *hijo de Changó*.[53] For Martiatu, recognition of the difficulties that such a love usually entails is key to understanding the two characters' relationship.

In concert with the sentiments expressed both here and through the series of *imágenes* in the first *cuadro*, Yuyo and Tino also reiterate the notion that to be 'un hombre' requires the overt expression of male superiority and control. For Yuyo, in spite of his entreaties and professed desire to leave his wife in order to be with María Antonia, when the latter tells him there was nothing to their sexual encounter and is incredulous that he could have believed there was, he exclaims, '¡Yo soy muy macho pa'que te burles de mí!' [I'm too much of a man for you to make fun of me!] and reduces her to the status of a common whore: 'Para lo único que sirve una mujer como tú, es para hacer gozar' [The only thing a woman like you is good for is screwing] (979, 982). Later in the same *cuadro*, Tino, no older than a teenager, repeats the sentiment, telling María Antonia that he can teach her what a real man does with a woman like her and responding to her laughter by ostentatiously grabbing his crotch and warning her, 'No te rías, ¿eh? No permito que ninguna mujer se burle de mí' [Don't laugh, if you know what's good for you. I don't let any woman make fun of me] (989–90).

Each of these characters behaves in a manner that reinforces their machismo and that present in the wider community, expressing various forms of masculinity with which María Antonia interacts. Some of these are fixed, such as the representation of the quintessential Cuban *macho* in Julián or the punitive masculinity Batabio embodies as a figure of authority who imposes certain patriarchal notions present in Santería. Faced with both of these, María Antonia remains defiant and intransigent: she rejects the deference for Santería and the *babalao* that Batabio requires by refusing to conform to the norms he dictates, and violently confronts Julián during each of their encounters, finally ending their tempestuous relationship when she murders him towards the play's close. For his part, Yuyo, infatuated as he is with the protagonist, is ready to leave his family in order to maintain what he believes to be a budding relationship. His actions convey a masculinity based on a sense of male entitlement, allowing him to act in this manner in spite of the fact he is married and a father. María Antonia capitalizes on his infatuation to serve her needs, asserting her *hembrismo* by rejecting him once he has fulfilled his purpose of keeping her company for a night, and so provokes his anger. In contrast, Carlos states that he does not wish to act in the manner forced upon him by his parents and the wider community, who require him to claim the violent masculinity outlined above. By orienting his character towards education and literature, Hernández Espinosa exemplifies in Carlos a type of masculinity that is not based on an idea of physical or hierarchical superiority by virtue of being a man but rather one that seeks to find a female companion with whom to raise a family. However, the social context of the *barrio* in which the play takes place does not permit such an expression of masculinity, presenting it as failed when challenged by poverty (as in the *manigua*) or by the neighbourhood bully or when he is emasculated by Julián and publicly rejected by María Antonia.[54] Having contemplated a future with Carlos that proved impossible, María Antonia then rejects the masculinity he embodies, forcing him in turn to recognize its failure and adopt the machismo that had seen his adolescent self assert those qualities he and others associated with manliness to then murder his teenage adversary. Ultimately, therefore, the various masculinities these characters portray lead to the acceptance — if reluctant in the case of Carlos — of the violent masculinity required of them by the social and/or religious contexts they inhabit.

María Antonia is, for the most part, defiant in the face of this machismo, refusing to accept its imposition and valorizing her womanhood. Orphaned and in the care of La Madrina from a young age, she recalls that the lack of opportunity to finish her education and thus her leaving school while still a girl was a direct consequence of not having a father who could provide for her:

> MARÍA ANTONIA [...] 'María Antonia, hija, desde ahora en adelante tengo que llevarte conmigo a la colocación'. '¿Por qué?' 'Ya has crecido y hay que trabajar'. 'Manuela, la hija del carpintero, es más grande que yo y su madre la lleva al colegio'. 'Sí, pero su padre trabaja'. 'Y tú también trabajas, Madrina'. 'Pero él gana más que yo'. (1001)

> [MARÍA ANTONIA [...] 'María Antonia, child, from now on I have to take you to work with me'. 'Why?' 'You've grown up and you have to work'. 'Manuela, the carpenter's daughter, is older than me and her mother takes her to school'. 'Yes, but her father works'. 'And you work, too, Madrina'. 'But he earns more than I do'.]

María Antonia's violent response to this, born out of anger, led to a consultation with a *babalao* who told La Madrina 'que Oshún era dueña de mi cabeza [...]. Me abrió las puertas y me dijo: "Hija de Oshún, compórtate como tal y que ella sepa refrescar tu Eledda"' [Ochún was my *orisha de cabecera* [...]. He opened the doors for me and told me: '*Hija de Ochún*, act accordingly and may she know to refresh your *eleddá*'] (1001). As María Antonia recounts, this led to further marginalization centred on her body. Continuing into adulthood, she is trapped within what Menéndez has called the 'triangle' that represents historical marginalization in Cuba, that is, she is a woman, black and poor.[55] This is a gendered inferior position, constantly reinforced and reiterated through the impositions placed on her body within this *machista* framework outlined above. Her attempts to escape take the form of her violent rejection of this patriarchal control, and she focuses on her body as the seat of power and subjugation, and consequently as the site of the struggle for self-definition. However, as Martiatu observes, in spite of her confronting machismo in such a manner, the weak point that María Antonia shares with Ochún is that she loves to the point of downfall, and this ensures that for much of the play she remains subordinate to Julián, as Ochún was to Changó.[56] Even immediately prior to murdering him, when Julián tells María Antonia he is leaving to pursue his boxing career abroad, she pleads, 'No, mi negro, no te vayas. Haré lo que quieras.

Tú eres mi macho, mi dueño. Yo soy tu esclava' [No, *mi negro*, don't leave. I'll do whatever you want. You're my man, my master. I'm your slave] (1027).

In Herrera's epilogue, 'Conversación con María Antonia (cuarenta años después)', the author underlines María Antonia's lack of choice regarding how she could react to her situation, which is rendered as a conversation between María Antonia and Herrera:

> — Tú hablas conmigo de violencia y no te das cuenta de que fue todo lo que tuve, lo único que me ofrecieron de regalo el día de mi nacimiento.
> — La aceptaste, fue como un reto, y tú...
> — ¿Yo qué? ¿Había para mí otra cosa?[57]
>
> ['You speak to me of violence and you don't realize that it was all that I had, the only thing that they gave me as a gift the day I was born.'
> 'You accepted it, it was like a challenge and you...'
> 'I what? Did I have any choice?']

Unable to respond in any other way due to her entrapment in an inherently violent context, the defiance María Antonia embodied was her only option. From her marginal position, she had to fight in order not to be completely subsumed and rendered powerless by those whose actions she perceived to control her. Indicative of this is her manner of speech in interactions with all the male characters in the play. The hierarchy between Batabio, La Madrina and María Antonia, reinforced through modes of address and deference (or lack thereof), places the protagonist at the bottom, not least because she is a non-initiate of Santería, in spite of her identification — and attempt to live — as an *hija de Ochún*.[58] Having been deemed a 'desorejá' (in this context, 'stubborn whore') by Batabio and a *puta negra* by the community for embodying the 'happiness' she regards as characteristic of the *camino de Ochún*, she cannot escape this double damnation and yells, '¡Yo no creo en esa mierda!' [I don't believe in that shit!] (1035–36). Elsewhere, when faced with the prospect of Yuyo and Carlos stabbing her on separate occasions, instead of cowering she taunts them both, instructing them to only brandish a weapon if they are going to use it (985, 1035). In this fashion, María Antonia appropriates and replicates the actions of those attempting to control her, a conclusion that was noted by Menéndez herself upon leaving the 1967 premiere of the play and overhearing an audience member exclaim, '¡Es mucho hombre esa mujer!' [She's such a man, that woman!].[59] Originally uttered in praise of Gertrudis Gómez de Avellaneda in the nineteenth century, this phrase reflects the gender discrimination against which María Antonia fights since it reinforces the primacy of men over women. However, despite this, it also reflects the path the protagonist takes for much of the play since circumstances force her to pitch *hembrismo* against machismo and thus she is restricted in her struggle by the very framework that she attempts to escape.

The context of possession, both sexual and spiritual, problematizes this framework of control. As an *hija de Ochún*, María Antonia's body already constitutes a site of interaction between the *orisha* and the physical world, embodying the essence of Ochún through her actions. Possession is further indicative of the two entities' inextricability and reinforces the importance of the body within the discourse of control. Considering sexual possession first, this has been traditionally viewed, albeit problematically, in terms of male and masculine domination and possession, especially so within the Cuban context depicted in the play. However, in much the same way as María Antonia seeks to appropriate *machista* violence in order to fight against it and gain perceived agency, she is shown to take control in this domain too. For example, after rejecting Yuyo's advances in the first *cuadro* while also obtaining the necessary goods for La Madrina's *toque de santo* from him without payment, María Antonia later instructs him to come to her room that evening after she argues with Julián. The following day, content with the events of the previous night, Yuyo is once again rejected by María Antonia, who tells him in no uncertain terms that he was merely a temporary replacement for Julián. Though Yuyo has 'possessed' María Antonia in a sexual sense, it is she who occupies the position of power here having enticed, enthralled, and then shunned him. This can be compared with the actions of Yuyo's wife, who performs the role expected of her within this construct and comes to plead with her husband to return. Injured, with his masculinity challenged, he threatens to kill María Antonia in order to prove himself in front of the assembled crowd, which results in her undermining him again, as outlined above. As such, although María Antonia gains agency and seemingly subverts the constraints that forbid such actions, the corollary of this is the imposition by Yuyo and the wider community of further sanctions upon her body. She is called 'una cualquiera' [a whore], reduced to the status of prostitute and ostracized within the *barrio* (981). The reinforcement of patriarchal notions of permitted behaviour on behalf of the wider community is not only effectuated in this instance; on the contrary, María Antonia later recalls that, 'Los bares cerraban sus puertas; las mujeres tiraban agua a la calle y hacían limpieza a sus maridos. Las madres soltaron a sus hijos a la calle; me los echaron como perros rabiosos' [The bars closed their doors; women threw water into the street and performed cleansing rituals on their husbands. Mothers let their sons out into the street, setting them on me like rabid dogs] (1001). María Antonia's position here can be interpreted in two opposing ways. Firstly, by performing this role, she arguably reinforces the very patriarchal norms against which she struggles as, in Butler's terms, her performance has itself become a norm and thus vitiates the power that she has seemingly obtained.[60] Secondly, and contradictorily, rather than being further empowered in possession, María Antonia is reduced to the receptacle, as it were, sought out by men not for her beauty but rather in order to satiate their desires through the act of possessing her.[61]

This embodiment of the essence of Ochún that has seen her subvert patriarchal norms and challenge multiple forms of masculinity has concomitantly provoked the restrictions that have been placed on her body. María Antonia recounts that the treatment marginalizing her from the community was a result of her keeping to the path she saw prescribed for her, and although she was following the trajectory of Ochún, she became a pariah. Cabranes-Grant asserts that 'María Antonia uses *santería* only for erotic purposes', a perspective in part shared by the wider neighbourhood community as they perceive her to be using *brujería* to entrap their husbands.[62] However, this is only a partial presentation of both Ochún and the protagonist. In much the same fashion, Julián attempts to force María Antonia to act as he wishes in order to both control her and 'deflect attention from his masculine flaws'.[63] He claims that as an *hija de Ochún*, 'Tú no naciste para ese carácter. Las hijas de Oshún nacieron para endulzar las aguas y enloquecer el viento' [You weren't born to be of such character. *Hijas de Ochún* were born to sweeten the waters and madden the wind] (969). María Antonia rejects such impositions upon her agency, retorting that Julián should keep his distance and better, leave for the gym. The reinforcement of her entrapment is based not on divination, therefore, but on the presentation of an incomplete picture which ignores the inherently contradictory nature of Ochún's character. In Herrera's epilogue, María Antonia critiques this very characterization, ready to counter what she believes is Herrera's insinuation that *hijas de Ochún* are given to pleasure-seeking and little else.[64] In this vein, Martiatu writes that Ochún:

> Puede ser amorosa y protectora de las mujeres embarazadas y de los niños y en otras ocasiones se muestra voluble, caprichosa, malvada o traicionera. Puede reinar en el universo del amor, de las pasiones, pero también en el de la muerte y el odio. Puede ser a la vez luminosa y oscura.[65]

> [Can be loving and the protector of pregnant women and of children, and on other occasions she proves to be fickle, capricious, wicked and disloyal. She is able to reign in the universe of love, of passion, but also in that of death and hatred. She can bring both light and darkness at the same time.]

Although the happiness and voluptuousness of Ochún are key elements of her character and often those of her initiates, as an *orisha* with multiple *caminos*, neither she nor her children can be reduced to the specific characteristics that Julián claims. María Antonia embodies Ochún more completely than those around her would like, and her overriding wish to define herself and escape from the patriarchal construct that binds her is both aided and thwarted by this fact.

By writing his protagonist and Ochún in this manner, Hernández Espinosa interrogates the popular presentation of Ochún in wider Cuban society and, to a certain extent, rewrites the *pataki* detailing the relationship between Ochún and Changó. Firstly, Ochún, through her association with the Virgin of Caridad del Cobre, occupies the position of Cuba's patron saint, most often depicted as a *mulata* with a light complexion and straight hair (though Cros Sandoval writes that in some *ilé* she is perceived to be a black woman with kinky hair).[66] Ochún is also associated with money, and so the playwright's decision to make explicit that María Antonia is a black prostitute who lives in poverty and to write her as the embodiment of Ochún therefore critiques the racial and economic symbolism ascribed to Ochún in the popular imaginary as a figure that unites the Cuban nation.[67] Along with this, Hernández Espinosa challenges the manner in which *hijos/as de Ochún* are described and thus the image portrayed both of the *orisha* herself and of the wider Cuban population with whom she is associated. Bolívar Aróstegui states that children of Ochún, while sensual and friendly individuals who enjoy dancing and *fiestas*, make an effort to comply with public opinion, a quality to which they assign great importance.[68] María Antonia does not, however, as she seeks to escape the male-oriented hierarchy that dominates the secular and religious contexts she inhabits and, in so doing, questions the validity of such partial and biased portrayals of *hijas de Ochún*. This change is then reinforced by Hernández Espinosa's rewriting of the *patakí*, which inscribes his play into the tradition of orality in Santería and other African-derived religious traditions noted in Chapter 1.

In his above-cited interview with Christilla Vasserot, Hernández Espinosa described part of his work as the writing and invention of *patakí*, providing as examples two of his plays, *Odebí el cazador* and *Obá y Shangó*.[69] During this conversation he explains that he is an artist and not a folklorist, and comes to the conclusion that the beauty of the world of Santería is the freedom and openness within it that enables him to do this work. Although he does not explicitly name *María Antonia* as one of his plays in which he has made use of this opportunity, his rewriting of *patakí* in this work is clear. Menéndez, for one, suggests that *María Antonia* is an example of the dynamic nature of oral tradition within Santería, and that Hernández Espinosa's rewriting of the relationship between Ochún and Changó is not only further evidence of this, but also a corollary of his protagonist being an *hija de Ochún* who resists societal norms.[70] Instead of María Antonia allowing her love for Julián to dictate her acceptance of his abandonment on the terms he sets out, this in spite of the sacrifice she had already made for him by going to prison for a crime he committed, she murders her lover in a direct clash of *hembrismo* and machismo, and so attempts to break the cycle of this *patakí* repeating itself in her relationship with Julián. At this moment, María Antonia reconfigures the myth that would have seen her inherit a legacy from Cumachela, whereby the latter's desertion by her lover after she asked him for what he could not give her would have become María Antonia's abandonment by Julián for the same reason.

Performing the role of *hija de Ochún* as she views it, María Antonia moves seamlessly between the public and private spheres, transferring her sexuality into the public domain and destabilizing the public/private dichotomy accepted in contemporary Cuban society as depicted in the play. For her, separation between the outside world and the home did not exist, and the absence of a definitive division between the two contributed to men's increasing vulnerability.[71] In keeping with the conclusions drawn in Chapter 1, Santería itself has challenged the traditional construct whereby Afro-Cuban religion was both maintained in and confined to the domestic sphere, and consequently gendered female through its link with this space. As noted above, Hernández Espinosa presents both Santería and the position of black women therein in such a manner that he challenged the reductive presentation of the religion as *brujería* and a source of comic stereotypes, which had been commonplace in previous theatrical works.[72] In the public space of the theatre, therefore, María Antonia continues to challenge this divide, undermining male authority in this space in which male characters violently subjugate her and designate her a *puta*. Refusing to allow men to dominate her as they wish, María Antonia attempts to grasp the power with which they have hitherto defined her body by maintaining her control over it at all costs, as we have seen with Julián,

Yuyo, Pitico, Tino and Carlos. Her performance of Ochún both undermines and reinforces this construct, and so, in order to effect change, the conflict must reach its peak in her murder. For her, this is both an act of defiance and resistance, as Herrera's text reiterates. Furthermore, María Antonia's treatment at the hands of the community mirrors that suffered by Ochún when she fulfils their wishes and entices Ogún back from seclusion in the forest by using her seductive powers and sweet honey. Despite the community's initial gratitude as they could now once again be prosperous, over time 'la gente no recuerda ese gesto de Ochún, y fueron ellos mismos, cuando ya tuvieron el hambre saciada, rebozantes la barriga, quienes emplearon la fuerza recuperada para señalarla' [the people do not remember that gesture of Ochún's, and it was the same people who, when their hunger was sated and their stomachs lined, used their energy thus renewed to point the finger at her].[73] In much the same way, the community wish María Antonia to perform the role of Ochún but ostracize her for the very fact of doing so.

Within the religious context of Santería, Batabio is a key example of the imposition of norms upon María Antonia's body. Excoriating her for rejecting the laws of this world, he concludes that she lost her *aché* by gallivanting about and focusing on the pleasures of the flesh, and so scolds her for forgetting that 'la cabeza es la que lleva al cuerpo' [it is the head that leads the body] (1035). Contrary to the *babalao*'s suggestion that she has wilfully lost her head, for María Antonia her head is all that she has left: while she believes in Santería, she is unable to accept the displacement of her human spirit through *orisha* possession. She participates willingly in the *toque de santo* for Ochún and dances to invoke the *orisha*, but when she feels she is about to be mounted, she breaks the circle and flees. Conversing with Yuyo immediately afterwards, María Antonia describes spirit possession as a means of domination, stating 'Mi cabeza no le pertenece a nadie. ¿Viste cómo me la quisieron robar? Por un minuto creí perderla. Oshún no encuentra cabeza y me busca, pero no se la voy a dar, aunque en ello me vaya la vida' [My head doesn't belong to anybody. Did you see how they wanted to steal it from me? For a moment I thought I would lose it. Ochún doesn't find a head and looks for me, but I'm not going to give it to her, even if it costs me my life] (978). In spite of the potential power invested in possession performance outlined above, for much of the play María Antonia considers it another way in which she loses agency.

Looking to the performance of the scene in closer detail, the seemingly oppressive nature of spirit possession for María Antonia is made even clearer. The ceremony is taking place in order to take the statue of Caridad del Cobre/Ochún to the river and refresh her, 'para que [María Antonia] no pierda la cabeza' [so that [María Antonia] doesn't lose her head]. Having been *despojada* (ritually cleansed), María Antonia goes into the river with the *iyalochas*, dancing, singing and laughing along with the *iyalocha* who has been mounted by Ochún. They process in a similar fashion back to La Madrina's house, and, as the stage direction describes, having arrived:

> La danza va in crescendo. *El Akpwón canta persistentemente sobre María Antonia, que está a punto de caer en trance. Para precipitar la posesión hace sonar sobre ella una campanilla de metal amarillo. María Antonia trata de escapar, pero las Iyalochas a la*

Oshún le hacen un cerco. El Akpwón le conversa al oído. María Antonia da un grito y violentamente rompe el cerco. Huye. (978)

[*The dance crescendos. The Akpwón sings persistently over María Antonia, who is about to fall into a trance. In order to precipitate her possession, the Akpwón rings a bell made of yellow metal over María Antonia. María Antonia tries to escape, but Ochún's iyalochas make a circle around her. The Akpwón speaks into her ear. María Antonia cries out and violently breaks the circle. She flees.*]

From both an auditory and visual standpoint, María Antonia is once again defined by external agents. The conflict is centred on the difference in perspective regarding what constitutes 'perder la cabeza': for La Madrina and the wider Santería community it means María Antonia's death and the reclamation of her *eleddá* by Ochún; for María Antonia, however, it is the inability — temporary as it may be — to remain in control of the way in which her body performs its role. In the secular context, although others have ascribed meaning to her bodily performances and deemed her actions contrary to the norms of society, María Antonia has maintained conscious control over her actions, albeit with the restrictions imposed by her marginalized position in the community and wider Cuban society. Furthermore, as possession is a gendered performance in which the *caballo* takes on a female role, those precipitating the manifestation of the *orisha* through dance and sound cues are aligned with the male-gendered role of the *orisha* and thus further contribute to María Antonia's subjugation. Although Hagedorn is careful to underline that the music performed for the *orisha* is not 'inherently female or male', she does suggest that 'the sexualized characterization of *oricha* possession seems to refer [...] also to the way in which the empowering musical sound [...] penetrates the possession vehicle — through the ears, the skin, the head'.[74] Despite the fact that María Antonia is not mounted on this occasion, the symbolically male-gendered auditory cues coupled with the physical delineation by the *iyalochas* of the space in which she can move serve to create an oppressive situation which María Antonia experiences as a loss of both power and agency.

After having been rejected once again by Julián, who following his boxing match had gone to celebrate at the *bar de los muelles* (dockside bar) without conveying any message to her, María Antonia runs to La Madrina's house from where, by means of a bodily ritual, she flees and finds herself in the *manigua*. Encountering Cumachela in its depths, the interaction between the old woman and María Antonia reiterates the latter's inescapable death as their journeys continue to be inextricably entwined. The two characters hold a conversation but at times speak together, which can be interpreted in opposing but complementary fashions. Firstly, this can be perceived as constituting a battle between the two individuals in which María Antonia is shown in conflict with the paternal authority of Ikú (though presented as a woman), as is demonstrated by their speaking at the same time and so both inherently fighting to be heard. Conversely, it also presents María Antonia and Cumachela as one entity, and so indicates that María Antonia has been dominated by the male authority of Ikú.

In coming to the *manigua*, María Antonia's body has facilitated her transportation to a liminal space in which it seems she may be able to explore a possible future without many of the restrictions placed on her outside this context. In contrast to bodily possession — both spiritual and sexual — the two *cuadros* that take place in a clearing of the *manigua* focus on possibility conceived in the mind. As Carlos discerns, María Antonia is trying to escape, not only from her daily life but also from herself. He ascribes his own feeling of helplessness to her: 'uno necesita a veces ser dueño de algo, y cuando no se es dueño de nada, ni de sí mismo, uno se echa a correr' [sometimes you need to be a master of something, and when you're master of nothing, not even yourself, you run away] (998). Both are victims of the patriarchal norms of society, and the scene leads to simultaneous soliloquies in which each recounts his or her own trajectory to this point. These soliloquies establish a connection between their separate experiences and point to the impossibility of a future together, itself explored further in the seventh *cuadro*. Narrated at the same time, Carlos's and María Antonia's stories are fused into a single account that moves beyond socioeconomic concerns to focus on *machista* attitudes. Carlos's family had the money to keep him in school and buy books, in contrast to María Antonia having been orphaned and cared for by her *madrina*, with financial hardship resulting in the premature end to her education. However, marginalized for not conforming to social norms, they were both forced into a violent response to the constraints placed on them: Carlos was required to kill the gang leader to prove his manliness, while María Antonia was further marginalized to the extent that violence was the only option still available to her. The result for both of them was sexual initiation and the concomitant appropriation of power and further subjugation this entails. By virtue of its liminal nature, then, on the one hand the *manigua* offers both individuals a space with inherent potential for resistance. On the other, however, this potential is thwarted by the impossibility of transferring the ideas constructed therein to the space they ordinarily inhabit. While welcome respite, the possibility of change cannot be realized.

This lack of potential is established at the same moment that Carlos's and María Antonia's stories are being woven together. While the soliloquies make explicit a connection between the two characters' past and future trajectories, the fact that they are simultaneous also illustrates that a joint path will be defined by conflict since, as a result, neither of the stories is intelligible in its own right and their performance demonstrates that the violence portrayed in each becomes directed at the other. This violence will become manifest in the closing scene of the play when Carlos stabs María Antonia and she goads him in the same way that she did Yuyo and Pitico. Therefore, their escape from the contexts in which they feel helpless and constrained by those around them in turn serves to reinforce the violence they have fled. Furthermore, the interweaving of their accounts and the mutual understanding between the two hitherto strangers suggest that this situation is equally damnatory for others in their position.

In the second scene set in this clearing, Carlos and María Antonia play a game that explores the possibility of a life together. Consisting of a series of snapshots of life as a couple — or 'dreams' as María Antonia calls them (1017, 1038) — the promise depicted in the first is at once marred by Carlos's insistence that María Antonia stay at home, clearly delineating the public and private spaces along gendered lines and once again placing María Antonia in a subordinate role (1013). As the game progresses, the situations the couple describe increasingly reflect their current realities: poverty-stricken, María Antonia's body is again defined by others, though in this case she is the unhappy housewife whose role is to clean and bear children; meanwhile, Carlos works increasingly longer hours on failed attempts to create the magic cement that was to make them rich. Moreover, despite the potential at the outset, their relationship mirrors the unhappy marriage of Yuyo and Mathilde, he a father unable to provide for his family who then seeks solace elsewhere, and she attempting to make do in increasingly desperate poverty. Returning to Butler and the manner in which gender is constructed, she writes that it is 'instituted through a *stylized repetition of acts*' and the 'possibilities of gender transformation are to be found [...] in the possibility of a different sort of repeating, in the breaking or subversive repetition of that style'.[75] As such, potential for change is harnessed through slightly different repetitions in the manner in which gender is performed, and in so doing, possibility is created through this subversive repetition. In the case of Carlos and María Antonia, however, each repetition results in the reinforcement of the previous stylized act, whose failure was necessary in order for the one which follows to commence. Rather than subvert the restrictions placed upon their actions within the community, the potential for escape offered by the liminal space of the *manigua* proves only to reinforce them. The impossibility of a future free from these impositions, indicated by the penetration of the other's soliloquy with the violence recounted in one's own, is restated here by the increasing subjugation of both characters to the fact that their repeated stylizations failed to offer an escape.

In addition to María Antonia's bodily performance of Ochún and thus her link to death through Cumachela's own embodiment of Ikú, this connection with death is also found in Ochún's association with the cemetery in one of her *caminos*. Most importantly, it is too exemplified through the manner in which María Antonia dies: stabbed in the vagina by Carlos at the same moment at which she is mounted by her *orisha de cabecera*. In her discussion of the ritual elements of the play, Martiatu highlights that in Santería, death signifies a change rather than a definitive end.[76] As she explains, the symbolic death that a neophyte undergoes as part of their initiation, which then leads to their rebirth as an *iyawó*, is repeated on a spiritual plane whereby the spirits of the dead continue to interact with the living, and as such death itself is the assurance of birth. This performance of life and death through the body by means of the subjectivities that inhabit and penetrate it is linked to the performance of María Antonia's sexuality in which her body is mounted and penetrated by a number of entities: herself, Julián, Yuyo and finally Ochún and Carlos at the same time. This close link between death and sexuality is an important aspect of African-derived religious traditions in the Caribbean, with the Gede exemplifying their coexistence in Vodou, and various *caminos* of different *orisha* in Santería associated with death and the cemetery alongside the amorous relationships they maintain. Georges Bataille has theorized the connections between sex and death in depth, writing that, 'Le passage de l'état normal à celui du désir érotique suppose en nous la dissolution relative de l'être constitué dans l'ordre discontinu' ('The transition from the normal state to that of erotic desire presupposes a partial dissolution of the person as he exists in the realm of discontinuity'), thereby linking the liminal experience of death to that of eroticism.[77] In their introduction to a selection of Bataille's works, Fred Botting and Scott Wilson render this liminality more explicit, concluding that, 'In eroticism the poles of life and death, being and nothingness, fullness and emptiness are one, dissolved like subject and object in the insensible totality of things'.[78] Furthermore, as Baudrillard highlights, for Bataille sexual excess itself leads to death, a notion Foucault reiterates, drawing on Greek philosophy, in his second volume of *Histoire de la sexualité* [The History of Sexuality].[79] The intertwining of these two notions and their importance in analyzing the various texts studied in the different chapters of this book is the central theme explored in Chapter 5. However, at this point, it is important to foreground the link between María Antonia's sexuality and her death in particular, and that together they contribute to the liminality of her body both within the context of the play and the wider environment of Santería.

In addition to María Antonia's double possession at the moment of her death, the link between sex and death is further underlined by the protagonist's relationships with Yuyo, Carlos and Julián. With Yuyo, his emasculation upon being rejected leads him to threaten María Antonia with a knife, claiming that he is ready to possess her in this fashion as a corollary of no longer being permitted to penetrate her sexually. Such a clear juxtaposition of the two is expressed the previous day when María Antonia finds Julián behind the marketplace: seeking to resolve their conflict, María Antonia tells Julián she would be capable of killing him, to which he replies '¡Mátame!' [Kill me!] and then they kiss (971). With Carlos, however, it is the mythical nature of the *manigua* that initially draws these two concepts together, a link made clear when he murders her at the play's close. In this space of possibility that quickly becomes the opposite, Carlos and María Antonia contemplate a sexual relationship, but these reflections have already been prefaced by María Antonia's meeting with Ikú and concludes with her acceptance of her impending death. The liminal space of the *manigua* then also becomes a site where sex and death coalesce.

Subversion in Death and Sacrifice

Thus far, we have seen that María Antonia's struggle against male-oriented hier-archies has continued throughout the play, at points reinforcing these hierarchies and at others undermining them. The final three *cuadros*, which take place between María Antonia's room and La Madrina's house, depict Julián's death at the hands of the protagonist and the latter's murder by Carlos. This climax also constitutes the point at which María Antonia's body is most extensively subjected to patriarchal violence and that, through her performance of both ritual and gender, she most clearly subverts the very norms imposed upon her. The two characters' deaths have been a key element of previous analyses of the play, which either signal María Antonia's predetermined death as a reimposition of patriarchy due to her *hembrismo* and thus the failure of her quest for self-definition or, while recognizing this, conclude that she is finally free from the constraints against which she had unsuccessfully struggled. For his part, Fulleda suggests, in reference to a series of plays which focus on Santería, that within the religious context, María Antonia's death would not have been predetermined but rather a result of the human condition and her own free will.[80] In contrast, González and Amado del Pino classify her death as inescapable, linking the unavoidable nature of her demise to the religious construct in which she participates.[81] Other critics conclude that, since there is no future possibility for an improvement in María Antonia's situation or for her to be free of the restrictions placed on her actions to that point, the protagonist chooses death and for her it constitutes both an escape and liberation.[82] Along with the numerous condemnations of María Antonia's actions and threats to her life, Ikú's omnipresence in the play and coexistence with the protagonist underscores the certainty of her death, an event that María Antonia unquestionably precipitates and for whom it constitutes a form of escape. However, as the following analysis shows, though María Antonia reinforces the established patriarchal construct present in Santería and seeks to break free from it in death, she goes one step further and, in her performance, both gains agency and subverts the very system that has condemned her.

As has been established, María Antonia's reaction to Julián's announcement of his departure is inevitable given the social context in the play that requires masculine domination to be countered with violence. Yet, Julián's murder at the hands of his lover is indicative of her appropriation of the agency he represents at this point and her subversion of the male-oriented system of Abakuá. Earlier in the play, María Antonia performs a ritual in order to place an *amarre* on Julián and tie his fate to hers, which is then validated when he dies from consuming the powder she put in his *chequeté* (a ritual drink made with fermented corn). At this point, she taunts Julián, telling him as he collapses that it is 'por ti que rezas. [...] Es por ti que llora Ekue' [for yourself that you are praying. [...] It is for you that Ekué cries], before lamenting the impossibility of their continuing to live (1029–30). María Antonia, unwittingly or not at the point of performance, thus ensures her lover's death by binding him through this ritual and voicing her desired outcome, 'Que ande detrás de mí como el muerto detrás de la cruz' [That he follow behind me like the dead man behind the cross] (992). The audience observes Ikú immediately consent to María Antonia's request, since, upon completion of the ritual, María Antonia is transported to the *manigua* where she meets Cumachela singing a funeral dirge. By taking control of Julián's destiny in this fashion, María Antonia once again demonstrates her defiance in the face of his belief that, as a man and *hijo de Changó*, he is free to leave her. Although there is an inherent contradiction in the idea that she has destroyed her love as a result of her refusal to be subjected once more to a framework that has designated her a *puta*, María Antonia is unable to react any differently without once again suffering the consequences that both she and Cumachela before her already have. Furthermore, María Antonia murders Julián to the sound of the Abakuá *nkrikamo* drum, which speaks for Ekué. Without going as far as suggesting that this act serves to avenge the murder of Sikán, María Antonia does establish her control over a *ñáñigo* to the sound of the very drums that speak this voice, and thus symbolically rejects the abovementioned misogyny inherent in the ritual space of the Abakuá. With this in mind, by dismissing the rules of the Sociedad in such a fashion, the vengeance they dictate for the murder of one of their own is invested with further meaning as it serves to reassert the misogynistic premises upon which the sect is founded. Though Tino, a young *ñáñigo*, does not kill María Antonia himself, James suggests that by witnessing it and announcing her death, this 'might be read as a symbolic necessity marking [his] passage into manhood [...] who [...] therefore replaces Julián within this cosmos'.[83]

In spite of the violence María Antonia suffers and the requirement that Julián's murder be avenged, her actions in the final *cuadro* see her subvert the constraints others place on her. Firstly, having sensed the presence of death and been warned of its impending arrival on numerous occasions, she tells La Madrina after Batabio has ordered her to leave his house that, 'No me basta esta vida, no la quiero. Necesito otro mundo. ¿Dónde está? Que vengan a buscarme, me encontrarán contenta y sabrosa' [This life isn't enough for me, I don't want it. I need another world. Where is it? Let them come and look for me, they'll find me content and alive with pleasure] (1036). Rather than flee as her godmother implores, María Antonia states, 'No. A tu casa me irán a buscar. Diles a los tamboreros que no dejen de tocar. Oshún quiere alegría' [No. They'll come looking for me at your house. Tell the drummers not to stop playing. Ochún wants happiness] (1036). While death constitutes an act of corporeal subjugation, both its inevitability and her invitation for it to happen reduce its potency as a fate imposed upon her. By claiming the unavoidable outcome, she then nuances a situation that would otherwise be conceived solely in terms of gender-based violence. Instead, she renders a more complex reading of the situation as it becomes framed as an inescapable yet subjective bodily performance at the centre of which she has actively positioned herself.

The way in which María Antonia performs her role when Carlos arrives exemplifies this further. Importantly, prior to his arrival at La Madrina's house during the ceremony, Carlos has once again been presented in feminized terms. In reference to his appearance alongside María Antonia in the *bar de los muelles*, Cabranes-Grant writes, 'This double feminization — a woman repels him, and a man literally kicks his arse — implies that Carlos is marked as a lesser male, an ostracized subject'.[84] This is reinforced by the women in the bar, who mock him as if he were a young boy, followed by Cumachela, who, upon offering him the knife that will become the murder weapon, repeats the words from the ninth 'image' in the prologue that echo those his father said to him: 'Es mejor ir pa'la cárcel que pal hoyo' [It's better to go to prison than to the grave] (1023). Carlos returns to 'reinstate his masculinity' and María Antonia simultaneously diminishes it, challenging his authority in a situation that is repeated from her altercation with Yuyo.[85] Rejecting Carlos's forceful advances, which elicits the same response of '¡Yo soy muy macho pa'que te burles de mí!' [I'm too much of a man for you to make fun of me!] (1038), María Antonia's voluptuous dance for Ochún becomes increasingly provocative as she removes her clothes. Though he has already threatened her with the knife, it is not until María Antonia goads him with '¡Nunca saques un arma si no vas a usarla!' [Never brandish a weapon if you're not going to use it!] and shouts '¡Dale!' [Go on!] that Carlos reacts to her provocations, at which point he thrusts the knife into her vagina, finally possessing and killing her by stabbing her in what many in the community consider to be the essence of her being as a *puta negra*. It is clear that, from his perspective, he only acts this way due to the societal pressure for him to do so in order to prove his masculinity; in a mirror image of machismo forcing María Antonia to destroy her love, Carlos is forced to destroy his. In this instance, however, María Antonia is shown to subvert the same masculinity thus reinstated as, in a similar way to Drewal's analysis of spirit possession above, though María Antonia is possessed by Carlos by means of the knife and he in turn is obligated to do so in order to re-establish his masculinity, she is shown to exert power over him and influence the manner in which he acts.

It is at this point that María Antonia is mounted by Ochún, an event that, as Cabranes-Grant outlines, poses a series of important questions regarding her agency. He reflects:

> But it is only when she dies that María Antonia's *oricha* claims her at last. [...] Is this a choice that María Antonia embraces willingly, or is she being possessed by default? [...] Is María Antonia offering Ochún a magnificent gift only for a few seconds, or is she becoming part of the god's energy? In other words, is María Antonia being absorbed into the general pulsations of *aché*, or is she experiencing a last-minute redemption, a final confirmation of the right of *santería* to guide her *camino* or path?[86]

Framing his questions in terms of the influences that define María Antonia in this scene, Cabranes-Grant captures a key aspect of the relationship between *santero/a* and *orisha*, that it is bi-directional. An important element of this relationship is the participation of the devotee in the process of spirit possession, and thus the possibility for self-definition inherent within it. As such, the question is not just one of whether María Antonia willingly submits to the *orisha* or not, but rather one that recognizes the empowerment of the practitioner alongside her submission. Indeed, as Dayan underscores in reference to spirit possession in Vodou, 'the loa cannot appear in epiphany, cannot be made manifest on earth without the person who becomes the temporary receptacle or mount', a process that she describes as an 'experience of election' and of 'communion'.[87] In this vein, María Antonia's performance of the agency she wrests from others also comes from the space between the notions of submission and self-definition that exists in the ritual of *orisha* possession in Santería.

The process of propitiation that precedes the moment a *santero/a* is possessed involves the active participation of the practitioner by invoking the *orisha* through songs and dance. Following the *orisha*'s manifestation through the adherent's body, they are offered the clothing they desire. María Antonia, having rejected possession by Ochún previously, dances for the *orisha* whilst wearing the latter's shawl and using her fan, before continuing her dance as she disrobes in provocation of Carlos.

She both invites and permits possession by Ochún, therefore, rather than solely choosing whether to submit to it or not, and in performing this role, the strength she displays further undermines the primacy of machismo. Although Carlos stabs her while he desperately embraces her, she does not die in his arms in an image of complete submission. Instead, she removes herself from the physical restriction his embrace imposes and continues to dance both for and as Ochún, before falling to the ground dead. Once again, as the link between the physical and spiritual, María Antonia influences both: she embodies Ochún, presenting herself visibly and willingly to the *orisha*, which then allows her to make a final gesture of defiance to the patriarchal norms that have enforced her death. Actively seeking, provoking and accepting it, she does so on her own terms. In so doing, she both gives something to Ochún and becomes part of Ochún; her *eleddá*, and thus her *aché*, becomes part of the *orisha* and is guided by the *orisha*.

This is not to suggest that the patriarchal norms of secular machismo and Santería are not reinforced, as this is clearly also the case. María Antonia dies at the hands of both of these, with her body destroyed in order for her affront to social and religious norms to be appeased. Doubly possessed — and thus symbolically doubly dominated — the masculine primacy in both contexts is reasserted. The insistence of Batabio and *Ifá* that she must die for having rejected 'la ley con que tiene que vivir aquí' is equally brought to fruition, as Batabio's reminder to María Antonia that she has forgotten that 'es la cabeza la que lleva al cuerpo' is demonstrated to be the case. María Antonia acted in the sensual and sexual manner that she thought an *hija de Ochún* should, but not having allowed Ochún to become *asentada* nor having been initiated as such, though comprehensible from María Antonia's point of view, has meant her body has been seen to rule her head. Within the context of Santería, María Antonia has not respected the necessary reciprocity of the *orisha-*practitioner relationship, and Ochún can indeed be considered to have reclaimed María Antonia's *eleddá*. However, María Antonia's sacrifice within this context also enables her to become the symbol of resistance against the patriarchy around which it is constructed, as the numerous iterations of the play and its protagonist testify. The separation of María Antonia's head from her body, though signalling the end of her physical life, enables her entry into communion with Ochún and her continued manifestation through the *orisha*, as the multiple renditions of her story, her enduring presence in the streets of Havana, and Herrera's epilogue all indicate.

In spite of Ochún's reclamation of María Antonia's *eleddá*, the fact that she did so in such a visible fashion and facilitated María Antonia's final defiant act points to the *orisha*'s tacit support for María Antonia's struggle and understanding of its legitimacy. As such, although María Antonia's perceived lack of respect for the *orisha* and refusal to heed their advice ultimately leads to her demise, by portraying the scene in this manner, Hernández Espinosa also posits that, in addition to recognizing the patriarchal construct of Santería, there is room therein to critique this accepted tradition, as he has done by reworking the *pataki*. In 'Conversación con María Antonía', Herrera clarifies the perception that María Antonia has become one with Ochún, the former presenting herself through her avatars who appear as 'una mujer de piel oscura, viste de amarillo suave contrastando con su pelo fuerte y duro, encanecido' [a woman with dark skin, dressed in soft yellow contrasting with her bold and strong greying hair].[88] At the same time, she underlines that María Antonia remains a distinct entity within the association between the two, and that the manner in which both are presented has been influenced by the other. The support Ochún demonstrates should not be interpreted as a suggestion that María Antonia's violent reactions against all that she regarded as oppressive are necessarily considered proportionate and legitimate in themselves, but rather that Ochún recognizes that her grievance against the impositions upon the female body within a male-dominated context is valid. Herrera and María Antonia continue to discuss this violence, which María Antonia emphasizes was the only thing she inherited upon her birth, a reflection that leads her to ponder how, without being a fortune teller, she could have known 'que el mundo giraba y que en uno de sus giros entrarían cambios' [that the world was turning and that in one of its turns change would come about].[89] Yet, it was precisely by changing something in one of these *giros* — her acceptance of the reciprocity of the possession performance — that a change was brought about. As such, it was by modifying an element integral to the 'stylized repetition of acts' that an opportunity to subvert the system was made possible, which then provided an escape for the protagonist.

Furthermore, this cycle of *giros* continues for others too, as the play and Herrera's text both demonstrate. The cyclical nature of *María Antonia* has been noted above, with its structure one that sees the reappearance of Batabio's house in the final *cuadro* indicating a return to the action portrayed in the play's prologue. There also exist several moments at which lines are repeated in the dialogue, pointing to further possible returns to previous scenes. Carlos's repetition of Yuyo's assertion '¡Yo soy muy macho pa'que te burles de mí!' and María Antonia's reply, along with the latter asking Cumachela '¿Quién es Carlos?' [Who is Carlos?] in the *manigua* and later in the final *cuadro*, constitute moments at which the action could be replayed. Likewise, the description of Cumachela as the erstwhile María Antonia, two characters with whom death is inextricably bound but who remain present throughout the play, not only ties together the fates of these two characters and their later avatars, but also speaks to the longstanding cycle of repeatedly forcing certain women into the binds of a role over which society maintains control, and so can simultaneously desire and despise, entreat and condemn to death. On one level, these points of cyclical repetition reiterate the inescapable nature of María Antonia's situation, and on another, they show that the action itself is inescapable as it is re-performed, just with different protagonists. To this end, Herrera writes that María Antonia makes the same observation, stating, 'Género, raza y estado social van a crear muchas María Antonia, que de acuerdo con su siglo y su milenio, así será explotada, violentada, así morirá y así matará' [Gender, race and social standing are going to create many María Antonias, who in accordance with the century and millennium, will be exploited and violated in this manner, will die this way and will kill this way], a sentiment Hernández Espinosa has also shared in his interview with Kaity (2011).[90] Accordingly, María Antonia's appearance to Herrera and others, her reappearance in 1990s Cuba at the end of Giral's film, and continued presence on the streets of Havana illustrate the further reaches of her defiance of male domination and that her death in the play did not represent the end of her resistance.

The manner in which María Antonia precipitates her death and the perception of it as predetermined come together with this notion of continued resistance to frame her murder in terms of a sacrifice. In response to Herrera's lament of the way events developed, María Antonia notes, 'No podía ser de otra manera; yo estaba marcada por la letra de mi nacimiento. [...] Yo fui la escogida, y lo que te va a tocar no lo cambia nadie, no lo borra nada' [It couldn't have been any other way; I was marked by the letter of my birth. [...] I was the chosen one, and no one can change your lot, nothing can sweep it away].[91] Having suffered these bodily impositions, María Antonia's experience becomes a story of resistance which is repeated and reinforced through its performance by the many other María Antonias who follow. However, the account must be retold if it is to have any effect, as the protagonist exhorts to Herrera:

> — También ese es tu empeño: saber y que sepan la verdad de historias así, como la mía.
> — Y la de Ochún; siempre el sacrificio que no se va.[92]

> ['That is also your task: to know and to make sure others know the truth of such stories, like my own.'
> 'And Ochún's; ever the enduring sacrifice.']

Yet, more than simply retelling the stories, these subsequent María Antonias symbolically perform them anew. In her book chapter 'Novel Insights: Sex Work, Secrets and Depression in Angie Cruz's *Soledad*', Donette Francis writes, 'actions under one instance of domination do not forever alter the system of dominance and therefore often have to be repeated'.[93] Similarly, here, those who follow then embody María Antonia through the performance in their own liminal spaces of gender, *orisha* possession, or both. These new performances increasingly subvert the male supremacy that has defined their bodies in every repetition of the act, with its own idiosyncrasies and individual characteristics, as María Antonia did in her re-rendering of Cumachela's tale. While not suggesting that María Antonia becomes an *orisha* herself who mounts *santeros/as* by means of spirit possession, the embodiment of her essence whereby successive generations are not her, but not not her in their own performances allows this resistance to continue.

Returning to Montero's novel *Del rojo de su sombra* and the context of Vodou and Gagá, the reader sees a similar notion of sacrifice and inescapable death espoused by its protagonist, Zulé. At the narrative's close, Zulé is murdered by her servitor and spurned lover, Jérémie Candé, while she is mounted by Ezili and he by Carfú. Her sacrifice, just as inevitable and predetermined from the outset as María Antonia's, serves to protect her *gagá* and prevent its consolidation with that of Similá Bolosse. As a powerful and well-respected *manbo*, Zulé rejects the alliance Similá proposes that would see her lose power and influence as he transports his shipments of narcotics through her *batey*. The result of her murder at the hands of Jérémie Candé, however, is the negation of Similá's right within a patriarchal hierarchy to exact his revenge for her refusal to submit, further undermined by Zulé rising to be with her *mèt tèt* and becoming the conduit 'through which man ascends and gods descend'.[94] While Zulé's sacrifice ensures the well-being of her religious community and prevents the imposition of a male-dominated framework associated with the Duvalier dictatorships and their violent Macoute militia, María Antonia's permits the cycle of resistance against the patriarchy forced on women like her in both secular and religious contexts to continue, by means of repeated performances. Neither text removes, or indeed is able to remove, the restrictions placed on women as a result of the accepted norms in society or those present in the religious traditions in which they participate. However, the protagonists' sacrifices do enable their subversion to continue.

The manner in which María Antonia performs ritual and gender serves to both reinforce and subvert the patriarchal hierarchy critiqued in the play. Rather than constituting 'una apología al machismo, a la prostitución y a la santería cubana' [a justification for machismo, prostitution and Cuban Santería], charges that Curbelo Mezquida notes were levelled against the play following its premiere, *María Antonia* establishes an insightful critique of each of these, emphasizing the unsatisfactory but inescapable nature of male domination within them.[95] María Antonia's body is the site of interaction between the physical and spiritual, the public and private, and despite the restrictions placed on the manner in which she can perform her gender, the performative nature of Santería and its presentation in the play provide a context in which the protagonist is able to appropriate both power and agency. By viewing the play and Santería ritual through the lens of performance theory that frames María Antonia as an agent who retains her subjectivity and engages with both the multiple iterations of that which is performed and those observing the performance, this allows a reading in which María Antonia manages to subvert the secular and religious male-dominated contexts so prevalent within them. Her performance of Ochún draws on several of her *caminos* and, as Herrera's epilogue shows, sees her reject the mindfulness of conforming to public opinion that Bolívar Aróstegui cites as characteristic of children of this *orisha*. At the same time as critiquing such a characterization, Hernández Espinosa takes advantage of the opportunity Santería offers for creativity and rewrites the *pataki* of Ochún and Changó, which then aids María Antonia's resistance by means of her association with, but not subsumption by, the avatars of her crowning *orisha*.

Conversely, the protagonist's performance of ritual also constricts her. Relinquishing power by conforming to the norm, María Antonia is unable to escape her death and her body is once again subjected to the violence of male supremacy. In spite of this, by confronting her fate in a manner which further enables her to exercise her agency as an individual, María Antonia's death is a sacrificial act that allows the essence of her resistance to be repeatedly embodied by the many María Antonias who have followed on stage, in film and narrative, and on the streets of Havana. In this way, the act is re-performed by others who also influence it, reframing it in a continually evolving fashion, and thus reiterating the dialogue and actions of subversion. The negotiation between the internal and external influences that operate on and through María Antonia's body — the violence to which she is subjected, her own defiance, the community's perception of her, the gendered performance of *orisha* possession — reflects these same conflicts within the character and in the religious traditions with which she interacts. Destabilizing the accepted primacy of male-oriented hierarchies through her performance, María Antonia's sacrifice has thus ensured that her resistance continues.

Notes to Chapter 2

1. Vasserot 1998: 46.
2. Fulleda 2003: 179.
3. See, for example, Martiatu Terry (1992); (1998); and Martiatu (2000); (2009).
4. Martiatu 1984: 37–39. It should be noted *María Antonia* followed on from the success of Brene's aforementioned *Santa Camila de La Habana Vieja* (1962), in which Santería was a central theme. For analysis of the two plays and the wider context in which they are situated, see Pino (2004) and Martiatu Terry (1992).
5. Cabranes-Grant 2010: 129.
6. Caballero 2004: 153–54.
7. See González Mandri (2006) and Humphrey (forthcoming), 'Ikú, Cumachela and the Figure of Death in *María Antonia* by Eugenio Hernández Espinosa'.
8. Herrera 2004: 167.
9. Astles 2009: 29.
10. Benedicty 2012: 299; Strongman 2008: 14.
11. González Pérez 2003: 204.
12. Balbuena Gutiérrez 2003: 99.
13. *María Antonia* is divided into eleven *cuadros* preceded by a prologue. Although the most common English equivalent to *cuadro* in theatre is 'scene', it is particularly noteworthy in the context of this play that *cuadro* also means 'painting' or 'tableau', since each *cuadro* is a snapshot of a scene in the characters' lives that can be replayed at various points in the work. This structural element is emphasized in the first *cuadro*, which is comprised of thirteen different *imágenes* (images) in addition to the main scene.
14. Cros Sandoval describes the difference between the newly and fully initiated thus: 'There are several categories of priests and priestesses in Santería. The new, or recent initiates, are called *iyawós* and are at the lowest level. The *babalochas* (males) and *iyalochas* (females) are above them. They are people who have been initiated for more than a year and have full priesthood credentials' (2006: 99).
15. Astles 2009: 34.
16. Taylor 1994: 14.
17. Schechner 1985: 110.
18. Turner 1969: 95.
19. Schechner 2002: 58; 1985: 110. The observation that Ian Maxwell makes regarding the term 'stage' as a conceptual space within which performance takes place and the simultaneous warning he sounds against the overuse of the term equally apply here (1998: 78–79).
20. Bell 1992: 16.
21. Ibid.: 200, 222.
22. Drewal 1992: 182.
23. Rizk 2001: 289.
24. Bell 1992: 222.
25. Beliso-De Jesús 2015: 189, 193.
26. Martiatu 2004a: 38.
27. Curbelo 2004: 128–29.
28. Ibid.: 123.

29. I examine the decay and ruination depicted in the play and film, and the narrative of death that runs through them, in the aforementioned article, 'Ikú, Cumachela and the Figure of Death in *María Antonia* by Eugenio Hernández Espinosa'.
30. Curbelo 2004: 37–38.
31. Lumsden 1996: 38, 184–86.
32. Martiatu 2004a: 38.
33. Ibid.: 50.
34. Clark 2005: 66.
35. James 2009: 48.
36. Cros Sandoval 2006: 138.
37. James 2009: 48.
38. Davies 1993: 290.
39. James 2009: 48.
40. Wedel 2004: 110.
41. Fernández Robaina 2008: 54–56.
42. González-Wippler 2004: 105.
43. James 2009: 48.
44. Both Beliso-De Jesús (2015) and Mary Ann Clark have explored this hierarchy in Santería, and for Clark it is based for the most part on the level of initiation and aptitude rather than anatomical gender (2005: 27, 64–70). However, in spite of Clark's conclusion that *Ifá* divination is not as central to Santería as is often contended, in this instance La Madrina perceives that recourse to *Ifá*, and thus to a male priest, is the only possible course of action if María Antonia's death is to be prevented.
45. Bolívar Aróstegui 1990: 95.
46. Hagedorn 2010: 147; see Kaity's 2011 documentary *Seguimos*.
47. Martiatu 2004a: 45.
48. See Davies 1993: 289, González 1998: 554, and Menéndez 2004: 82–83.
49. Martiatu 2004a: 47.
50. Bolívar Aróstegui 1990: 112; Davies 1993: 290; Martiatu 2004a: 43.
51. Martínez-Echazábal 1994: 18.
52. Cabrera 1969: 141.
53. Martiatu 2004a: 51.
54. The *manigua* is an area of thick woodland that here represents a magical or mythical space (Davies 1993: 293).
55. Menéndez 2004: 90.
56. Martiatu 2004a: 45.
57. Herrera 2004: 156.
58. Several critics have suggested that María Antonia has been initiated into Santería or has had initiation prescribed as the manner in which she would avert the death she faces. These include: Fulleda, who states that 'María Antonia puede no despeñarse si corona su cabeza' [María Antonia can prevent her demise if she undergoes initiation] (2003: 179); Martiatu Terry, who writes, 'In María Antonia, [...] the heroine is able to save her life by means of her initiation into Santería' (1998: 56); and Conrad James, who conflates La Madrina's plea to '"Cleanse her from the inside. Uproot her and plant her again"' in the prologue (and thus chronologically at the play's close) with the 'pursuit of the path of Oshún' which is prescribed in María Antonia's childhood (2009: 49, 66). It would seem that María Antonia has not been fully initiated, however, as she indicates herself when talking to Carlos in the *manigua*: 'Quieren que yo me haga santo' [They want me to be initiated] (1012). Furthermore, the fact that both María Antonia's and La Madrina's requests for the protagonist to be born again would also suggest that she has not already been through this process. As will be explored below, it is María Antonia's death that symbolically marks her initiation into Santería, as Martiatu has also suggested (1992: 939–40).
59. Menéndez 2004: 88.
60. Butler 1988: 531.
61. Martiatu 2004a: 66.

62. Cabranes-Grant 2010: 129.

63. James 2009: 47.

64. Herrera 2004: 166.

65. Martiatu 2004a: 43.

66. Cros Sandoval 2006: 241.

67. In addition to María Antonia and others who have described her as 'negra', original director Roberto Blanco cast Hilda Oates, a black actress, to play the role of María Antonia.

68. Bolívar Aróstegui 1990: 121.

69. Vasserot 1998: 46.

70. Menéndez 2002: 223.

71. Menéndez 2004: 80.

72. Martiatu 2005: 22–23.

73. Herrera 2004: 167.

74. Hagedorn 2010: 147–49.

75. Butler 1988: 519–20.

76. Martiatu 1984: 43.

77. Bataille 1987: 23; 1986: 17.

78. Botting & Wilson 1997: 13.

79. Baudrillard 1976: 240–41; Foucault 1984: 141.

80. Fulleda 2003: 179. The plays Fulleda refers to are, in order: Carlos Felipe, *Réquiem por Yarini* (1960), Eugenio Hernández Espinosa, *María Antonia* (1964), José Ramón Brene, *Santa Camila de La Habana Vieja* (1962), Rolando Ferrer, *Lila, la mariposa* [Lila, the Butterfly] (1963), Gerardo Fulleda León, *Chago de Guisa* (1992), Elaine Centeno, *La piedra de Elliot* (1993) and Virgilio Piñero, *Electra Garrigó* (1948).

81. González 1998: 551; Pino 2003: 186–87.

82. Martiatu 2004b: 7; Pogolotti 2004: 26.

83. James 2009: 45.

84. Cabranes-Grant 2010: 132.

85. Ibid.: 133.

86. Ibid.

87. Dayan 1997: 19.

88. Herrera 2004: 155.

89. Ibid.: 156.

90. Ibid.: 165.

91. Ibid.: 160.

92. Ibid.: 167.

93. Francis 2011: 60.

94. Fernández Olmos 1997: 280.

95. Curbelo Mezquida 2009: 17.

CHAPTER 3

Women, Haitian Vodou and Reconstitution of the Self

In her analysis of Rosario Ferré's first collection of stories, *Papeles de Pandora* (translated as *The Youngest Doll*), Cynthia Sloan adopts the Puerto Rican author's own image of the 'sartén', or frying pan, used in 'La cocina de la escritura' (Ferré 1980) ('The Writer's Kitchen', Ferré 1986), to explain her depiction of women's agency and construction of identity. Sloan writes:

> In order to engage and confront the identity that is imposed upon them, women need to enter 'the frying pan.' From there, it is on to the fire where, like the mythical phoenix, they can resurrect themselves from the remains of their former selves.[1]

Despite the differences in setting and context, the image Sloan employs to describe women's resistance to and subversion of patriarchal constructs in which they are confined is of particular relevance to Haitian author Kettly Mars's work. Across many of her texts, Mars explores these struggles within the framework of Haitian Vodou, be it in her debut novel *Kasalé*, her post-earthquake *Aux frontières de la soif* [At the Borders of Thirst], or numerous of her short stories. Her 2008 novel *Fado* — the central text examined in this chapter — focuses on the body as the site of multiple interactions in both the physical and spiritual realms, and depicts the process through which her protagonist manages to reconstitute her fractured self. Set in a context of Haitian Vodou interwoven with Portuguese fado, the novel depicts a childless, recent divorcée's exploration of her sexuality as she traverses a series of fragmented physical and conceptual spaces. Her brokenness exemplified by her butchered and wounded body, Anaïse/Frida undermines the male-centred framework that categorizes women as wives/mothers or whores, conflating both of these notions and embodying the essences of the *lwa* Ezili Freda and Ezili Dantò.[2] By means of her multifaceted female sexuality, she negotiates the concepts of corporeality and multiple subjectivity, then engages with the notion of death as conceptualized within Vodou in order to avoid reinscription into the patriarchal system she has sought to undermine.

Comprising thirty-three short, unnumbered chapters, *Fado* begins soon after Anaïse's now ex-husband and current lover, Léo, left her upon the news that his mistress had conceived. Their divorce is presented as largely the result of Anaïse's apparent inability to bear children, itself related to her repeated rape and two forced abortions as a teenager. Anaïse then starts to work as a prostitute at Bony's in the 'bas-ville' [lower town] of Port-au-Prince, where she manifests the persona of Frida. Both personas conceive with their respective lovers, and the novel closes with Bony and Léo poisoned by Frida and Anaïse, respectively, who themselves take the same poison. The relationship between the two is fluid: at times they become a single entity, at others they are separate, but both inhabit the same body and ultimately choose what they describe as 'freedom' ('liberté' (Mars 2008: 109), 'délivrance' (105)) in their return to Ginen.[3]

In her review of the novel, Hanétha Vété-Congolo notes the numerous dualities upon which *Fado* is constructed, explaining these as a dual personality, a double life and murder, and a dual presentation of women.[4] Indeed, the author has described it in conversation with Nadève Ménard as a story that shatters the boundaries between reason and madness, that is, the deconstruction of a psychological dichotomy, and this is cited as a central theme by Vété-Congolo (2010a), Marvin Victor (2008), as well as on the book jacket itself.[5] Moving beyond reason and madness, when viewed through the lens of Vodou spirituality, Anaïse/Frida not only draws together the *lwa* Ezili Dantò and Ezili Freda, but also reflects the twin *lwa*, the *marasa*, 'twins' who engender a third entity which then speaks to the tripartite nature of the *marasa* known as the *marasa twa*. As Joëlle Vitiello observes, 'Le mystère, la folie et la religion s'entrecroisent comme des voix issues du même corps [...]. L'entrecroisement des destins féminins et masculins [...] se déroulent sur fond de musique portugaise langoureuse et languissante, entre douleur et plaisir, entre vie et mort' [Mystery, madness and religion are interwoven as voices coming from the same body [...]. The interweaving of male and female destinies [...] unfolds against the backdrop of sultry and languid Portuguese music, between pleasure and pain, between life and death].[6] It is the point at which these paired notions coalesce, the corporeal space where the spiritual and physical coexist, that the protagonist explores the dualities of her character and knits together her sense of self.

On one level, the multiple dualisms that Anaïse/Frida encapsulates are indicative of her fragmentation: she is the spurned wife and the whore, the bourgeois professional resident of the uptown Port-au-Prince suburb of Pétionville and the marginalized denizen of the city slum. However, the bodily violations that Anaïse has suffered are both reason for and proof of her physical and psychological fracturing. In the opening chapters of the novel, she recalls that a headmaster known to her family repeatedly raped her as a teenager and that, at the age of fifteen, this led to two forced abortions only six months apart. Anaïse describes the abortions as 'butchery' and recounts that the second time, she felt the doctor's knife 'grattant, délogeant la vie de mes fibres' [scraping, dislodging the life from the fibres of my flesh] (49). Deciding at this point that she would never become a mother, she refuses to tell her father for fear of rejection, of her own fragility, of her body, and of the complicity she feels despite herself. Anaïse's apparent sterility as a result of the ordeal is a key factor in her remaining childless, in addition to her conscious decision not to become a mother. Moreover, her feeling of physical dismemberment and violation is replicated on a psychological plane through the blame and mental fragility she ascribes herself.

Conceptually, these events further subjugate Anaïse when viewed within the patriarchal frameworks that the novel depicts as present in contemporary Haitian society. Adrienne Rich, among others, notes that, with the exception of certain examples such as cloistered nuns, the '"childless" woman has been regarded [...] as a failed woman', since she is unable to fulfil her 'natural' role of mother as it has been traditionally conceived.[7] Rejected by Léo for this reason, Anaïse is further fractured when he leaves her for his pregnant mistress, which she describes as the loss not only of a man in her house but also of the illusion of power she thought she had held. Throughout her marriage, Anaïse had viewed her sexual relationship with her husband as one of 'fulfilling her duties', a perception that contrasts with the narrative present of the novel during which their daytime trysts as lovers are expressions of their passion and ardent desire. Through the lens of the male-dominated construct she describes, Anaïse sees herself as having lost any agency she believed she had, unable to fulfil the roles of wife, mother or lover. She deems herself 'broken', as does her husband, and the figure to whom she has tied her notion of power departs. Anaïse's status as an 'unnatural' woman positioned alongside the negation of life and motherhood, despite the abortions being both secret and forced, then continues in the 'failed' woman she considers that she has become as an adult.

Anaïse's subsequent reconstitution of this fractured self is a multi-layered process, one that is evident in the imagery the protagonist uses to describe her exploration and valorization of her sexuality. She frames her sexual relationship with the brothel's owner as follows: 'Avec Bony, je recolle mes fragments épars. Quand nous faisons l'amour, je redeviens un corps, une tête, quatre membres et un sexe soudés par le plaisir' [With Bony, I stick my scattered fragments back together again. When we make love, once again I become a body, a head, four limbs and a vagina knit together by pleasure] (31). Drawing together the disparate parts of her body, Anaïse/Frida states that she is a 'real woman' and one with whom she had not previously been acquainted (21). Having her broken front teeth replaced after they had been knocked out by a drunk client — an event that further indicates her physical fragmentation — highlights on a physical level the reconstitution she is to experience on the spiritual plane through her engendering of the *marasa twa*. Her later pregnancy, though problematic for the protagonist, and the events leading up to it see her negotiate the duality she comprises by confronting the physical and socio-political violence to which she has been subjected, thereby resolving these issues in a manner that, as an individual, enables her to view her concept of self as a woman who is able to function outside the restrictive male-dominated order. As such, she not only reconstitutes her sense of self but also delineates a space in which she can reject such domination.

Entitled *Fado* and bookended by the voice of Amália Rodrigues, the text renders the plurality of Haitian popular culture more complex by introducing this lusophone musical genre so closely associated with Portugal, and with Lisbon in particular. Mars grounds her narrative in a setting that is both transatlantic and inextricable from the sea, and incorporates the timeless nature of fado and Vodou into the form and content of her novel. In so doing, the author presents a hybrid context for her narrative that both reflects and assists the protagonist's numerous physical and spiritual journeys and the development of her multiple subjectivities. As a musical genre, fado is the product of a series of cultural exchanges that have come together to form a 'mythology' regarding its origins, that is, a variety of accounts which persist in the popular imaginary.[8] As Lila Ellen Gray reports, fado has a range of originary myths in popular belief: it was derived from the music of the troubadours, invented by the Moors, or sung by 'homesick sailors on boats during the Discoveries'; it came from the streets, from the brothels of Lisbon, from Africa, from Brazil.[9] To this end, José Ramos Tinhorão's *Fado: dança do Brasil, cantar de Lisboa* [Fado: Dance of Brazil, Song of Lisbon] (1994) points to the transatlantic origins of the musical form and the influence of African-derived cultural practices in the Americas upon it, an analysis regarded as 'convincing' and 'tightly argued' in subsequent scholarship.[10] Incorporating fado into her novel, Mars creates a cultural construct that not only reflects the multiple influences present in Haitian popular culture, but also looks outside this using a cultural form that links Brazil, Portugal and Africa. Indeed, these links are explicit from the outset, with the opening reference to fado and Amália Rodrigues followed by the lyrical lines, 'Mon lit tel le Tage et mon corps tour de Belém, témoins d'un destin funeste qui faisait voile pour le Bénin' [My bed like the Tagus and my body the Tower of Belém, witnesses of a fateful destiny which set sail for Benin] (13). Benin (modern-day Dahomey and considered by many the seat of Vodou) represents Ginen in the narrative, the physical and spiritual place to which Anaïse and Frida return, thereby reinforcing the link within the transatlantic context of fado already forged by the slave trade.[11] The protagonist describes fado as a faithful friend that does not miss any of their maritime departures, using the shared notion of departure and return via the sea that is integral to both Vodou and fado to bridge the two. Replicating the journeys on and beneath the waves in the undulating rhythms characteristic of this music, the trade between Africa, the Caribbean and Europe that these journeys reprise also conceptually underscores the perceived African and Afro-Brazilian roots of fado. In this vein, the bridge thus built between Haiti and Brazil is one already established in contemporary religious, social and political contexts, albeit a relationship of a somewhat ambivalent nature. Within the framework of African-derived religions in the Caribbean, Brazilian Candomblé is closely related to Cuban and Puerto Rican Santería and stands alongside Haitian Vodou, while in the political arena, Brazil remained at the head of the military arm of the United Nations peacekeeping mission in Haiti, MINUSTAH, for the majority of its existence.[12] In this hybrid context, the author provides her protagonist with a space in which she can express her multiple identities and explore the mobility between discrete sites within this space that she is afforded.

Mirroring the two discrete milieux inhabited by Anaïse/Frida, uptown Port-au-Prince and the city slum, historically fado has also straddled these distinct spaces, developing from a musical genre associated with the poor and the popular classes to become professionalized and performed in bourgeois settings.[13] This transition is personified in the lives and careers of two famous *fadistas*, Maria Severa Honofriana and the aforementioned Amália Rodrigues, the latter of whom, Richard Elliott writes, embodies a 'central mytheme' of fado as, representing the 'popular classes' in the sense of lumpen proletariat, she herself sold fruit 'on the streets of Lisbon in the years immediately preceding her discovery and subsequent fame'.[14] As fado became professionalized by force under the authoritarian government of António Salazar, it was removed from its 'true home' in the poor neighbourhood of Mouraria and 'placed [...] in the more respectable bourgeois environs of the grand Avenida da Liberdade'.[15] Fado thus also bridged the divide the reader sees in Mars's novel, with its continuation outside the sanctioned space necessarily clandestine and Amália herself becoming, over time and following a period of adjustment after the regime's downfall in 1974, the voice of fado that traversed the economic divisions in Lisbon society.[16]

Kimberly DaCosta Holton describes Maria Severa Honofriana as 'the legendary fado vocalist, instrumentalist and lyricist whose life span paralleled fado's first appearance in Lisbon'.[17] A prostitute and resident of Mouraria, the conflation of fado, prostitution and the city slum in the single body of Severa is reprised in Mars's novel, as Amália Rodrigues's music both accompanies and precipitates Anaïse's embodiment of Frida the prostitute, denizen of the 'bas-ville', and her concomitant manifestation of the *lwa* Ezili Freda. Central to this metamorphosis, Anaïse/Frida tells her ex-husband and current lover that she was born as Frida the day she met Bony at a birthday dinner, before noting that there were 'les sanglots d'un fado chanté par Amália Rodrigues attachés à nos ombres' [the sobs of a fado sung by Amália Rodrigues anchored to our shadows] (15). In the following chapter, Anaïse states that for two weeks she was the only one to occupy Bony's bed, the period of time it took for Anaïse to become Frida (17). The fact that music heralds Anaïse's embodiment of Frida is reminiscent of the way in which *lwa* are called to mount a *vodouyizan*, through singing and playing the *tanbou*. For Anaïse, this process takes two weeks and occurs while she is lying down, similar to the initiation ceremony (*kanzo*) in Vodou that involves between three and twenty-one days' seclusion during which neophytes often lie on mats on the floor.[18] Seeping from her pores, Frida then inhabits the same body as Anaïse, and from this point onwards she is repeatedly accompanied by fado music. Fado transcends Anaïse/Frida's body, therefore, serving as the musical cue for her embodiment of the essence of the *lwa*, approximating the physical and conceptual spaces and facilitating movement between them. Together, Vodou and fado enable the protagonist to cross the divisions between spaces defined by class and propriety, a notion that brings to mind Severa herself since fado provided her an opportunity to access higher social circles, albeit to a limited extent, through her love affair with the Count of Vimioso.[19]

Moreover, the embodiment of the essence of fado that these two women represent complements the notion of embodiment in Vodou. It is often said that one is born a *vodouyizan*, that individuals are ordained to serve the *lwa* before they are born, even if an individual chooses not to propitiate the *lwa*. Similarly, Gray writes that 'a fadista is born with *fado na alma* (fado in the soul)', an observation complemented by Eduardo Sucena's description of fado as the 'expressão da alma simples do povo' [expression of the very soul of the people].[20] Resident in, and an expression of, the soul, fado is thus embodied, an idea further reinforced by Júlio Dantas who recounts that Severa once proclaimed, 'A Mouraria, sou eu! O fado, sou eu!' [I am Mouraria! I am fado!].[21] Apocryphal or otherwise, this assertion encapsulates the idea that the *fadista*'s body is inhabited by fado and that by means of this embodiment, fado can then engender movement between conceptual spaces, unbound by the specifics of place or historical event. In this manner, the movement between the enclosed spaces of Anaïse's house and Bony's brothel is framed by her visceral experience of fado, with both spaces constituting sites in which the protagonist's body is inhabited by Frida/Ezili Freda and Anaïse/Ezili Dantò. Vodou and fado thus serve as complementary constructs that intertwine to form a complex framework in which the female body is the site for the interactions and negotiations of space, the exploration of sexuality and the resultant reconstitution of the fractured self. Lending its name to the title of the novel, fado permeates Mars's text, framing it with the voice of Amália Rodrigues, that 'throaty voice [which] intones a politics of polyphony and perseverance' synonymous with fado itself.[22]

The Body, Multiple Subjectivities and Configurations of Womanhood

By writing a female protagonist that traverses a number of physical and conceptual dualities, Mars situates her novel in a long tradition of doubling in Haitian literature, a device that has been used both to reinforce patriarchal categorizations and representations of Haitian women in this context and to subvert these same restrictive categories. Régine Latortue uses Marie Chauvet and Nadine Magloire as key examples of female Haitian authors who seek to transgress the strictures of the discrete archetypes of '"l'ange" (the peasant and proletariat woman, the passive bourgeoise)' and '"la bête" (the bourgeoise, when she is not passive as she is supposed to be)' by their refusal to conform.[23] She notes that this dialogue has been placed within the city scape, a theme that Vitiello highlights in her analysis of Yanick Lahens's works in which the distinctions between the bourgeois 'ville haute' — the uptown suburb of Pétionville, nestled on the hill above Port-au-Prince — and 'la ville basse' or 'la capitale' are collapsed.[24] Evidenced in Lahens's novel *Dans la maison du père* [In the Father's House] (2000) and numerous of her short stories such as the 1994 collection *Tante Résia et les dieux* [Aunt Résia and the Gods], this desire to bridge the divisions in the urban space has been noted in Mars's works, along with the deconstruction of the aforementioned dichotomous presentation of female characters. Mars has been described as an author who affirms the beauty and truth of her multicultural heritage,[25] and has herself observed that 'la femme dans les livres, elle n'est pas une héroïne ni une femme abattue qui n'est pas forte. [...] On est tous [...] des êtres complexes. L'être humain est complexe par définition' [The female protagonist in books isn't just a heroine nor just an oppressed woman who lacks strength. [...] We are all [...] complex people. Human beings are complex by definition].[26] By writing a complex female protagonist who resists the oppositional categories imposed in texts that reinforce this binary construct both in the female body and in physical space, these authors complicate the simplistic representation of women in Haiti that Latortue has described, one which she terms 'the projection of an ideology created by male bourgeois society'.[27]

The 'subordination of the feminine', to use Jean Franco's words, by imposing such roles on women, is not particular to Haitian literature, of course; the phallologocentric semiotic diagram Franco outlines in reference to Latin American literature, whereby the four female archetypes of the virgin mother, the virgin, the mother and the whore are positioned in the four corners of a quadrangle centred on the phallus, has long been in place and recognized.[28] Indeed, in relation to works by Marta Brunet and Rosario Ferré, María Inés Lagos-Pope describes doubling within their female protagonists as an articulation of 'la experiencia femenina al aludir, específicamente, a la división del mundo de la mujer en compartimentos estancos y al subrayar las restricciones que a ésta le ha impuesto la sociedad patriarcal' [the female experience by alluding, specifically, to the division of the world of women into watertight compartments and by underlining the restrictions to which she has been subjected by patriarchal society].[29] In *Fado*, Mars combats these strictures and focuses on the female body as the space in which and the means by which her protagonist resists such an imposed categorization. Consequently, Anaïse/Frida seeks to displace the phallus as the sole agent in this framework, without denying the place it continues to hold in contemporary Haitian society. The interaction of the multiple aspects of Anaïse/Frida's character — different 'mes', in Audre Lorde's terms — which may seem to be in opposition, results in a constructive process, as Lorde suggests is indeed possible.[30]

In keeping with Lorde's use of the term different 'mes', the interaction between the two personas in *Fado* does not remain that of the self with the other, as might be suggested by Anaïse being displaced by Frida in the novel. Surging from a place within Anaïse that she had long occupied, Frida repeatedly interacts with Anaïse in order for the self (Anaïse) to be reconstituted through her embodiment of the other (Frida). However, as Kelly Oliver writes in *Colonization of the Psychic Space*, subjectivity is not the definition of oneself in opposition to the other, but rather is attained through the continual interaction of the self with the other in a relational manner.[31] In Mars's novel, while the self is Anaïse prior to the narrative present, the interactions between Anaïse and Frida lead to a questioning of which one is self and which one is other, resulting in a presentation of both as self and as other. This self and other are themselves the products of the abovementioned patriarchal construct that has created such a dichotomy — that of the spurned wife and the whore — and the bourgeois professional in contradistinction to the marginalized resident of the city slum. In bringing these together, Mars both deconstructs the compartmentalization of women's identity to which Lagos-Pope refers, thus challenging the restrictions placed on the manner in which they are permitted to act, and highlights that rather than a conflation of two personas, the self her protagonist manages to reconstitute is one of a complex, multifaceted woman comprising multiple, interacting 'mes'.

In this manner, Anaïse/Frida embodies the concept of multiple avatars of the *lwa*, whereby a *lwa* comprises numerous 'personae', each of which has specific characteristics and which interact with and complement each other.[32] Especially pertinent in this regard, Ezili Dantò and Ezili Freda are often likened to sisters and, as two avatars of the popular and powerful *lwa* Ezili, they can work together for a common goal. Yet, as one of the most contradictory and arbitrary *lwa*, 'a spirit of love who forbids love [and] a woman who is the most beloved yet feels herself the most betrayed', the short-lived harmony may be broken at any time by the manifestation of the fierce rivalry that exists between the two.[33]

In the Catholic chromolithographs with which many *lwa* are associated, Ezili Dantò is depicted by the Mater Salvatoris or the Virgin of Czestochowa, a black virgin carrying a child. Within the context of Vodou, this child is identified as Anaïs or Anaïse, the daughter of Ezili Dantò. The persona of Anaïse in *Fado* is therefore associated with the *lwa* of motherhood via her daughter, while her character is informed by this *lwa*, particularly in her relationship with and conceptualization of motherhood. Furthermore, by writing a character called Anaïse who moves beyond the boundaries of the male-conceived dichotomy of women associated with Ezili Dantò and motherhood as related to the 'dark-skinned peasant or proletarian woman',[34] Mars not only references the protagonist of Jacques Roumain's canonical work *Gouverneurs de la rosée* (1944), Annaïse, she also rewrites this representation to illustrate that the latter's depiction of womanhood within this dichotomy must be interrogated (as both Latortue (1990) and Mars (2010b) have stated). In reference to Ezili Dantò, Anaïse/Frida embodies the *lwa* both in her maternal actions towards Léo and the other prostitutes at Bony's and through her status as a spurned wife, which then reflects the relationships Ezili Dantò is said to have maintained with her lovers. For example, although she never marries and is fiercely independent in this regard, Ezili Dantò maintains a relationship with Ogou, 'a warrior spirit pictured as a hero, a breathtakingly handsome and dedicated soldier'.[35] However, Ogou is also untrustworthy and Ezili Dantò knows she cannot depend on her lover. In a similar fashion, Léo has a comfortable job in a bank, Anaïse works as a graphic designer, they live in the 'haute ville' and Anaïse does not foresee the end of their marriage. As an embodiment of Ezili Dantò, it might seem that the protagonist's desire not to have children is incongruous with her representation of this *lwa*. However, Ezili Dantò always has the interests of children at heart, even if it involves her own suffering and, having been shattered by the experiences of repeated rape and two abortions, Anaïse must assert her independence from the patriarchal construct that has caused her pain and rejection. In addition to being a mother, Ezili Dantò is also a warrior and the chromolithograph shows her with three scars on her cheek. Various accounts exist of how she sustained these scars, be they wounds inflicted by Ezili Freda due to their rivalry over lovers, as Brown and Fernández Olmos and Paravisini-Gebert note, or the result of Ezili Dantò protecting her child from kidnap by the violent and jealous Ezili Mapiang (another avatar of Ezili) as Déita recounts.[36] Moreover, commonly they are also ascribed to her having 'fought fiercely beside her "children" in the Haitian slave revolution' during which she was wounded.[37] These are scars that Anaïse bears beneath the skin, and her apparent inability to conceive is just one of the consequences and long-standing reminders of the violence that has been forced upon her body. As problematic as it will be demonstrated to be below, the fact that she ultimately does conceive marks the conception of the reconstituted self through her actions as Ezili Freda, although this symbolically reinscribes her into the oppressive context from which she sought — and continues to seek — freedom.

Brown has described Ezili Dantò as 'an independent, childbearing woman with an unconventional sexuality that, on several counts, flouts the authority of the patriarchal family', a portrait similar to that which Otero paints of her counterpart in Santería, Yemayá (see Chapter 1).[38] However, whilst Ezili Dantò is essential to the way that Anaïse/Frida challenges the patriarchal construct in which she is depicted, it is in her expression of her sexuality through her embodiment of Ezili Freda rather than her association with Ezili Dantò that the reader witnesses the protagonist's undermining of the restrictions placed on her thus far. In addition to the similarity in name highlighted by Vitiello, Ezili Freda's sensuality and propensity for having many sexual partners is reflected in the manner in which Anaïse's behaviour changes when she becomes Frida.[39] Remembering her years of marriage, Anaïse states, 'Je remplissais mes devoirs par routine' [I fulfilled my duties out of routine], believing that Léo was remaining faithful to her, and she was suddenly awakened from her 'marital torpor' and 'the straightforwardness of conjugal life' by the announcement of his departure (20). In the narrative present, however, Anaïse/Frida uses her sexuality in order to gain the sense of power that she thought she possessed. This illusion of power that was predicated on her 'fulfilling her [marital] duties out of routine' exemplifies Anaïse's status as a woman whose sexuality has been suppressed within a context that has expected her to act as the archetypal wife, maintaining conjugal relations with her husband and providing children.

As Lorde writes, the erotic and female sexuality as a source of power have been negated by their presentation as 'a sign of female inferiority' and by women being 'made to suffer and to feel contemptible and suspect by virtue of its existence', resulting in the erroneous belief 'fashioned within the context of male models of power' that 'only by the suppression of the erotic [...] can women be truly strong'.[40] Indeed, as Myriam Chancy has stressed, despite the participation of women in Haitian society, 'Sexuality takes on a striking importance [...] for it is the ultimate site of women's subjugation and is, by extension, the site of possible empowerment'.[41] It is equally important with regard to defining identity, as it is through her exploration of her sexuality that Anaïse/Frida manages to reclaim her subjectivity and thus the power to define her own identity. This notion — key in *Fado* — has been explored by Mars in her previous novel *Kasalé* (2007), in which Sophonie, its protagonist, chooses to become a partner of the *lwa* Agwe manifested through Athanaël.[42] Thereby 'embrac[ing] her femininity and sensuality', she 'discover[s] all the dimensions of an undivided womanhood' to subsequently give birth to a daughter conceived on a mythical plane between Lasirèn and Athagwe, thus enabling the Vodou heritage of the *lakou* [familial compound] to continue from the current matriarch Gran'n to the new generation.[43] Lasirèn is the consort of Agwe (also called Athagwe in *Kasalé* (31)) and is considered to be closely related to the avatars of Ezili. Depicted as a siren or mermaid, she 'is believed to bring good luck and wealth from the bottom of the sea', which Fernández Olmos and Paravisini-Gebert note sometimes results in her being known as 'Ezili of the Waters'.[44] In this regard, Mars illustrates this close relationship between Lasirèn and the Ezilis in her short story 'Et tant pis pour la mort' [And That's Too Bad About Death] (2014), writing a female protagonist who embodies characteristics of Ezili Dantò, Ezili Freda and Lasirèn, and who is named explicitly as the latter two of these in reference to both her sexuality and her sirenic allure. Notably, however, while Anaïse/Frida in *Fado* and Malory in 'Et tant pis pour la mort' both grasp the sexuality and sexual identities characteristic of their associated *lwa*, Sophonie in *Kasalé*, in contrast, is presented as somewhat passive in her relationship with Athanaël (Athagwe), as Vété-Congolo underlines.[45]

In these terms, the spurned wife versus whore dichotomy represented as two subjectivities who share the same corporeal space can be viewed as an example of what Strongman denotes as the 'transcorporeal conceptualization of the self' characteristic of African-derived religions in the Caribbean.[46] Anaïse and Frida inhabit the same body as two distinct personas who inform each other both as self and other. While the body does then serve as the site of interaction between the physical and spiritual in the same manner as it does in the other novels discussed here, in *Fado* the focus is on the multiple subjectivities that inhabit it and the different spaces it traverses, as well as it constituting a nodal point between the public and private spheres. In the first chapter, Anaïse describes Frida as an ever-present entity who has long dwelt within her body, remarking that, 'Je lui donne voix. Je lui érige quatre murs où exister, je la légitime' [I give her a voice. I provide her with four walls in which to exist, I legitimize her] (15). Thus presented as a duality, the female body is not only a means through which to engage with other individuals and spaces, it also functions as the location in which Anaïse and Frida can interact. A divided yet single whole, though fractured and dismembered, her body then constitutes both the site and the means for transcending the dichotomies in status and space.

Space and Sexual Identities

By traversing a series of fragmented spaces, Anaïse/Frida's body enables the intersection of the socio-political, spiritual and psychological, thus permitting the interrogation of each. With regard to the spurned wife versus whore dichotomy, its embodiment in a single corporeal entity by Anaïse and Frida is reflected in and explored through the interactions between Ezili Dantò and Ezili Freda in numerous ways. On one level, the rivalry between the two represents the conflict and impossibility of coexistence that has been created between the traditional literary representations of the Madonna and whore. However, the two are also complementary, as evidenced by the description of Frida and Anaïse as *marasa* articulated by the latter at the novel's close when she refers to Frida as her twin sister, her other self (109). This notion of coexistence is mentioned explicitly at several points in the narrative: at the outset Anaïse ponders the question she believes Léo really wants to ask, 'Qui es-tu devenue, Anaïse?' [Who have you become, Anaïse?] (14), whilst elsewhere Frida is described as a presence that has manifested itself from within Anaïse's being. Moreover, in the seventeenth chapter — the halfway point of the novel — the two temporarily collapse into one without distinction as the narrative recounted by Anaïse moves seamlessly from the 'I' as Anaïse at home to the 'I' as Frida at Bony's (58–61).

Anaïse's status as the spurned wife and divorcée has ramifications for the manner in which she interacts with society, however. Having lost her illusion of power, the persona of Anaïse retreats from all but necessary interaction with society beyond the four walls of her house. She works from home and avoids the streets of Port-au-Prince, streets 'qui tuent sans discrimination' [that kill indiscriminately] and are 'peuplées d'êtres à mi-chemin entre l'humain et la bête' [populated with beings halfway between humans and beasts] (22). As Anaïse, therefore, she is no longer able to interact with this society from which she feels completely alienated, to the extent that she ceases to recognize herself and others as belonging to the same human race. She sees the men as 'hommes-caméléons', chameleons that change their temporal outward identities to suit their surroundings, and the women as 'femmes-couleuvres', non-venomous but malicious snakes that are perfidious by nature. This is a further example of the duality of the body and therefore no different in this specific respect to Anaïse/Frida, but rather than being restitutive, the association of wider society with chameleons or snakes renders them both deleterious and other. In so doing, Anaïse then views herself as other to society, mirroring the manner in which she was treated when raped as an adolescent, objectified and dehumanized to the extent that she thought her father would reject her out of disbelief. Subject to the restrictions she perceives wider society imposes upon her, the persona of Anaïse withdraws from this context.

While Anaïse then becomes Frida, those non-lovers with whom she does interact in the 'haute ville' continue to view her as Anaïse the divorcée. One of these, her female neighbour, spies on her from the window, not able to comprehend the 'perverse bonds' that hold a divorced man to his wife nor to countenance the 'unspeakable things' that go on between them (68). In much the same fashion as above, the neighbour is presented as other; she is a rat with small gleaming eyes who spies from the window, her tail coiled around the metal bars, and as such, represents the disapprobation of Anaïse's actions on behalf of wider bourgeois society. Moreover, Anaïse's presentation as other is made explicit here, not only as a corollary of her disassociation from the 'bêtes' that surround her, but also with her being described — like María Antonia in Chapter 2 — both as a predator who thirsts for sex with women's husbands and as easy prey for these men, since they believe she must now be available to satisfy their sexual desires. As such, she is subjected to the patriarchal construct which rejects and marginalizes her 'pour délit de défaut d'homme' [for the crime of lacking a man] (69), yet within which she becomes the object of male desire because of this very characteristic. Harry, Léo's friend, attempts to court Anaïse, attracted by the 'vibration' given off by, in his words, the body of a satisfied woman (34), and later tries to force her to kiss him until she sinks a letter opener into his face (94). Throughout, therefore, the reader witnesses bourgeois society's impositions on the manner in which women within this environment are supposed to act and repudiation of those who do not conform, while legitimizing the actions of men like Harry towards Anaïse. Although this example is in a different socio-political context to María Antonia in Hernández Espinosa's play, it is notable that the aforementioned conflict between María Antonia and the women within her community is replicated both here and between Frida and Natacha, a newcomer to Bony's brothel. In the latter of these instances, Natacha's arrival and favourable treatment by the owner threatens the sense of camaraderie that exists between the prostitutes already working at his establishment, Frida included.

In the face of this rejection by bourgeois society and the long-standing effects of Anaïse's rape as an adolescent, the persona of Frida comes to the fore, thus enabling the protagonist to undermine this patriarchal authority by exploring her sexuality whilst continuing to function in the spaces of the bourgeois neighbourhood and the 'bas-ville'. Following this account, Anaïse expresses her desire to 'unlearn her fear' and invokes Frida, asking if she is afraid of living in that part of town (50). In Frida we see a woman who is the opposite of Anaïse, one who does not 'fulfil her marital duties' but rather appropriates a sexual being for herself. Casting off her 'oripeaux d'épouse' [wifely rags], which have confined her in this subordinate position, Anaïse/Frida asserts that Léo would now discover in her the true woman that she is (21). Here, her womanhood is directly linked to her sexual relationship with Léo, in which she takes the leading role. The divorce was necessary for Léo to become her lover, and in this position she describes him as eating from her hands and giving her everything she asks of him, unable to recognize the woman to whom he had been married. For Léo, his relationships with the two women in his life are very similar to before: he has both a wife and a mistress, but they now fulfil opposite roles. In this way, therefore, nothing of the patriarchal construct has changed; Babeth and Anaïse/Frida still occupy the defined positions of wife/mother and mistress/whore. However, as the lover, Anaïse/Frida has not only appropriated 'the true woman' resident inside her but in this position she exercises the power that she perceived as lost. Continually returning to the house that was once his, yet that is sufficiently unfamiliar due to the changes both in furnishings and in Anaïse so as to resemble a first visit, Léo then becomes subservient to Anaïse/Frida to a certain extent due to the power she now wields. 'Tu ne savais pas que ton corps pouvait tant brûler' [You didn't know your body could burn so much] she ponders as she mentally addresses Léo, affirming his desire as an ardour that he cannot fathom and pleasure from which he emerges confused (23). For the protagonist, however, this unidentified quality by which Léo is so enthralled is the result of 'le fado et Bony et *Bony's* de la rue des Fronts-Forts' [fado and Bony and *Bony's* on Fronts-Forts Street] (22). In short, it is Frida.

Comparable to María Antonia's position, whose actions as a protagonist both reinforce and subvert the male-dominated construct by which she is confined, Frida's status as a prostitute can also be read both as a result of further imposition of patriarchy through Bony and as an undermining of it. As part of the two-week 'initiation' period referenced above during which Anaïse/Frida must be moulded into the woman Bony and the clients desire, it was necessary for her to 'reperdre ma virginité, ou plutôt la retrouver' [lose my virginity once again, or rather to recover it] (17). In order to return to a position prior to having been raped, Anaïse must symbolically unlearn her experiences as this persona and then relearn how to function as the woman Bony and the clients desire. Later in the novel, Frida notes that, in the interests of business and to ward off troublesome expressions of camaraderie between the 'girls', Bony must impose his will upon them. Within this framework, Frida has the illusion of power that Anaïse had: she claims Bony as her own since she 'commande à son désir' [has command over his desire] and tries to convince Anaïse that he would never betray her trust (40). This is not the case, however, as becomes apparent when Bony takes in Natacha, a new, young prostitute whom Frida considers her rival. Furthermore, although Anaïse and Frida recognize each other as subjectivities residing together in the protagonist's body, Anaïse does not feel able to mention Frida to those with whom she does interact such as her friend Maryse, her long-term gynaecologist Gladys, or even Léo for that matter; such dialogues between the two remain internal. In this regard, Frida is presented as a sexually liberated individual when considered in comparison to Anaïse, but one who outwardly functions solely within the restrictive phallologocentric framework outlined above.

In contradistinction to this, however, the fact that Anaïse/Frida manages to gain a position of agency both at Bony's and with Léo points to the subversion of this very construct. At Bony's, Frida procures a position in which she manages to move beyond that of merely one of his working girls to be recognized as his mistress. In spite of the manner in which Bony manages his establishment whereby he maintains sexual relationships with all the prostitutes who work there, Frida obtains a preferential status aided undoubtedly by her love of fado. While the others dislike this music, preferring merengue and *konpa*, fado becomes part of Frida's being, integral to her sense of self just as Ezili Freda is. For Bony, fado encapsulates the soul of his business and his life overall, inextricable from the establishment that he inherited from his mother where Amália Rodrigues can be heard whenever he is present. Internalizing the singer, Frida describes fado as providing her with 'une grande liberté d'être' [a great freedom of being], albeit with momentary anxieties, and it comes to represent her ability to exercise a level of agency she was unable to exert previously (27). As such, she is able to enjoy a privileged position with Bony, working with clients but occupying his bed more than the others, and also to capture Léo's interest more than she did as his wife, both of which are attained by virtue of her embodiment of Ezili Freda and fado. Moreover, she moulds Léo into the lover she wants, one who desires her as the true woman expressing herself from within rather than as a wife and potential mother. Although Anaïse/Frida learns 'à l'aimer en plein jour' [to love him in broad daylight] partly out of necessity, since he can only visit her during his lunch break, she reconfigures this as a further example of the expression of her sexuality as central to her being, leaving to Babeth 'la nuit, l'obscurité, la pudeur des draps' [the night, the darkness, the modesty of the sheets] (28).

Furthermore, Anaïse/Frida's refusal to kiss Léo, Bony or any of her clients under any circumstances, or indeed to allow them to kiss her in spite of any supplication or increased payment they offer, serves to defy the restrictive archetype of the whore she has been ascribed. Her lips are 'rebellious' (18), and her decision represents a seemingly minor but significant stance on her part that allows her to exercise authority within a context in which she is outwardly defined by male desire. Her insistence leads to her body becoming fractured even further when a drunk client knocks out her front teeth after she bites off the tip of his tongue, which he is trying to force into her mouth. Her subsequent reluctance to smile is a reminder of the violence she suffered, but she does not abandon her resolve in the face of this adversity. Although she is marked physically as a reprisal for her refusal to completely submit, the assertion of her agency in this way reiterates on each occasion her challenge to the very authority that has repeatedly injured her.

The rejection of the category of whore as an homogeneous identity is a further example of how the phallologocentric framework in the novel is undermined. The four archetypal identities afforded women in literature as outlined by Franco above are reductive in nature, with women assigned to four possible roles whose interaction can only be through the male figure. However, the idea of multiple femininity illustrated in *Fado* is not restricted to the dual subjectivities representative of Ezili Dantò and Ezili Freda who come together in the body of the protagonist; the women in the novel are portrayed both as individuals and a collective whole who together exert a level of authority over the men presented as their 'maîtres'. Frida observes that the prostitutes working at Bony's constitute 'une seule femme à plusieurs corps, à plusieurs mystères' [a single woman comprising several bodies, several mysteries] (25), that is, the multiple aspects of femininity that can inhabit numerous bodies or equally — as the protagonist herself illustrates — a single body. The concept of womanhood in this context, itself linked to the *lwa* through Mars's use of the word 'mystères', is necessarily complex, unable to be represented as a single category of prostitute.[47] Furthermore, this femininity transcends the categories via each woman's sexuality, as illustrated by the connection Frida shares with an unnamed scorned wife who kills her husband at the brothel:

> Étrangement, je me suis connectée par la pensée à cette femme, j'ai senti le long de mon bras, sur le parcours de mon échine, dans chaque pore de ma peau la vibration du coup fatal qu'elle a porté. Un orgasme. Le premier spasme de l'orgasme. (39–40)

> [Strangely, I was connected telepathically to this woman, I felt the vibration of the fatal blow she had given along the length of my arm, over the course of my spine, in every pore of my skin. An orgasm. The first spasm of an orgasm.]

Anaïse/Frida notes that it was as a woman that the wife had avenged her husband's rejection and therefore his relegation of her to the status Anaïse held at the novel's opening. Yet Anaïse/Frida experiences this connection as sexual *jouissance*, 'une libération absolue' [a complete liberation] which can be felt due to her being a woman (40). In this fashion, therefore, Mars suggests that what Anaïse/Frida seeks in straddling the divide between spurned wife and whore, linking the two via the female body rather than through the phallus, is not only the freedom from this restrictive construct on an individual level but also as a collective, multifaceted female identity. In so doing, she simultaneously points to the multiple aspects of an individual's personality — Lorde's different 'mes' — that constitute the complexity that is the female protagonist she portrays.

In bridging the divide between these two archetypes, Anaïse/Frida's body crosses the boundary between the uptown, bourgeois neighbourhood and the downtown city slum, reinforcing by means of her sexuality the link already forged by Vodou and fado. As Krista White has emphasized, the erstwhile dichotomy of Ezili Freda being associated with the bourgeois woman and Ezili Dantò with the proletariat is no longer valid, writing that such 'strict association of each lwa with a particular class of woman is too simple'.[48] Rather, the manner in which Haitians identify with these two *lwa* is far more complex and individual since they have been, and continue to be, defined through a series of interactions between the numerous subjectivities that comprise the two groups.[49] However, by drawing together Vodou and fado as Mars does and using Ezili Freda's sexuality associated with Frida becoming a prostitute, the novel undermines the division between the two spaces and the restrictive notions of permissible behaviour held by the urban elite as it brings the actions pertaining to the city slum into this space as a reconstitutive force. With regard to Anaïse/Frida, she embodies fado as she embodies Ezili Freda, and both make the move from Bony's to her house in the 'ville haute'. Here, it is both Frida and fado that Léo finds 'dans la peau d'Anaïse' [in Anaïse's skin], and these are the source of the sexual power she exerts over him (26).

The character of 'l'Empoisonneur' [the Poisoner] also explores this concept of a multifaceted identity within a single body that manages to transcend these discrete spaces of bourgeois neighbourhood and city slum. Described as 'l'homme-caméléon' (99), therefore symbolically related to the world outside the defined spaces of Anaïse's home and Bony's, l'Empoisonneur's body is inhabited by a different spirit each time Frida visits: a seductress ('l'Empoisonneur-femme'), a senator ('l'Empoisonneur-sénateur'), an ardent poet ('l'Empoisonneur-poète') and finally as himself ('l'homme-caméléon'). As observed before in reference to many of the characters discussed, this individual also exemplifies the notion of the body as a conduit for the interaction of the physical and spiritual planes. Of particular note, however, is that this single character crosses numerous socio-political divides by being able to represent these three personas in addition to his own by means of a single physical body. In Montero's *Del rojo de su sombra*, Similá comprises the roles of *bòkò*, the *lwa* Belié Belcán and Toro trois-Graines, and the Macoutes, and through these various elements of his character is at times a lover, at others an enemy, and at still others a colleague together with whom Zulé performs spiritual work. While embracing different roles, Similá is not shown to traverse the socio-economic and socio-political divisions as l'Empoisonneur of *Fado* does, however. Upon arriving at his house, Frida observes 'ses muscles proéminents et la bosse indécente de son sexe nu sous le tissu fin' [his prominent muscles and the indecent imprint of his naked penis under the thin fabric], continuing to note his virile and manly body before naming him 'l'Empoisonneur-femme' and focusing on his feminine accoutrements (82). As 'une femme en chaleur, espérant la rosée d'un homme' [a lustful woman, awaiting the dewdrops of a man] (83), he is related to prostitution and therefore embodies the socio-political group represented by Frida, while equally exemplifying the fluid concept of gender and sexual identity in Vodou practice. On subsequent occasions, l'Empoisonneur is a senator and a poet, as such belonging to both the political and artistic elites. This 'homme-caméléon' both draws these spaces together and functions in each of them, and so complements the role Anaïse/Frida plays in traversing the divide between the bourgeois professional and the prostitute, the uptown neighbourhood and the city slum.

The manner in which l'Empoisonneur complicates gender and sexual identity invites a brief comparison with the protagonist of Rita Indiana's 'novela de ciencia-ficción *eco-queer*' [science fiction, eco-queer novel] *La mucama de Omicunlé*, discussed in the Introduction and Chapter 1.[50] As noted previously, Acilde Figueroa's transition from a female to male body is simultaneous with his initiation as a child of Olokún, an androgynous *orisha* who is part woman/man, part fish and master of the sea, an event that occurs in the dystopic not-too-distant future of 2027 in the Dominican Republic.[51] Within the context of a complex, trans-Caribbean framework of African-derived religions, indigenous religious practices and Catholic iconography, the incarcerated former prostitute Acilde is replicated at two points in the past, as an adult male in 1991 and as a seventeenth-century buccaneer. Acilde, Giorgio and Roque occupy discrete corporeal spaces, yet much like the different *caminos* or 'personae' of the *orisha* and *lwa*, these multiple avatars have varying sexual and gender identities and are of differing socio-economic status. It is Acilde's work as a runaway androgynous prostitute following the 'corrective rape' she suffers as a teenager that enables her to obtain the drug Rainbow Bright in order to transition from a woman to a man, which then precipitates his acceptance of the mission to save the marine environment by means of his male avatars born in the past but linked mentally to the narrative present. As Giorgio, he marries an heiress and founds an eco-tourism and environmental conservation project on the northern Dominican coast, leading him to invite an artists' collective to the property in order to celebrate the official launch of the venture. As Roque, leader of an all-male group of buccaneers who later has a late-night tryst with a new member (himself an avatar of a colleague in the artists' collective), he encourages the newcomer to make prints using cowhide and blood collected during their hunting expeditions. These prints, produced in the Caribbean with hallmarks of Spanish artist Francisco Goya's work yet more than a century before the latter appeared in Europe, would later be 'discovered' by Giorgio, and their sale would ensure the conservation project's future.

Returning to l'Empoisonneur, he also transcends the discrete spaces of the uptown neighbourhood and city slum in the novel by means of the poison he gives Frida. Intended to cause a painless demise, the poison is used by Anaïse/Frida to first kill Bony and Léo and then commit suicide, an act that undermines the superior position that the elite ostensibly holds. Poisoning, as Pierre Pluchon notes, was a common crime of which black slaves were charged, with the best known *empoisonneur* in the eighteenth century being Makandal (who, Moreau de Saint-Méry observed, through his popularity lent his name to poisons and poisoners in general).[52] Later considered — in Haitian popular culture, at least — to be an important figure in the burgeoning struggle for independence, Makandal was popularly described as not having perished at the stake but as having metamorphosed into a mosquito, and subsequently becoming a Vodou spirit.[53] Linked to the overthrow of colonialism and the rejection of domination by white slave masters, l'Empoisonneur further exemplifies the deconstruction of the male-female/dominator-dominated binary upon which the colonial powers considered Saint-Domingue to be based. In this context, the poison provides Anaïse/Frida with the ability to choose between 'la vie et la mort, la délivrance et la damnation' [life and death, deliverance and damnation] for Bony, Léo and herself (109). In this manner, he assists Anaïse/Frida's subversion of the patriarchal construct by supplying the poison, while the poison itself becomes the means through which these two spaces are conflated in death. Furthermore, this poison is the sole physical object in the novel that moves between the two discrete spaces of Bony's brothel and Anaïse's house. Appearing in Anaïse's bathroom cabinet in the last chapter and being used in the same manner by her and Frida, it symbolizes the identical final decision that they both make, and thus the most complete intersection of these two spaces.

Motherhood, Sexuality and Reconstitution of the Self

In addition to linking discrete spaces, the female body provides the 'four walls' in which the distinct subjectivities of Frida and Anaïse can coexist, informing and interacting with each other; yet it is simultaneously an agent in the novel by means of the sexuality it expresses. While the body serves as this defined active space, it is itself enclosed for much of the novel between the four walls of Anaïse's house or Bony's brothel. In much the same way as Claudia Tate notes in her introduction to *Black Women Writers at Work*, these 'geographical boundaries merely represent the physical limits of her quest' and Anaïse/Frida's 'destination [...] is not a place but a state of mind'.[54] Mars encapsulates this notion in her choice of epigraph, a couplet from Amália Rodrigues's fado 'Nem ás paredes confesso' [Not Even to the Walls Will I Confess], which introduces the interior nature of the journey the reader will witness. The fact that the body is distanced from society in such a manner highlights that 'her journey is an internal one', which focuses on her awareness and sense of self and foregrounds the 'intense introspection' Tate underlines as necessary for the protagonist to be able to relate to herself.[55] This awareness through reflection on the multiple aspects of one's identity and the actions carried out through an exploration of sexuality allow Anaïse/Frida to draw her fractured body together without viewing the different subjectivities as mutually exclusive. In so doing, she denounces the confinement and imposition of patriarchal society upon women, thereby freeing her to articulate her story beyond the walls by which she has been hitherto contained.

The unexpected end of Anaïse's marriage to Léo gives the protagonist the impetus to seek the change that she accomplishes in the novel. Meeting Bony at a birthday dinner shortly afterwards, his blasé approach to discussing the business he runs in this bourgeois context awakens Frida within Anaïse's being. The protagonist describes this event in terms of subjugation due to her inability to repress the desire to follow him, and the involuntary nature of her response when confronted with the strength of Frida's manifestation within her is likened to that of sweat running from her pores (15). While it is Bony who awakens the personification of Anaïse's sexuality, what is important at this point is the possibility he represents for her negated sexuality to enable her to break free from the restrictions that stifle her. She is not 'subjugated' by him per se, though he is the person she follows and the one with whom she is 'initiated' as a prostitute. Rather, this aspect of her self is asserted as Frida so that she can challenge the oppressive framework in which she lives. Nevertheless, although Anaïse accepts this willingly, she does also become subject to the patriarchal hierarchy in place in the brothel, as demonstrated above, in spite of the fact that she does so in order to 'délivrer mon corps. L'ouvrir' [free my body. Open it up] (17). Anaïse's body represents her sense of self, and so while on one level she must be moulded by Bony and becomes virginal again, on another she reappropriates her body from the violence meted out to it and to her self. As a result, she frees it from this oppression and opens it up, positioning herself as an active agent in her sexuality. The protagonist then uses the sexuality she gains to delineate an idea of femininity outside the very constructs to which she has been subjected.

Anaïse/Frida articulates this reconstitutive aspect of her sexuality while she ponders the significant role fado now plays for her. Listening to Amália Rodrigues, she muses that, although she does not understand the lyrics, 'elle me parle de ma vie, de cet enfant que je n'ai pas désiré, de tous les départs qui m'ont amputée d'un morceau de moi-même' [she speaks to me of my life, of that child that I didn't want, of all the departures which have cut from me a piece of myself] (30). Fado connects with her on a basic level and with its 'mots écorchés, aux accents fissurés' [flayed words, with ruptured accents], it represents the visceral fracturing of her sense of self expressed in 'une mélancolie fêlée' [a cracked melancholy]. However, it also participates in her recovery, continuing to play in the background as she knits the scattered fragments of her body together through pleasure. Each of the 'departures' from her life — her innocence through rape, her children through the two forced abortions, her sense of power at home by her husband replacing her with a younger, child-bearing woman, and even her front teeth because she refused to completely submit to a client's wishes — have been framed in a context of male dominance. Through the expression of her sexuality, Anaïse manages to weave her sense of self back together, a self originally fractured by her oppression within multiple patriarchal configurations of femininity.

In addition to her sexual liberation, this reconstitution is replicated on a physical level by the replacement of Anaïse/Frida's front teeth, a procedure paid for by Bony. Reinforcing the complex presentation of the protagonist, this event underlines that she is not positioned in opposition to the frameworks she seeks to undermine but participates in them in a way that enables their reconfiguration, thereby offering a space in which women are able to define their own concept of self. One of the objectives Frida seeks is to forge a relationship with Bony in which she can be described as his mistress, and although the dental procedure he pays for is evidence of his desire to define her — indeed, Bony is surprised by his own generosity — the result is the very outcome that Frida has been pursuing: upon seeing her with her new teeth, Bony is moved to recognize her as one apart from the others in his employ. Moreover, the integral nature of this procedure to the reconstitution of her body and therefore her self is demonstrated earlier in the same paragraph, as Bony muses that Frida has in fact become a new woman. While this is problematic since Bony considers that he has both physically and conceptually refashioned her on his terms, Frida remains an active participant in their relationship, expressing her sexuality in a particularly intense manner, 'comme si c'était le dernier acte qu'elle posait sur terre avant la fin du monde' [as if it were her final deed on earth before the end of the world] (63). At this point, Anaïse/Frida participates in a process of suggesting, in Sloan's terms, 'new configurations of meaning by reappropriating and reinventing images of women', which is achieved by engaging with and confronting the identity imposed on her and so determining an alternative.[56] This is not always as successful as first envisioned, however, as once Frida attains this privileged position, Bony then acts as Léo did with each of his wives, taking another mistress and in so doing subjecting these women to the male-dominated hierarchy.

Anaïse/Frida's adoption and reconfiguration of motherhood is a further front on which the protagonist mounts her challenge to the phallologocentric framework that Franco delineates. As noted above, in this construct the circumscribed archetype of 'mother' can only be accessed via the phallus. However, in *Fado*, the protagonist accesses both the framework and the notion of motherhood through her reconfiguration of this very concept, drawing together Ezili Freda and Ezili Dantò as distinct yet mutually reliant subjectivities who inform each other and whose interactions allow her to create meaning. In her discussion of Julia Kristeva's work, Oliver writes, 'Women are put in the paradoxical position of having to endorse a social code that devalues them and represses the maternal body as something natural rather than cultural'.[57] Anaïse suffers in light of this very paradox — whereby Léo rejects her because she seems unable to fulfil her 'natural' role and bear children — but also has been subject to a more complex paradox since her body was devalued and violated at the hands of a doctor when she did perform this very function and conceived after having been raped. In light of her decision never to have children and her subsequent apparent sterility, Anaïse/Frida then assumes a maternal role with respect to Félicia, one of the prostitutes at Bony's, and at times describes her relationship with Léo in maternal terms. Importantly, Frida is also described as a woman who does not have, and has never wanted, children — in keeping with Ezili Freda — and Anaïse 'n'a pas su être mère' [didn't know how to be a mother] (21). However, in this context in which Ezili Freda is pre-eminent, the reader sees the influence of Ezili Dantò as the *lwa* of motherhood, in conjunction with the overall concept of Ezili who represents sisterhood between women, since Frida loves Félicia as if she were her own. Throughout the novel, Frida treats Félicia as she would a daughter, listening many times to her repeated nightmare of her father's death, but each time as if it were the first, and caring for her when she falls ill. Faced with the absence of desire to have her own children, even if she were able, the notions of motherhood and sisterhood are conflated and conceptualized as the former, thus moving beyond the idea of a 'natural' social code in which children are necessarily born of the womb to one which reflects more closely the idea of motherhood encapsulated by Ezili Dantò. If it is the exploration of sexuality within an overarching context of Vodou which binds women together in this novel, then Anaïse/Frida's age and embodiment of Ezili Dantò places her in a position of spiritual motherhood with regard to the other women working at the brothel, similar to that of a *manbo* who fulfils a motherly role for the 'children' she initiates, or indeed in that of an 'other mother' where kinship is unrestricted by biological or familial ties.[58] This then manifests itself most clearly in the relationship between Félicia and Frida, the former both a young girl and a woman who has missed out on adolescence, which then enables Anaïse/Frida to collapse the discrete categories of mother and whore while simultaneously subverting the hierarchy that insists that motherhood is a 'natural' role necessarily attained through a woman's procreation. Moreover, Frida has maternal feelings for each of the girls alongside whom she works, although she finds these sentiments hard to reconcile with the 'douleureuse et jouissive complicité' [painful and pleasurable complicity] that binds them all together as women who share a single man (25). Instead of rejecting this role, Mars's protagonist draws on the notion of other-mothering and redefines motherhood within a context of female sexuality and Vodou, which then allows her to fulfil a role for which she was rejected as incapable on her own terms.

In contrast, in the eighteenth chapter Bony entreats Frida, 'Viens, [...] j'ai envie de te faire un enfant' [Come, [...] I want to make you a baby] (64), and she realizes she is pregnant two chapters later. Anaïse/Frida also conceives Léo's child, a necessary event on the one hand as they both inhabit the same body, but one which is presented in a complex manner. Firstly, Anaïse/Frida's pregnancy indicates the conception of something new immediately following the abovementioned point at which the two personas are most closely linked. In reference to Mars's earlier novel *Kasalé*, this is similar to the symbolism conveyed by Sophonie's pregnancy and the subsequent birth of her daughter by means of the *lwa*, who enabled Sophonie to conceive in the spiritual realm by joining her with the father Athanaël (son of Agwe/Athagwe, master of the waters) through the river that passed by the *lakou*. Here, the process of conception, pregnancy and birth of 'l'enfant de l'eau' [the water's child] (42), as Gran'n describes her, signals the rebirth of the *lakou* as the ailing matriarch had foretold, and thus the continuation of the dwindling practice of Vodou in the community after her death.

Returning to Anaïse/Frida's pregnancy, the notion of bearing Léo's and Bony's child is also problematic, however, since to do so would reinscribe the protagonist into the patriarchal construct that she has sought to challenge and reconfigure through the alternative concept of motherhood outlined above. Upon being informed by her gynaecologist that she is pregnant despite the odds, Anaïse whispers, 'Gladys... je suis morte' [Gladys... I am dead] (89). Although indicative to a certain degree of Frida's and Ezili Freda's own desire not to have children, more importantly this event, along with the more frequent appearance of the young and ambitious Natacha at Bony's, prompts the re-emergence of the persona of Anaïse who taunts Frida when she insists Bony will not betray her confidence (78). Originally rejected by Léo for her apparent sterility, Anaïse/Frida has managed to delineate this alternative concept of motherhood both with Léo and at Bony's. However, if she now accepts the male-dominated 'natural' perception of motherhood and continues as Bony's mistress, she is denied any agency in these two relationships, rendering them male-dominated once again. The reassertion of Anaïse in this context along with her statement regarding her impending death therefore signifies on a symbolic level that giving birth would undo the progress Anaïse/Frida has made in managing to reconstitute her body and thus her sense of self. This additionally draws on one of Ezili Dantò's characteristics, who, as a mother to many, seeks the benefit of her children over her own well-being. If, then, giving birth to the child would force Anaïse/Frida back into this framework in which women are subjected to the restrictions that she has sought to undermine, Mars's protagonist has no choice but to reject this outcome and seek an alternative; that is, the death of Léo and Bony who are readying to abandon her and her own departure from the physical world, itself conceptualized as 'délivrance'.

This link between pregnancy, maternity and death can be viewed in light of the symbolism evoked by scholars such as Simone de Beauvoir (1949) and Julia Kristeva (1987), in which pregnancy and motherhood equate to death, or indeed Trinh T. Minh-ha's observation that through such a reduction to the 'infant-producing organ', patriarchy is imposed on and in the woman's body.[59] Anaïse/Frida's pregnancy and mothering of Félicia can be seen in a similar vein, with her pregnancy engendering her physical undoing in addition to her conceptual reconstitution. On one level, therefore, the restitution of the body's capability to conceive which indicates the reversal of the physical damage that resulted from her rape and abortions is itself harmful since it connotes her death. Similarly, Anaïse's position as a mother figure to Félicia leads to a similar outcome, eliciting her desire to accompany her 'daughter' on the latter's journey to the sea to recover her *bonanj*. Deconstructing Félicia's madness by reclaiming this from the sea, both women must then choose death in order to be reborn.

On another level, however, Anaïse/Frida's conceiving is an illustration of the *marasa twa* and Anaïse's ultimate reconstitution of her self. The *marasa twa* are the tripartite twin *lwa*, with the twins born together considered sacred and powerful as a dual entity and the third twin, the one born afterwards called the *dosou/dosa*, 'believed by many Haitians to be even "stronger" [...] than the twins themselves'.[60] The concept of twins is frequently explored in Haitian and Haitian diasporic literature: Mars indicates the power of the *marasa* in much of her work, particularly in *Kasalé* and in her short story 'Lobo', while twinning is key to Deyita's *Esperans Dezire*, Edwidge Danticat's *Breath, Eyes, Memory* and Lilas Desquiron's *Les Chemins de Loco-Miroir* (published in English as *Reflections of Loko Miwa*), to name but a few.[61] Furthermore, in her article 'One Plus One Equals Three: *Marasa* Consciousness, the *Lwa*, and Three Stories', Toni Pressley-Sanon (2013) examines this notion of the *marasa* and *dosou/dosa* and applies her analysis to three stories from the 2011 anthology *Haiti Noir* edited by Edwidge Danticat. With regard to *Fado*, the *marasa* are evident in the various dualities that have been explored here — Anaïse/Frida, the spurned wife/whore, the bourgeois/city slum, life/death, Ezili Dantò/Ezili Freda — a point Anaïse makes most clearly near the novel's close when she calls Frida her twin before referring to 'le secret des *marassa*' [the secret of the *marasa*] (109). As the most closely and commonly identified of the two Ezilis, both complementary and contradictory, Dantò and Freda already form a type of *marasa*, as Pressley-Sanon also contends in her article. This is complemented by the association between the *marasa* and Ezili Dantò, *lwa* of motherhood who cradles her daughter.[62] However, 'le secret des *marassa*' is embodied by the *marasa twa*, the *dosou/dosa* who comes afterwards and in the case of *Fado*, binds these together in a manner that renders the two more than the sum of their parts. This *dosou/dosa* is the child Anaïse/Frida conceives, the *mystère* she bears: 'je sentais que mon sang, ma chair, mes os, mes cheveux nourrissaient un mystère' [I felt that my blood, my flesh, my bones, my hair were feeding a mystery] (72).

In his introduction to *Fragments of Bone*, Bellegarde-Smith cites the well-known Haitian formulation with regard to the *marasa* that Pressley-Sanon uses in the title to her later article: 'one plus one equals three'.[63] Discussing the notion of this third twin as a necessary part of the *marasa*, Benedicty-Kokken writes that it invokes the '"jamais deux sans trois" — "never two without three" rule', whereby the *dosou/dosa* exists alongside the other two, 'not quite birthed into full existence, but always present'.[64] She compares the tripartite nature of the *marasa twa* to the dialectic of 'thesis' and 'antithesis' followed by 'synthesis', and explains that, in a similar vein:

> The role of the marasa is to work out conflict, conflict between persons, between forces, between a standard order of things and a changing order. The marasa as a cosmological and philosophical concept serves as an arbitrating force in the worlds of persons and communities constantly downtrodden by globalizing forces from slavery to the neocolonially inflicted environmental forces of destruction.[65]

In *Fado*, the dual subjectivities that dwell within the body of Anaïse are drawn together by both of them conceiving and both choosing to administer and take the poison Frida sought from l'Empoisonneur. Although the vial itself is described as constituting and containing 'le chemin secret qui relie les *marassa*' [the secret path that joins the *marasa*] (104), it is an external object that represents the 'third twin' developing in Anaïse/Frida's womb. The protagonist discovers the vial in her bathroom cabinet in the final chapter of the book, having traversed the divide between the discrete spaces of Bony's brothel and Anaïse's house and upon grasping it, she connects directly with the unborn child:

> Un arc-en-ciel inattendu me traverse de part en part et distille dans ma poitrine un bonheur presque insupportable. Mais bien vite les couleurs se brouillent, diluées en une masse rouge, un ectoplasme sanguinolant qui bouge en moi, m'absorbe de l'intérieur. La fiole vit entre mes mains. Je repose mon front contre le miroir du petit meuble. Je me regarde jusqu'au fond de mon abîme. (108)

> [An unexpected rainbow shoots right through me and secretes a happiness in my chest that becomes almost unbearable. But quickly the colours fade, diluted in a red mass, a blood-coloured ectoplasm that moves inside me, absorbs me from the inside. The vial is alive in my hands. I rest my forehead against the mirror of the small unit. I look at myself, look to the bottom of my inner abyss.]

Addressing Frida directly through the *marasa twa* and seeing her via the mirror against which she rests her forehead, Anaïse then asks if she knows the secret of the *marasa* and repeats the words l'Empoisonneur uttered to Frida, that she has in her hand both life and death, deliverance and damnation (109). This third entity — the unborn child, the vial and the poison, the alternative notion of motherhood, the collapsing of the bourgeois neighbourhood and the city slum — is therefore the secret of the *marasa*. It is only at this point, the novel's close, that the persona of Anaïse comes to realize this with clarity at a moment of 'intense introspection', looking 'au fond de mon abîme' and seeing the image of herself, Frida and the unborn child reflected in her mind's mirror as one. As such, while *Fado* does explore these dualities, the outcome is in fact the embodiment of the *marasa twa*, that one plus one equals three, and the reconfiguration of these as represented in the third entity, the *dosou/dosa*, is the most propitious of all. Moreover, this notion is reflected in the structure of *Fado*; the novel is written in thirty-three chapters and it is in the last of these that Anaïse addresses Frida (and the reader) as 'tu', asking, 'connais-tu enfin le secret des *marassa*?' [do you finally know the secret of the *marasa*?] (109). The tripartite twins are therefore explored and their secret posed to the reader in the final chapter which, if enumerated, would be headed '33', a double-digit number comprised solely of the figure three.

Similarly, the twinning observed here is a central theme in Indiana's *La mucama de Omicunlé*. Firstly, as noted previously, Yemayá and Olokún are key *orisha* in this novel, with Esther and Eric both children of Yemayá and Acilde initiated in the novel as a child of Olokún. The original twinning of Acilde reborn from the water as Giorgio reflects not only the nature of Yemayá born from Olokún, but also that of the twin *orisha*, the Ibeyi. A boy and a girl born to Changó and Ochún, they are adopted by Yemayá who raises them as her own. This relationship is reflected in that between Esther and the protagonist, as the former becomes the mother figure for Acilde, who also embodies numerous gender identities in the ways outlined above. Furthermore, Acilde's three avatars as himself, Giorgio and Roque serve as an iteration of the *marasa twa* who seek to resolve the conflict between the spiritual and physical realms in which the residence of Olokún and Yemayá, *orisha* of the sea, has been completely destroyed and rendered uninhabitable to all forms of marine life. The 'moment of resolution or completeness [...] integral to the marasa concept', as Pressley-Sanon describes it, is born of the simultaneous suicide of Acilde and Roque, which transfers the self from the narrative present in 2037 (since by this point Acilde has been incarcerated for ten years) to the life Giorgio leads in 2001.[66] It is left to the reader to decide if the future environmental crisis and the resultant conflict are averted, or indeed whether or not Acilde's death marks that very resolution. What is clear, however, is that for Acilde and his unpredictable crowning *orisha* Olokún, the *dosou/dosa*, the moment of completeness, is to continue as Giorgio in order to forget the rejection and pain Acilde feels in the future and thus, perhaps also mitigate the rejection and humiliation that Olokún experienced at the hands of his love interest, Orisha-Oko.

A further dualism in *Fado* to which Vété-Congolo points is that of life and death, within which she describes the presentation of Anaïse/Frida as a 'peinture de la femme assassinant l'homme après la trahison et pour la libération' [portrait of the woman killing the man following her betrayal and for her freedom].[67] The presentation of this dualism embodied in a single female character is aptly exemplified in the analysis that Frida provides of the abovementioned unnamed wife killing her cheating husband. Having been rejected and replaced by a prostitute, the wife has been left with the couple's children and nursing a sense of wounded pride, a situation compounded by the lack of monetary assistance from her husband. Motivated by deprivation of the pleasure they once shared but aware that he was able to find it with another woman, the wife is constrained within a male-dominated construct that allows her husband to obtain elsewhere that which he no longer felt he could find at home, but denies her the same opportunity. Her reaction is to attempt to dismantle the phallologocentric framework in which she feels trapped by removing the sole agent within it, her husband. However, although she achieves this and therefore her liberation, she does so in a manner that destroys the framework without providing an alternative. This does not allow the wife to reconfigure the construct, but rather she remains subject to it despite the physical absence of the central focus. In this instance, there is no transformation of the framework, just a reaction against it.

To a certain extent, this critique can be applied to Anaïse/Frida, who kills both Léo, because he is about to leave her again, moving abroad with his new wife and son, and Bony, due to his replacing her with Natacha. In this situation, Anaïse/Frida acts as Ezili Freda might have done, exacting revenge against her lovers for having spurned her once again. However, Mars offers a more complex reading in this instance, using the concept of death in Vodou to present an alternative construct in which Anaïse/Frida can continue to undermine this framework in a fashion that does not solely constitute a reaction against it, although this alternative does necessitate her own physical demise. Dispatching Léo and Bony to 'la mort' and 'damnation', Anaïse/Frida departs for 'la vie' and 'délivrance'. As shown, continuing to live would require Anaïse/Frida either to be reinscribed within the restrictive construct of natural motherhood that she has sought to undermine, or to subject her body once again to the butchery and dismemberment of abortion. In order to maintain her reconstituted sense of self, her only option is to depart in a death that would signify life, a damnation that would be deliverance.

In her foreword to the third edition of Brown's *Mama Lola: A Vodou Priestess in Brooklyn* — itself the *dosa* of the three editions — , Michel underlines that the death of a Vodou initiate is the beginning of:

> His or her voyage of return to Ginen, [...] the realm of the unborn and the afterlife, where ancestors who have passed from this life to the next reunite with those not yet born [...]; where the conjoining of spirits — old and new — creates a seamless tapestry of past, present, and future that is then brought to this earth to shield and strengthen the living.[68]

In returning to Ginen in this fashion, Anaïse/Frida manages to continue to undermine the hierarchy that she challenged through her embodiment of Ezili Freda and the *marasa twa*, although it required her departure from the physical world. Furthermore, in so doing she ties together the alternatives she has delineated through her body with the spirit world, symbolically linking the seat of the world of the *lwa* with her struggles, and providing a construct in which women can be invested with agency and thus continue to challenge male privilege that has divided womanhood into discrete spaces in Haitian society. Anaïse/Frida was not able to prevent her physical demise as to do so would be to accept the re-fracturing of the self, and it is this self that is signified by the *marasa twa* that she conceives. Consonant with the previous readings of the deaths of Zulé in *Del rojo de su sombra* and, to a certain extent, María Antonia in Hernández Espinosa's play, death considered from this perspective in *Fado* does not constitute for Anaïse/Frida the imposition of male domination, but rather the choice not to submit to it.

An important element of this journey and the entity that binds Vodou and fado, life and death, Ginen and Haiti, is the sea, the means of spiritual and physical departures. Described by Régine Michelle Jean-Charles as 'un lieu de contradiction, de complexité et de confort' [a place of contradiction, complexity and comfort], the sea is inherently related to the passage of the soul to Ginen and thus the transition to the next stage of life.[69] Further, it remains both pertinent and powerful as an ever-present reminder of the death and horrors of the Middle Passage, while, more recently, carrying off the 'boat people' who flee the archipelago in search of a better life. With regard to just a selection of the texts discussed here, the link between life and death engendered by water is evident in *Kasalé*, where it precipitates Gran'n's demise and is the means by which Sophonie and Athanaël's daughter is conceived, while in *La mucama de Omiculé* its multivalence extends from it being the site of regeneration for both Acilde and his avatars to representing the multiple physical and conceptual deaths that Indiana's novel portrays. In Santos-Febres's *Sirena Selena vestida de pena*, the journey across the Mona Passage, albeit by air, is the incipient moment for the *bolerista*'s future success, and his accomplishments on the margins of Puerto Rican and Dominican society are in part ensured by his embodiment of

Ochún and Yemayá, accompanied (if only by virtue of his name) by one of their counterpart *lwa*, Lasirèn.

In *Fado*, the sea at Port-à-l'Écu, site of Félicia's father's zombification and her subsequent haunting by him, has held Félicia's *bonanj* prisoner since her childhood journey to the mainland to work as a *restavèk*.[70] Confronting the sea in death will then allow her *bonanj* to also make the journey to Ginen and release her from torment. Doing so with Anaïse/Frida, the trio then form a further instance of the *marasa twa*, reinforcing the mother-daughter bond between Anaïse/Frida and Félicia, and thus validating the alternative notion of motherhood formulated through the protagonist's actions. This is reiterated by Anaïse/Frida's earlier assertion that she carries within her 'la mer de Port-à-l'Écu' [the sea of Port-à-l'Écu] (96), the long association between the homonyms 'mer' [sea] and 'mère' [mother] encapsulating here the fluidity of motherhood and the connection between Frida and Félicia forged therein, along with the notion that maternity is related to the bountiful sea and the link the waters create between motherhood and death. While neither Frida nor Anaïse is depicted taking the poison, their deaths are marked by their final appearances closing with departures to the sea, accompanied by a softly playing fado sung by Amália Rodrigues and whose undulating rhythms replicate the very waves to which they will succumb. The novel closes with Anaïse joining Frida and Félicia, thus cementing the relationship between the three, and she shuts her eyes to see, dancing on the inside of their lids, 'le bleu des vagues qui m'emportent vers Port-à-l'Écu' [the blue of the waves which carry me towards Port-à-l'Écu] (110). Polysemous by nature, the sea then serves as another (feminine) body in which the numerous dualities explored in the novel collapse to constitute a space of possibility, as Jean-Charles suggests.[71]

In sum, the female body in *Fado* not only serves as the site of interaction between the physical and spiritual worlds, but more importantly is the space in which the male-dominated dichotomies regarding women's identity can be challenged and undermined within a context that is itself hybrid. Encapsulating the seemingly disparate contexts of fado and Vodou within her protagonist's body, the author employs a threefold approach whereby the body, music and religion each signify the crossover between the discrete subjectivities of Anaïse and Frida — the spurned wife and the whore, the bourgeois professional and the denizen of the city slum. The narrative interweaves the contexts of fado and Haitian Vodou to draw together the history of an ostensibly European musical genre with African-derived religious practices, and so renders the presentation of them both more complex, be they in isolation or together. As such, it delineates a spiritual context that resonates with the protagonist and in the different socio-political contexts the narrative comprises (Haitian, Brazilian, West African, Portuguese) while seeing Anaïse/Frida traverse divisions in space, class and social propriety. In bringing these together, the protagonist is able to produce meaning and effectuate the reconstitution of her fractured sense of self, represented by the dismembered body, and draw together in that body the different 'mes' it comprises. This is achieved largely through the exploration of her sexuality, and in so doing Anaïse/Frida appropriates agency in areas in which she has been oppressed and restricted. Importantly, however, the complexity of these issues is retained and, while subverted, the patriarchal frameworks are shown still to be extant. Nevertheless, in spite of this and the fact that the protagonist's physical demise is unavoidable, Anaïse/Frida's negotiation of the different spaces outlined and her challenge to the constructs in place offer a reading that goes beyond the duality of reason and insanity and sees Mars's protagonist collapse the still extant phallologocentric framework, at least in part.

Notes to Chapter 3

1. Sloan 2000: 46.
2. The body of Mars's protagonist is inhabited by two subjectivities, Anaïse and Frida. 'Anaïse/Frida' will be used when referring to her as a single entity.
3. In Haitian Vodou, Ginen is conceptualized both as Africa and as the realm of the *lwa* and of the dead.
4. Vété-Congolo 2010a: 914.
5. Ménard 2011: 231.
6. Vitiello 2011: 369–70.
7. Rich 1977: 251.
8. Interview with Rui Vieira Nery by João Miguel Tavares, cited in Gray 2007: 121.
9. Gray 2007: 106.
10. Holton 2002: 113; Elliott 2010: 23; see also Nery (2004) and Gray (2007).
11. Vété-Congolo 2008: 128.
12. In April 2017, the United Nations Security Council announced that MINUSTAH would close by the following October; MINUSTAH was succeeded by the United Nations Mission for Justice Support in Haiti (MINUJUSTH) on 16 October 2017.
13. Elliott 2010: 15.
14. Ibid.: 15–16.
15. Ibid.: 15.
16. Cook 2003: 23; Elliott 2010: 53. The traversal of these divisions can also be seen in Perdigão Queiroga's 1947 film, *Fado: história d'uma cantadeira* [Fado: A Singer's Story]. The film depicts the rise to relative fame of its *fadista* protagonist, Ana Maria (played by Amália Rodrigues), and the restrictive patriarchal norms with which she is forced to contend as a woman from a lower socio-economic class working in this environment.
17. Holton 2002: 110.
18. Brown 2006: 14.
19. Holton 2002: 110.
20. Gray 2007: 113; Sucena 2002: 29.
21. Sucena 2002: 24.
22. Holton 2002: 116.
23. Latortue 1990: 182.
24. Vitiello 2004: 185.
25. Étonnants-Voyageurs 2011.
26. Mars 2010b. This excerpt is taken from a longer comment made by Mars during the 'Les spectres du passé' [Ghosts of the Past] panel on 24 May 2010 that was one of a series of panels held at the Étonnants-Voyageurs Book Festival in Saint-Malo, France, 22–24 May 2010.
27. Latortue 1990: 182.
28. Franco 1988: 507.
29. Lagos-Pope 1985: 735.
30. Tate 1983a: 102.
31. Oliver 2004: xvii–xviii.
32. Desmangles 1992: 95.

33. Dayan 1995: 59.

34. Latortue 1990: 183.

35. Brown 2010: 235.

36. Brown 2010: 256; Fernández Olmos & Paravisini-Gebert 2011: 131; Déita 1993: 272–74.

37. Brown 2010: 229.

38. Ibid.: 228–29.

39. Vitiello 2011: 369.

40. Lorde 1984: 53.

41. Chancy 1997: 127.

42. *Kasalé* was originally published in 2003 by Presses de l'Imprimeur II in Port-au-Prince.

43. Vété-Congolo 2010b: 309. The term *lakou* (lit. courtyard) refers to a small village built around a shared yard or to a shared residential compound, the latter of which is often familial.

44. Fernández Olmos & Paravisini-Gebert 2011: 126–27.

45. Vété-Congolo 2010b: 308–09.

46. Strongman 2008: 14.

47. *Mystères* is another term used to refer to the *lwa*, with the main room or building housing the altar to the spirits in a *peristil* called the *kay mistè* [house of mysteries]. Symbolically, therefore, Mars creates a further link between Bony's and the Vodou pantheon via the sexuality of the former's residents.

48. White 2000: 75.

49. This is a process that continues and exemplifies the fluid nature of the religious tradition, in which the *lwa* influence the perceptions of adherents and vice versa. Two pertinent examples of the multiple ways in which this has been witnessed are the conversations surrounding gender roles and participation of women noted in Chapters 1 and 2 and those examining the nature and extent of gay men's participation in Vodou rites and ceremonies. For further discussion, see the edited volumes by Bellegarde-Smith (2005a) and Bellegarde-Smith & Michel (2006), as well as Anne Lescot and Laurence Magloire's documentary *Of Men and Gods* (2002).

50. Duchesne Winter (2015).

51. In keeping with Indiana's practice in the novel, female personal and possessive pronouns (she/her/hers) are used here when referring to the period before Acilde's transition, and male pronouns (he/him/his) afterwards.

52. Pluchon 1987: 178.

53. It bears reiterating from Chapter 1 the importance in Caribbean literature of Cuban writer Alejo Carpentier's novel *El reino de este mundo* [The Kingdom of This World] with regard to the presentation in literature of the image of Makandal and his believed ability to metamorphose. The coexistence of and interaction between the physical and spiritual planes in Haitian culture forms a part of the context of *lo real maravilloso* in his novel, of which Makandal's and Boukman's status as *lwa* and the former's metamorphosis are important elements.

54. Tate 1983b: xx.

55. Ibid.: xx, xxiv.

56. Sloan 2000: 46.

57. Oliver 2004: 135.

58. Indeed, non-biological motherhood and the concept of 'other mothers', based on cultural notions of kinship that go beyond biological or familial ties, are common themes in Caribbean and African-American literature. For further discussion, see works such as Patricia Bell-Scott's edited volume *Double Stitch: Black Women Write About Mothers and Daughters* (1993), Angelita Reyes's *Mothering Across Cultures: Postcolonial Representations* (2002) and Sharon Abbey and Andrea O'Reilly's edited volume *Redefining Mothering: Changing Identities and Patterns* (1998).

59. Trinh 1989: 36–37.

60. Courlander 1960: 32.

61. The Kreyòl novel *Esperans Dezire* was published using the Kreyòl spelling of the author's name, Deyita; her volume *La Légende des Loa du Vodou haïtien*, written in French and also referenced here, was published under the French spelling, Déita. It should be noted that, in spite of this difference, the author of these two publications is the same.

62. Houlberg 2005: 19.
63. Bellegarde-Smith 2005b: 11.
64. Benedicty-Kokken 2015a: 231.
65. Ibid.: 231–32.
66. Pressley-Sanon 2013: 119.
67. Vété-Congolo 2010a: 914.
68. Michel 2010: xviii–xxvi.
69. Jean-Charles 2011: 175.
70. A *restavèk* (literally, 'stay-with') is 'a child taken into virtually indentured service by a well-to-do family in Haiti; many poor families have felt forced to place children as *restavèk*' due to monetary concerns (Coates 2006: 193).
71. Jean-Charles 2011: 176.

CHAPTER 4

Destructive Masculinity,
Vodou and the State

In this chapter, my analysis serves as a counterpoint to those offered thus far in which African-derived religions in the Caribbean provide women and other marginalized groups with the opportunity for resistance. When viewed together, the protagonists of Montero's, Hernández Espinosa's and Mars's texts, to name just three among those examined, simultaneously deconstruct, reinforce and subvert patriarchal frameworks in the social, political and cultural contexts they inhabit. At this juncture, however, the focus turns to the alignment of Vodou with destructive masculinity through the François Duvalier and Jean-Claude Duvalier dictatorships, an authoritarian regime that began with François Duvalier's election to the Haitian presidency in 1957, was bequeathed to his son upon the father's death in 1971, and finally came to an end fifteen years later upon Jean-Claude Duvalier's ouster in 1986. Papa Doc, as François Duvalier was commonly known, was the embodiment of religious and political authoritarian power drawn together into a single entity, incorporating Vodou — the traditional locus of resistance — into his regime and thereby removing the space which potential detractors could inhabit to instead use it to suppress opposition. In conjunction with this, the regime was predicated on a gendered hierarchy in which violent repression by the state and its apparatus, most notably the Tonton Macoutes, was presented as masculine (and any opposition therefore as feminine), a framework presided over by the dictator as the omnipotent representation of masculinity. The imposition of power by François Duvalier, either in person or via intermediaries, has been framed in these gendered terms, examples of which highlight the constructed nature of gender within this power relationship and exemplify the notion of destructive masculinity.

The analysis that follows examines two principle themes: François Duvalier's subsumption of nation, state and religion (Vodou and Catholicism, and to a lesser extent Protestantism) into a single masculine entity; and the manner in which fictional renditions of the regime explore the notions of destructive masculinity and sexuality to demonstrate the effects of the dictator's use of Vodou to negate any possibility of resistance and opposition, thereby focusing power in a singular, male-gendered individual. The corpus of works in Haitian literature that invoke these themes is extensive, from before, during and after the period of dictatorship. The discussion here will focus on three main texts whose intersections are particularly instructive with regard to the two main themes identified; these are Marie Vieux-Chauvet's *Folie* [Madness] (2005, first published 1968; the third novella in her Haitian trilogy *Amour, Colère et Folie*, the first two of which will also be discussed),[1] Franck Fouché's play *Général Baron-la-Croix ou Le silence masqué* (1974) and Kettly Mars's novel *Saisons sauvages* (2010a).[2]

As an important note, although this chapter draws on notionally historical or biographical works written about the Duvalier regime, it does not seek to debate the merits of the fictional over the factual or vice versa, or to compare notions of form and veracity. This stance is drawn from the work of Avery Gordon, among others, in *Ghostly Matters: Haunting and the Sociological Imagination* (2008), where she emphasizes the indistinct nature of the division between fact and fiction. As she underlines, the representation of experienced events is mediated and constructed, while fiction pertaining to such events draws on these accounts, also reconstructing and mediating them in order to incorporate them into the text.[3] Here, then, the biographical monographs referenced provide historical and cultural background beside which the novels and plays can be read, while these fictional texts portray an experience of the regime that conflates the various levels of interaction between both the spiritual and physical and the state apparatus and individual.

Furthermore, there is no intention to suggest that the association of the political establishment with religious ideologies and/or institutions — either explicit through profession of belief or practice, or implicit through measures such as greater formal acceptance of hitherto marginalized religious practices — was a new phenomenon in post-independence Haiti (or indeed in the wider postcolonial Caribbean) when it was employed by François Duvalier. For example, despite of the role Vodou was regarded to have played in the Haitian Revolution, the newly independent republic continued the norm imposed by the former colonial power and which the latter ostensibly rejected during its own revolution: that is, it declared itself to be officially a Catholic state. This is a status quo that has remained in force despite the documented practice of Vodou by Dessalines, the later legal recognition of Vodou by Faustin Soulouque, as well as its practice and/or espousal by subsequent presidents and politicians.[4] In the wider Caribbean, the colonial practice of association between the political establishment and Christian religious institutions — be they Catholic or Protestant — has also continued, serving to align, symbolically at least, the state with these religious ideologies.[5] To this end, the election in 1990 of liberation theologist and then Catholic priest Jean-Bertrand Aristide to the office of president in Haiti serves as one such example; while in relation to policy, a more recent example would be the (albeit unofficial) undertaking made on 6 May 2012 by then president Michel Martelly to 'remettre "Haïti à Jésus de Nazareth"' [rededicate Haiti to Jesus of Nazareth] at a Protestant conference in Delmas, Port-au-Prince.[6] Moreover, such an alignment with Catholicism and Protestantism illustrates a non-espousal, in official terms at least, of those traditions linked to African heritage in the Caribbean, and therefore the latter's political marginalization. In Haiti, this has been illustrated by the recognition of the African influence on popular culture evidenced in the increasing corpus of literature, theatre and music that draw on these elements, while it could be said that official culture, which focused on the perspectives and actions of the elite, especially with regard to politics, has been much more oriented towards a European or North American ideal.

As a result, although François Duvalier also did not enshrine his alignment with Vodou in law, the manner in which he incorporated it into the dictatorial establishment and so exerted authority over the religion differentiates this context from those previous and contemporary to it. For example, while Dessalines is said to have practised Vodou and, as Paul Christopher Johnson notes, has become a spirit associated with Ogou, he did persecute *vodouyizan* and this religious tradition 'was not part of the indigenizing process of state-making [Dessalines] envisioned'.[7] Under Duvalier, however, the distinction between Vodou and the state was blurred; Vodou and its practitioners became both 'constitutive' of the state 'and a cipher of it, but always without official recognition'.[8] In preparation for the subsequent literary analysis, the first section that follows will explore this conflation of Christian and Vodou religious traditions with the notion of the Haitian nation in the figure of François Duvalier.

Duvalier, Vodou and the Nation

In her revised and republished analysis of Haiti under the Duvalier regimes, *Haiti: A Shattered Nation* (originally published in 1988 as *Haiti: The Duvaliers and their Legacy*, with an updated edition in 1991),[9] Elizabeth Abbott cites the *Catéchisme de la Révolution* [Catechism of the Revolution] that François Duvalier ordered to be printed in which he presents himself as an embodiment of the nation:

> 'Who are Dessalines, Toussaint, Christophe, Pétion and Estimé?' went the new catechism.
> 'Dessalines, Toussaint, Christophe, Pétion and Estimé are five founders of the nation who are found within François Duvalier.'
> 'Is Dessalines for life?'
> 'Yes, Dessalines is for life in François Duvalier.'[10]

Rewriting the catechism thus, Duvalier inscribes himself as divinely appointed, encapsulating the essence of the nation through his embodiment of its five founding fathers in a similar fashion to the Christian notion that Jesus embodies the essence of God the Father. Furthermore, in so doing, he also binds the notion of the Haitian state to himself, thereby claiming in effect that he is the nation, an assertion echoed in Mars's *Saisons sauvages* by Roger, the brother of the protagonist, when he states, 'En fait, depuis Duvalier, la notion de gouvernement remplace celle de l'État. Donc, Duvalier étant le chef du gouvernement, c'est lui l'État' (Mars 2010a: 40) ('In fact, since Duvalier came to power, the notion of the government is replacing the notion of the state. So Duvalier, as head of the government, is also the state', Mars 2015: 23). Moreover, although the catechism follows the format of that of the Church, Duvalier also ties Catholicism together with Vodou through his reference to Dessalines (also a *lwa*) separately from the others, conflating nation and religion and inscribing himself as the personification of them all. In so doing, he embodied and thus aligned the notions of power, nation and Haitian religious traditions.

In 1963, François Duvalier declared, 'I am already an immaterial being', presenting himself as divinely appointed in the Christian tradition while placing himself alongside Henri Christophe and Dessalines, the latter of whom had entered the Vodou pantheon and the essence of both of whom Duvalier claimed he embodied.[11] Publishing as part of his *Catéchisme de la Révolution* a rewritten version of the Lord's Prayer, which opened with 'Notre Doc qui êtes au Palais National pour la Vie, que Votre nom soit béni par les générations présentes et futures' [Our Doc who art in the National Palace for life, hallowed be Thy name by the present and future generations], Duvalier publicly reiterated — as the dictator Rafael Trujillo had previously in the neighbouring Dominican Republic — his embodiment of the divine and therefore his position as divinely appointed.[12] Duvalier later reinforces this appointment in his *Mémoires d'un leader du Tiers Monde* [Memoirs of a Third World Leader], where he recalls the manner in which the rebels of Jeune Haïti were crushed in 1964 with a reference to the biblical cleansing of the temple by Jesus, who ordered the money changers who had turned it into a 'den of thieves' to leave. Duvalier writes, 'Nous sommes entrés dans ce temple, et nous avons fustigé et chassé les vendeurs pour vous dessiller les yeux' [We entered the temple, and we thrashed and chased out the merchants in order to open your eyes].[13]

Having previously studied and published on Vodou as an ethnologist, Duvalier also capitalized on his position as an *oungan* while fostering the idea that as president he 'was one with, was possessed by, was Baron Samedi, incorporating the master of life and death into his own person'.[14] Staging himself theatrically as this Gede *lwa*, Papa Doc made a show of being ridden by his *mèt tèt*, at which times he would present information he had gleaned from his network of spies as knowledge passed to him by the *lwa*. Although spirit possession is necessarily performative and therefore inherently 'theatrical' — notions explored in Chapters 1 and 2 — it is important here to examine in further detail the suggestion implicit here that Duvalier purposefully manipulated Vodou in the process of creating this image. On the one hand, it is not unusual to present similar characteristics in one's personality or appearance as one's *mèt tèt*; indeed, similarities in temperament at least are not uncommon at all. However, the idea that a *vodouyizan* would capitalize on this association with a particular *lwa* to the extent of consciously propagating an impression that practitioner and *lwa* were one and the same also suggests that the adherent may be one of the few who '*pran poz*', that is, 'act disingenuously as if possessed'.[15] As such, while the dictator's 'pro-Vodou' credentials, in Richman's terms, are not in question, his motivations for these certainly are.[16] Abbott, Johnson, Richman and Ferguson have all suggested that Papa Doc propagated a 'myth of promotion' with regard to Vodou, developing a 'reputation not only for "practicing Vodou" but also for incorporating the practices and priesthood in his ruthless politics'.[17] It is not the intention here to evaluate the legitimacy of his links to Baron Samedi within the context of Vodou belief and practice, nor of any influence the *lwa* may have had in his regime (indeed, Papa Doc, like Dessalines, has become a *lwa* himself: Lwa 22 Os [Lwa 22 Bones]).[18] That said, various observers, be they academics, Haitians interviewed by Abbott, authors and playwrights or others, have concluded that, to a greater or lesser degree, Duvalier appropriated the religious tradition and aligned himself with Baron Samedi in order to gain and maintain political power.

Duvalier's presentation of himself as both nation and spiritual entities incarnate is referenced in numerous fictional texts which draw on the events of this period. One such example, Fouché's *Général Baron-la-Croix*, is described by VèVè Clark as a 'satirical biography' and overtly parodies his declarations to this effect.[19] Although different stylistically to Fouché's earlier *Bouqui au paradis* [Bouqui in Paradise] with regard to the proverbs and riddles found in the former work, as described by Carrol F. Coates, *Général Baron-la-Croix* does continue the playwright's use of Haitian folklore and Vodou, especially through its protagonists.[20] The play was written and published in exile, and is subtitled as 'une tragédie moderne en deux calvaires, vingt-huit stations et une messe en noir et rouge' [a modern tragedy in two calvaries, twenty-eight stations and a mass in black and red]. This pointed observation underscores the dualism embodied by the protagonist, le Chef, through the double reflection of Calvary and the fourteen stations of the cross, before the Catholic and Vodou traditions are enmeshed one with the other in the final mass that has been transformed from the Easter celebration of Christ's resurrection into an uncontrollable, apocalyptic sacrament in the national colours of Duvalierist Haiti. This dualism of both the oppositional powers in Christianity and the mix of this with Vodou is further underlined in the XVIIIe Station when a passerby observes: 'Mon cher ami, [...] aujourd'hui Dieu et Satan marchent la main dans la main comme des frères jumeaux. Quant aux dieux vaudous, n'en parlons pas. Bons comme mauvais, ils dansent ensemble, font l'amour sous le même péristyle' [My dear friend, [...] God and Satan now walk hand in hand like twin brothers. As for the Vodou gods, let's not talk about them. Good and bad, they dance together, make love under the same *peristil*] (Fouché 1974: 72). Through the protagonist's embodiment of Baron-la-Croix, Papa Doc is also associated with this Gede *lwa* that has variously been described as related to Baron Samedi through brotherhood, as one of his avatars, or simply another of his names.[21] The abovementioned *Catéchisme de la Révolution* is countered in the XIXe Station at the end of the first *calvaire*, titled 'Un credo athée' [An Atheist Creed], in which an alternative revolutionary creed is recited disavowing the 'mythes inventés par la peur' [myths invented through fear] and 'paroles des faussaires qui derrière leur masque de justiciers crachent sur leur peuple mépris' [words of the fraudsters who behind their masks as upholders of the law spit on their despised people] (74). Le Chef asks Baron-la-Croix to grant him power for two thousand years, once again referencing the perception that Duvalier believes himself to be divine, which, when ridiculed by his advisors, leads to their arrest and execution. His appointment as a deity is also shown to have been bestowed by the *lwa* himself, who accords this divine right with the declaration that every 'chief' is a god in the making and that le Chef is a god who just does not know it yet (16).[22] Frantz-Antoine Leconte also parodies Duvalier's perceived divine status in his play *La République* (1998). Here, Le Leader is described as an apostle of the revolution and salvational father of the Republic, a figure against whom irreverent discourse is considered blasphemy by citizens willing to denounce members of their own family using such terms, as does Obéiry's mother near the play's close (Leconte 1998: 30, 124). Of note here is the suggestion that Duvalier's divine status is bestowed on his son, too, as Fouché also asserts in his play. Instead of le Chef himself begetting his son, it is Baron-la-Croix who performs this act, and thus the playwright draws a further direct link between this Gede *lwa* and the Duvaliers, namely with Jean-Claude, François's heir.

Continuing with this theme of characters' self-perception and outward presentation, the only point at which le Chef's given name, Dokossou, is spoken, he insists that he is called 'Baron-la-Croix'. The protagonist is never mounted by the *lwa*, however, only juxtaposed with him through the latter's disembodied, nasalized voice. This vocal quality is important as it brings le Chef together with both the Gede and François Duvalier himself, given that it is an attribute that they all share. Beyond shared physical traits, from the unmistakeable voice to le Chef dressing as Baron-la-Croix and Duvalier as Baron Samedi respectively, it is also symbolically important that, as politicians, both the protagonist and his inspiration call upon the Gede to help in matters of government, as these *lwa* are said to organize themselves in a similar hierarchical system comprising barons and ministers. Furthermore, le Chef's interpellation of the *lwa* for help in his installation as dictator mirrors the purported summoning of the especially mighty and malevolent spirits from Trou Foban to reside in the Palais National, an event which took hold in the popular imaginary as illustrated in Mars's *Saisons sauvages* when Raoul Vincent, head of the Tonton Macoutes, contends:

> Papa Doc lui-même avait attendu trois mois, après sa proclamation comme président d'Haïti, avant de prendre logement avec sa famille dans cette demeure écrasante. Il lui avait fallu tout ce temps pour exorciser des couloirs les esprits de toute nature convoqués par ses prédécesseurs et y installer les siens. (229–30)

> [After being proclaimed president of Haiti, Papa Doc waited three months before moving into this overwhelming residence with his family. He needed all that time to purge the hallways of the spirits his predecessors had summoned and to usher in his own.] (168)

Moreover, in *Bouqui au paradis*, Fouché's critique of the regime is framed as a series of four 'mensonges' [lies] and one 'vérité' [truth] in which the protagonists are Bouqui and Malice, two figures from Haitian folklore. Bouqui is repeatedly duped by Malice in a scheme to extort money from him by means of Vodou; the latter, it transpires in the first tableau of 'Première vérité', is in the employ of Maître-Terre [Master Earth]. Although this earlier play is less overtly detailed in its presentation of Duvalier as having misappropriated Vodou than is *Général Baron-la-Croix*, it does reiterate the critique that the association of the regime, and of Duvalier in particular, with Vodou ritual and practice is somewhat opportunistic. Indeed, this is an observation that runs through other of Fouché's works and, as will be demonstrated below, is a common theme in both reports and fictional renditions of the period.

To this end, Abbott suggests that, after having observed that in the present Vodou was the perpetuation of the African past and in the past it had been the inspiration for the Haitian Revolution, 'it was only a short step for Duvalier to extrapolate to the future, and to what vodoun could do for him'.[23] The pragmatism herein implied does not necessarily undermine the extent to which the dictator's implicit profession of faith was truthful. Johnson addresses this issue when he relegates 'the division between "real" religion and the specious "use of" religion [...] to venues outside academe', concluding that ' "real belief in" versus mere "use of" the religion [are] ultimately intractable questions'.[24] By presenting himself as both divinely appointed and an embodiment of Baron Samedi, Papa Doc therefore manages to align both religious and national power. In so doing, he seeks to direct and control others' perception of both him and his government; that is, he seeks to present himself as a president who 'simultaneously honors Vodou's cultural significance, claims total allegiance to the Vatican as a marker of Haiti's political modernity, and contributes to his citizens' awe of his terrifying and mystifying persona by claiming divine characteristics'.[25] Duvalier himself recognizes this deliberate juxtaposition and perceived promotion of the two religious traditions when he writes that he 'soulignai[t] le rôle historique du vaudou comme facteur d'unité spirituelle' [was underlining the historical role played by Vodou as an agent of spiritual unity] while emphasizing 'comme fait définitivement acquis l'appartenance du peuple haïtien à la civilisation latine et aux croyances du christianisme' [as a well-established fact the Haitian people's affiliation to Latin civilization and to Christian beliefs].[26] Subsuming Vodou, Catholicism and, as Richman argues, Protestantism into the state thus, Papa Doc completes his conflation of the religious and political with the nation, thereby ensuring he is able to control them.[27] The links between these three religious traditions and their oversight by Duvalier are signalled in *Saisons sauvages* as a state of affairs discernable by those oppressed by the regime. Prior to his incarceration, Daniel writes, admittedly from his professed Communist perspective, in his diary entry of 1 November 1962: 'Pendant ce temps catholiques et vaudouisants se livrent une guerre larvée tandis que le mouvement protestant s'insinue sournoisement dans l'arrière-pays' (83) ('Meanwhile Catholics and [vodouyizan] have been waging a latent war, while the Protestant movement is furtively infiltrating the backcountry', 57).[28]

Presenting himself as divinely appointed by the Christian God, a personification of Baron Samedi within Vodou, the embodiment of Haiti's forefathers and therefore the nation itself, and the sole rightful head of all state apparatus, Duvalier was then able to consolidate his position of power by knitting all of these together in a single entity, namely himself. In contrast to those such as Fanon and his contemporaries who called for a break from colonial rule through the recognition of political and cultural plurality in the Caribbean, Papa Doc sought to establish a regime that symbolically drew heavily on that imposed by the colonial powers since, although he was elected president, the general Haitian population were divested of any political and religious power unless they participated in, and therefore ascribed to, the politics of the regime. By writing *Catéchisme de la Révolution* and rewriting the Lord's Prayer, along with his acceptance of various titles including 'Apostle of National Unity', Duvalier portrayed his 'brand' of national unity as 'irreproachable' and 'sacrosanct', a process James Ferguson has termed 'supernatural messianism'.[29] When faced with the resistance of Catholic bishops appointed by the Pope, dissenting prelates were forcibly removed from both their positions and Haitian soil, causing further tensions with the Vatican. Re-establishing this relationship was dependent on recognition of the right enshrined in the 1860 concordat of the Haitian president to appoint all bishops and archbishops, subject to papal approval, a prerogative reiterated by the official protocol signed by the papal delegation sent to Port-au-Prince in July 1966.[30] Papa Doc had therefore reaffirmed that the Catholic Church could legitimately operate in Haiti, but simultaneously restricted any political commentary it could make by aligning the prelacy with the state and removing direct extra-territorial involvement therein. With regard to Protestantism, Harold Courlander and Rémy Bastien conclude that Duvalier's promotion of the development of the Protestant Church in Haiti, thereby undermining both Vodou and Catholicism, indicates that 'the relationship between Duvalier and religion [...] should be approached from the standpoint of the relations between church and state'.[31] For his part, Fred Conway posits that Papa Doc's welcoming of Protestants had the effect of people being drawn away 'from an allegiance to the Catholic Church without themselves presenting a monolithic front to the government'.[32] Reducing the external influence of the Church thus, the dictatorial regime both limited the potential for resistance from this important outside power and consolidated its own grip over each of the religions.[33]

In conjunction with undermining the influence of the Church on his regime and appropriating Vodou to present himself as a divine entity, the manner in which Papa Doc incorporated the already extant nationwide network of Vodou temples and practitioners into the state apparatus and the image he portrayed of the *lwa* participating in his regime enabled him to further cement and maintain his hold over the nation. He established a nationwide militia answerable directly to him, officially known as the Volontaires de la Sécurité Nationale [National Security Volunteers], but more commonly referred to as the 'Tonton Macoutes'. This sobriquet itself is significant as it refers to the 'bogeymen of Haitian folk belief' who would kidnap boys and girls at night and put them in their *makout*, or straw satchels, to carry them away. However, the Tonton Macoutes are also associated with Zaka (also known as Azaka or Kouzen Zaka [Cousin Zaka]), a *lwa* often affiliated with Gede but with distinct characteristics. *Lwa* of agriculture, 'he wears a straw hat, a blue denim shirt, trousers with one leg rolled to his knee, and a machete attached to a strap placed about his waist', an outfit ostensibly similar to the denim uniforms of the Duvalier's militia.[34] Meanwhile, the sunglasses the Macoutes wore serve as a further symbolic association with the Gede, and their red kerchiefs 'indexed [...] the *kako* armies who resisted U.S. invasion in 1915'.[35] For Brown, however, the identification of the Macoutes with Zaka is heavily ironic given that the 'stories of corruption, intimidation, and violence that surround the Makout' are quite the opposite of the 'gentle spirit' that is this particular *lwa*.[36] In this regard, Desmangles makes an intriguing comparison between Gede and Zaka:

> Unlike Gede, Zaka's speech is neither eloquent nor his gestures clever enough
> to incite laughter. Gede speaks defiantly with bold vulgarity, whereas Zaka
> is inarticulate [...]. Gede is most often boisterous whereas Zaka is passive and
> quiet. In short, this unsophisticated and gauche 'peasant Pan' (Deren 1972: 110)
> is the sort of character whom Gede would ridicule.[37]

Symbolically, therefore, the relationship between the *lwa* mirrors that between
their homologous figures in the dictatorial state — Baron Samedi (a Gede spirit)
and Duvalier, and Zaka and the Macoutes respectively — whereby the Macoutes
are seen to be in a subservient position and less learned than the 'President for
Life'. Furthermore, Desmangles continues to underline a closer affinity between
'the Haitian peasant' and Zaka than between the former and Gede since, 'although
Gede produces laughter by clowning, his presence creates a sinister atmosphere
which no laughter can obscure'.[38] This then serves to reinforce the hierarchy within
the Macoutes, whereby a large number of Macoutes were subservient to Duvalier
and his comparatively few commanders. As the following analysis of literary texts
shows, it is the proximity between Vodou and the state coupled with that between
the Macoutes and the general population that is represented as the most common
interaction between the dictatorship and the majority of Haitians at the time.
While the somewhat removed figure of Duvalier was sinister and represented fear,
the pervasive climate of fear that infiltrated communities was in turn enforced on
a local level by the Macoutes who circulated, and often lived, among the people
they intimidated. In short, they were 'staged as being "of the people" through the
imagery of the most populist loa, even as they were tools of repression'.[39] This then
constitutes a further important aspect of Papa Doc's duplicitous use of iconography
in Vodou as he symbolically links the agents of his regime to the popular Gede,
therefore subsuming the popular with the state by means of this religious tradition.
Furthermore, the recruitment of volunteers from the community rendered the
space in which Vodou ritual is performed — the community itself — one that was
now occupied by the regime, thereby both corrupting and dominating it as a site
of possible resistance.

   Moreover, due to the Tonton Macoutes' proximity to the wider Haitian
population, in fictional renditions of the period they come to be representative of
Duvalier in their positions at the point of interaction with the regime, in addition to
becoming associated with the Gede. As such, while Zaka is distinct from the Gede
and Baron Samedi, in practice the Tonton Macoutes are depicted as exhibiting
aspects of both groups of *lwa*, peasants for the most part who symbolically represent
the Gede by becoming part of the state apparatus headed by Baron Samedi. One
such example is le Gorille [the Gorilla], *chef de section* [section chief] in Chauvet's
Colère [Anger] which, although purportedly set during the American occupation
of Haiti, clearly critiques the Duvalierist state and the violence meted out by it.
In this novella, le Gorille is the head of the militia, clad completely in black, who
occupy the Normils' land. In order to secure its return, Rose, Louis Normil's
daughter, must submit to le Gorille, which results in her repeated sexual violation
by the Macoute. During one of their daily encounters, le Gorille confides to Rose
that previously he was 'un mendiant pouilleux' ('a flea-ridden beggar') before he

became a figure of authority, 'méprisé, honni par les inaccessibles têtes de saintes de ton espèce' (Vieux-Chauvet 2005: 253) ('despised, shunned by haughty little saint's faces like yours', Vieux-Chauvet 2009: 245).[40] As a Macoute, le Gorille represents the violent nature of the Duvalier regime, also becoming associated with the Gede in the process, and thus the sinister side of the Gede is foregrounded as a result. Consequently, while there does exist a critique of the Macoutes in works like *Amour, Colère et Folie* and *Saisons sauvages*, their position as intermediaries of the state and thus of Duvalier who embodied that very state means that a critique of the Macoutes also serves as one of the dictator himself.

Mars foregrounds this proximity in *Saisons sauvages* through Raoul's thoughts during his frequent visits to the National Palace. On his way to the presidential residence, he reflects, 'Avec ses hommes et femmes habillés de l'uniforme de gros bleu, Duvalier ne craignait rien. Ils portaient la toile rude de Papa Zaka et symbolisent la force tellurique du dieu paysan' (227) ('With his men and women in their coarse, blue uniforms, Duvalier feared nothing. They wore the rough fabric of Papa Zaka and symbolized the earthly force of that peasant god', 166). Importantly, in such a discussion of the alignment of Vodou and the state, Raoul continues to note that male and female Vodou priests 'étaient devenus des auxiliaires précieux du pouvoir, convoqués souvent en consultation au palais national au même titre que maires, préfets de police et chefs de sections rurales' (227–28) ('became precious auxiliaries of power, often called upon to consult at the National Palace alongside mayors, police chiefs, and leaders from rural areas', 166). In his study of the incorporation of the network of *oungan* and *manbo* into the Duvalier regime, Michel Laguerre states that the 'two Duvalier administrations appropriated the political aspect of Voodoo' and 'brought the Voodoo church openly into the political process'.[41] This 'recruitment of voodoo priests as espionage agents' is nothing new, as Laguerre later contends, but rather 'a common phenomenon throughout Haitian history'.[42] The process therefore saw all the religious frameworks already in place subsumed — to a greater or lesser degree — by the dictatorial state, as non-Haitian Catholic dissenters were expelled to be replaced by handpicked bishops, Haitian Protestant pastors (it has been claimed) joined the Macoutes while North American missionaries avoided involvement in political affairs, and *oungan* and *manbo* across the country also enlisted.[43] Vodou priests, male and female, were also invited into the palace and as Mars underlines above, served as advisors in addition to informants and religious practitioners. This continued under Baby Doc, with the invitation of a group of *oungan* and *manbo*, including the longstanding spokesperson for Vodou on the national stage until his death in 2015, Max Beauvoir, invited to the palace in January 1986 to advise the President in the midst of the popular unrest. Indeed, the meetings Beauvoir and others had with Baby Doc are represented in Mayra Montero's *La trenza de la hermosa luna* (1987), already examined in Chapter 1. In her novel, the main *oungan* for Gonaïves under Papa Doc is seen as completely acquiescent to the latter's demands, but his son, Papa Marcel, *oungan* in the narrative present of the novel, seems to have a more complex relationship with the regime whereby he has links to the Macoutes but also supports the removal of Baby Doc from power.

As such, Papa Doc conflates *oungan* and Macoute and thus, 'le père spirituel est devenu père fouettard' [the spiritual father became the bogeyman].[44] In so doing, the framework of Haitian Vodou, presented in the texts analyzed in Chapters 1 to 3 as a locus of resistance, is dominated by the very organ that feared such opposition: the government as embodied by Duvalier. This 'nationalization' of sorts, a term not necessarily synonymous with promotion, also conceptually undermined another characteristic of Vodou (and other related African-derived religious traditions) that has formed a central tenet of the analysis offered thus far: its status as a locus for female agency and participation. While not restricting participation to men, the association of nationalism with masculinity has been well established (as Joane Nagel (1998) summarizes), and such an association must therefore align those religious traditions associated with and subsumed by the nation with that very notion of (nationalist) masculinity. Subordinating women within this male-dominated framework, the nation thus perceived is a construct in which women's roles continue to be defined by the father figure, a process that readers observe in the texts examined here. As will be demonstrated below, Duvalier's regime employed this dichotomy and gendered those it subordinated as feminine, with errant members of this subordinated class subjected to further violence. As for Duvalier himself, he embodied the notions of *père spirituel*, apostle of national unity and immaterial representation of Baron Samedi (the epitome of masculine sexuality presiding simultaneously over the realms of sex and death) in a single entity intimately linked with violence and destruction. Michel-Rolph Trouillot succinctly summarizes such a conflation of state apparatus in Duvalierist Haiti as follows: 'If the nation could be reduced to the state, if the state could be reduced to the Executive, if the Executive was only the chief of state, then the chief of state was the nation', a truncating process that, as he notes, 'necessitated violence without limit'.[45] It is to this violence and destruction dispensed by means of appropriating Vodou and wielding it as an integral yet subservient component of the Duvalier regime that this analysis now turns.

Violence, Destruction and State Terror

The association of nationalism with masculinity and the perception of the nation as a male-headed household are necessarily bound up with concepts of power and violence. Women, of course, have long been aligned with the nation as the symbolic mothers of the nation or as the physical body of the nation, both of which are subordinate to the masculinized institutions of the state and nationalism. In Haiti, although women are the 'pillar[s] of society', as N'Zengou-Tayo and Bergan and Schuller (2009), among others, have demonstrated, they still remain in a subordinate position as they are simultaneously dominated by these institutions and subjected to the power accorded through the apparatus of the nation.[46] Since the nation under Duvalier was conceptualized as having been subsumed into the dictator's very being, not only was the nation gendered masculine but, necessarily, so was the omnipresent dictatorial regime. In her discussion of power and violence, Hannah Arendt argues that, although these concepts are opposites, they are intimately connected, with violence unsustainable without power to undergird it.[47] Furthermore, she observes that while 'violence can destroy power [...] it is utterly incapable of creating it'. By means of explanation, Arendt writes: 'The extreme form of power is All against One, the extreme form of violence is One against All. And this latter is never possible without instruments', since 'everything depends on the power behind the violence'. For a totalitarian regime, this power base is 'the secret police and its net of informers'.[48] In her discussion of patriarchy, bell hooks draws violence and masculinity together, writing that the patriarchal system 'insists that males are inherently dominating [...] and endowed with the right [...] to maintain that dominance through various forms of psychological terrorism and violence', especially over females.[49] As a result, patriarchy 'supports, promotes, and condones sexist violence', which when applied to a regime predicated on a perception of itself as a gendered dichotomy then associates domination — and therefore violence — with masculinity and subjugation with femininity (as Teresa de Lauretis has also observed).[50] Those totalitarian regimes — the extreme form of violence in Arendt's conceptualization — of which the Duvalier dictatorship is an example, remain gendered masculine therefore, not only through the association of the concept of nation they embody with masculinity but also as a result of the notion of violence as inherently intertwined with that of masculinity when considered within this patriarchal construct.

Moreover, not only is this power and violence therefore conceptually perceived as masculine, the necessarily gendered nature of the relationship between those wielding such power and those subjected to it is also constructed as a dualism, that of 'activity and passivity, masculinity and femininity'.[51] In so doing, notions of masculinity held by any of those subjected to this violence are thereby negated as they are emasculated and, from the regime's perspective, their masculinity is violated and destroyed. This is not to suggest that femininity is the destruction, and therefore absence, of masculinity, but rather that the notion of masculinity as perceived by those in power is conceived out of violence and that within the dualism of those who violate and those who are violated, the former are masculine and the latter are thus gendered feminine. As Carolle Charles highlights in reference to state manipulation of gender categories and ideologies in Haiti, 'the repressive state can use gender symbols and discourses as a central element in asserting power and domination', itself a process evident elsewhere in the Caribbean.[52] Returning to the idea of violence and totalitarian regimes, therefore, the destruction inherent therein reaches its peak when such a regime dominates through terror. Having destroyed all opposition, in such a situation violence destroys power and therefore attacks the very base on which the regime is predicated: 'the police state begins to devour its own children, [...] yesterday's executioner becomes today's victim'.[53] Terror is then the illustration par excellence of the constructed nature of the gendered dichotomy of state power and violence, as those gendered masculine as part of the regime are emasculated and become gendered feminine as part of the process of their destruction. By virtue of its compound nature, the term 'destructive masculinity' used in this chapter could be interpreted in various ways. However, in the contexts in which it is employed here, destructive masculinity is intended to encapsulate this compendium of violence, terror, abuse of power and appropriation of the state and nation, each framed as tools of those gendered masculine within the dichotomy outlined above. As will be made apparent, this is a notion very much present in the literary texts analyzed below.

First, in reference to the historical and biographical monographs cited above, Abbott uses the inherently violent notions of 'mastery' in her description of Duvalier's destructive masculinity, which he draws together with Vodou: 'In vodounesque Haiti, Duvalier knew he had to do more than propitiate some spirits. If he were to succeed in gaining complete mastery of his people, he needed Haiti's most powerful spirits by his side'.[54] In similar terms, she later writes, 'As profoundly important as his mastery of Haiti's spiritual world was, Duvalier never neglected brute physical force', which he imposed through his network of Macoutes unhindered by 'the eunuch army'.[55] Here, as elsewhere, Papa Doc is described as both manipulating and violating the image of the *lwa* in Haiti and abroad, and violently oppressing the Haitian people. To this end, Duvalier's association with Baron Samedi undoubtedly served to enhance the dictator's image as the figure who controlled death. However, as Brown observes, Gede 'presides over the realms of sex, death, and humor', the former juxtaposed with the rumours of Papa Doc's impotence in later life (one of the themes which forms the basis of *Général Baron-la-Croix*).[56] Outside the country's borders, as many publications, novels and films were to attest, the image of Vodou presented was one which linked 'the "barbarism of the Duvalierist political regime" with "the 'diabolic' character of this 'black sect'"'.[57]

For their part, Bernard Diederich and Al Burt invoke the Vodou concept of zombification in their assessment of Duvalier's use of Vodou and the *lwa* of death.[58] The popular image of the *zonbi* controlled by the nefarious and self-interested practitioners of Vodou has been portrayed as emblematic of the religion both within Haiti and beyond its borders, be it in literary, filmic, journalistic or academic works too numerous to detail. In this vein, the implication is not that Duvalier zombified the population by capturing their *tibonanj* and thus, as a *bòkò*, commanded the empty vessels that they had become (this being one of the popular perceptions of what a *zonbi* is). Rather, in the case of Duvalier, the image evoked is one of complete subservience to the regime, in keeping with the idea that the *zonbi* is 'symbolic of the Haitian experience of slavery, of the separation of a man from his will, his reduction to a beast of burden at the will of a master', and of the history of colonization.[59] With regard to the *lwa*, Déita has described Baron Samedi as the one responsible for, and able to perform, zombification, symbolically significant given Papa Doc's association with this *lwa*.[60] Moving into fictional renderings of the regime, Similá, Macoute *bòkò* in *Del rojo de su sombra*, is said to have long had *zonbi* under his jurisdiction,[61] and Mars's protagonist Nirvah in *Saisons sauvages* explains the experience of Haitians under Duvalier as, 'Nous sommes déjà devenus des zombies. Pour vivre une vie en apparence normale, il ne faut pas avoir d'opinion, il ne faut pas se révolter contre l'arbitraire, contre le terrorisme d'État' (96) ('We've already become zombies. In order to live a seemingly normal life you mustn't have an opinion, you mustn't rebel against anything arbitrary, against the terrorism of the state', 66). The image of the *zonbi* as the destroyed individual is personified in Marie's description of her mother Nirvah who, having been subjected to the psychological manipulations and sexual whims of the *chef des macoutes* Raoul Vincent, is like a ghost, wandering the house seemingly in search of something but never succeeding in locating whatever it is she seeks (178). Destroyed by those working for Duvalier, Nirvah has been subjected to the zombification she earlier criticized as she unsuccessfully sought the release of her detained husband by attempting to fight the state apparatus from within by means of a sexual liaison with Raoul.

Released the same year as *Saisons sauvages* was published, Arnaud Antonin's film *Zombi candidat à la présidence, ou Les Amours d'un zombi* [Zombi Presidential Candidate, or A Zombi Love Story] (2010) critiques the idea of Duvalier having zombified the nation even further with a group of Port-au-Prince's political elite deciding to nominate Pierre Zephirin, a newly escaped *zonbi*, to the presidency. Ultimately unsuccessful in their scheme as Pierre withdraws his candidacy, the premise of the film is succinctly communicated in one of its opening scenes by a pastor who questions the validity of the *zonbi* giving a press conference and ponders as to when the 'shadows' that envelop the country will disappear. Although the film sees Pierre resist the impositions of both the politicians and Baron Samedi, the question regarding the possibility for opposition (contestation from within) to this image of the zombified nation continues to resound throughout. This theme of zombification and politics is one that screenwriter of *Zombi candidat à la présidence* Gary Victor has explored elsewhere in his fiction, for example, in his short story 'Nuit de chance' [A Lucky Night], published in the collection *Treize nouvelles vaudou* [Thirteen Vodou Short Stories] (Victor 2007: 43–55). Drawing more on the macabre representation of Vodou in Hollywood-style depictions, as N'Zengou-Tayo observes, in 'Nuit de chance' senatorial candidate Kerou makes a pact with a *bòkò* in order to assure his successful election, but as a result, becomes a *zonbi*.[62] In contrast to Victor's screenplay, however, the short story closes with the author's satirical note that, 'dans un pays où la folie est la norme, personne ne s'en rendit vraiment compte' [in a country where madness is the norm, no one really realized] (55).

Such a situation in which the use of Vodou becomes politically expedient in order to obtain a position of power is one of the main themes running through Victor's earlier novel *Clair de manbo* [Manbo Light] (1990). The title is adapted from the popular French folk song 'Au clair de la lune', the first verse of which the author uses as his epigraph. However, he changes the last couplet to directly invoke the *lwa* by pluralizing the last word: 'Ouvre-moi ta porte | Pour l'amour de Dieu' [Open your door to me | For the love of God] becomes 'Pour l'amour des dieux' [For the love of the gods] (Victor 1990: 11). In the novel, Hannibal Serafin returns to Haiti from exile in North America in order to stand in the presidential election, styling himself 'Président des Générations Futures' [President of Future Generations] as just one of a string of other titles that are all reminiscent, and satirically critical, of Duvalier (53).[63] To ensure his success, Hannibal is advised that he should propitiate the *lwa* Agwe through *manbo* Madan Sorel, but the local *bòkò* Djo Kokobe, banished from the community by spiritual means, sees this as an opportunity to become the local rural police chief and so intimidates Hannibal into ensuring that he obtain this position in exchange for assistance. On the one hand, therefore, Vodou in this novel is presented as a means of intimidation intimately related to politics, although, as becomes apparent, there is space for opposition through Vodou in the community. This opposition is manifested by the cosmic battle between Djo and Madan Sorel that results in both their deaths, and like Zulé's demise in *Del rojo de su sombra*, Madan Sorel's is too presented as sacrifice. When isolated, however, Djo's intimidation of Hannibal takes the form of an overnight siege of Hannibal's residence, provoking the latter to fear for his life, believe the protection of Agwe that he enjoys to be ineffectual, and so accept Djo's terms. Hannibal's forced captivity and violent manipulation at the hands of the *bòkò* constitute a microcosm of the larger siege of the nation by Duvalier, during which the embodiment of masculinity terrorizes the doubly feminized resident — as the object of masculine violence simultaneously identified with the domestic space — who is confined by the four walls of his violated abode. Emasculated thus, the only way for Hannibal to reassert the masculinity that he thought he had ensured by installing himself as supreme leader of the nation is to join forces with the violator. Here, Vodou is therefore portrayed as both the mechanism and the means through which destructive masculinity is employed to guarantee control over the state and its people.

The notion of siege then leads to the concept of terror often used in descriptions of François Duvalier's regime, in biographical and historical accounts and fictional texts alike. Abbott titles one of the eleven chapters of her work directly discussing the Duvaliers 'The Height of the Terror', while Trouillot, Micial Nérestant, Ronnie Scharfman, Régine Isabelle Joseph and Ferguson, among others, all directly reference the notion of terror under the dictatorship.[64] In the literary domain, le Chef in *Général Baron-la-Croix* maintains his hold on power by eliminating the advisors who suggest that he sounds like a mythomaniac when presenting himself as a god (as Baron-la-Croix told him he was) and that he should work for the good of his people. Baron-la-Croix's advice, however, is that 'La force seule est vraie. L'histoire en mains, on peut dire que la force est le sésame de la politique. Avec elle, le mot impossible n'existe plus' [Violence is the only truth. With history in hand, it can be said that violence is the key to politics. With violence, the word impossible no longer exists] (18). The *miliciens*, his squadron of terror, are themselves dressed as Gede spirits, named 'gouverneurs de la mort' [masters of death] (35), and described as *loups-garous* ('werewolves', with the emphasis placed on their ability to transmogrify from otherwise indistinguishable members of the community into ferocious animals).[65] In other words, they are Duvalier's Macoutes. The play's final scene, 'Messe en noir et rouge', is consonant with Arendt's notion of terror as complete violence which destroys power and therefore itself. Catholicism, Vodou, politics and madness are collapsed into one, and the notion of power onto which le Chef has clung so tightly is destroyed by the source of the power le Chef believes he has wielded, Baron-la-Croix himself (119–21). Impotent in the face of this all-consuming last act of violence, le Chef yells to his petrified wife that the Silence which he had made emblematic of his reign but then destroyed in a bid to maintain control is returning to consume the very notion of power it enforced. Le Chef and his wife, gripped with terror, then freeze as silence falls and the macabre laugh of Baron-la-Croix rings out for the last time.

In *Saisons sauvages*, Nirvah describes the terror enforced and embodied by Duvalier and his Macoutes in similar terms: 'De temps en temps la révolution dévore l'un de ses fils, semant le trouble et la confusion dans le cercle des proches' (172) ('From time to time the revolution devours one of its own, sowing trouble and confusion from within', 124). Moreover, terror becomes self-perpetuating as, in an effort to avoid becoming the victim of violence, those who suffer then denounce those around them in a bid to deflect the arbitrariness of destruction under terror onto another individual. However, by its very arbitrary nature, as Nirvah underlines, no one but the man administering terror can escape it since he 'obéit souvent à d'occultes pulsions ou à de simples lubies et peut faire disparaître du jour au lendemain son serviteur le plus fidèle' (189) ('appears to obey occult impulses and mere whim, and is capable of eliminating his most faithful servant overnight', 137). By embodying all the organs of government and the nation — religious traditions included — and thereby the epitome of masculinity, Duvalier, 'the madman in power' (137), also manages to remain above such arbitrary acts of violence as the blame for the terror imposed by his agents falls on them rather than the President. For example, Maxime Douville, Minister of Finance and Economic Affairs, does not direct his anger for the execution of members of his family during the *vêpres jérémiennes* [Jérémie Vespers] at Duvalier, the Macoutes or the military, but rather at Raoul Vincent as the person who discharged the dictator's orders. By subsuming all loci of resistance into the state, embodied by himself, and promoting the denunciation of one's colleagues and members of the community through a climate of terror, Duvalier is presented in *Saisons sauvages* as above the reproach of even the ministers affected by his brand of destructive masculinity, these men who can see the workings of the regime. In reference to this novel in particular, therefore, it would seem that when the state violence employed by the Duvalierist regime is considered in terms of masculinity and femininity, there exists the continued threat of subjection to feminization through the destruction of one's masculinity. This then foments the desire to reassert one's masculinity through the easiest form of destruction, that is, of a colleague on an equal footing (as shown here by Maxime and Raoul) or of citizens outside the framework of power, as will now be explored.

The notion of terror with regard to the Macoutes and the wider Haitian population has been highlighted as a key theme in Chauvet's *Amour, Colère et Folie* by numerous scholars (including, among others, Dayan, Scharfman, Jean-Charles, Chantal Kalisa and John Walsh).[66] In her discussion of terror in the trilogy, Scharfman highlights the manner in which the regime fractured society by rendering impotent any organization that might promote opposition: 'The other [...] is watching me, but never to share anything. S/he is there, threatening to denounce me without me knowing. In terror paranoia reigns: all solidarity is forbidden. [...] In Chauvet's world gone mad, power afflicts, inflicts violence arbitrarily'.[67] The fracturing of society reaches as far as the family unit, which risks decimation should any member be accused of plotting against the regime. As *père spirituel* and father of the nation, symbolically Duvalier occupies a position of distant but omnipresent patriarch whose authority is then imposed by his agents, the Macoutes. In reference to *Colère* and its female protagonist Rose, Jean-Charles writes:

> Under the conditions of terror fear obliterates the option of consent within this model; that is, Rose's actions are motivated by fear and must be viewed in the context of *la terreur*, during which the private lives and belongings of Haitian citizens no longer belonged to them.[68]

This appropriation of citizens' 'private lives and belongings' extended to their own bodies, all of which were systematically violated and destroyed. Given the focus of this section on destructive masculinity and Vodou, the majority of the following analysis will centre on Chauvet's third novella, *Folie*, as it constitutes the point of the trilogy at which violence and destructive masculinity coupled with Vodou become absolute. However, by means of introduction and exposition of these concepts in the work as a whole, this discussion will now turn to the two preceding novellas, *Amour* and *Colère*.

In her article which seeks to underscore the effect of state terror on the female protagonists of *Amour* and *Colère* — Claire and Rose respectively — and therefore on Haitian women in general under the Duvaliers, Chancy criticizes as oversimplistic the assertion that Claire and Rose gain agency through their associations with Ezili and describes Chauvet's 'vision' in her trilogy as 'ha[ving] a depth charged with a realism that cannot be dismissed or subsumed under an analysis that merely shifts the ground from character to god, or from story to myth'.[69] However, as Dayan has argued, analyzing *Amour* and *Colère* through the characterizations associated with Ezili 'goes beyond any false dichotomizing, as she prescribes and responds to multiple and apparently incoherent directives'.[70] Through Ezili, complex narratives of Haitian women's lives are presented in which the individual and the *lwa* come together rather than the mythological masking women's lives and rendering them invisible by means of romanticization or mythologization. The 'dualité' that Claire sees in herself — daughter of a Vodou practitioner but fervent believer in the Catholic faith, sexually active in her dreams and fantasies but still a virgin at the age of thirty-nine — is indeed a reflection of two avatars of Ezili: the *mulâtresse* Ezili Freda, sensual *lwa* of love and sexuality, and the black Ezili Dantò, fierce revolutionary warrior who is said to eschew men despite presiding over the realm of motherhood, both of whom are associated with different incarnations of the Virgin Mary. However, Dayan has also described Claire's doubling as that of Ezili Freda and Ezili Je Wouj, the latter the old, stooped Ezili who schemes and therefore represents the element of women to be 'abhorred'.[71] As the agent of state terror in *Amour*, Calédu, the local Macoute chief, keeps a stranglehold over the community, whipping Dora Soubiran's genitalia so fiercely she can barely walk a week later (37), and summarily executing Jacques le fou in the street in front of the procession for the Feast of the Virgin (46–48). Moreover, he violates Claire both in public when he pierces her with his gaze and in her dreams when he rapes her with his 'phallus énorme', a weapon that transforms into a knife with which to murder her (125–26, 147). In his position, Calédu reinforces the subjugated status of the population, fracturing both the community and Claire's family unit, and violently assaulting her in public when she is awake and privately as she sleeps. Here, Chauvet's protagonist manages to revolt against this patriarchal authority, taking the knife given to her by her sister's husband as a love token and stabbing Calédu. In so doing, 'this violent phallic gesture,' Scharfman concludes, 'allows Claire to become the aggressor, both father and Calédu, thereby destroying the whip, the rape, [...] the cruelty to which she had been subjected'.[72] However, as Renée Larrier observes, Claire's subsequent return to her locked room undermines this 'act of resistance', a symbolic appropriation of masculinity, as any position of power she gained is immediately negated by her confinement and the forced subjugation to the regime that Rose suffers in the following novella, *Colère*.[73]

If Ezili is present through Claire's duality in *Amour*, Dayan suggests that Rose's story is that of 'the Virgin, Mary Magdalene, or Saint Theresa', which 'recalls Erzulie, the goddess cursed by the Church as whore but whose generosity knows no bounds'.[74] Only daughter in the Normil family, Rose accompanies her father at his behest to lodge an official complaint against the government militia's occupation of the family's land, which, by her rejection of her father's prohibition and therefore her submission to le Gorille alone, results in her abovementioned repeated sexual violation as a form of payment in exchange for the plot that has been taken. In this manner Rose's body becomes 'annexed' to the land, thereby converting her from a person into property and designating her as an object that then must be 'ravished' in an image of 'woman's passivity or submission [...] necessary for the ideology of nation building to be effective'.[75] Duvalier's project of nation building — that is, a personal fiefdom over which to wield power — is no different, and it requires those gendered feminine to be passive and submissive. In this regard, some describe Rose's submission to her violation as an action she willingly takes, and so the subsequent liberation she perceives as a result of it suggests that she obtains a form of power oppositional to masculine violence. For her part, Jean-Charles critiques this very notion in her assertion that terror negates the possibility of consent. In spite of any perceived opposition through Rose's portrayal of her ordeal, Jean-Charles contends that it still constitutes the masculine destruction of the feminine through rape 'because of the conditions under which she "agrees" and the circumstances of each encounter'.[76] Rose's experience therefore connotes the destruction of her body and the violation of her psyche; as Scharfman posits, she suffers degradation but at the same time becomes 'an active, complicit collaborator in this degradation'.[77] The violence she is subjected to is therefore not 'gendered violence as a tool to *avoid* other forms of violence' (my emphasis), but rather gendered violence which both represents and forms part of other forms of violence, as well as being complicit with them.[78] In Dayan's terms, 'Chauvet [...] reveals that [Rose's] violation is *always* sexualized, and that it has been accomplished not only by the black intruder, but by her mulatto family' too, this despite her family not being active participants in the acts of sexual violence to which she is subjected.[79] Further to this, in the context of this wider discussion of destructive masculinity, the violation of individuals and family units by the state is then also both sexualized and gendered violence. In *Amour* and *Colère*, the narratives have focused on female protagonists violated by male aggressors who represent the state; in *Folie* this final notion is also destroyed as the male protagonist is feminized in a context in which 'degradation, claustrophobia, paranoia, and derangement reach their paroxysm'.[80] Importantly, it should be noted that male characters in both *Amour* and *Colère* are feminized by means of state violence, too; for example, Jacques le fou is killed by Calédu in *Amour*, and Rose's father and brother are positioned in opposition to the regime during their struggle to regain their land in *Colère*. Prefigured thus, in *Folie* this theme does indeed 'reach [its] paroxysm' through René, the protagonist.

In her article '"The Origins of Totalitarianism": From Resistance to Human Rights in Marie Chauvet's *Les rapaces*', Benedicty-Kokken looks beyond gender in *Folie* and Chauvet's subsequent novella *Les Rapaces* [The Raptors] to analyze the characteristics of a resistance to totalitarianism that has become a '*fait accompli*', to then concentrate on how Chauvet's characters both 'emerge from classes that are not their own' and 'meditate on the futility of resistance to a despotic regime'.[81] Meanwhile, in her 2011 lecture at Barnard College, 'The Gods in a Trunk, or Chauvet's Remnants', and subsequent further developed article, Dayan examines animality in the novella and the collapse of distinctions between animals and humans, sacred and profane, in a context where humanity is a political project and 'the upright and the "reasonable" systematically stigmatize the subjugated as threating and superfluous'.[82] However, in light of the above analysis of Duvalier's destructive masculinity within a framework of Vodou explicitly interwoven with Catholicism, it is important to explore the ways in which gender is interpolated in *Folie*, especially as a consequence of the gendered violence and emasculation to which the protagonist is subjected. From the outset, René occupies a dehumanized space in which the violence of the regime extends from the physical and psychological to the very structure of the narrative and its content. In contrast to *Amour* and *Colère*, where the reader witnesses the continual decay of each of their narrative contexts, society in *Folie* has fractured to such an extent that the sieges laid in the first two novellas have long been in place come the last. Holed up in a stinking shack with his two friends (and later joined by a third), René narrates the story of their ultimate demise at the hands of the Macoutes in a Haiti where, as Dayan indicates, the divisions between the physical and spiritual, reason and insanity, human and animal have completely collapsed.[83] Convinced of their persecution by 'les diables' [the devils], René confines the starving group of poets to this tiny space where, isolated from the outside world, honey that has been offered to the *marasa* is the only source of nourishment and, with water rationed, *kleren* (cheap, unrefined white rum) is the only liquid to slake one's thirst and stave off hunger.

Beginning with the interweaving of Vodou and Catholicism, this is evidenced most clearly by the perceived omnipresence of the *diables* who patrol the town, be it in the street or in the poets' hideouts. In the first of his three essays on *Folie*,

Maximilien Laroche points to the polyvalence of the term, underlining that *diables* takes on different meanings in Christian and Vodou contexts.[84] With regard to the former, the poets often describe these devils as being clad in black and having horns and red tails, descriptions which they even juxtapose with references to Vodou. However, it should also be noted that in Kreyòl the term *djab* encapsulates both the idea of a devil that has horns and a tail and the notion of an 'evil' spirit in the context of Vodou. Although the novella and the trilogy as a whole are written in French, the text does include various terms derived from Kreyòl such as *cocobés* (cripples), *simples* (ritual actions and/or gestures associated with Vodou) and *bon ange* (*bonanj*), to give just three examples. As such, while terms such as *diable* convey the meanings commonly understood in standard French, their meaning is also imbued with that ascribed to them in their original context, which, in this case, serves to reiterate the inscription of this novella into both the Catholic and Vodou traditions in Haiti. Indeed, the repeated denomination of the Macoutes as *diables* is prefaced in *Amour* and *Colère*: Jacques le fou calls Calédu 'Satan' (46), and the Macoutes driving in the stakes which separate the Normils from their land are dressed completely in black (165), an association that Dayan makes more explicit by using the very word 'devils' to describe them.[85] In addition, Laroche deconstructs the notion of the *marasa* — invoked by the '*plats-marassas*' in the shack with René and his friends — in a particularly instructive fashion in his analysis, underlining how this concept exists threefold between four poets all looking towards the *métropole* with regard to their artistic production: Jacques and André are *frères de sang*, a twinning broken by Jacques's death during the siege; André and René are *frères de nationalité* when perceived in comparison to Simon (a Frenchman); and René and Simon are *frères de l'âme*, given the similarities seen between the two by Jacques and André.[86] As such, while they are writing in what they perceive to be a French tradition, notions associated with Vodou define their existence, both as three pairs of twins (thus doubly linked to the concept of the *marasa*) and as victims of the *diables/djab*.

Educated out of the Vodou and Kreyòl he saw as his inheritance from his black mother by the French Catholic sisters and brothers at the schools he attended, René considers his relationship with the *lwa* as one of expediency. He writes, 'Autant amadouer les loas et les mettre aussi de mon côté' (301) ('Might as well wheedle the *loas* and have them on my side as well', 291). However, in a context in which the regime — in this case, a *noiriste*, nationalist dictatorship portrayed as an embodiment of Vodou — seeks to crush anything perceived as outside of its control, René's orientation towards France in education and poetry identifies him as a target for elimination. As such, whether the *diables* really are roaming the streets and laying siege to the poets' shack is not what is most important here; the offensive the regime is leading decries the poets for the very ideas they will potentially write about in their work. In a similar context, the wife of le Chef in *Général Baron-la-Croix* describes the nature of this oppression thus:

> Ce sont des exaltés, les poètes. Ils sont plus à craindre qu'aucun autre pour la paix de la cité. Je ne redoute pas tant un revolver dont on arme la main malhabile d'un ignare qu'un seul chant de révolte de ces poètes maudits. En un

rien de temps ça peut vous ameuter une foule et vous mettre le feu aux poudres.
[...]
   On ne sait jamais ce qu'ils cachent derrière leur tête de fous, ces intellectuels.
(105–06)

   [Poets, they're fanatics. They are to be feared more than any other with
   regard to maintaining calm in the city. I dread a revolver in the clumsy hand
   of an ignoramus less than a single call to revolt from those damned poets. In no
   time they can stir up the crowd and ignite a rebellion. [...]
   You never know what they're hiding inside those crazed heads of theirs,
   those intellectuals.]

In this instance the only poet left in the city — described as harmless by the
functionaries of the regime — is shot on the orders of le Chef as a precautionary
measure while his case is investigated. As poets, René and his group of friends
in *Folie* and this single remaining poet, victim of Fouché's le Chef, represent
an elite educated in a system oriented towards France, if not physically situated
within its borders. On one level, this conflict between the nominally postcolonial
state and the Francophone poet reiterates that outlined by, among others, Frantz
Fanon in *Peau noire, masques blancs* [Black Skin, White Masks] (1952) between the
Antillean who rejects what France represents and the one who returns from France
having completely adopted the former colonizer's ways. However, in this context
of a violent dictatorial state which seeks to eliminate that which it cannot both
circumscribe and control, the poet here constitutes a source of either resistance
through his articulation of ideas from outside or opposition by expressing ideas not
sanctioned by the state. As illustrated in both of these works, the mere potential
for non-adherence is enough to warrant elimination: the unnamed poet in *Général
Baron-la-Croix* is said to be harmless while the four friends in *Folie* have not
produced anything worthy of wider recognition.

   Moreover, the targeting of the intellectual perceived to reside outside the control
of the state serves to further underscore Duvalier's duplicitous use of Vodou and
Catholicism, whereby his explicit alignment of religion and state and his imposition
of a violent dictatorial regime are themselves reminiscent of the colonial period.
Concomitantly, his appropriation of Vodou in order to remove this religious
tradition as a possible site of resistance aligns his otherwise symbolically Western-
oriented regime with that which the colonizer rejected: the influence of Africa.
While the purpose here is not to question the extent to which Duvalier's practice
of Vodou was an expression of genuine belief, the manner in which he conflated
it with these colonial notions and apparatus and used it as a means to impose a
destructive, masculine-gendered regime might suggest that the persecution of the
intellectual, as represented here in a literary context by the poet, focused more
on the latter's potential to fall outside the control of the state rather than there
existing an inherent conflict between the intellectual and the regime's above-cited
ideological stance. This is illustrated by René, an individual who recognizes his
dual heritage — French and Kreyòl, Catholic and *vodouyizan* — and therefore
seemingly embodies the influences upon which Duvalier draws, yet he is still
targeted by the dictator through his Macoutes due to the potential threat he

poses as one who might articulate an alternative idea of the Haitian nation. *Folie* opens in the throes of battle, with René momentarily imagining his poetry as his weapon: 'Je vais, drapé de majesté ancestrale, ouvrir d'un coup de pied cette porte et marcher jusqu'à eux. Dessalines! Pétion! Toussaint! Christophe! J'appelle à l'aide nos héros indomptables' ('By the glory of our forebears, I'm going to do it, kick the door open and walk up to them. Dessalines! Pétion! Toussaint! Christophe! I call on our indomitable heroes for help'). Drawing on the forefathers of the Haitian state just as Duvalier did, he recalls that through poetry, 'enfermé dans le Parnasse haïtien' ('shut away in my Haitian Parnassus'), he sought to create 'un Dieu bien haïtien, moitié blanc, moitié noir, mélange de Christ et de Legba [...] pour, à coups de machette imaginaires, tracer le sentier de la liberté [...] et gravir l'inaccessible colline du rêve' (300) ('a truly Haitian god, half-white, half-black, a blend of Christ and Legba [...] to hack a path to freedom with an imaginary machete [...] and climb the unreachable hill of dreams', 290). However, as he articulates at the beginning of the novella, this is but a dream and poetry is not a weapon he can use, as it is incompatible with, and therefore forbidden by, those who wield power. In this manner, Chauvet reinforces the idea that persecution in *Folie* focuses on the dichotomy imposed by the Duvalierist state which rejects any construction of the nation through pluralism, as Duvalier himself is that nation. Similar to Dayan's earlier observation, there exist for the regime two groups: those who form part of the state apparatus and those who are positioned outside it, the latter of whom can only be against the regime when viewed through the dichotomous paradigm it espouses. Formulated in other terms, then, these two groups are those gendered masculine and those rendered feminine.

The omnipresent threat of persecution due to the group's status manifests itself in René's perception that they are constantly under siege. This results in an attack on his sanity, which is the only weaponry he fully considers his own, and its breach is thus one example of the *folie* to which the title refers. Within the context of the trilogy, any limited amount of agency that Rose might have had within the constraints placed upon her by being forced to act as she did in *Colère* (such as any freedom she perceived that she gained through her actions) is completely negated here as René's psychological state worsens due to the incessant onslaught from the *diables* he believes are hounding him because of his self-professed vocation. Duvalier's omnipresent regime has created such a climate of terror that the mere threat of violence — the presence of Macoutes in the street — is enough to completely destroy any possibility of rational thought and action.

A key example of the blurring of the distinctions between reason and insanity is René's concern for the corpse lying in the street, which he reiterates on several occasions through the novella. Initially convinced that he saw the *diables* shoot the man in front of him, René then believes it must be Saindor, the owner of a bodega by the sea, before questioning whether it is the body of a dead dog when he dashes outside to get water and coal. Never sure whether it is in fact Saindor or just a dog, it is only after René runs out into the street and throws a Molotov cocktail — the act that leads to his arrest — that an outside voice exclaims, 'Hou!

comme ce cadavre de chien pue!' (357) ('Ugh, that dead dog over there stinks!', 349). More important than whether the body is that of Saindor or just a dog is the issue of René and his group's dehumanization as a consequence of a situation that has made it possible that this corpse could feasibly be either. Referring to this passage, Dayan ponders whether 'the creature crawling with worms turns out to be a dog and nothing but a dog', before asking 'does the distinction between human corpse and animal carcass matter?'[87] She poses a pertinent question here, and her observation underscores that the association of man and dog throughout the text and the destruction of both entities in this fashion have reached such a level that they have an equivalent non-human status. As a result, not only is René's body violated through starvation, the restrictions placed on his freedom of movement and finally his execution, his entire sense of self is destroyed as the notion of personhood is no longer a defining characteristic that differentiates him from an animal. Not only has Duvalier's destructive masculinity gendered René feminine through its violation of his body and mind therefore, it has completely dehumanized the other to such an extent that, as Anne Marty concludes, the very fact of being alive in this literary context becomes a plot against the state.[88] It is here, then, that terror begins to attack itself as Arendt's theory requires: as keeper of the cemetery presiding over the transition between life and death as well as the space in between, Baron Samedi embodied by Duvalier, helped by his *djab*, begins to attack life, the very power base upon which his position is predicated. For without life there can be no death, and without death, no cemetery.

This destruction of the fabric of the regime is further represented by the manner in which Chauvet writes her text. *Amour* is written as a series of journal entries, and *Colère* in the format of book chapters. The first book of *Folie*, however, seems to consist of lengthy streams of consciousness punctuated by dialogue between the four poets, while the second begins with the breakdown of even this narrative structure into a script that details their arrest before ending with what amounts to a transcription of their interrogation and execution, both from René's perspective. Drawing together Fanon's call for nation building through cultural production in the Caribbean with the notion of nationalism as gendered masculine, the conflict depicted in this novella could be perceived as one between two forms of masculinity, both of which seek to delineate an idea of nation. However, from the perspective of the dictatorship, there is no alternative form of masculinity to that which it has itself espoused, that is, what has been termed destructive masculinity here. Other concepts of masculinity are negated since those not subscribing to Duvalierism are subjected to violent repression, fail in their assertion of an alternative, and become gendered feminine. It has already been established that any potential for René's poetry, or that of his group, to counter the dictatorial state in *Folie* is nothing but a dream; their sporadic attempts to do so fail in the face of state terror which attacks their sanity, and they are ultimately killed by agents of this same oppressive regime.

In a similar vein, the manner in which René's death is recounted returns to the complete marriage of Vodou and Catholicism in this novella, and reiterates the poets' failure to counter the Duvalierist regime. Likening it to the crucifixion of Christ, René is executed at the hands of the *diables/djab*, and at that point implores the Christian saviour, 'fais que notre mort serve à quelque chose et empêche nos noms de sombrer dans l'oubli' (382) ('let our deaths mean something and don't let our names become lost in oblivion', 373). At the height of his *folie*, René's death also becomes a moment of prescience: the downfall of the Duvalier dynasty would indeed come at the hands of those that both Papa Doc and Baby Doc had sought to silence and dominate, the emasculated army, the Catholic Church, the representatives of Vodou and most importantly, the Haitian population itself. Perhaps, as the *lwa* suggests in *Général Baron-la-Croix*, when faced with complete destruction, 'La folie parfait, c'est la sagesse' [perfect madness is wisdom] (18). However, in the narrative present, René's death further illustrates his failure to assert an alternative notion of masculinity and of nation. By calling on Christ and drawing a parallel between the manner of their deaths, the protagonist symbolically inscribes his death into François Duvalier's own national discourse since, in a Duvalierist narrative, the latter has presented himself as the embodiment of the Christian God in addition to Baron Samedi. In this novella, then, Chauvet depicts not only the rendering of René as feminine and the destruction of the notion of personhood through terror, but also the negation of any alternative form of masculinity and the collapse of the division between the realms of the dead and the living for a regime that presents itself as presiding over this distinction. Having symbolically destroyed the feminine, the prediction can only be that the course of terror must then lead to the regime's self-destruction.

Destructive Masculinity and Sexual Subjugation

The destructive masculinity reinforced through Vodou discussed above is an important theme in *Saisons sauvages*. Raoul, in his position of Secretary of State in charge of the Macoutes, is depicted from the outset in a position of masculine authority over a female petitioner upon whose vulnerability he preys. Having been kept waiting for four hours and ten minutes, when Nirvah is admitted to the Secretary of State's office, she addresses him as 'Son Excellence', immediately reinforcing the gendered hierarchy which he has already begun to exploit. Nirvah is acutely aware of the gravity of her situation and knows that, since she is 'en butte à la colère légitime de l'autorité absolue' (15) ('up against the legitimate anger of the provoked absolute authority', 5), Raoul has the power to, in her words, 'save or destroy' her. This absolute authority upon which the regime is predicated is inherently gendered, and is a construct that can be imposed irrespective of an individual's sex (though, it is worthy of note that the majority — though by no means all — of those participating in the state apparatus were indeed male). With regard to women within this framework, Charles writes:

> The Duvalierist state [...] restructure[d] and redefine[d] gender roles and representation with two constructed categories of women: a reappropriated historical gender symbol represented by a rebellious slave woman, Marie

> Jeanne, who as a new constructed category [...] became an integral part of
> the state paramilitary forces; and, parallel to the new 'Marie Jeanne,' another
> woman — the enemy of the state and nation. Women who were not loyal to
> the Duvalierist cause were defined primarily as subversive, unpatriotic and
> 'unnatural'.[89]

The first category, of which Madame Max Adolphe became emblematic in her role
as commandant of Fort Dimanche, has, at least in the literary works studied here,
been subsumed by the singular presentation of those state apparatuses in which they
participated (such as the Fiyèt Lalo, the female section of the Macoutes). This group
of women are most commonly represented in these fictional accounts as *miliciennes* (or
in the case of *Général Baron-la-Croix*, just as 'la Femme' [the Wife]), if differentiated
at all. The second category, however, are those such as Yvonne Hakime-Rimpel,
raped and left for dead as a result of her outspoken rejection of Duvalier's politics,
or Mars's protagonist Nirvah, disloyal to the regime solely by association. It is
the targeting of the latter group that Trouillot contends differentiated Duvalierist
violence from that of previous regimes in Haiti, that is, 'the complete disappearance
of the protection traditionally conferred by femininity' since 'everyone knew —
and François Duvalier wanted it known — that women could fall victim to state
violence. The unusual became the principle'.[90] Furthermore, as is the case with
Nirvah and her children, 'political innocents', women, children, and the elderly,
became targets despite any relationship to a political suspect being 'nonpolitical',
and so the defence that these ties were solely familial, religious or social was no
longer valid.[91]

In such a climate in which gender polarizes the positions of violator and violated,
corporeal markers of femininity become potential sites of violation if associated
with the subservient. Nirvah makes this observation when she rejects the idea of
asking the Secretary of State if she can use his toilet:

> Je n'ose pas lui rappeler que j'ai un corps, un appareil urinaire, une vulve. [...]
> Je ne le veux pas m'imaginant dans la pièce à côté, vulnérable et dénudée.
> Cette fonction de ma féminité me semblerait dans cet instant une faiblesse, une
> menace contre mon propre corps. (17)

> [I don't dare remind him I have a body, a urinary tract, a vulva. [...] I don't want
> him to imagine me in the next room, vulnerable and denuded. This function
> of my femininity would seem like a weakness at that instant, a threat to my
> own body.] (6)

Nirvah fears that reminding Raoul Vincent that she is a woman would increase the
risk of his raping her, rape under Duvalier often used as punishment or, in Jean-
Charles's terms, 'simply a recreational activity for the Tonton Macoutes'.[92] Such acts
of arbitrary sexual violence reinforced the climate of terror in Duvalierist Haiti,
and it is to the regime's use of sexuality as a means of subjugation, particularly in
contexts where it is aligned with Vodou, that this analysis now turns.

As has been noted, the sexual violence meted out by male Macoutes over female
citizens is a recurrent theme in fictional works exploring Haiti during the François
and Jean-Claude Duvalier years. Indeed, Mars's exploration of this issue places her

novel in a literary tradition stretching from the years of the dictatorship — with one such example being Chauvet's seminal trilogy published in 1968 — to the present day, a tradition that includes other works analyzed in this and other chapters such as Montero's *Del rojo de su sombra* and Victor's *Clair de manbo*. However, a notable way in which *Saisons sauvages* differs from the others mentioned here is the fact that its female protagonist's fate is open-ended in nature. In these other texts, either the female protagonists are depicted as dying (such as Rose in *Colère*, Zulé in *Del rojo de su sombra* and Madan Sorel in *Clair de manbo*), or their death is implicit. An example of this latter instance is Claire in *Amour*, who, having killed the *chef de section*, is unlikely to escape the same fate, or Cécile in *Folie*, whose execution is implied at the end of the novella. In comparison, *Saisons sauvages* ends with Nirvah and her family having been stopped at a Macoute roadblock on their way to the Dominican border, and the reader is not told of the outcome. To this end, Mars responds to Christian Tortel's interview question asking why she did not write one of her main characters as an heroic victim as follows: 'Les victimes héroïques sont mortes sous la dictature. Je m'attache surtout à comprendre ceux qui y ont survécu' [The heroic victims died under the dictatorship. What I seek most is to understand those who survived it].[93] This survivor is Nirvah, whose experience of sexual violence initially develops in a similar manner to that of Rose in *Colère*, as will be demonstrated below. However, as a mother whose violator falls out of favour with the regime and as a survivor, Nirvah's story continues beyond the final lines of Chauvet's novella (as Jean-Charles also observes), the point at which Rose dies.[94]

One of the ways in which both Macoute chiefs in *Colère* and *Saisons sauvages* impose their power is by sexually assaulting and raping adolescent virgins, including the daughters of the plaintiffs who petition them. Through these acts of sexual violence, they not only violate their victims' bodies sexually and possess them for the first time, but also violently disregard the notion that respectability is tied to a daughter's virginity and simultaneously destroy the idea that parents can protect their children. In *Colère*, le Gorille checks that Rose has not lied about her virginity when he first meets her, then, dripping with sweat to the extent that she already felt defiled, 'Il s'enfonça en moi d'un seul coup terrible, brutal et, aussitôt, il râla de plaisir' (252) ('He rammed himself into me in one rough terrible thrust, and immediately groaned with pleasure', 244). In comparison, immediately after Nirvah leaves Raoul's office, he contemplates the extent of the power that he wields, noting that Nirvah had come to him for that very reason. For Raoul, his power is a drug, one 'dont il ne pouvait plus se passer à présent' ('he could no longer forego at this point') and of which he retains the trophies in his collection of 'mouchoirs tachés du sang de jeunes vierges qu'il dépucelait en les violant' (25) ('handkerchiefs stained with the blood of young virgins he deflowered as he raped', 12). As a result, possessing Nirvah, who represents all that he despises, is what he desires most. However, both Rose and Nirvah see their sexuality as the only means through which they can attempt to obtain what they want: the return of her father's land in the case of the former, and the release of her husband in that of the latter. As Jean-Charles indicates above, although other critics have suggested that Rose — and therefore by association other women — can ostensibly give her consent in such circumstances and therefore may seem to retain an element of agency, the nature of the climate of terror negates any notion of agency since there is no other option.[95] Agency can only be gained if the balance of power shifts and these women can begin to engineer the situation to their own advantage. For both Rose and Nirvah, this is not presented as a possibility.

Furthermore, even if Rose and Nirvah regard the use of their sexuality as a means to obtain what they want, it is clear as the narratives progress that the process of repeatedly being subjected to the destructive masculinity that both men employ has ramifications for the women beyond those imposed on their bodies. In *Colère*, the reader witnesses the extreme violence Rose suffers, with her whimpers of pain met with le Gorille's promise that, 'Je t'ouvrirai jusqu'à ce que mon poing entier y passe' (252) ('I'll open you up until my entire fist goes in', 245), and whose hands she feels 'sur mon corps [...] dans mon corps, fouillant ma chair sans vergogne' (253) ('on my body [...] Inside my body, shamelessly probing my flesh', 245). Her daily submissions to him destroy her resolve and she repeatedly states that she is already dead. By the end of the chapter in which her ordeal is recounted, she has become a 'panthère lascive et insatiable' ('lascivious and insatiable panther') compared to him, 'un pauvre chien [...] qui [...] adopte l'attitude d'un loup [...] qui aboie et qui mord pour prouver qu'il est autre chose qu'un chien' (260) ('a poor dog [...] who turns into a wolf [...] who barks and bites to prove that he's something other than a dog', 252). As such, the end of the month sees her both physically and psychologically destroyed, which is demonstrated by the change in her response to her rape: it begins as resistance through passivity, passes through an intermediary stage of contemplating the possibility of sexual pleasure were the situation different, before concluding with her self-perception as an animal alongside him.

In comparison, Nirvah describes her sexual relationship with Raoul in *Saisons sauvages* as one from which she derives pleasure, albeit a pleasure with 'unexpected dimensions' that he 'm'a injecté nuit après nuit, dans le froid de la chambre, en prenant possession de l'endroit et de l'envers de mon corps, en me violentant souvent' (211) ('infused me with night after night in the cool bedroom, possessing my body front and back, often assaulting me', 154). Here, Raoul conceptually replaces her incarcerated husband as a result of the intense pleasure she recognizes that he arouses in her; yet, the image of Nirvah's complete destruction is subsequently portrayed when she physically craves his sexual violence despite mentally trying to reject it. During his deployment to the Grand'Anse department to direct the massacre that would become known as the *vêpres jérémiennes*, Raoul takes the opportunity to propitiate his *lwa* Sogbo (also known as Sobo). Associated with thunder and lightning, this *lwa* is described as often violent and destructive in his Petwo manifestation, characteristics the reader sees in Raoul. Furthermore, in reference to Desmangles's observation that Sogbo 'can cause death to persons who harbor' him, Raoul falls increasingly out of favour with the regime in the period following the ceremony, and this process does indeed result in his death.[96] Prior to his political downfall, however, Nirvah confronts Raoul on his return from Jérémie and demands to know whether he was also sexually abusing her children. At this point, he flies into a rage, denies any interest in her son and bombards her with a series of questions about her daughter without answering any himself, forcing her to look at their image in the bathroom mirror as he yells at her and saps her life with his eyes. He sows doubt by asking if something so egregious could have happened right in front of her eyes, and if so, whether her daughter, Marie, was forced to submit or had sought him out as Nirvah herself had. In such a state, confused and physically restrained, Nirvah feels Raoul's erect penis pressing against her buttocks, evoking a visceral sensation of turmoil in her stomach produced by the conflict between her resolve not to give in to him and the inability to deny the physical desire she feels. She then describes what happens as follows:

> Raoul se détache de moi enfin. Je me retourne vers lui, lui tends mes bras, croyant qu'il va m'enlacer, que nous allons tomber sur les carreaux de la salle de bains et nous prendre avec toute cette rage qui nous fait si mal. Mais il s'éloigne en regardant sa montre. Sans un regard il me laisse, récupère dans la chambre son arme et sa serviette en cuir et s'en va. (245)

> [Raoul finally releases me. I turn toward him, hold out my arms, thinking he's going to embrace me, that we're going to fall onto the bathroom's tiled floor and take each other with the rage that is hurting us so much. But he moves away, looking at his watch. Without a glance, he leaves me, takes his gun and leather briefcase from the bedroom, and goes.] (179–80)

In an image of complete subjugation (the opposite of María Antonia's defiance as depicted at the end of Hernández Espinosa's play), Nirvah is rejected, having been lied to about Raoul's sexual relationships with her children and rendered complicit in her entire family's denigration. Importantly, as Jean-Charles suggests, Mars appears to 'avoid casting the blame on Nirvah for this situation' by providing clues to the reader — but not to the protagonist — of Raoul's sexual history at the beginning of the novel, such as his abovementioned collection of handkerchiefs stained with young virgins' blood.[97] Nevertheless, in spite of any understanding on the reader's behalf, Nirvah is made to believe she is responsible for her family's abuse and humiliation, a situation seen above in *Colère* when the terror Rose faces forces her to believe she is too complicit in her own degradation.

This episode in which Nirvah's ideas of being in control of her body and of being able to protect her children are destroyed directly follows Raoul's return from Jérémie. He is initially reinvigorated by both the massacre and the ceremony for his *mèt tèt*, leaving Grand'Anse with a feeling of invincibility to later describe Nirvah and her children as his real family. However, Raoul senses that his position within the regime and with Nirvah is in danger when he visits Duvalier at the Palais National, a prospect that would see his masculinity challenged. His fears are temporarily allayed when he relives the events of the previous few days by recounting them to Nirvah, and he feels both reenergized and calmed by this reiteration of his masculine status. As such, in spite of the imminent threat to his position within the state apparatus, the moment of his most violent outburst resulting in Nirvah's destruction directly follows the point at which his masculinity as a destructive agent of the Duvalierist regime is reinforced, coupled with his propitiation of his *lwa*.

A similarly destructive male sexuality is also shown in *Del rojo de su sombra* and *Clair de manbo*. Firstly, in *Del rojo de su sombra*, Similá's semen is regarded as deleterious, illustrated by the warning Zulé receives against having sex with him and reinforced by the fact that she terminates the resultant pregnancy, acknowledging the event with a single, bitter comment: 'Se acabó la meaja de ese negro' (106) ('That black man's seed is finished', 88). Furthermore, the manner in which Similá has sex with her — although it is consensual — is described in violent terms, 'Similá Bolosse la destazó así mismo, como se destazaban los careyes de la costa, la revolcó sobre los taburetes derribados y la sometió mil veces, haciéndola besar la tierra' (91) ('Similá Bolosse slaughtered her just as turtles on the coast are slaughtered, he conquered her among the overturned stools, he subdued her a thousand times, making her kiss the ground', 73). In coming to her *batey*, Similá is not only seeking to cure the sores he carries, but also to forge an alliance between his *gagá* — and by extension his *ounfò* near Lac de Péligre — and Zulé's in order to secure a route by which to traffic the narcotics passing through post-Duvalierist Haiti. Unsuccessful in his attempts to forge such an alliance, Similá then undertakes to destroy Zulé in battle, bathing in the blood of a hundred goats in order to propitiate Lokó Siñaña and leading his band of Macoutes in their search for her. In this context, although Similá does not manage to cow Zulé and she dies at the hand of Jérémie Candé mounted by Carfú, the destructive masculinity bolstered by Vodou with which he attempts to render her subservient is a direct inheritance from the Duvalierist state. Moreover, to return to Zulé's abortion, had the protagonist carried her child to term, it would have embodied a liaison between her and Similá that is not borne out by the events the novel depicts. In this way, the rejection of the pernicious effects that the proposed alliance between the two would have had for Zulé and her legacy, that is, her *sosyete*, is foreshadowed by this bodily process of repudiating his toxic influence.

With regard to Djo Kokobe in *Clair de manbo*, he is also a malevolent *bòkò* who seeks to subjugate and destroy Madan Sorel both out of revenge and to remove any opposition to the terror he intends to impose on the region that he controls as police chief. Calling the *manbo* to him by attacking with a poisoned axe the sacred mapou tree which serves as her link to Ginen and the *lwa*, Djo Kokobe demonstrates that he has no reverence for the *lwa* who reside in and commune with the physical world through this tree. Moreover, he symbolically aligns himself both with the war on Vodou waged by the Church in the first half of the twentieth century — a campaign during which many sacred mapou were cut down — and the damaging environmental and cultural consequences that such actions engendered. Madan Sorel is physically maimed by Djo's assault due to the visceral connection she maintains with the mapou and so she confronts him at its base, at which point he forces her to prostrate herself and beg for mercy, before he details how he is going to rape her. By acting in this manner, Djo seeks to render Madan Sorel physically and spiritually subservient, and he becomes enraged when she suggests that he is both fearful and impotent when presented with her naked body. His masculinity injured thus, he throws himself on her and upon penetrating her, seals both their fates: to die at the hands of the *vèvè* on which they are lying, Djo's soul to burn and Madan Sorel to rise in communion with the *lwa* and the spirit of the *vèvè*. Viewed thus, Madan Sorel's and Zulé's sacrifices in order to protect their respective communities can be seen to be of a similar vein. They are both destroyed by notions of masculinity associated with power and the Duvalier regimes, but in the process, they come to represent the possibility of survival for those left behind.

With regard to Nirvah's denigration in *Saisons sauvages*, from the moment at which she submits herself to Raoul in order to save her husband, she is reduced to — and evaluated in relation to — the roles she fulfils: wife, sexual partner/ whore and mother. Moreover, she will be destroyed in each of these roles by the destructive nature of Raoul's masculine sexuality, notably more potent after his offering to Sogbo and his campaign in Jérémie. As outlined above, Nirvah no longer considers herself a faithful wife from the moment at which sex with Raoul becomes pleasurable, and thus, as a sexual partner likened to a whore, she is also destroyed. When earlier in the novel she visits her neighbour Solange, a *manbo* and a prostitute, Nirvah is told, 'Les foufounes des femmes, [...] c'est comme la faïence. Une fois lavées, elles redeviennent neuves. Nous ne gardons pas de trace, pas de marque dans nos corps' (125) ('Women's *foufounes* are like earthenware. [...] Once washed, they become new again. We keep no trace, no mark, on our bodies', 88).[98] Nirvah repeats this idea after she burns her husband Daniel's journal to prevent his further incrimination, describing her 'sex' as earthenware and reiterating that it is like new each time it is washed (174). However, as becomes apparent, Raoul's sexuality is also harmful and Nirvah's vagina does not become like new each time she washes it. Further, the marks left on her psyche are shown to be indelible, exemplified by the disjunction that exists between her body and mind whereby the former yearns to be violated and appears to act of its own accord while the latter rejects this corporeal desire. At this point, in the absence of proof to the contrary, Nirvah gathers her strength to be a mother to her children. Yet, having permitted Raoul access to her house, her two children have also been exposed to the danger he poses: he has repeatedly raped her daughter Marie, who conceives and suffers a botched abortion, which then threatens her life; meanwhile, he violates her son Nicolas's innocence by gaining his confidence through academic tutoring, before coercing him into a sexual liaison that Raoul justifies to himself by framing it as a relationship between an *erastes* (lover) and *eromenos* (beloved) common in Ancient Greece. Nirvah is thus shown to be unable to fulfil the roles by which she has defined herself throughout the novel, and the family's survival hinges on their escape from both Raoul and Duvalier's Haiti. Fighting for their very existence, Nirvah's only choice is to hire a jeep and driver and try to flee under cover of darkness into the neighbouring Dominican Republic, an attempt that is also foiled when they are stopped by the Macoutes just a few miles from the border. In these terms, therefore, Raoul's noxious masculine sexuality reinforced through his association with the regime and Vodou succeeds in destroying Nirvah completely, and although it can be inferred from Mars's above-cited statement that Nirvah and her family survive the dictatorship, the question remains as to with what sense of self they manage to do so. Will Nirvah be able to wash these experiences away as she suggests when she asserts, 'Je laverai chaque jour ma fente avec de l'eau et du savon et des feuilles de petit-baume' (240) ('I'll wash my hollows with soap and water and leaves of wild mint', 176)? This question remains unanswered.

Finally, this analysis returns to the notion of terror and its self-destruction examined above. Consistent with the regime's appropriation of Vodou as a means to enforce terror and destructive masculinity, Raoul seeks the help of his *lwa* Sogbo to enable him to overcome what he perceives to be Nirvah's own protection at the hand of the Gede. Earlier in the novel, the protagonist visits Solange, who herself serves Déméplè — a *nago* spirit that Rachel Beauvoir describes as *lwa* from Nigeria who are violent and like war — and she takes a cleansing bath under the instruction of the *manbo* during which she feels 'delivered' by Déméplè, Ezili Dantò, Ezili Freda and the wider body of *lwa* (162).[99] In spite of this experience and any alignment with the *lwa* it connotes, Nirvah goes on to resist the protections Solange offers for both her and her children. Subsequently, the protagonist explains the fit Raoul suffers when he touches her as epilepsy, reasoning that he rejects in favour of one that requires a sacrificial offering to Sogbo and thus his reinvigoration by means of the spirits. However, it is following his return from Chardonnières to propitiate the *lwa* that his abuse of Marie and Nicolas is discovered and the other ministers in Duvalier's cabinet seek to discredit and undermine him. Despite his increased level of protection, therefore, he is still vulnerable to attack from an individual he perceives as serving Gede (Nirvah) and one who embodies Gede through Baron Samedi (Duvalier). As such, although Vodou can serve to reinforce destructive masculinity and sexuality in the context of the Duvalier regime, in this particular situation in *Saisons sauvages* it is shown to be of no assistance when an individual loses their status as gendered masculine and is therefore placed in opposition to the dictatorship. To this end, in the strict dichotomy depicted in this novel where resistance is impossible as one cannot reside outside the control of the state and opposition from within is crushed, propitiating one's *lwa* can only be of benefit from a position that agrees with this same authoritarian framework of state control. In other words, Vodou can support the violence meted out by the Duvalier regime by reinforcing the notion of destructive masculinity, but once an individual is gendered feminine within the dualism inherent in representations of Duvalierist Haiti, any power accorded by Vodou is negated. Furthermore, in *Saisons sauvages*, as in other texts analyzed here, a belief in the power of Vodou by those within the regime when it is separated from the context of masculinized imposition of power through violence is portrayed as a source of self-destruction. Raoul, le Chef in *Général Baron-la-Croix* and Djo Kokobe all believe their power to be bolstered by their interactions with Vodou and the *lwa*, but this very confidence leads them all to attack the fabric of the system itself, which then leads to their downfall.

When viewed through the lens of destructive masculinity, therefore, literary renditions of state violence in the context of Duvalierist Haiti have underlined the gendered nature of the framework of dictatorial power and have capitalized on the appropriation of Vodou and Catholicism by the dictatorship to explore in greater detail the gendered violence inherent in the climate of terror created under the regime. As the head of state who presented himself as the embodiment of Baron Samedi, François Duvalier collapsed the spaces of the dead and the living within Vodou, while subsuming the religion — the traditional locus of resistance since the struggles of the Haitian Revolution — into the apparatus of the dictatorship. In this fashion, Duvalier annulled the possibility for resistance and simultaneously used the same religious framework as a means to crush opposition. Conflating religion, nation and state into the single figure he embodied, Duvalier thus became synonymous with his regime, one which his bogeymen, the Macoutes, came to symbolize due to their status as the agents of the state with whom the wider population interact. Furthermore, the gendered hierarchy of power upon which the notion of destructive masculinity is predicated illustrates that in spite of the fact that the overwhelming majority of those wielding power were male, this characteristic in and of itself did not prevent the feminization of those considered opponents and therefore their subjection to physical and psychological gendered violence in the same manner. The regime has also been associated with a notion of destructive sexuality whereby the imposition of sexual violence by those in positions of power is seen as deleterious, undermining in *Amour, Colère* and *Saisons sauvages*, at the very least, any sense of agency the women subjected to it perceived that they had. In such a context, not even membership of the state hierarchy could ensure one's safety from emasculation and the consequent subjection to violence, and so, in accordance with Arendt, the imposition of terror propagated the demise of these very agents of terror.

Jean-Paul Sartre states in his preface to Fanon's *Les Damnés de la terre* [The Wretched of the Earth] (1961) that the violence suffered under colonialism will be reflected and imposed by those educated in the nations that imposed that colonialism, a notion that Fanon explains himself later in the same volume.[100] Within this conceptual framework, the step that Duvalier took that went further than his predecessors, colonial and otherwise, was not just to recognize African-derived religious traditions as sites of potential resistance, but to eliminate this possibility by absorbing them into the state. Appropriated thus, Vodou no longer constituted a locus of resistance but rather was a part of the repressive state framework, a status that has been coupled in literature with destructive masculinity and violent male sexuality to explore the experiences of Haitians under the fixed dichotomy — Duvalierist or subversive, masculine or feminine — imposed by this dictatorial regime.

Notes to Chapter 4

1. As Thomas C. Spear highlights in his contribution to a special issue of *Yale French Studies* dedicated to this author, she has long been known by her readers as Marie Chauvet, the name under which she published the majority of her works. The hyphenated 'Vieux-Chauvet' used since 2004 for new editions and translations of her works was, in his words, 'invented to serve as a compromise among Chauvet's three children' (2015: 23). In keeping with the majority of existing and contemporary scholarship, the author will be referred to here as 'Chauvet'; any use of Vieux-Chauvet is intended solely to aid the reader's locating the relevant source in the Bibliography.

2. Translation by Jeanine Herman, published in 2015 as *Savage Seasons*. All translations of *Saisons sauvages* are taken from this edition, unless otherwise noted.

3. Gordon 2008: 26, 81.

4. See Chapter 1 for further discussion of the official status of Haiti as a Catholic state and the role of Vodou in the Haitian Revolution, including opposing arguments regarding the veracity of the accounts surrounding Boukman and the Bois Caïman ceremony and the role ascribed to Vodou during the uprising.

5. For further discussion of the alignment of politics and Christianity — in particular Catholic liberation theology and Protestantism — across what Jeff Haynes terms 'the Third World', including Latin America and the Caribbean, see his volume *Religion in Third World Politics* (1994: 98–121), and Leslie James's book chapter 'Text and the Rhetoric of Change', in *Religion, Culture, and Tradition in the Caribbean* (2000: 43–66). A pertinent example of the associations drawn between religion and nation state (or the representatives thereof) in recent Caribbean politics is that of Kamla Persad-Bissessar, former Prime Minister of Trinidad and Tobago, whose Hindu cultural upbringing has been counterpointed with her baptism into the Christian church as an early adolescent. This became the subject of particular scrutiny by the media when, during a trip to India in January 2012, she bent down and touched the feet of then President Pratibha Patil in a gesture of respect, provoking much discussion of her heritage and competing claims of the symbolism conveyed by this act for the citizens and government of Trinidad and Tobago.

6. See Amos Cincir's article in the Haitian newspaper *Le Nouvelliste*, 'Le Secteur protestant prend le président Martelly à son mot' (2012).

7. Johnson 2006: 423–24.

8. Ibid.: 424.

9. Abbott has described her book as 'a narrative told from the perspective of individual Haitians' that 'is not a scholarly book', though 'many of the stories in it are the stuff of primary historical material' (2011: 12). Intended for non-Haitians, it is the product of her bibliographical research and interviews she conducted at the time, made possible in part by her status as the wife of Joseph Namphy — and therefore the sister-in-law of Lieutenant General Henri Namphy (interim head of government immediately after Jean-Claude Duvalier fled) — and her job reporting for Reuters News Service (2011: 8). Due to the nature of the work, some critics, such as Robert Fatton Jr., have noted that in places 'it is difficult to ascertain the complete accuracy of Abbott's [...] rendition', thereby questioning by implication its complete reliability (2002: 63). However, such reservations have not prevented the book from being consistently referenced as a text that offers an insight into the workings of the François and Jean-Claude Duvalier regimes, the purpose for which it is cited here.

10. Abbot 2011: 140. This catechism also shares the format of the catechism of the antisuperstition campaigns of the 1940s, cited by McAlister (2006: 88). As such, Duvalier symbolically undermines the Catholic Church by reincorporating Vodou into the catechism through his inclusion of Dessalines.

11. Diederich & Burt 1972: 215.

12. Fourcand 1964: 37.

13. Duvalier 1969: 330.

14. Johnson 2006: 438.

15. Brown 2006: 13. *Pran poz* is the phrase used in Haitian Vodou for those who are considered to be 'faking' a possession, i.e. pretending that one is mounted by a *lwa*, which is a phenomenon recognized as possible in many African-derived religious traditions in the Caribbean as well as Vodou, Santería included. For further discussion in reference to Vodou, see Brown (2006), and with regard to Santería, see Hagedorn (2010).

16. Richman 2012: 274.

17. Ibid.

18. François Duvalier regarded twenty-two as his lucky number due to numerous important events falling on or deliberately scheduled for that day of the month, the first of which was his election to the presidency. For further discussion, see Laguerre (1989: 113–14, 123; 1982: 106) and Abbott (2011: 122–23). Duvalier's affinity for this number is parodied in Haitian diasporic author,

playwright and academic Frantz-Antoine Leconte's *La République* [The Republic] (1998), with it being used recurrently when referring to amounts or numbers of people in Le Leader's presence, and it is even the age of Le Leader's son.

19. Clark 1992: 784.
20. Coates 1996: 258. *Bouqui au paradis* was first written in Kreyòl in 1960 as *Bouki nan paradi*, while Fouché was still resident in Port-au-Prince. Following the playwright's exile to Canada, it was translated into French in Montreal in 1967 and published by Éditions de Sainte-Marie in 1968 (Fouché 1968: 137; Coates 1996: 256).
21. Déita 1993: 197; Hurston 1990: 214; Bourguignon 1969: 188.
22. The translation of 'chef' as 'chief' (or le Chef's title as 'Great Chief') is that offered by Coates in his 1996 article, 'Folklore in the Theatre of Franck Fouché'.
23. Abbot 2011: 70.
24. Johnson 2006: 426.
25. Heath 1999: 38.
26. Duvalier 1969: 45. It should be noted that Geggus, in reference to Laguerre's 1989 *Voodoo and Politics in Haiti*, has questioned the characterization of Vodou as a unifying factor under Duvalier, suggesting that it would have also fractured wider society (2002: 76–77). However, this does not undermine the argument that Vodou and Catholicism were juxtaposed within the concept of the nation.
27. Richman 2012: 274–77.
28. Herman uses 'voodooist' for the original 'vaudouisant' in her 2015 translation *Savage Seasons*, as she does 'voodoo' for 'vaudou'. In light of the efforts to change the spelling used in English to Vodou, which is the accepted spelling in much of contemporary scholarship and removes the pejorative and colonial (albeit still extant) overtones with which the word 'voodoo' is associated, any use of 'voodoo' or 'voodooist' in quotations from *Savage Seasons* has been altered.
29. Ferguson 1988: 49.
30. See Lora 2003: 1342–48. As noted above, the 1966 Protocol signed between Duvalier and the Vatican reiterates the 1860 concordat, which allowed Haiti to name its own bishops and archbishops. The Protocol, as reproduced in *Enchiridion dei concordati: due secoli di storia dei rapporti chiesa-stato* [Enchiridion of the Concordats: Two Centuries of History of Church-State Relations], decrees: 'Conformément au prescrit de l'Article IV du Concordat intervenu le 28 Mars 1860 entre la République d'Haïti et le Saint-Siège, Monsieur le Président à Vie de la République nommerait au siège actuellement vacant et à ceux qui le deviendront par démission des Titulaires, des Ecclésiastiques auxquels Sa Sainteté le Souverain Pontife s'engage à accorder l'institution canonique, après les avoir trouvés en possession des qualités requises par les Saints Canons' [As prescribed in Article 4 of the Concordat agreed on 28 March 1860 between the Republic of Haiti and the Holy See, the President for Life of the Republic will appoint to the currently vacant seat and to those that will become vacant due to the resignation of their incumbents, clergymen to whom His Holiness the Pope undertakes to accord canonical office, after having found them in possession of the qualities required by Holy Canon Law] (Lora 2003: 1344). This right was later renounced by Jean-Claude Duvalier on 8 August 1984, although the amendment recognized the prerogative of the Haitian government to object on political grounds to the Vatican's nomination and that, 'à tout moment, la consultation susdite sera effectuée avec la plus grande réserve' [at all times, the abovementioned consultation will be conducted with the utmost discretion] (see Lora 2003: 1624–26).
31. Courlander & Bastien 1966: 56.
32. Conway (1978), cited in Richman 2012: 274.
33. It could be argued that such caution was ultimately shown to be prudent from the perspective of the regime, given the involvement of the Catholic movement of liberation theology in the unrest leading to the deposition of Jean-Claude Duvalier. See, for example, Hurbon (2001: 118–19), Lawless (2002: 42–43) and Nérestant (1994: 207–45).
34. Desmangles 2010: 199.
35. Ramsey 2011: 251.
36. Brown 2010: 185.

37. Desmangles 2010: 199.
38. Ibid.
39. Johnson 2006: 430, n. 6.
40. Translation by Rose-Myriam Réjouis and Val Vinokur published in 2009 as *Love, Anger, Madness*. All further translations of *Amour, Colère et Folie* from this edition, unless otherwise noted.
41. Laguerre 1989: 102, 118. While the terminology used here might be considered problematic, such as the reference to a notion of a 'Voodoo church', Laguerre's underlying argument has been accepted for the most part by subsequent scholars.
42. Laguerre 1993: 138.
43. Richman 2012: 275.
44. Laroche 1998: 87.
45. Trouillot 1990: 179.
46. N'Zengou-Tayo 1998: 118.
47. Arendt 1970: 41–56.
48. Ibid.: 56, 42, 49, 50.
49. hooks 2004: 18.
50. Ibid.: 24; De Lauretis 1989: 240.
51. Kaufman 1995: 18; see also hooks 2004: 18–19.
52. Charles 1995: 158.
53. Arendt 1970: 55.
54. Abbott 2011: 95.
55. Ibid.: 166.
56. Brown 2010: 360.
57. Ramsey 2011: 251, citing Gérard Pierre-Charles, *Radiographie d'une dictature*.
58. Diederich & Burt 1972: 357.
59. Fernández Olmos & Paravisini-Gebert 2011: 153.
60. Déita 1993: 199.
61. As established in Chapter 1, although *Del rojo de su sombra* is set temporally during the *dechoukaj* that followed the fall of Jean-Claude Duvalier's dictatorship, Similá's status as a *bòkò* and his long-standing relationship with the Macoutes permits a comparison to be drawn between him and figures in the earlier Duvalierist regime.
62. N'Zengou-Tayo 2010: 42.
63. Other self-aggrandizing titles Hannibal suggests are 'le Rédempteur, le Libérateur, le Civilisateur, le Sauveur, le Bienfaiteur, l'Homme Providentiel, l'Homme Ultime, l'Homme du Pays profond, l'Homme de la Majorité Nationale, le Réconciliateur' [the Redeemer, the Liberator, the Civilizer, the Saviour, the Benefactor, the Man of Providence, the Supreme, the Representative of the Heartlands, the Man chosen by the National Majority, the Reconciler] (Victor 1990: 53).
64. Abbott 2011: 117–40; Trouillot 1990: 169; Nérestant 1994: 173–76; Scharfman 1996: 234; Joseph 2007: 145; Ferguson 1988: 91. It should be noted that Ferguson questions the prevalence of terror since he appears to divorce fear and hopelessness from terror itself, therefore suggesting the latter is only physical destruction which 'was infrequently used against the ordinary Haitian'. However, terror also comprises the fear of such destruction and the hopelessness engendered by the state terrorizing its avowed victims (1988: 91).
65. Anatol 2000: 49. 'Gouverneurs' has been translated as 'masters' in order to remain consistent with the English translation of Roumain's *Gouverneurs de la rosée* as *Masters of the Dew*.
66. Dayan (1991; 1996; 2011; 2015), Scharfman (1996), Jean-Charles (2006), Kalisa (2009) and Walsh (2014).
67. Scharfman 1996: 234.
68. Jean-Charles 2006: 7.
69. Chancy 2004: 310.
70. Dayan 1991: 240.
71. Ibid. Martin Munro explores another form of duality in Chauvet's narrator, describing Claire

as a 'distinctly chiastic narrator, [...] both seeing and seen, subject and object, her alienation determined largely in and through the body, by the dark shade of her skin' (2015: 49).

72. Scharfman 1996: 240.

73. Larrier 2000: 104.

74. Dayan 1991: 247.

75. Ibid.: 243.

76. Jean-Charles 2006: 7–8.

77. Scharfman 1996: 240–41.

78. Jean-Charles 2006: 7.

79. Dayan 1991: 243. For further analysis of the violence and rape that Rose suffers, and the implication of Rose's family — in particular her brother, Paul — in this, see Jean-Charles 2014: 70–83.

80. Scharfman 1996: 243.

81. Benedicty-Kokken 2015b: 59, 61.

82. Dayan 2015: 99.

83. It should be noted that the overlap of reason and insanity in *Folie* is distinct from that suggested by critics as the main theme in Mars's *Fado*. In *Fado*, possession by Ezili was permitted, and it enabled Anaïse to reconstitute her sense of self. Conversely, here the blurring of the two is the result of René's violation by those associated with the regime and the *lwa* through the Duvalierist state.

84. Laroche 1984: 21–22.

85. Dayan 1991: 243.

86. Laroche 1984: 23–25.

87. Dayan 2015: 97. It should be noted that Dayan continues to question the very distinction between human and non-human, suggesting that there be a 'reshuffle of our conceptual schemes' and a recognition of the constructed, political nature of boundaries that delineate notions such as humanity (2015: 98–99).

88. Marty 1997: 153.

89. Charles 1995: 140.

90. Trouillot 1990: 167.

91. Charles 1995: 139.

92. Jean-Charles 2006: 5.

93. Tortel 2010.

94. Jean-Charles 2014: 99. For further analysis of this intertextual relationship between *Colère* and *Saisons sauvages*, see Jean-Charles 2014: 88–99.

95. Jean-Charles 2006: 7.

96. Desmangles 2010: 203.

97. Jean-Charles 2014: 96.

98. The term *foufoune* (or *foufoun*) is one of the words for vagina in Kreyòl. It is neither translated nor glossed in Herman's translation.

99. Beauvoir 2003: 87. It should be noted that Mars does portray here the restitutive aspects of Vodou when it remains within the realm of the feminine; it is only presented as destructive per se when aligned with the masculinity of the regime.

100. Sartre 1991: 47.

CHAPTER 5

Until Death...
Sexuality, Death and the Sacred

In her analysis of the Gede, Brown observes that they are the spirits who 'preside [...] over the realms of sex, death and humor', which she later describes as 'the great social levelers'.[1] Often symbolized by an erect penis, skull and/or cross — the latter indicative of the tomb but also of the crossroads between life and death — the Gede reside in the cemetery and represent, through the conflation of these symbols and spaces, the notion in many African-derived religions in the Caribbean that sex and death are two sides of the same coin.[2] Indeed, the association of Gede with a *gwo zozo* ('big cock', as given by Brown) has been explored in the plastic arts of the Atis Rezistans artists' collective of Grand Rue in Port-au-Prince by scholars such as Katherine Smith in her book chapter 'Atis Rezistans: Gede and the Art of Vagabondaj' (2012), while Cosentino references the symbolism of the *gwo zozo* as an attribute of the Gede spirits in 'Envoi: The Gedes and Bawon Samdi' (1995).[3] This link between the Gede, sex and death has been discussed in Chapter 4 in relation to destructive masculinity and state terror, a key element of which is the use of sexual violence as a means of subjugation by the Macoutes as agents of the state apparatus under the Duvalier regimes.

Importantly, however, when considered outside this context, the Gede also represent the interplay between the visceral and transitional experiences of sex and death expressed elsewhere in the Vodou pantheon. Notably, the multiple avatars of Ezili include Ezili Freda and Ezili Dantò (both associated with sexuality) alongside Ezili Mapiang, each of whom is linked with death to varying degrees through her respective characteristics: Ezili Freda is vengeful, Ezili Dantò, a warrior and a mother, Ezili Mapiang, pernicious and corrupt. In Santería a similar correspondence exists among the *orisha*, especially Ochún, Yemayá and Oyá. The first two, like Ezili, have different *caminos* associated with sex and the dead: Ochún, *orisha* of love and sexuality, is related to the dead and mourns alongside Ikú as Ochún Awé, while Yemayá, *orisha* of motherhood, is associated with the dead both through her role as a mother and as Yemayá Asesú, the latter of whom 'recibe las ofrendas en compañía de los muertos' [receives offerings in the company of the dead].[4] Oyá, keeper of the cemetery and *orisha* who governs death, is the jealous wife of Changó who, in one *patakí*, is enraptured by his wife's slender and mature body to the extent that, once rescued from Ikú by Ochún, he turned down the *orisha* of love to rest in his wife's arms.[5]

As these examples illustrate, the close relationship between death and sexuality depicted in the literary works examined in this book is grounded firmly in the way these two notions interact and coexist within the context of African-derived religions of the region. In these texts, sexuality and death depend on and influence each other, either through their juxtaposition or, more intimately, by framing and informing the other, which then results in both notions being presented in a more complex fashion. As has been demonstrated, the female protagonists' deaths in *Del rojo de su sombra*, *María Antonia*, *Fado* and *Clair de manbo* form part of the discourse regarding their sexuality, each of which is discussed in further detail below. Equally, the interaction between death and sexuality is essential to the narrative in *Como un mensajero tuyo*, for example, where Aída's impending demise is directly related to her sexual relationship with Caruso, while Acilde's replication and death in *La mucama de Omicunlé* is intertwined with his and his avatars' sexual relationships with Eric Vitier, Linda and Argenis. Furthermore, in *Saisons sauvages*, Daniel Leroy's prolonged incarceration leads to his symbolic death due to his wife's decision to effectively replace him with the minister in charge of the Macoutes. In this latter instance, his wife maintains a sexual relationship with the minister, which then results in her own symbolic death both as a victim of rape who comes to desire her attacker and as a mother unable to protect her children from his sexual advances.

In Fouché's *Général Baron-la-Croix*, the figure of death makes his presence known on stage through the Gede spirit's disembodied nasalized voice, juxtaposed with le Chef who displays some of the spirit's other traits (see Chapter 4). Moreover, due to his impotence, the birth of le Chef's successor in the play is only made possible by the sexual liaison between his wife and Baron-la-Croix, an act in which le Chef must also participate and that engenders 'un monstre' [a monster] who is born after a gestation period of only nine days (86–87).[6] In contrast to Fouché's play, where the figure of death is not directly personified on stage, the character of Cumachela in Hernández Espinosa's *María Antonia* is the explicit personification of Ikú. An old, crazed woman who lives in the streets, Cumachela interacts with a number of characters in the play and encounters the protagonist when she enters the *manigua* in the fourth *cuadro*, itself an indication of María Antonia's inescapable demise and her conflict with the paternal authority of death (see Chapter 2). Importantly, as the figure of death, Cumachela conflates Ikú with sexuality: not only is she described as the erstwhile María Antonia, with all the sexual connotations such a description entails, she also speaks of her previous *marinovio* (a combination of the words for 'husband' and 'boyfriend') whom she murdered after he abandoned her in response to her request for marriage. Further, upon recounting this anecdote to Julián and the party assembled at the *bar de los muelles* — itself associated with raucousness and casual sexual encounters — Cumachela embellishes it with tales of her other sexual exploits, and later refers to the 'machos' who will be coming to dance with her (that is, the *íremes* that appear with her after Julián's murder in scene eleven) by using a term that connotes sexuality. In a similar vein, María Antonia's abovementioned encounter with Ikú/Cumachela takes place immediately after she has put an *amarre* on Julián having heard that he will leave Cuba to box abroad, and just before she meets Carlos, with whom she explores the possibility of a life together and who later murders her. The scene is framed by María Antonia's sexuality, which both the protagonist and Cumachela reference during the former's interrogation of Ikú/Cumachela, thus juxtaposing her sexuality with both her and Julián's impending deaths. Just as her physical demise is inescapable, so is the failure of her relationship with Julián that has contributed to it; as an *hija de Ochún*, María Antonia's rejection and abandonment by her lover, an *hijo de Changó*, is inevitable given its precedent in the *pataki*.[7] The manner of her brutal death at the hands of the spurned and emasculated Carlos then collapses the notions of death and sexuality, as does Julián's murder at the hands of María Antonia.

In addition to recognizing the interaction between these two concepts, the idea of death itself in these works must also be understood from within the context of Santería and Vodou. For *santeros* or *vodouyizan*, death is of course no less inevitable than for anyone else, a fact Montero highlights, for example, with the continual re-emphasis of the passage of time in *Como un mensajero tuyo* whereby Aída's impending death prompts the transcription of her story by her daughter, who then passes it on to the outside world when she herself is nearing death. Equally, this inevitability is exemplified by the many María Antonias that Hernández Espinosa and Herrera have seen and continue to see on the streets of Havana, each of whom continues in her own way the struggle of those who have preceded her. However, in the framework of these religious traditions, death does not constitute a finality that renders an individual no longer able to interact with the physical world, but rather it marks an individual's transition between the connected physical and spiritual worlds. In reference to Santería, Martiatu writes, 'La muerte es un cambio y no un fin. Los muertos pasarán a ese plano "infrahumano" que no los saca del mundo, sino que los lleva a seguir entre los vivos pero en otra condición' [Death is a change and not an end. The dead will move on to that 'infrahuman' plane which does not remove them from the world, but rather permits them to remain among the living in another form].[8] Similarly, in Vodou the dead journey to Ginen, 'where ancestors who have passed from this life to the next reunite with those not yet born' and the spirits 'past, present, and future [... are] then brought to this earth to shield and strengthen the living'.[9] This notion of death as a transition is reinforced by the symbolism that forms part of initiation into both religious traditions, most notably the period of seclusion from the outside world during which a novitiate symbolically dies, is re-born and then is presented to the religious community as a new member of their respective *ilé* or *ounfò*. The ceremonies performed upon and following the death of a *santero* or *vodouyizan*, during which the practitioner's spirit is disassociated from the body and both the spirit of the deceased and the *orisha de cabecera* or *mèt tèt* are propitiated by means of offerings, reinforce this notion of transition and signal the next stage in an adherent's religious experience. While death connotes the demise of the body and its physical yielding to the paternal authority of Ikú or the Gede, inherent within this process is the progression of the spirit into a space from which it can influence both the physical and the spiritual, the living and the dead.

The symbolism of death as a transition and as replicated in initiation is connected with ideas of sexual initiation and the transitions in an individual's life and experiences that this involves. Like death, such a transition is often conceptually associated with violence (corporeal and/or otherwise) and the accompanying symbolism of penetration. However, in the instances detailed in reference to *Fado*, *Colère* and *Saisons sauvages*, this first experience of sex for some of the characters involves additional violence — in these cases, that of rape — which then more closely associates their experience of sexuality with the concept of death. With regard to Carlos in *María Antonia*, this link was further underscored when his father rewarded him for killing the neighbourhood bully with a visit to a brothel so he could lose his virginity and cement his new position as a 'man'. This experience then evoked in him feelings of loss and bereavement due to his being forced to act in a way that he thought he was able to avoid, in order to secure his manly status in the eyes of his family and the community. As part of this process, death becomes inseparable from Carlos's acquisition of an approved masculinity, thus is derived from a violent sexuality.

In light of the above discussion, the remainder of this chapter will consider the manner in which the concepts of death and sexuality have been theorized from a European perspective and explore the theories proposed by scholars such as Georges Bataille and Jean Baudrillard, reframing them through the lens of African-derived religious traditions in the Caribbean. In so doing, the analysis will demonstrate that the conceptualization of death and sexuality within these worldviews, and in the literature that draws on them, is more complex than might be suggested by a reading that solely employs the frameworks these theorists propose. Subsequently, the chapter will turn to the multiple forms in which death can be manifest, exploring the key notions of prostitution and motherhood, rape and sacrifice, to then draw conclusions about the importance of using literary texts as a source of knowledge regarding the perception of death and sexuality in the Caribbean, and the ways in which such a viewpoint complicates the abovementioned male-oriented perspectives of these two concepts.

Theorizing Death and Sexuality

When considered through the lens of Afro-Caribbean spirituality, the conceptualization of death and sexuality is one that in some ways reinforces the manner in which they have been theorized by scholars like Bataille and Baudrillard, but in others both troubles and contests it. First, death and sexuality are both visceral experiences centred on the body, which ties them together in space with the corporeal experiences involved in African-derived religious traditions in the Caribbean. Second, there has long been a conceptual link between the two, as Foucault illustrates — to highlight just one example — when he draws on Ancient Greek philosophy in his reflection on the matter in *Histoire de la sexualité*. As he writes, the sexual act was not perceived as a solely positive experience, it was also seen as 'marquant la mortalité de l'individu' ('prefiguring the death of the individual'),[10] although this same act — linked to a form of sexuality as a mode of reproduction — might also permit that the individual 'd'une certaine façon [...] échappe à la mort' ('in a sense escape death').[11] For Bataille, on the one hand sexual activity and death are associated through the idea that 'l'affaissement consécutif au paroxysme final est tenu pour une "petite mort"' ('exhaustion following the final paroxysm is thought of as a "little death"'), with death 'le symbole du retrait des eaux qui suit la violence de l'agitation' ('the symbol of the retreating waters after the violence of the storm').[12] On the other, he defines *érotisme* [eroticism] as a distinct form of sexual activity independent of sex for the purpose of reproduction; although children may result from erotic pleasure, eroticism itself is a form *'qui ne peut servir à rien'* (*'which cannot serve any purpose'*).[13] The subjective experience of eroticism therefore brings pleasure as the opposite of death together with 'the foretaste of death' that is given by the depression that follows orgasm.[14] This interaction between eroticism and death is framed as one linked by the continuity they represent in comparison to the discontinuity of individuals, a symbolic link that for Baudrillard is forged through the exchange of energies and mutual excitement of each other that both involve, separate from the biological link between sex and death created in reproduction.[15] Constructed thus, the division between life and death, reproduction and eroticism, is the basis of a power framework in place in European and European-oriented societies that depends on the disruption of an exchange between the former two.[16] Manipulating the interaction with death through its prohibition then permits control over secondary divisions drawn along the same lines, such as 'soul and body, masculinity and femininity, good and bad', and so sex and death constitute a dichotomy from which power emerges.[17] In the context of the Duvalier dictatorships, such divisions imposed on the populace and control over them are an essential element of understanding the manner in which death has been conceptualized within this context and thus in the narratives that depict these regimes, as previously discussed.

Before examining this notion in further detail, it is necessary to consider the gendered nature of the alignment of death and sexuality. In the introduction to their edited volume *Death and Representation*, Elisabeth Bronfen and Sarah Webster Goodwin cite the title to Philippe Ariès's 1976 work *L'Homme devant la mort* (lit. 'Man before Death') as indicative of Hélène Cixous's later conclusion that, in the oppositional male-female binary, man is associated with life and woman with death.[18] The editors then reinforce this position and elaborate on the relationship between death and the female body outlined by Freud, to conclude that Western male-dominated cultural frameworks position death and women as 'radically other to the norm, the living or surviving male subject'.[19] It is this alignment between death and the behaviours and societal positions designated as 'feminine' within the dictatorial state that is evidenced in the texts explored in Chapter 4. Framed within the imposition of a strict gender-based dichotomy by the Duvalier regimes, these texts illustrate how the dictatorship relegated individuals considered to be outside the state apparatus to an inferior female-gendered status and maintained power over that division by means of state terror and violence. Those occupying this subordinate position were branded as antithetical to the professed aims of the regime — 'other to the norm' in Bronfen and Goodwin's words — and therefore contagious as a potential threat to authority. As a result, from the regime's perspective they were already considered dead. When Nirvah petitions Raoul Vincent for the freedom of her husband at the beginning of *Saisons sauvages*, Daniel Leroy, who has been incarcerated for Communist activities, becomes a bargaining chip for the minister. Already as good as dead from Raoul's point of view since he has no intention of releasing him, Daniel's death is symbolically reiterated by his physical absence throughout the entire novel, by Nirvah's burning of his diary which is the only tangible evidence of his existence in the text, and by the fact that Raoul comes to occupy Daniel's position within the family, however perverse this relationship with them might be. In a similar fashion, in Chauvet's *Folie*, René is incarcerated and ultimately executed, having been portrayed as gendered feminine within the abovementioned male-female dichotomy, while Rose's fate in *Colère* is sealed the moment she accompanies her father to lodge a claim for the return of the family's land. Indeed, Rose's brother Paul understands the inevitability of her destruction as soon as he learns of his father and sister's decision, to which he responds with the prophetic warning, 'Ne joue pas trop des fesses, [...] ça pourrait te coûter cher' (177) ('Don't wiggle your ass too much, [...] it could cost you dearly', 170). In addition to her imminent death as related to her sex, the association between Rose and death is reinforced when she describes le Gorille — already subhuman in name — as having become a dog who follows her around, which in one sense presents her as having negated his status as a human being through their daily sexual encounters. Furthermore, it is her daily rape by le Gorille that provides the impetus for Paul's attempt to kill his sister's aggressor and for their father's successful orchestration of the same man's murder. While not wishing to suggest that these examples indicate Rose's sexual agency (a position discussed previously), it should be recognized that from the perspective of the regime they do exemplify a further instance of the alignment between those gendered feminine and death, and so the symbolic power that the latter entails.

In both the context of Afro-Caribbean spirituality and the European theoretical framework, death is an inherently violent concept. Although it is described as a transitional process in Santería and Vodou, death is always violent to a certain degree since it requires the demise of the physical body which, upon becoming a corpse, is testament to the violence every person is destined to suffer.[20] Moreover, as Habermas, among others, emphasizes, this inherent violence is found in sexuality as it is in death, which Bataille contends draws the two together in a climax of excess, fuelling erotic ardour alongside the anguish that forms a part of both eroticism and death.[21] In her analysis of the role of women in Bataille's theorization of eroticism, Suzanne Guerlac highlights that the erotic object possessed by the male erotic subject 'must be not only a woman, but a woman as object', that is, a prostitute whose passivity is required.[22] This urge to possess the erotic object is also linked with death since, although possession itself does not signify death, Bataille contends that a lover will sometimes think of killing the object of his love if he cannot possess her, with this outcome being preferable to losing her.[23] Such a compulsion to kill the woman who cannot be possessed sexually is important when examining the deaths of Zulé in *Del rojo de su sombra* and of María Antonia. At this point it should be noted, however, that despite the fact that María Antonia pays with her own life the price for rejecting the gender-based framework that permits male dominance to the point of death, her actions when she kills her lover Julián see the play contest Bataille's gendered framework. By means of these actions, the text destabilizes the very notions that have been reinforced by the society in which María Antonia lives and questions the gender-based theorizations of death outlined above.

The character of Zulé has multiple interactions with death at various points throughout her life: as a young child her two brothers, mother, grandmother and stepmother drowned on separate occasions in the river at the foot of the Mayombe Hill, and later, after she had been promised to the *gagá* at Colonia Azote, she asked Coridón to work her eyes in order for her to descend to the world of the dead. Upon becoming *manbo* of her own *gagá* at Colonia Engracia, Zulé is associated with Gede Nibo (keeper of tombs) through her status as *dueña* of her *sosyete*, in the position of which she is sought out by a Dominican man searching for his wife who has been turned into a *zonbi* and taken to Lac de Péligre on the Haitian side of the border.[24] Already aligned with death in this manner, Zulé exemplifies the coexistence of the realms of the living and dead in Vodou, which contests the power construct posited by Baudrillard, demonstrating that the interplay between the two rather than their division can serve as a source of power, channelled in this instance through a female Vodou priest. As previously shown, Zulé's death at the hands of Jérémie Candé mounted by Carfú and associated with Ogou Feray is a complex event with multiple overlapping meanings. The first of these focuses on the notion of sacrifice, a key theme in Montero's novel to which this chapter will return below. At this point, however, the analysis will concentrate on the manner in which Zulé's death illustrates Bataille's observation above regarding the lover's murder of the unobtainable erotic object.

The moment of Zulé's death at the culmination of the *gagá*'s Easter procession is framed by her repeated sexual rejection of Jérémie Candé and her refusal to form an alliance with her former lover and current adversary Similá. While the scene has also been written as a conflict between the *lwa* as shown in Chapter 1, it must equally be viewed in terms of a struggle between two men and the woman who is, or represents, the object of their desires and who refuses to acquiesce to either of them. Beginning with Jérémie Candé, he is denigrated by Zulé on a sexual plane when she encourages his voyeurism and expression of passion through masturbation, yet repeatedly disparages them as 'cosas de chino' (108) ('things Chinamen do', 90). This is a denial of sexual agency that must be recognized as a contributing factor to his reasons for murdering her despite his being her loyal *sèvitè*. For Similá, Zulé represents the object of his desire as *dueña* of the *gagá* with which he seeks an alliance, a fact that is reinforced by the sexual relationship they have maintained and the juxtaposition of his goals of religious and sexual unions in order to ensure political hegemony. However, the severing of any possible ties between the two *sosyete*, prefigured by Zulé's abortion, signifies Similá's inability to realize his overlapping religious, political and sexual objectives. Rejected thus, his violence towards Zulé on the battlefield and promise to kill her is directly linked to his desire for the territory she represents in order to secure a smuggling route through the *bateyes* of the region. Consequently, it should be viewed as the result of the escalation of tensions provoked by her denying him the chance to possess her once again and to seal the alliance that she embodies.

In reference to María Antonia, her death is a direct consequence of Carlos's violent reaction to her public rejection of him. In this final scene of the play, he announces his arrival at the *toque* for Ochún by shouting '¡María Antonia! [...] ¡Vengo a buscarte!' [María Antonia! [...] I've come to find you!] (1037), a statement of intention that quickly leads to violence when María Antonia refuses to submit to the male authority he has attempted to assert. With no intention of leaving, María Antonia responds to Carlos's threat that he is 'muy macho pa'que te burles de mí' [too much of a man for you to make fun of me] — a repetition of Yuyo's earlier line delivered in similar circumstances — by dancing for Ochún and declaring provocatively, '¡María Antonia tiene sed, sed de hombre! ¡Tráigame un jarro lleno de hombres!' [María Antonia thirsts, thirsts for a man! Bring me a pitcher filled with men!] (1038). Conflating the notions of death and sexuality evident throughout the play thus, her declaration mimics the biblical description of Christ's penultimate utterance before his death, 'I thirst', and the subsequent provision of vinegar to drink. However, María Antonia formulates it as a proclamation of her sexuality and sexual agency, while her dance constitutes both one of death and a performance of her sexual agency as the erotic subject. Beginning with the dance, María Antonia courts death by drawing Carlos — who has been charged by Ikú with murdering her — into a position from which he can only react by killing her. She counters his machismo with her *hembrismo* and begins to dance provocatively for Ochún, removing her clothes, fully aware that it was her embodiment of the sensual, sexual and defiant nature of her *orisha de cabecera* expressed through her sexuality that had led to Batabio's declaration of her impending death. Rightly foreseeing that María Antonia's dance and accompanying verbal provocations would result in her physical demise, La Madrina petitions Yemayá and the other *orisha* for *aché* and for their blessing for her *ahijada*, further underlining that the protagonist's actions constitute a dance of death.[25] María Antonia's invocation of Ochún in this manner, which culminates in the *orisha* mounting her *caballo*, is also a possession performance through the propitiation of the *orisha* and the invitation for her to manifest herself. Importantly, however, as stated above, María Antonia's dance is an erotic performance of her sexual agency as the subject of desire, displacing Carlos from his position as the male erotic subject and claiming it for herself. Although Carlos's reaction is to destroy her by stabbing her in the vagina, this male domination does not negate the agency she exercises at the same time through her provocative dancing beforehand and the final image of defiance she displays afterwards. As a result, María Antonia's death is framed in terms of the murder of the unobtainable erotic object and as a punishment for defying male hegemony, both within a context of Santería. However, the presentation of sexual agency as intertwined with her death enables the protagonist to destabilize the gender-based construct that has castigated her thus. It is to the imposition and subversion of patriarchal frameworks governing sexuality as interwoven with notions of death that this analysis now turns.

Narratives of Motherhood and Prostitution

As discussed in Chapter 3, the concepts of motherhood and prostitution have often been rendered discrete within the phallologocentric order which has long governed the 'meanings borne by the feminine' in literature that draws on male-oriented societal constructs.[26] In the texts analyzed here, however, the dichotomy that formerly separated these performances and declarations of sexuality is collapsed, and the female characters comprise multiple roles and sexual identities that interact with and inform each other. This is particularly the case in texts like *Fado* and *Saisons sauvages*, which clearly show women traversing this divide, while other texts such as *María Antonia* have presented the mother and the prostitute as two separate but mutually dependent individuals. In *Fado*, the interplay between these two archetypal depictions of woman has been shown to be the source of Anaïse/Frida's power to knit together her fractured self. However, the focus here will centre on the manner in which motherhood and prostitution are both counterpointed and drawn together through death. As will be demonstrated, the interaction of the two with each other and with death, within the context of Santería and Vodou, provides a space where the spiritual and/or physical annihilation these roles connote in male-dominated theoretical models can be prevented.

As Kristeva highlights, the association between maternity and death harks back to the symbolism associated with the biblical Eve as the woman who is the mother of humankind but brought death into the world as the wages of her sin, as well as through Mary who gave birth to Christ in order for him to die.[27] In a similar fashion, as Goodwin writes, there has long been an association between the prostitute and death which, though analyzed and theorized by Freud, was 'already implicit' in the Bible through 'the location of the Whore of Babylon in John's apocalyptic vision of the end'.[28] Socially marginalized and perceived as the embodiment of '"depraved" sexuality', a prostitute occupies the lowest rung on the ladder of social hierarchy, representing 'the lowlife of the city's narrow streets and slums', from where she challenges the framework of society since she moves between notionally discrete social spaces.[29] Her position at the point where all levels of society converge means she is able to dissolve the divisions between them, which then confers on her a symbolic status similar to death — described by James Shirley in his seventeenth-century poem *Death the Leveller* — as one with whom all clients are rendered equal: upon interacting with her, the men are positioned on the same level, and by doing so they must recognize the same sexual desire that they each hold.[30] Consequently, within the framework of wider, male-dominated society a prostitute is considered to be diseased and haunting since she possesses the ability to negate privilege and status, while also constituting an external representation of the erotic self that therefore beckons men towards her.[31]

It must also be emphasized that motherhood and prostitution have both a subjective and plural nature, which these texts recognize. In reference to motherhood, the importance of spiritual and other-mothering in *María Antonia* and *Fado*, for example, has been outlined in earlier chapters. With regard to prostitution, on the one hand there are characters like Frida in *Fado*, who is a self-identifying prostitute who receives money in exchange for sex. In addition, however, the categorization of the 'woman's "unchaste" body' as that of a prostitute — a long-held tenet of societal frameworks which have labelled women expressing a perceived errant sexuality as whores regardless of the individual's own perception — is evident in several of these texts, most notably *Colère*, *Saisons sauvages* and *María Antonia*.[32] For Rose and Nirvah, those surrounding them view their submission to the Macoute chiefs as a transaction of the protagonists' sexuality (and in Rose's case, her virginity) for Louis Normil's land and Daniel Leroy's freedom, thereby denoting them as prostitutes. However, despite this relationship being perceived as transactional by others, it is important to reiterate that both women are raped by their aggressors and are not able to remove themselves from the destructive relationships forced upon them as part of 'the system of terror and culture of fear that reigned under Duvalier'.[33] For her part, María Antonia, though in a different context, is likened to a common whore due to the sexuality she expresses in fulfilling what she perceives to be her role as an *hija de Ochún*, a categorization she vehemently rejects. The designation of each of these women as prostitutes is one that has been imposed due to society's view of their bodies as 'unchaste' and the sexual desire unleashed by their attackers and/or lovers, rather than their self-identification as such.

Returning to *Fado*, the reconstitutive nature of motherhood and prostitution for Anaïse through the persona of Frida has already been established. However, Frida is also clearly associated with death: having enabled Anaïse to explore her sexuality by embodying the nature of Ezili Freda, Frida poisons Bony, and Anaïse, Léo, before they both swallow the poison themselves and depart for Ginen. Anaïse is herself associated with Ezili Dantò and, upon learning of her pregnancy, exclaims, 'je suis morte!' [I am dead!] (89). For her, motherhood would see her reinscribed into male-dominated relationships with both Léo and Bony since she would then be forced to fulfil the 'natural' role of woman — that of mother — a role which Simone de Beauvoir and Trinh T. Minh-ha, among others, have linked to a loss of agency and death. Importantly, the butchery Anaïse experienced as an adolescent was related to both her rape and the two abortions she was forced to undergo, the latter of which further aligns her conceptually with the idea of death. On the one hand, this is due to the deaths of the foetuses that are the result of such a procedure; on the other, it is the enforced death of her own potential to bear children at the hands of her attacker when the second abortion leaves her sterile. In this way, though her refusal to become a mother can be seen as propagating the destruction that resulted from these bodily violations, Anaïse/Frida ultimately progresses to occupy a space in which her physical death in fact enables her to maintain the integrity of the spiritual self she has knit back together. Death in *Fado* is therefore a complex and multivalent notion that reinforces its destructive nature with regard to the younger Anaïse and her two present lovers. At the same time, it offers a space in which Anaïse/Frida is able to prevent her re-fracturing by going through the transitional process that physical death in the context of Vodou permits, instead of being subjected to another abortion or to what she perceives as the restrictive role of mother.

In *Como un mensajero tuyo*, the link between motherhood and prostitution via sexuality and death is explored through Aída's embodiment and invocation of various *caminos* of Yemayá, in addition to the way in which her practice of Santería is framed. As an expectant mother, Aída explicitly refers to two of the multiple avatars of Yemayá (Yemayá Asesú and Yemayá Achabá) who protect Aída and Caruso's unborn daughter while Aída languishes in a cave, and in this way they provide for mother and daughter alike. Elsewhere in the novel, Yemayá mounts the protagonist in order for the latter to save Caruso from drowning in the Lagoon of San Joaquín, acting in the interests of her own love for Changó, Caruso's *orisha de cabecera*. Although Yemayá's motherhood and sexuality are thereby shown to be protective, some of the witnesses Enriqueta interviews view her mother's sexuality and involvement with Santería and Sanfancón as harmful, and they intimate that her actions are equally those of a prostitute. One example is the pharmacist who was a suspect in the bombing; he describes Aída in a disparaging tone, recalling that the newspapers had reported Caruso as having become involved with 'una china, una medio mulata que para colmo era santera' (106) ('a woman who was half Chinese and half mulatta, and if that wasn't bad enough, she was a *santera* too', 79). To complete the description, he adds, 'aquella mujer, una china que lo enredó, figúrese ('that woman, with her Chinese snares. Just imagine'). The distaste in his commentary for Aída and her conduct — ensnaring a married man using a mix of African- and Chinese-derived religious practices — evidences his perception of her as destructive. Not only does she embody the grotesque through her hybrid racial identity which places her firmly as 'other', the blame for Caruso's kidnap and subsequent demise is also laid squarely with her due to what the pharmacist believes were her underhand methods of seducing Caruso and the pernicious effects this had.[34] The pharmacist and those writing the newspaper he cites consider Aída, corrupting and diseased, to be symbolically, if not literally, little more than a prostitute, although she does not profess to be anything of the sort. As such, the combination of Aída's sexuality and imminent motherhood are presented as both protective and deleterious, related to — and simultaneously bridging the divide between — motherhood and prostitution, life and death.

As noted above, in *María Antonia* the mother and the whore are counterpointed as two separate characters, La Madrina and María Antonia respectively. Similarly to Aída, however, María Antonia does not describe herself as a prostitute; in fact, she asserts the contrary in an argument with Julián: 'Yo no soy ninguna puta de San Isidro' [I'm not one of those whores from San Isidro] (1025). In spite of this, from the perspective of the majority of those in the community where she lives, her actions are indeed those of a *puta*, for which her alignment with death and her resultant physical demise are considered to be proportionate, if not desirable. This designation, repeated elsewhere in the play such as when Yuyo describes her as nothing but 'una mujer [...] para hacer gozar' [a woman [...] good for screwing] (982), indicates the grammar of control extant in wider society that in this instance seeks to define María Antonia against her wishes. While it elicits her fierce denial and violent response, this framework more generally attempts to cow women into remaining within the defined spaces of particular roles such as mother or prostitute. By describing María Antonia as a whore, the community is then able to blame the protagonist herself for her own death and for the destruction of others. Meanwhile, the motherly figure of La Madrina seeks to support her *ahijada*, but also participates in the restrictive framework of Santería that condemns her.

La Madrina's identification with Batabio and the punishment of death that he pronounces against María Antonia is evident from the play's outset when she petitions the *babalao*, 'Bórrela por dentro. Arránquela de raíz y siémbrela de nuevo' [Cleanse her from within. Pull her up, roots and all, and sow her anew] (947). She views María Antonia's sexual exploits and attitude towards the *orisha* as the source of the problems that have led her to become associated with death and Ikú/Cumachela, and so to murder Julián. Consequently, La Madrina pleads with Batabio to forcibly remove the shadow of physical death from her charge and re-form her in an image that would be both pleasing to the *orisha* and the wider Santería and secular communities. However, such an action would constitute María Antonia's symbolic death by removing the defiance and *hembrismo* that characterize her, and so although on one level La Madrina seeks to ensure what she considers to be María Antonia's physical well-being by preventing her physical demise, on another, through her petition, she is supporting the very death she seeks to avoid. La Madrina is also limited by her reluctance to contradict the *babalao* as a figure of authority in Santería, which is a characteristic typical of her *orisha de cabecera*, Yemayá.[35] As a result, rather than troubling the framework that associates motherhood and sexuality with death, as Anaïse/Frida does, La Madrina is depicted as complicit in María Antonia's inescapable physical and possible spiritual death, despite the fact that the latter is avoided by María Antonia's acceptance of Ochún's manifestation through spirit possession immediately before she dies. The conflict between the two characters continues throughout the play, but lessens in the final scene as the immediacy of María Antonia's death becomes reality, and La Madrina assists the protagonist in her propitiation and invocation of Ochún. Nevertheless, the two never manage to reconcile themselves completely with one another, which itself reflects the impossibility of harmony between Yemayá and Ochún that is encapsulated in the *patakí* and possession performance (as highlighted in earlier chapters). With this in mind, it is important to underline that such a conclusion is not intended to suggest that La Madrina's complicity in María Antonia's death is indicative of the animosity that exists between the two *orisha* as Changó's lovers, but rather in the context of motherhood (Yemayá) clashing with sexuality (Ochún).

In this regard, numerous community members perceive María Antonia's sexuality to be similar to that of a prostitute, and thus they consider it to be dangerous. Courted and rejected by Yuyo and Julián, María Antonia is regarded as a necessary part of their sexual lives but one to be dominated as the male subject seeks to dominate death. This is in keeping with Goodwin's description of a prostitute's sexuality 'as socially undesirable and as illicitly desired', and the prostitute herself as a woman who embodies both the 'other' and the erotic self that desires her.[36] Indeed, the outcome for Julián of his relationship with María Antonia is his own murder when his machismo comes into direct conflict with her *hembrismo*. Conflating different *caminos* of Ochún thus, María Antonia then draws her sexuality and sensuality together with death, as the *orisha* herself does too.

'Le viol dans la violence': Rape, Death and Sacrifice

Bound together with the depiction of motherhood and prostitution in a number of these texts is the sexual violence suffered by many of their protagonists. As mentioned above, Rose, Nirvah and Anaïse are all raped by their aggressors and are unable to remove themselves from the destructive relationships into which they are forced. In her monograph *Conflict Bodies: The Politics of Rape Representation in the Francophone Imaginary*, Jean-Charles (2014) examines rape as a literary trope employed in texts depicting conflict zones in Haiti and other postcolonial francophone nations. As she writes in a section titled 'Le viol dans la violence' [Rape within violence], the theoretical framework of her project is underpinned by 'the embedded containment of *viol* in *violence*', that is, the French word for 'rape' as the constituent element of the word *violence*.[37] Notably, Jean-Charles observes that 'the feminine noun [*la violence*] becomes masculine when it designates the violation of women [*le viol*]', thereby collapsing the masculine and feminine notions into one.[38] Just as rape and violence are thus 'interdependent', so too is rape intertwined with the way in which violence has been both inflicted on bodies in the conflict zones she examines and depicted in literary renditions of the same.

Such a conflict exists in *María Antonia*, where the clash between machismo and *hembrismo* leads in the final act to the protagonist's murder by Carlos, thus exemplifying the link between rape, sacrifice and death indicated above. As mechanisms by which society removes women as active participants, rape and sacrifice subordinate women to men through physical domination, thereby connoting their symbolic or physical death. Necessarily violent and debilitating, rape is presented in these texts as a means to inflict punishment, among other objectives, and it serves this purpose in Hernández Espinosa's play. Here, it reaches its most excessive form in the brutal murder that María Antonia suffers, in which the very symbol of her defiance is violated. This act then establishes complete male dominance over the physical representation of her errant sexuality. While her expression of contempt for the machismo that requires Carlos to act in this manner ensures his response — she tells him, as she did Yuyo, '¡Nunca saques un arma si no vas a usarla! […] ¡Dale!' [Never brandish a weapon if you're not going to use it!

[...] Go on!] (1039) — such goading does not constitute a specific invitation for a violent death, nor does it exculpate Carlos for violating her as he does. In addition to her bodily destruction, this intimate assault also seeks to punish María Antonia for having rejected the passivity that the community requires of those collectively deemed 'prostitutes'. As a corollary, it attempts to deny her any notion that she had of a multifaceted identity or sexual agency.

Similarly, Rose's agreement to exchange her virginity and young body for her father's land in *Colère* does not lessen the charge of rape against le Gorille nor the destruction of her body that it entails. She too suffers physical annihilation, in which her violent rape by le Gorille every day for a month violates her so thoroughly that it leaves her dead at the novella's close. As Chancy concludes, although Rose is limited by the class privilege that she seeks to maintain by submitting herself to le Gorille, the 'atrocities committed against her young body are hateful and irreversible', leading her to lose everything, 'including her self-respect'.[39] The manner in which the abovementioned exchange is agreed also exemplifies the collusion of the legal institutions in the physical and spiritual annihilation of women since, by accompanying her father to the lawyer's office, the lawyer sees Rose as potential payment for the Normils' having contradicted the state and lodged the petition for the return of their land. Her destruction and the extent of le Gorille's violence are then evidenced by her contemplating the possibility of a long-term relationship with her aggressor, as does Nirvah in *Saisons sauvages*. For Rose, it is not only her self-respect that is violated as a result, but also her humanity. At the end of Part Two of the novella, she views herself as a 'panthère lascive et insatiable' ('lascivious and insatiable panther'), one half of the 'couple bestial fait pour s'entendre' (260) ('beastly couple, made for each other', 252) that she forms with le Gorille. Reduced to the same bestial status that her aggressor holds, she descends to her inescapable death alongside him, subjugated by his violent and animalistic sexuality.

In *Fado*, the destruction inherent in rape leaves Anaïse sterile and powerless, and the violence her body suffers is described in terms of butchery and fracturing. Anaïse was not only defenceless when faced with her rapist, she was also put in a position from which she could not seek help since she did not think her father would believe her account. Any agency she thought she had was negated as a result, and this experience contributes to the failure of her marriage given that she cannot provide Léo with the son he desires. She notes that her sense of power as a married woman was an illusion, and so here at the beginning of the novel, her rape has already rendered her symbolically dead: she has sex with her husband out of a sense of 'marital duty', is unable to fulfil the role of mother that he expects of her, and, following their divorce, invites the pity of her neighbours and the unwanted flirtatious conduct of her boss. In short, her childhood experience has left her unable to fulfil the obligations placed on her by society to participate as it requires. It is not until Anaïse begins to explore her sexuality as an active participant that she manages to challenge the norms of bourgeois society which have designated her a failed woman. In so doing, she reconstitutes her sense of self, from which she draws the strength to refuse to be drawn back into such a framework when she conceives.

Initially intertwined with her repeated violation, death is then transformed into a transitional process, based on her exercising her sexuality, that permits liberation from the violence to which she has been subjected and the constraints thus imposed. As Jean-Charles charges in her introduction, the silences surrounding rape and its representation must be interrogated and unsettled, which is intrinsically linked to being able to hear 'the "subaltern" "speak" about sexual violence' in literary and real-world contexts.[40] In *Fado*, this narrative is voiced by Anaïse/Frida through the actions she takes. As concluded in Chapter 3, it is by expressing her sexuality framed by Vodou spirituality that Anaïse/Frida bridges the divide to find life in death, deliverance in damnation.

This idea of reconstitution leads us to consider the concept of sacrifice and its presentation within the frameworks of Santería and Vodou. In this context, it is a notion that provides the possibility for redemption in contradistinction to the physical destruction that rape and male-oriented eroticism engender. Texts such as *Del rojo de su sombra*, *Clair de manbo* and *María Antonia* run counter to the conclusion by Bataille that a necessary element of sacrifice is that 'the offering is rescued from all utility'.[41] For Bataille, the process of sacrifice is linked to sexuality through the association already extant between death and sexuality, as well as the idea of continuity contained therein.[42] Moreover, they are intertwined through the way in which the sacrificial victim is penetrated and laid open to the violence involved in the ritual. This is similar to the idea that, within the framework of eroticism, a woman is the object of the violence fashioned upon her by the male erotic subject. In such a context, it is necessary therefore for the person sacrificed to be a passive woman who is denied agency as the erotic object and whose death expresses a finality that precludes any subsequent utility, since in sacrifice she passes back to the immanence from whence she came.[43] The texts studied here dispute this formulation of sacrifice as in each example the female protagonist exercises her agency, has maintained a link with the physical world by virtue of its coexistence with the spirit world, and continues to be of use after her death. In *Del rojo de su sombra*, Zulé confronts her impending death as *dueña* of her *gagá*, having already rejected the entreaties of members of the community to avoid a confrontation with Similá and the latter's repeated offers for an alliance, itself contrary to the interests of her *sosyete*. Aware of the risk she faces by refusing to cede to the *bòkò* and then briefly vacillating on the battlefield, Zulé's sacrifice at the hands of Jérémie Candé/Carfú ensures the continued independence of her *gagá* and sees her obstruct in death the violence of patriarchal domination that Similá represents.

This safeguarding of a *manbo*'s community through her sacrifice is found at the close of Victor's *Clair de manbo*, where Madan Sorel lures the *bòkò* Djo Kokobe to her *peristil* with the promise to submit to his sexual domination after he has attacked the mapou that links her to the spirit world. Tricking him by lying on the cloth covering the *vèvè* that is the source of her power, Madan Sorel ensures that Djo's fate is sealed as soon as he penetrates her: the assault awakens the *vèvè*, which then unravels itself to encompass the two of them, killing them both and destroying Djo's soul with its power. In an act that expresses her sexual agency and her position as both erotic subject and object, Madan Sorel sacrifices herself in order to prevent the *bòkò* presiding over the region, thereby assuring the well-being of her lover Sonson Piripit and the wider community. Although María Antonia's death in Hernández Espinosa's play is not for the benefit of the Santería and secular communities amongst which she lives, it can be seen as a necessary step in the continuation of the struggle against male dominance and control of women's sexuality. Complex in its presentation since it both connotes the imposition of male authority and its subversion, her death and simultaneous possession by Ochún are framed as her physical destruction for transgressing the norms of Santería and secular society, but also as the possibility that is offered to the many María Antonias who follow to further undermine the construct that requires them to deny sexual agency in the face of machismo. By means of her association with the *orisha*, she is then able to return and offer advice within the context of Santería, as Herrera depicts in 'Conversación con María Antonia (cuarenta años después)'.

Through an exploration of death and sexuality across the fictional works studied, it becomes apparent that the inescapable contemplation of death alongside sexuality serves to illuminate a discourse in Caribbean fiction that sees the coexistence of these two notions indicate possibility for women instead of complete annihilation on both the physical and spiritual planes. Based on notions of female sexual agency and of death as a transitional process, these fictional texts reflect the complex manner in which sexuality, death, prostitution, motherhood and sacrifice are formulated through Santería and Vodou. Victims and survivors of sexual violence are able to voice their experiences within these frameworks as well, permitting their narratives to be heard. For some, the inescapable death that their repeated physical violation connotes sees them reduced to subhuman figures, thus categorizing them alongside their aggressors as well as denying their agency as living humans. For others, Santería and Vodou permit the expression of their sexuality on their own terms, and thus serve to contest death and sacrifice as the negation of utility in spite of the violence inherent in these individuals' subjugation. In conjunction with the other religions and religious traditions invoked in this discussion — and the book as a whole — the texts examined thus convey the resistance that has long been an integral part of, and indeed a founding notion within, African-derived rites and practices in the Caribbean. Moreover, although the literary texts studied are but a sample of a wider corpus of works, they articulate a series of narratives that constitute an important source of knowledge which must be taken into account when seeking to conceptualize gender and sexuality from a Caribbean perspective.

Notes to Chapter 5

1. Brown 2010: 360–61.
2. See Beasley 2010: 43; Smith 2012: 125; Brown 2010: 357, 368.
3. Brown 2010: 358.
4. Bolívar Aróstegui 1990: 96.
5. Lachatañeré 1992: 23–26.
6. This takes place in the XXIe Station, titled 'Un successeur né d'une étoile et du rire de Baron-la-Croix' [A successor born of a star and Baron-la-Croix's laughter] (84–87). The fruit of a

pregnancy much acclaimed in the following scene, the monster then born is later regarded a genius, in a direct parody of descriptions of Jean-Claude Duvalier's childhood and adolescence (88–90; 112–16).

7. Martiatu 2004a: 51.
8. Martiatu 1984: 43.
9. Michel 2010: xvii, xxvi.
10. Foucault 1984: 141; 1990: 125.
11. Ibid. 1984: 152; 1990: 135.
12. Bataille 1987: 101; 1986: 100. This 1986 edition of Mary Dalwood's English translation of *L'Érotisme* is entitled *Erotism: Death and Sensuality*, in spite of the translation of *érotisme* as 'eroticism' in the text. The original 1962 translation was entitled *Death and Sensuality: A Study of Eroticism and the Taboo*. The present discussion will employ 'eroticism' as the term found most commonly in translations and criticism of Bataille, while the wider concept of sexuality incorporates eroticism within it.
13. Bataille 1976: 12; 1991: 16.
14. Bataille 1986: 102.
15. Baudrillard 1976: 237, 241.
16. See Baudrillard 1976: 221–26.
17. Bronfen & Goodwin 1993: 17.
18. Ibid.: 5. The English translation of Ariès's work is titled *The Hour of Our Death*.
19. Ibid.: 13.
20. Bataille 1987: 47.
21. Habermas 1987: 230; Bataille 1987: 64; 1976: 88.
22. Guerlac 1990: 92–93.
23. Bataille 1987: 25.
24. Deive 1988: 139.
25. The translation of the term *ahijada* in English is 'goddaughter', while 'La Madrina' is 'godmother'. However, as the woman who raised María Antonia in the absence of her parents, the relationship between La Madrina and the protagonist is also similar to that of a mother and daughter. La Madrina petitions 'Yemayá Olókun, madre de agua' [Yemayá Olokun, mother of the waters] with the invocation in Lucumí: 'wanaché ilé wanaché abalonké wanaché aina wanaché Beyi Oro. Wanaché Dáda. Wanaché taekué kaidé alabá konkido. Oloddumare!' (1039). In her *Anagó: vocabulario lucumí (el yoruba que se habla en Cuba)*, Cabrera states that this invocation asks for *aché* and the blessing of the *orisha* and of the Ibeyi (twins) (1970b: 315).
26. Franco 1988: 507.
27. Kristeva 1987: 239.
28. Goodwin 1993: 157.
29. Ibid.: 158.
30. The first verse of Shirley's poem reads: 'The glories of our blood and state | Are shadows, not substantial things; | There is no armour against Fate; | Death lays his icy hand on kings: | Sceptre and Crown | Must tumble down, | And in the dust be equal made | With the poor crookèd scythe and spade' (in Quiller-Couch 1901: 296).
31. Goodwin 1993: 159.
32. Ibid.: 158.
33. Jean-Charles 2006: 7.
34. As shown in Chapter 1, Aída's and her daughter Enriqueta's Chinese and black racial heritage links them with Jérémie Candé. Due to this specific hybridity they are considered as the dangerous 'other', destructive yet strangely appealing, and therefore rejected by the different levels of society.
35. Bolívar Aróstegui 1990: 95.
36. Goodwin 1993: 159.
37. Jean-Charles 2014: 56.
38. Ibid.: 55.
39. Chancy 2004: 311.

40. Jean-Charles 2014: 5, 12.
41. Cited in Botting & Wilson 1997: 213.
42. Bataille 1987: 91.
43. Botting & Wilson 1997: 213.

CONCLUSION

This book has drawn together a number of Cuban, Haitian and other Caribbean novels and plays in order to analyze the manner in which issues of resistance, gender and sexuality are explored in these works within the frameworks of Santería and Vodou. Focusing on the central theme of the body as the point at which many discourses intersect, it has demonstrated the importance of foregrounding the voice of the marginalized when constructing a narrative that seeks to recognize women as active participants in Caribbean society and historical discourse. The consequent acknowledgement of the plurality of experiences that such a narrative provides and questioning of patriarchal discourses so often espoused by dominant voices in society then enable the complex nature of religious, social and political life in Cuba, Haiti and the wider Caribbean to be more fully appreciated. Moreover, by writing works of fiction positioned within African-derived religious traditions, the authors of these texts are able to draw on worldviews that permit the collapse of divisions within concepts such as gender, sexuality and sexual identities, womanhood and identity politics within an interconnected, trans-Caribbean space, while recognizing the contiguous nature of the physical and spiritual planes and of life and death. In so doing, they provide a space for resistance, as well as a complex and arguably more complete rendering of contemporary lived experiences in the region when compared to official discourse which has limited, if not written out, these narratives. By way of drawing conclusions, this final section will look to the contemporary political and social contexts in Haiti and Cuba and the continuing narratives surrounding gender, sexuality and resistance that have been articulated in fiction and personal testimony. In so doing, it will signal some of the ways in which these concepts continue to intersect in present-day narratives across the Caribbean, both within the context of African-derived religions and beyond.

On the 12 January 2010, the devastating earthquake that struck Port-au-Prince, Gressier, Carrefour, Léogâne and other surrounding towns and villages in Haiti claimed up to 316,000 lives and injured thousands more.[1] The *goudougoudou*, a Kreyòl term used to denote the earthquake, led to a peak population of 1.5 million people living in internally displaced persons' (IDP) camps — many for several years — and an ever-increasing death toll due to inadequate shelter and safety, subsequent natural disasters and a deadly cholera epidemic (the latter a previously eradicated disease in Haiti which was reintroduced by MINUSTAH troops).[2] The responses to the earthquake and its aftermath by ordinary citizens, statespersons, celebrities, the media and governmental and non-governmental entities on the national and international stages has been analyzed in detail, but here I want to turn to works undertaken by Haitian authors, scholars and activists in the months and years that followed.[3] In a collection of essays on which she had been working prior to the earthquake but that was published the following September, Edwidge Danticat employs Albert Camus's phraseology to charge that writers 'create dangerously', an exhortation that she interprets as one of memorial, one which sees writers, 'in the face of both external and internal destruction, [...] still trying to create as dangerously [...] as though each piece of art were a stand-in for a life, a soul, a future'.[4] This 'revolt against silence', in Danticat's words, is for Martin Munro in his analysis of the collection 'as much, if not more, about style and the act of writing [...] as it is about outward, political gestures of insubordination'.[5] In a similar vein, scholar and performance artist Gina Athena Ulysse has called for resistance through the act of creation, repeating on numerous occasions that 'Haiti needs new narratives', a 'refrain' that thus earnt its place as the title of her trilingual 'post-quake chronicle'.[6] These representations of Haiti, however, are not just 'to explicate its myriad contradictions', but also to 'fill the lacuna of stories from Haitian perspectives with counter-narratives about the earthquake and its aftermath'.[7]

Indeed, the imbalance between 'mainstream constructions of the disaster' and these counter-narratives has been somewhat ameliorated in the years that have followed, with 'critical perspectives' incorporated into human rights reports, anthropological analyses and collections of oral histories that '[center] the voices and lived experiences of Haitian and Diaspora women'.[8] In his monograph *Humanitarian Aftershocks in Haiti*, Schuller not only points to other scholars who have sought to do this, with Myriam Chancy and Gina Athena Ulysse among them, but also is careful to structure his text around extended transcripts of interviews he and members of his team conducted in the IDP camps, allowing 'these people's analyses and lived experiences' to serve as the overarching narrative in his book.[9] For their part, editors of *Lavil: Life, Love and Death in Port-au-Prince* Peter Orner and Evan Lyon (2017) too foreground the voices of their participants in a collection that is almost exclusively comprised of oral testimonies accompanied by short biographies. Beyond the necessary transcription and translations into English, the editors eschew explanations and interpretations of the accounts they collated, preferring instead 'to help debunk oversimplified notions of life in Haiti and in Port-au-Prince in particular, by providing a curious reader with a multiplicity of voices from the city' (20).[10] As Danticat states in her foreword to the volume, 'the voices here [...] speak for themselves, [...] tell their own stories' and in so doing offer testimonials that examine life after the earthquake but also situate lived experience within a wider trajectory of recent Haitian political and social history.[11] The latter of these is particularly important, since, as Schuller, Chancy, Ulysse, Danticat and Orner and Lyon all indicate in their work, the earthquake — while devastating — was one among a series of natural and 'unnatural' disasters, to use Schuller's term, that Haiti has suffered from the colonial period to the present day.[12] In order to counter reductive, oversimplified characterizations such as the oft-repeated line that 'Haiti is the poorest country in the western hemisphere', a space must be provided for these voices to articulate their experiences and appropriately contextualize the earthquake and its aftermath within a larger narrative.

Throughout this book we have witnessed some of the many impositions made upon women's bodies and different ways in which women have resisted subjugation to violent patriarchal social and political frameworks. Sexual and gender-based violence suffered by women has been a key theme voiced through many of the narratives analyzed here and is one that continues in post-earthquake literature. Importantly, as Jean-Charles reminds us, it is imperative to avoid 'the pitfalls that only associate rape with moments of political unrest or instability' since rape and sexual violence must be named 'as a facet of gender oppression and politics no matter the situation surrounding its occurrence'.[13] With this in mind, she points to reports such as *Our Bodies Are Still Trembling: Haitian Women's Fight Against Rape*, published collectively in July 2010 and updated in January 2011, which detail the ways in which grassroots women's groups have sought justice for those who have suffered sexual violence.[14] She writes that 'the testimonials included illustrate that victim/survivors are speaking subjects and are not mute or muted objects of political rapes'; by giving them a voice, this 'disrupts the notion of survivors confined to silence' and also indicates that 'the silence in question belongs to a broader cultural tendency that ignores the narratives of rape'.[15]

The focus Jean-Charles places on survivors — and on women more generally — as 'speaking subjects' is a key concern expressed in Haitian author Makenzy Orcel's work. His 2016 novel, *L'Ombre animale* [Animal Shadow] (2016a), recipient of numerous literary prizes, comprises the reflections of a dead woman for whom the mere fact of her demise is not particularly remarkable, but rather the perspective and relationship that she is able to articulate between life and death — and life in death — now that she has passed away.[16] In an interview with Augustin Trapenard on his *Boomerang* radio show, Orcel remarks that it had always struck him that women were ever-present in Haitian society but little heard (2016b). He describes this as a 'silence assez pesant' [quite heavy silence] and continues to state that 'moi, je voulais éclater, briser ce silence... leur donner une voix' [personally, I wanted to smash, shatter this silence... to give them a voice]. Indeed, it is in death that Orcel's narrator finds her voice and is able to explore both her lived experience and that of others, leading to a deeper understanding of their circumstances. Having died, 'cette nuit-là j'ai eu l'impression de découvrir le village pour la première fois, je dirais qu'il s'est révélé à moi comme s'il m'avait toujours été étranger' [that night I had the impression of discovering the village for the first time, I would say that it revealed itself to me as if, for me, it had always been foreign] (Orcel 2016a: 213). With this new perspective, the narrator examines her relationships with her father, Makenzy, and the object of her desire, Orcel, reflections she makes with the drumming that punctuates Vodou ceremonies continuing in the background.[17] Through 'le langage des tambours' (the language of the *tanbou*) whose 'rythme se frayait un passage secret' [rhythm cleared a secret passage], the narrator perceives the blurred distinction between reality and dreams in which Orcel was not physically but only spiritually present (212). Later, still accompanied by the *tanbou*, she then recounts the ways in which Makenzy had betrayed his people to the 'salivating wolves' for remuneration, be it in convincing them that the 1978 massacre of Creole pigs was justified or that the anti-superstition campaign which attacked Vodou was 'un obstacle à la civilisation' [an obstacle to civilization] (217). Similarly to the protagonist of Kettly Mars's *Fado* who departs in a death that signifies life, a damnation that is deliverance, Orcel's narrator here is only able to explore life in death due to her demise prior to the novel's start since — in the author's own words — 'le vivant, [...] il n'a aucun pouvoir sur le passé, le futur n'existe pas. Et le mort, il est dans la vérité, il domine tout, il comprend tout' [the living [...] have no power over the past, the future doesn't exist. The dead are in truth, they master everything, understand everything].[18]

For Orcel in *L'Ombre animale*, therefore, the mere fact of being alive is not necessary for his female narrator to gain a voice or to be a survivor. This interplay between life and death is a key theme in his first novel, *Les Immortelles* [The Immortal Women] (2010), which was first published less than a year after the earthquake.[19] Dedicated to 'toutes les putes de la Grand-Rue emportées par le violent séisme du 12 janvier 2010' [all the whores of the Grand-Rue carried off by the violent earthquake of 12 January 2010] (Orcel 2010: 7), the novel recounts the story of an unnamed prostitute, 'la petite', who is killed during the earthquake and whose account is told through first-hand narration by an unnamed friend and fellow prostitute. By writing la petite's story, Orcel not only gives her the voice that she was denied in life and at the moment of her death, but also breaks the silence imposed on the other prostitutes of Grand-Rue in the aftermath of the earthquake; as the narrator charges the writer transforming her oral history into a written account, 'je raconte cette histoire pour que toi, l'écrivain, [...] tu immortalises toutes les putains de la Grand-Rue emportées par *cette chose*' [I'm telling this story so that you, the writer, [...] immortalize all the Grand-Rue hookers carried off by *that thing*] (45). Furthermore, through the voices of all the *immortelles* working on Grand-Rue, Orcel foregrounds the many unnamed and marginalized individuals who died in the earthquake and whose stories were not told in public accounts of the event. This 'tension [...] between the need for silence [...] and [the] equally pressing desire to bear testimony' is key to Marvin Victor's debut novel *Corps mêlés* [Tangled Bodies] (2010) too, as Munro (2014: 96) writes.[20] Narrating a mother's loss of her daughter, the novel also explores the close relationship between life and death, with the daughter's burial in the rubble of their house serving as the impetus for Ursula's telling of her own story: her difficult conception and subsequent birth in the sea, the interplay between 'sex, love, bodies and death' and indeed the link of 'motherhood and [...] womanhood to trauma and death'.[21] Continuing the narratives that interweave sexuality, motherhood and death examined throughout this book, these post-earthquake novels fulfil their objective of allowing the silenced to be heard and resisting the hegemony of the 'mainstream constructions of the disaster' noted above.

When discussing women as 'speaking subjects' in this particular context, it is worth briefly considering the narrator's designation of the earthquake as '*cette chose*' in *Les Immortelles*. As Schuller observes, the words in Kreyòl for 'catastrophe' and 'disaster' are often avoided by commentators in Haiti when speaking about the earthquake, which was also long the case for the specific term for earthquake in Kreyòl, *tranblemanntè*. Instead, 'it was known as various names, including *Douz*

(12), *bagay la* (the thing), *evenman nan* (the event) or *goudougoudou* (an onomatopoeia mimicking the rumbling sound of the earth moving)', terms used out of respect for those who died and also to avoid evoking memories of the event.[22] The narrator's choice of *'cette chose'* — a French-language version of the Kreyòl *bagay la* — underscores that she too is a speaking subject who decides to honour la petite through her avoidance of the term earthquake and, in so doing, maintains a distance from the event but a proximity to la petite and the other victims. Earlier in the novel, she denotes the building in which la petite was entombed as 'ce monstre' [that monster] (32), this structure being the physical manifestation of the earthquake that killed her. Orcel uses the same term repeatedly in the chapter of *L'Ombre animale* titled 'la nuit des loups' [the night of the wolves], in which he explores the occupation of Haiti as 'un des visages du néocolonialisme' [one of the faces of neocolonialism].[23] These 'salivating wolves', or indeed 'monsters' as they become (217), represent the neocolonial policies of the United States in Orcel's novel, whereby individuals — here Makenzy — are paid to undermine the community's welfare in order to benefit the neocolonial power, which in turn devours its subjects (227). The image of the monster that has long ravaged Haiti is one that filmmaker Raoul Peck (2013) invokes in his documentary *Assistance mortelle* [Fatal Assistance], describing 'la dictature de l'aide' [the dictatorship of aid] — that is, the longstanding, overwhelming presence of NGOs and international/United Nations entities on the ground in Haiti — as 'violente, arbitraire, aveugle, imbue d'elle-même; un monstre paternaliste qui balaie tout sur son passage' ('violent, arbitrary, blind, full of itself; a paternalistic monster that sweeps away anything in its path').[24] The effects of this subjugation of the Haitian state and its citizens are such that scholars of disaster vulnerability and response have employed the term 'unnatural disaster' to denote the consequences of the exploitation and isolation of Haiti and the subsequent neoliberal and/or neocolonial policies that national and international entities have implemented.[25] The 'massive urban migration [to] and slumification of Port-au-Prince' engendered by these policies resulted in a higher overall death toll and an increase in the number of IDPs who were housed in camps.[26] If in Orcel's novels we hear the voices of those consumed by the 'monstre' of neocolonial policies in Haiti, in Kettly Mars's first post-earthquake novel, *Aux frontières de la soif* (2013), these voices speak of the ongoing consequences of these policies, from the precariousness of daily life in the IDP camps to the exploitation and commodification — alongside the solidarity — of their residents.[27]

In *Aux frontières de la soif*, Mars depicts the movements of her male protagonist, Fito, between the spaces occupied by those working on behalf of NGOs involved in the relief effort — such as Fito himself — and the Canaan IDP camp, which he frequents at night in order to bury his grief and frustration in the nubile bodies of young girls. The pimp whom Fito contracts to procure these girls regards them as goods to be sold, reducing them to 'la chair tendre [qui] se vendait au prix de la faim et de la soif' [tender flesh which was sold at the price of hunger and thirst] (Mars 2013: 94). For their part, the girls recount the difficulties of surviving the earthquake and then the IDP camps, outlining the circumstances that led them to work for 'l'oncle' [the uncle], as the pimp is known. In Schuller's discussion of the 'gender of aid', the testimonial of his interviewee Malya Villard-Appolon describes a similar situation, whereby in order to receive ration cards distributed in the camps, 'a young girl in need is forced to sleep with the person [...]. What does she get with this card? A little rice'.[28] Employing Peck's notion of 'la dictature de l'aide', a parallel can be drawn between the girls in Mars's novel, those in Villard-Appolon's account and Rose in Chauvet's *Colère*, whose rape is analyzed in Chapter 4 within the frame of destructive masculinity and sexual subjugation. As Jean-Charles underscores in reference to Rose's repeated sexual violation, 'under the conditions of terror fear obliterates the option of consent' and so the extent to which Rose is free in her choice to exchange her body for her family's land is questionable, especially given the context of a dictatorship in which women's bodies were seized by the state and the ways in which she seeks to avoid complete submission to her rapist.[29] Some of the girls in *Aux frontières de la soif* also speak of having chosen to work for l'oncle; however, as exploited and dehumanized subjects of a larger social and political system that denies the ability to choose, they too inhabit a space in which their agency is curtailed. Such an observation intersects with the analysis of death, sexuality, rape and prostitution offered in Chapter 5, which underscores the wider frameworks of sexual violence extant outside situations of political unrest and authoritarian regimes that Jean-Charles charges us as readers to recognize. In this regard, the manner in which Vodou permeates both Orcel's novels and Mars's earlier works is also evident here, notably in the way in which doubling is central to the girls' experiences when they have sex with clients.[30] The *marasa* and *marasa twa* that are central to Anaïse/Frida's reconstitution of self in *Fado* are reflected in the dissociation of Ketia from her body in this novel, a process through which she becomes the victor in a spiritual battle with a demon and is saved by the ingenuity of her *loup-garou* or *soucouyan* grandmother (the latter of whom is reminiscent of Madan Sorel in Gary Victor's *Clair de manbo* discussed in Chapter 4).

Moving beyond literature and testimonials that foreground Haitian voices, the 2010 earthquake and other natural and 'unnatural' disasters — both in Haiti and the wider region — are key concerns in Cuban, Dominican and other Caribbean narratives published in the same period. In his chronicle and photojournalistic essay, *Puertos príncipes: temblemos todos* [Port-au-Princes: May We All Tremble] (2015), Puerto Rican journalist and photographer Huáscar Robles Carrasquillo summarizes his experiences reporting shortly after the earthquake, recounting his first-hand observations of the aftermath of the disaster while framing it by his prior and subsequent work with Haitians who were resident in or visiting Puerto Rico. In his discussion of sexual violence in the IDP camps researched on a subsequent visit, Robles Carrasquillo reflects on the myth propagated about them as 'cuna de lobos y centro de iniquidades' [the cradle of wolves and centre of wickedness], while attempting to portray a complex image of the social and political realities lived therein.[31] For his part, Cuban author and poet Orlando Andrade examines the circumstances of an earlier period of violence and unrest in his novel *Mesyè Prezidan* [Mr President] (2014), namely that of the 2004 overthrow of former Haitian president Jean-Bertrand Aristide. Exploring the notion of power within this context Andrade's narrative comprises prose, poetry, theatrical dialogue and monologue, changing format in a manner akin to Chauvet's *Folie*, a novella that too scrutinizes the concept of power, but in Duvalierist Haiti. As texts that depict the crossing of boundaries and divisions, both literally and conceptually, *Puertos príncipes* and *Mesyè Prezidan* evoke an image that Munro employs in concluding his analysis of *Corps mêlés* and *Les Immortelles*: 'one might say [...] that the earthquake has reopened various kinds of frontiers and brought into sharp focus the frontier related elements of Haitian and Caribbean living that are the unfinished legacies of the past'. This experience, he continues, 'communicates the idea that the post-earthquake frontier is at once a place and a time that render uncertain and unclear the boundary between life and death, human and animal, past and present and home and exile'.[32] Such frontiers, Munro underlines, have long been in place and as this book has demonstrated, have been important sites of enquiry for authors writing narratives that draw on African-derived religions like Santería and Vodou.

Turning to the physical border between Haiti and the Dominican Republic, Maria Cristina Fumagalli writes that 'literary and artistic interventions [...] do not always support dominant discourses', with the texts she focuses on identifying the 'borderland [...] as a multi-ethnic contact zone and a transnational territory'.[33] This is particularly the case, Fumagalli notes, when examining religions such as Haitian Vodou and Dominican Vodú, as we have seen in reference to Mayra Montero's novels discussed in Chapter 1. Rita Indiana's work is especially important in this regard, one example of which is her music video 'Da pa lo do' [There's enough for both] (2010) that Fumagalli later analyzes. Constituting one of Indiana's responses to the 2010 earthquake, the video rejects the notion of inherently irreconcilable differences between Dominicans and Haitians and instead depicts a single representative from each nation who embraces his counterpart on the border. This event is facilitated and presided over by Indiana, who here embodies the associated religious figures of the Catholic Virgin Mary, the *lwa* Ezili Dantò and her Dominican Vodú/Gagá counterpart, Metresilí. Representing each of these at once, the border she straddles thus becomes a site of unity rather than hostility, with the blue and white mantle under which these three religious figures come together replacing the divisive 'veil' of the border.[34] Moreover, through the pendant worn by the Virgin Mary/Ezili Dantò/Metresilí figure, the video invokes the twin *lwa* — the *marasa* and *marasa twa* — reinforced by triads formed in the video, symbolizing two nations who imagine themselves as part of the same island.[35] This traversing of borders and particularly the Haitian-Dominican border, is a recurrent theme in Indiana's novels, both in terms of the physical movement of people and goods as well as the interconnectedness of religious practices and traditions. In *La estrategia de Chochueca* [Chochueca's Strategy] (2003), *Papi* (2005), *Nombres y animales* [Names and Animals] (2013) and *La mucama de Omicunlé*, the precariousness of daily life for Haitians and Dominicans of Haitian descent in the Dominican Republic is a recurrent theme, both groups of which are increasingly presented as undesirable or expendable commodities. As noted in the Introduction, this trend culminates in the negation of their humanity in *La mucama de Omicunlé* when, on its opening page, they are showered with lethal gas and collected in refuse trucks. Presented within the novel's dystopian framework as a potentially logical conclusion of official Dominican policy that denies citizenship rights to Dominicans of Haitian descent, Indiana's criticism of the numerous manifestations of anti-Haitianism in the Dominican Republic, as well as the manner in which Dominican society regards the border, is clear not only in her literary work and music videos, but also her journalistic articles and activism.

The complex, trans-Caribbean framework of African-derived religions, indigenous religious practices and Catholic iconography that Indiana presents in *La mucama de Omicunlé* underscores one of the ways in which regional narratives have highlighted the interconnected nature of the region. In her testimonial of the Cuban response to the 2010 earthquake, *Haití en la memoria* [Haiti Remembered] (2014), historian Gloria María León Rojas emphasizes the depth of these ties between Haiti and Cuba in particular. Her text focuses on Cuba's long-standing involvement in Haiti by providing Cuban and Cuban-trained medical personnel and showcases the government-funded aid response through the Escuela Latinoamericana de Medicina [Latin American Medical School] and the Brigada Artística Cubana [Cuban Artistic Brigade]; however, one chapter of the book is dedicated to recounting her personal experience as a teenager with Vodou practice in her native Matanzas and drawing links with the rites and rituals performed in Haiti.[36] The testimony's laudatory tone of the ideology underpinning the international mission aside, León Rojas's chronicle does exemplify the crossing of physical and conceptual frontiers (as Benítez Rojo and Díaz-Quiñones have theorized) that we see in *La mucama de Omicunlé* and Montero's works, not least *Como un mensajero tuyo* and *Del rojo de su sombra*.

Further afield, these links forged through religious practices enable those resident *lòt bò dlo* (lit. on the other side of the water) to maintain ties with the region, a notion explored in numerous works by diasporic Caribbean authors. Cuban and Haitian voices in the diaspora are both numerous and varied, many of which have been analyzed in detail; the small number mentioned here are intended only as examples. With regard to Santería, its role in connecting Cubans in the United States with those on the island is exemplified in Cristina García's *Dreaming in Cuban* (1992) and *The Agüero Sisters* (1997), while it serves as the site of a spiritual depiction of the Bay of Pigs invasion in Raúl de Cárdenas's *Los hijos de Ochún* [The Children of Ochún] (1999). For its part, Vodou serves as a spiritual bridge across the waters and as a site of enquiry in Danticat's *Breath, Eyes, Memory* (1996) and *The Dew Breaker* (2004), Chancy's *Spirit of Haiti* (2003) and Dany Laferrière's *Pays sans chapeau* (2007, first published in 1996) (*Down Among the Dead Men*, 1997).[37] African-derived religions in each of these texts permit a form of coexistence with those 'back home', as it were, be it via spiritual connections between individuals on different sides of the Caribbean Sea, such as Pilar and Celia's relationship in *Dreaming in Cuban*, or in the manner in which Haiti and its diaspora are depicted as the intertwined yet conflicting *marasa*, like in *Breath, Eyes, Memory*. García's use of the Ibeyi in Santería to formulate the relationship between Cuba and its diaspora in *The Agüero Sisters* is indicative of the theme running through all of these works of the multiple levels at which there is disjuncture between the two inherently linked but physically separate groups. As sisters who are *hijas de Ochún* and *de Changó* respectively, the authenticity of Constancia's visceral experience of Cuba in the diaspora — both through Santería and in the wider secular and consumerist North American context — is questioned when counterpointed with that of Reina, who embodies the voluptuousness of Ochún and physically interacts with Changó while she works as an electrician for the Revolutionary government. For Constancia, however, her relationship to Ochún — representative of Cuba and invoked in Miami by both the *babalao* and Constancia herself — is somewhat strained: the destruction the *babalao* sees in Constancia during a *consulta* points to the problems she faces regarding her Cuban identity when divorced from everyday life on the island and thus she must physically return to Cuba in order to resolve these interrelated issues. The presence of Ochún in the diaspora and this fracture of the Cuban population exemplified by the Agüero sisters are also explored in Cárdenas's *Los hijos de Ochún*. Written as a conflict among the *orisha*, the play sees Ochún's body, which is indicative of the physical and cultural space of Cuba, rent by the divided spaces of Miami and Havana.

For each of these authors, Santería and Vodou offer a space for the transmission of knowledge regarding familial histories and experiences, Afro-Cuban and Afro-Haitian culture and integral aspects of everyday life in Cuba and Haiti that inform an individual's perception of what it means to be Cuban or Haitian. This *conocimiento* or *konesans* — ritual knowledge gained through initiation and immersion into the rites and practices of Santería and Vodou respectively — is shown to be an intimate understanding that can only be consolidated by direct interaction with the different protagonists' forebears and/or close reacquaintance with the Cuba or Haiti left behind. *Breath, Eyes, Memory* and *The Dew Breaker* both frame this as spiritual twinning, with Ka's father in the latter describing her as his *tibonanj* and using their journey to Florida to lead her to an understanding of her personal and cultural history as a Haitian born in the diaspora to an exiled Macoute. It is this lack of *konesans* that is indicative of Old Bones's twenty-year absence from Haiti in Laferrière's autobiographical *Pays sans chapeau*, in which his journey to the world of the dead serves as the premise for a much wider exploration of what being Haitian signifies for him and the numerous people he meets. As his novel illustrates, the *konesans* required to access and then return from the 'curious other world among us' (Laferrière 1997: 210), that 'pays où personne ne porte de chapeau' (Laferrière 2007: 270), is gained by way of a first-hand exploration of the multiple layers that comprise the Haitian worldview and a rediscovery of the protagonist's own Haitian identity.[38] Finally, in Chancy's *Spirit of Haiti*, Carmen is called back from Montreal to Haiti by the *lwa* when the corporeal link between her dual cultural heritage manifests itself in the new life she carries. Having met Léah who embodies this notion of *konesans* or *conocimiento* as a blind daughter of Ochún symbolically linked to Yemayá and the Ezilis, Carmen completes the process of initiation into Vodou and it is at this point that she affirms to her unborn child the essential part that Haiti plays in both of their identities.

In short, therefore, consideration of these works from across the Caribbean and its North American diasporas offers further lines of enquiry that enhance the analysis provided here. Contemporary narratives of natural and unnatural disasters — both real and imagined — have forged further connections across the region, while foregrounding the continued importance of African-derived religions as a context in which the tensions between concepts such as death, survival, dehumanization, sexuality, prostitution, motherhood and sexual violence can be articulated and processed. Providing a space for women's and other marginalized individuals' voices to be heard, these novels, testimonies and artistic interventions enable their narrators/protagonists to become 'speaking subjects', resisting hegemonic discourses that would otherwise see them silenced. Santería, Vodou and associated African-derived religious traditions are therefore not only a source of *conocimiento* or *konesans* across the Caribbean, but are also key to understanding the complexities of Cuban, Haitian and wider regional conceptualizations of life and death, power, gender and sexuality as represented in literary texts.

Much of this concluding chapter has focused on the effects of the 2010 earthquake and its aftermath on representations of political and social life in Haiti, including the 'dictatorship of aid' that the international community has imposed during the years that have followed. The period between my research trips to Cuba that bookended this project has also seen notable shifts in international engagement and presence in the region. These have included the reestablishment of diplomatic ties between the United States and Cuban governments — and the subsequent cooling of the warmth of these relations under the new administration — as well as an influx of visitors from the island's northern neighbour that remains above pre-2014 levels. In the aftermath of Hurricanes Irma and Maria, the migration flow of Puerto Ricans to the United States due to the longstanding economic crisis on the island has dramatically increased, while as Naomi Klein (2018) outlines, the politics of disaster capitalism coupled with US colonial policies have become ever more entrenched.[39] Concomitantly, the uncertainty surrounding the Temporary Protected Status for Haitians in the United States put in place following the 2010 earthquake has seen some protected persons seek haven elsewhere, while others contemplate their potential forced return. Unsurprisingly, as after the earthquake in Haiti, Puerto Rican authors and artists such as Mayra Santos-Febres (2018), Edgardo Miranda-Rodríguez (2018a; 2018b) and Awilda Sterling Duprey (2018) are already drawing on African-derived and indigenous religious practices to make sense of Hurricane Maria and its aftermath through embodied, gendered and racialized representations.

In such an environment where interactions continue to increase between populations across the Caribbean and those *lòt bò dlo*, an understanding of the presence, form and function of Santería and Vodou both in literary works and as an inextricable element of Caribbean life and culture is indispensable. Here I have sought to demonstrate some of these complexities, most notably with regard to the manner in which gender and sexuality have been formulated within the Caribbean. Likewise, I have foregrounded the essential contribution made by fictional texts drawing on Santería and Vodou in incorporating the voices of women into the public space of debate. These texts exemplify the crucial roles that women continue to play in society by resisting male hegemony and articulating narratives that are marginalized in male-oriented official accounts. Acknowledgement of this discourse and of the ongoing nature of the conversations they outline is fundamental when seeking to understand the functions of religious traditions in Caribbean society. Equally important is the recognition of women's participation in defining the manner in which they and their sexualities are represented. As sites of resistance and repositories of collective memory, Santería and Vodou continue to serve as a framework through which to question the primacy and exclusivity of official histories, while providing a space for alternative narratives and women's voices to be heard.

Notes to the Conclusion

1. In the introduction to their edited volume, Mark Schuller and Pablo Morales cite official estimates of the number of those who lost their lives as 'up to 316,000' (2012: 1), while Raoul Peck cites figures of 230,000 dead in his 2013 documentary, *Assistance mortelle* [Fatal Assistance]. As Robert Muggah and Athena Kolbe state in their *Los Angeles Times* article, 'Haiti: Why an Accurate Count of Civilian Deaths Matters' (2011), the Haitian government increased its original estimate from 230,000 to 316,000 on the first anniversary of the earthquake, while the 'USAID contractor Tim Schwartz estimated between 46,000 and 85,000 in an unpublished report in May 2011. Small Arms Survey estimated 158,000' (Schuller 2012: 195).
2. Schuller 2016a: 2.
3. To mention just a small number of sources, see, for example: the many works by anthropologist Mark Schuller (2012; 2015; 2016a; 2016b; 2017); Schuller & Morales's edited volume (2012); Munro's edited volume (2010); and Ulysse (2015).
4. Danticat 2010: 13, 20.
5. Ibid.: 11; Munro 2014: 30.
6. Ulysse 2015: 31. Ulysse's *Why Haiti Needs New Narratives: A Post-Quake Chronicle* was published as a single volume in English, Kreyòl and French, a decision made in order to allow Ulysse's essays to reach as wide an audience as possible, both in Haiti and abroad. This sentiment is indicated in a note at the beginning of the Kreyòl translation: 'nou swete tradiksyon an ap pemet lektè kreyolofon yo apresye liv la' [we hope that the translation allows Kreyòl-speaking readers to appreciate the book] (130).
7. Ulysse 2015: 157, 77.
8. Schuller 2016a: 109.
9. Ibid.: 14. To this end, Schuller examines and critiques the position of anthropologists in Haiti — himself included — and the desire to ground narratives in the lived experience of Haitian participants in his book chapter, 'The Anthropological Uses of Haiti: A *Longue Durée* Approach' (2016c).
10. Orner & Lyon 2017: 20.
11. Ibid: 13.
12. Schuller 2016a: 27.
13. Jean-Charles 2014: 68.
14. The initial July 2010 report was published by the Institute for Justice and Democracy in Haiti, the TransAfrica Forum, MADRE, the University of Minnesota Law School and the University of Virginia School of Law. The updated January 2011 version was published by MADRE, the International Women's Human Rights Clinic at the City University of New York School of Law and the Institute for Justice and Democracy in Haiti.
15. Jean-Charles 2014: 68.

16. It should be noted that, in its English-language promotional materials, the publisher has used both *Animal Shadow* and *The Bestial Shadow* as translations of *L'Ombre animale*; see Zulma (2016) and (2017). I have chosen *Animal Shadow* as it is the title to which Zulma gave most prominence in these materials.

17. The author has described this doubling between himself and the two characters as part of the 'dialogue du clair et de l'obscur' [dialogue between light and dark]. He continues, 'moi, je voulais vivre cette expérience donc je me suis coupé en deux. [...] Makenzy, qui est un personnage sombre, très bizarre, et Orcel, qui est plus ou moins lumineux, qui aime le voyage, la mer et tout. Et donc ça m'a permis de vivre aussi l'expérience du livre' [as for me, I wanted to live this experience, so I cut myself in two. [...] Makenzy, who is a shadowy, very strange person and Orcel, who is bright, more or less, who likes travelling, the sea and such. So that allowed me to live the experience of the book too] (2016b).

18. Orcel 2016b.

19. Originally published with Montreal-based publishing house Mémoire d'encrier, *Les Immortelles* was re-published in 2012 with Zulma.

20. Munro 2014: 96.

21. Ibid.: 97, 96.

22. Schuller 2016a: 20.

23. Orcel 2016b.

24. Cited in English in Walsh 2015: 195.

25. See Schuller 2016a: 19–44.

26. Ibid.: 43.

27. It should be noted that, while Mars's *Saisons sauvages* appeared in bookstores on 4 February 2010, by virtue of the timescale of publication and its release less than a month after the earthquake, it fits more closely within the categorization of 'earlier Haitian literature' than 'postquake Haitian literature', to employ Mark Cruse's terms (2013).

28. Schuller 2016a: 102.

29. Jean-Charles 2006: 7–10.

30. I discuss this example of *marasa* consciousness and draw parallels with Danticat's *Breath, Eyes, Memory* in my book chapter 'Capital Prostitution: Voices from the Shadows in Post-Earthquake Haitian Fiction' (2019). This chapter also further analyzes the narratives of prostitution in *Les Immortelles* and *Aux frontières de la soif.*

31. Robles Carrasquillo 2015: 118.

32. Munro 2014: 120, 121.

33. Fumagalli 2015: 19.

34. Ibid.: 353. In her introduction, Fumagalli describes the Haitian-Dominican border as a veil, using the image employed by Edwidge Danticat's protagonist Amabelle Désir in *The Farming of Bones* (2015: 3).

35. Fumagalli 2015: 353–54.

36. León Rojas 2014: 88–94.

37. It is important to note that in Haiti the phrase 'pays sans chapeau' (lit. country without a hat) is employed to refer to the world of the dead. The novel's title in English provides a more overt reference to this.

38. In the English translation this phrase is rendered as the preceding quotation: 'curious other world among us' (210). A literal translation of the French would be 'country where no one wears a hat'.

39. Klein (2007) outlines and examines the notion of disaster capitalism in her earlier book, *The Shock Doctrine: The Rise of Disaster Capitalism*. This has been one of the neoliberal and neocolonial policies long employed in Haiti and the 2010 earthquake served as a further pretext for its escalation.

BIBLIOGRAPHY

ABBEY, SHARON, and ANDREA O'REILLY (eds). 1998. *Redefining Motherhood: Changing Identities and Patterns* (Toronto: Second Story Press)

ABBOTT, ELIZABETH. 1988. *Haiti: The Duvaliers and Their Legacy* (New York: McGraw-Hill)

—— 1991. *Haiti: The Duvaliers and Their Legacy*, rev. edn (New York: Simon and Schuster)

—— 2011. *Haiti: A Shattered Nation* (New York: Overlook Duckworth)

ALEGRÍA PONS, JOSÉ FRANCISCO. 1993. *Gagá y vudú en la República Dominicana: ensayos antropológicos* (Puerto Rico: Ediciones El Chango Prieto)

ANATOL, GISELLE. 2000. 'Transforming the Skin-Shedding Soucouyant: Using Folklore to Reclaim Female Agency in Caribbean Literature', *Small Axe: A Caribbean Journal of Criticism*, 7: 44–59

ANDERSON, BENEDICT. 2006. *Imagined Communities: Reflections on the Origin and Spread of Nationalism*, rev. edn (London: Verso)

ANDRADE, ORLANDO. 2014. *Mesyè Prezidan* (Santiago de Cuba: Editorial Oriente)

ANGLADE DE AGUERREVERE, LUCÍA. 2005. 'Dar voz al silencio: la mujer y la santería en *Las hermanas Agüero* de Cristina García, *Como un mensajero tuyo* de Mayra Montero, y *Querido primer novio* de Zoé Valdés' (unpublished doctoral dissertation, Boston College)

ANIM-ADDO, JOAN. 1996. 'Audacity and Outcome: Writing African-Caribbean Womanhood', in *Framing the Word: Gender and Genre in Caribbean Women's Writing*, ed. by Joan Anim-Addo (London: Whiting & Birch), pp. 210–24

ANTONIN, ARNAUD (dir.). 2010. *Zombi candidat à la présidence, ou Les Amours d'un zombi* (n.p.: Original Production)

APTER, ANDREW. 1991. 'Herskovits's Heritage: Rethinking Syncretism in the African Diaspora', *Diaspora: A Journal of Transnational Studies*, 1(3): 235–60

ARENDT, HANNAH. 1970. *On Violence* (New York: Harcourt Brace & Co)

ARNDT, SUSAN. 1998. *African Women's Literature: Orature and Intertextuality*, trans. by Isabel Cole (Bayreuth: Bayreuth African Studies)

ASTLES, CARIAD. 2009. 'African Presence in Cuban Theatre', in *African Theatre: Diasporas*, ed. by Christine Matzke and Osita A. Okagbue (Woodbridge: James Currey), pp. 26–38

AYORINDE, CHRISTINE. 2004. *Afro-Cuban Religiosity, Revolution, and National Identity* (Gainesville: University Press of Florida)

BALBUENA GUTIÉRREZ, BÁRBARA. 2003. 'La ritualidad en las danzas de la regla de Ocha', in *Rito y representación: los sistemas mágico-religiosos en la cultura cubana contemporánea*, ed. by Yana Elsa Brugal and Beatriz J. Rizk (Madrid: Iberoamericana), pp. 97–108

BARNET, MIGUEL. 1996. 'La posesión', *Tablas*, 4: 14–15

—— 1997. 'La Regla de Ocha: The Religious System of Santería', in *Sacred Possessions: Vodou, Santería, Obeah, and the Caribbean*, ed. by Margarite Fernández Olmos and Lizabeth Paravisini-Gebert (New Brunswick, NJ: Rutgers University Press), pp. 79–100

BARRITEAU, EUDINE (ed.). 2003. *Confronting Power, Theorizing Gender: Interdisciplinary Perspectives in the Caribbean* (Kingston: University of the West Indies Press)

BASCOM, WILLIAM. 1972. *Shango in the New World* (Austin: University of Texas)

BASTIDE, ROGER. 1971. *African Civilisations in the New World*, trans. by Peter Green (London: C. Hurst & Co.)

BASTIEN, RÉMY. 1966. 'Vodoun and Politics in Haiti', in *Religion and Politics in Haiti*, ed. by Harold Courlander and Rémy Bastien (Washington, DC: Institute for Cross-Cultural Research), pp. 39–68

BATAILLE, GEORGES. 1962. *Death and Sensuality: A Study of Eroticism and the Taboo*, trans. by Mary Dalwood (New York: Walker)

——— 1976. 'L'Histoire de l'érotisme', in *Œuvres complètes*, vol. 8 (Paris: Gallimard), pp. 7–165

——— 1986. *Erotism: Death and Sensuality*, trans. by Mary Dalwood (San Francisco: City Lights Books)

——— 1987. 'L'Érotisme', in *Œuvres complètes*, vol. 10 (Paris: Gallimard), pp. 7–270

——— 1991. 'The History of Eroticism', in *The Accursed Share: An Essay on General Economy*, trans. by Robert Hurley, vols 2–3 (New York: Zone Books), pp. 13–191

BAUDRILLARD, JEAN. 1976. *L'Échange symbolique et la mort* (Paris: Gallimard)

——— 1993. *Symbolic Exchange and Death*, trans. by Iain Hamilton Grant (London: Sage Publications)

BEASLEY, MYRON M. 2010. 'Vodou, Penises and Bones: Ritual Performances of Death and Eroticism in the Cemetery and the Junk Yard of Port-au-Prince', *Performance Research: A Journal of the Performing Arts*, 15(1): 41–47

BEAUVOIR, RACHEL. 2003. *Savalou E* (Montreal: CIDIHCA)

BEAUVOIR, SIMONE DE. 1949. *Le Deuxième Sexe* (Paris: Gallimard)

BELISO-DE JESÚS, AISHA. 2015. *Electric Santería: Racial and Sexual Assemblages of Transnational Religion* (New York: Columbia University Press)

BELL, CATHERINE. 1992. *Ritual Theory, Ritual Practice* (Oxford: Oxford University Press)

——— 1997. *Ritual: Perspectives and Dimensions* (New York: Oxford University Press)

BELL-SCOTT, PATRICIA (ed.). 1993. *Double Stitch: Black Women Write About Mothers and Daughters* (New York: Harper Perennial)

BELLEGARDE-SMITH, PATRICK. 2005A. 'The Spirit of the Thing: Religious Thought and Social/Historical Memory', in *Fragments of Bone: Neo-African Religions in a New World*, ed. by Patrick Bellegarde-Smith (Chicago: University of Illinois Press), pp. 52–69

——— 2005B. 'Introduction: What If History Were Written by the Vanquished', in *Fragments of Bone: Neo-African Religions in a New World*, ed. by Patrick Bellegarde-Smith (Chicago: University of Illinois Press), pp. 1–12

BELLEGARDE-SMITH, PATRICK, and CLAUDINE MICHEL. 2006. 'Introduction', in *Haitian Vodou: Spirit, Myth, and Reality*, ed. by Patrick Bellegarde-Smith and Claudine Michel (Bloomington: Indiana University Press), pp. xvii–xxvii

BELLEGARDE-SMITH, PATRICK, and KATE RAMSEY. 2012. 'Media Alerts', *Journal of Haitian Studies*, 18(2): 28–33

BENEDICTY, ALESSANDRA. 2012. 'Towards an Intellectual History of Possession: Reading "la crise" as a Textual Space in Vodou and André Breton's Haitian Lectures and *Nadja*', *Studies in Religion / Sciences Religieuses*, 41(2): 280–305

BENEDICTY-KOKKEN, ALESSANDRA. 2015A. *Spirit Possession in French, Haitian, and Vodou Thought: An Intellectual History* (Lanham, MD: Lexington Books)

——— 2015B. '"The Origins of Totalitarianism": From Resistance to Human Rights in Marie Chauvet's *Les rapaces*', in *Paradoxes of the Postcolonial Feminine*, ed. by Kaiama L. Glover and Alessandra Benedicty-Kokken, special issue of *Yale French Studies*, 128: 57–73

BENÍTEZ ROJO, ANTONIO. 1989. *La isla que se repite: el Caribe y la perspectiva posmoderna* (Hanover: Ediciones del Norte)

——— 2003. 'Creolization and Nation-building in the Hispanic Caribbean', in *A Pepper-pot of Cultures: Aspects of Creolization in the Caribbean*, ed. by Gordon Collier and Ulrich Fleischmann (Amsterdam: Rodopi), pp. 19–27

BERGAN, RENÉE, and MARK SCHULLER (dirs). 2009. *Poto Mitan: Haitian Women, Pillars of the Global Economy* (Watertown, MA: Documentary Educational Resources)

BOLÍVAR ARÓSTEGUI, NATALIA. 1990. *Los orishas en Cuba* (Havana: Ediciones Unión)

BOTTING, FRED, and SCOTT WILSON. 1997. 'Introduction', in *The Bataille Reader*, ed. by Fred Botting and Scott Wilson (Oxford: Blackwell), pp. 1–34

BOURGUIGNON, ERIKA. 1969. 'Haïti et l'ambivalence socialisée: une reconsidération', *Journal de la Société des Américanistes*, 58: 173–205

BRANDON, GEORGE. 1993. *Santeria from Africa to the New World: The Dead Sell Memories* (Bloomington: Indiana University Press)

BRATHWAITE, EDWARD KAMAU. 1974. *Contradictory Omens: Cultural Diversity and Integration in the Caribbean* (Mona: Savacou Publications)

BRENE, JOSÉ RAMÓN. 1992. 'Santa Camila de La Habana Vieja', in *Teatro cubano contemporáneo: antología*, ed. by Carlos Espinosa Domínguez (Madrid: Centro de Documentación Teatral; Sociedad Estatal Quinto Centenario; Fondo de Cultura Económica), pp. 465–554

BRERETON, BRIDGET. 1998. 'Gendered Testimonies: Autobiographies, Diaries and Letters by Women as Sources for Caribbean History', *Feminist Review*, 59: 143–63, <http://www.jstor.org/stable/1395728> [accessed 7 June 2010]

BRERETON, BRIDGET, BARBARA BAILEY, and VERENE SHEPHERD (eds). 1995. *Engendering History: Caribbean Women in Historical Perspective* (London: James Currey)

BRONFEN, ELISABETH, and SARAH WEBSTER GOODWIN. 1993. 'Introduction', in *Death and Representation*, ed. by Sarah Webster Goodwin and Elisabeth Bronfen (Baltimore, MD: Johns Hopkins University Press), pp. 3–25

BROWN, KAREN MCCARTHY. 1997. 'Systematic Remembering, Systematic Forgetting: Ogou in Haiti', in *Africa's Ogun: Old World and New*, ed. by Sandra Barnes, 2nd edn (Bloomington: Indiana University Press), pp. 65–89

——2006. 'Afro-Caribbean Spirituality: A Haitian Case Study', in *Vodou in Haitian Life and Culture: Invisible Powers*, ed. by Claudine Michel and Patrick Bellegarde-Smith (New York: Palgrave Macmillan), pp. 1–26

——2010. *Mama Lola: A Vodou Priestess in Brooklyn*, 3rd edn (Berkeley: University of California Press)

BRUGAL, YANA ELSA, and BEATRIZ J. RIZK (eds). 2003. *Rito y representación: los sistemas mágico-religiosos en la cultura cubana contemporánea* (Madrid: Iberoamericana)

BURTON, RICHARD D. E. 1997. *Afro-Creole: Power, Opposition, and Play in the Caribbean* (Ithaca, NY: Cornell University Press)

BUTLER, JUDITH. 1988. 'Performative Acts and Gender Constitution: An Essay in Phenomenology and Feminist Theory', *Theatre Journal*, 40(4): 519–31

——1993. *Bodies That Matter* (London: Routledge)

CABALLERO, RUFO. 2004. '*María Antonia*: la linealización del montaje vocal', in *Una pasión compartida*, ed. by Inés María Martiatu (Havana: Letras Cubanas), pp. 149–54

CABRANES-GRANT, LEO. 2010. 'Possession, Gender and Performance in Revolutionary Cuba: Eugenio Hernández Espinosa's *María Antonia*', *Theatre Research International*, 35(2): 126–38

CABRERA, LYDIA. 1954. *El monte: igbo finda, ewe orisha, vititinfinda* (Havana: Ediciones C. R.)

——1969. 'Ritual y símbolos de la iniciación en la sociedad secreta Abakuá', *Journal de la Société des Américanistes*, 58: 139–71

——1970A. *La sociedad secreta abakuá: narrada por viejos adeptos*, rev. edn (Miami: Editorial C. R.)

——1970B. *Anagó: vocabulario lucumí (el yoruba que se habla en Cuba)* (Miami: Cabrera y Rojas)

——1980. *Yemayá y Ochún: Kariocha, iyalorichas y olorichas* (New York: Ediciones C. R.)

CÁRDENAS, RAÚL DE. 1999. 'Los hijos de Ochún', in *Presencia negra: teatro cubano de la diáspora (antología crítica)*, ed. by Armando González-Pérez (Madrid: Betania), pp. 143–201

CARPENTIER, ALEJO. 1969. *El reino de este mundo* (Montevideo: Arca)

CASTELLANOS, ISABEL. 2001. 'A River of Many Turns: The Polysemy of Ochún in Afro-Cuban Tradition', in *Òṣun Across the Waters: A Yoruba Goddess in Africa and the Americas*, ed. by Joseph Murphy and Mei-Mei Sanford (Bloomington: Indiana University Press), pp. 34–45

CASTELLANOS LLANOS, GABRIELA. 2006. *Sexo, género y femenismo: tres categorías en pugna* (Cali: Manzana de la Discordia Editores)

CHANCY, MYRIAM J. A. 1997. *Framing Silence: Revolutionary Novels by Haitian Women* (New Brunswick, NJ: Rutgers University Press)

—— 2003. *Spirit of Haiti* (London: Mango)

—— 2004. '"No Giraffes in Haiti": Haitian Women and State Terror', in *Écrire en pays assiégé: Haïti: Writing Under Siege*, ed. by Marie-Agnès Sourieau and Kathleen M. Batulansky (Amsterdam: Rodopi), pp. 303–21

CHARLES, CAROLLE. 1995. 'Gender and Politics in Contemporary Haiti: The Duvalierist State, Transnationalism, and the Emergence of a New Feminism (1980–1990)', *Feminist Studies*, 21(1): 135–64

CHEN, EDITH WEN-CHU. 2008. '"You are like us, you eat *plátanos*": Chinese Dominicans, Race, Ethnicity, and Identity', *Afro-Hispanic Review*, 27(1): 23–40

CINCIR, AMOS. 2012. 'Le Secteur protestant prend le président Martelly au mot', *Le Nouvelliste*, 9 August 2012, <http://www.lenouvelliste.com/article4.php?newsid=107946> [accessed 21 August 2012]

CLARK, MARY ANN. 2004. 'Ambiguities in Santería Possession Trance: Challenges to the Unitary Self', in American Academy of Religion Annual Meeting, San Antonio Texas 20–23 November 2004, <http://www.aarmysticism.org/documents/Clark.pdf> [accessed 10 August 2011]

—— 2005. *Where Men Are Wives and Mothers Rule: Santería Ritual Practices and Their Gender Implications* (Gainesville: University Press of Florida)

CLARK, VÈVÈ A. 1992. 'When Womb Waters Break: The Emergence of Haitian New Theater (1953–1987)', *Callaloo*, 15(3): 778–86

COATES, CARROL F. 1996. 'Folklore in the Theatre of Franck Fouché', *Theatre Research International*, 21(3): 256–61

—— 2006. 'Vodou in Haitian literature', in *Vodou in Haitian Life and Culture: Invisible Powers*, ed. by Claudine Michel and Patrick Bellegarde-Smith (New York: Palgrave Macmillan), pp. 181–98

CONNER, RANDY P. 2005. 'Rainbow's Children: Diversity of Gender and Sexuality in African-Diasporic Spiritual Traditions', in *Fragments of Bone: Neo-African Religions in a New World*, ed. by Patrick Bellegarde-Smith (Chicago: University of Illinois Press), pp. 143–66

CONWAY, FRED. 1978. 'Pentecostalism in the Context of Haitian Religion and Health Practice' (unpublished doctoral dissertation, American University)

COOK, MANUELA. 2003. 'The Woman in Portuguese Fado-singing', *International Journal of Iberian Studies*, 16(1): 19–32

COOPER, CAROLYN. 1993. *Noises in the Blood: Orality, Gender and the 'Vulgar' Body of Jamaican Popular Culture* (London: Macmillan)

COSENTINO, DONALD J. 1993. 'Vodou Vatican: A Prologomenon for Understanding Authority in a Syncretic Religion', *Caribbean Quarterly*, 39(3/4): 100–07

—— 1995. 'Envoi: The Gedes and Bawon Samdi', in *Sacred Arts of Haitian Vodou*, ed. by David J. Cosentino (Los Angeles: University of California Los Angeles Fowler Museum of Cultural History), pp. 399–415

COURLANDER, HAROLD. 1960. *The Drum and the How: Life and Lore of the Haitian People* (Berkeley: University of California Press)

COURLANDER, HAROLD, and RÉMY BASTIEN. 1966. *Religion and Politics in Haiti* (Washington, DC: Institute for Cross-Cultural Research)

CROS SANDOVAL, MERCEDES. 2006. *Worldview, the Orichas, and Santeria: Africa to Cuba and Beyond* (Gainesville: University of Florida Press)

CRUSE, MARK. 2013. 'Place in Haitian Literature Since the 2010 Earthquake', *The Geographical Review*, 103(4): 469–83

CURBELO, ALBERTO. 2004. 'La voz del otro: tradición y oralidad en El Cerro de *María Antonia*', in *Una pasión compartida*, ed. by Inés María Martiatu (Havana: Letras Cubanas), pp. 117–37

CURBELO MEZQUIDA, ALBERTO. 2009. 'El alba del negro en el teatro cubano', in Eugenio Hernández Espinosa, *Quiquiribú Mandinga: selección y prólogo de Alberto Curbelo Mezquida* (Havana: Letras Cubanas), pp. 5–32

DANTICAT, EDWIDGE. 1996. *Breath, Eyes, Memory* (London: Abacus)

——2004. *The Dew Breaker* (London: Abacus)

——2010. *Create Dangerously: The Immigrant Artist at Work* (Princeton, NJ: Princeton University Press)

DAVIES, CATHERINE. 1993. '*María Antonia*: tragedia cubana, tanto africana como hispana', in *Actas del Primer Congreso Anglo-Hispano. Tomo II: Literatura*, ed. by Alan Deyermond and Ralph Penny (Madrid: Castalia), pp. 287–97

DAYAN, COLIN. 2011. 'The Gods in a Trunk, or Chauvet's Remnants', presentation given at Barnard College, New York, 21 November 2011, <http://www.youtube.com/watch?v=M_W8kagMAB4> [accessed 18 May 2012]

——2015. 'The Gods in the Trunk, or Writing in a Belittered World', in *Revisiting Marie Vieux Chauvet: Paradoxes of the Postcolonial Feminine*, ed. by Kaiama L. Glover and Alessandra Benedicty-Kokken, special issue of *Yale French Studies*, 128: 92–112

DAYAN, JOAN. 1991. 'Reading Women in the Caribbean: Marie Chauvet's *Love, Anger, and Madness*', in *Displacements: Women, Tradition, Literatures in French*, ed. by Joan DeJean and Nancy K. Miller (Baltimore, MD: Johns Hopkins University Press), pp. 228–53

——1995. *Haiti, History and the Gods* (Berkeley: University of California Press)

——1996. 'Erzulie: A Women's History of Haiti?', in *Postcolonial Subjects: Francophone Women Writers*, ed. by Mary Jean Green, Karen Gould, and Micheline Rice-Maximin (Minneapolis: University of Minnesota Press), pp. 42–60

——1997. 'Vodou, or the Voices of the Gods', in *Sacred Possessions: Vodou, Santería, Obeah, and the Caribbean*, ed. by Margarite Fernández Olmos and Lizabeth Paravisini-Gebert (New Brunswick, NJ: Rutgers University Press), pp. 13–36

DE FERRARI, GUILLERMINA. 2007. *Vulnerable States: Bodies of Memory in Contemporary Caribbean Fiction* (Charlottesville: University of Virginia Press)

DE LAURETIS, TERESA. 1989. 'The Violence of Rhetoric', in *The Violence of Representation: Literature and the History of Violence*, ed. by Nancy Armstrong and Leonard Tennenhouse (London: Routledge), pp. 239–57

DE MAESENEER, RITA. 2004. 'Los caminos torcidos en *Sirena Selena vestida de pena*, de Mayra Santos-Febres', in *El artista caribeño como guerrero de lo imaginario*, ed. by Rita De Maeseneer and An Van Hecke (Madrid: Iberoamericana), pp. 127–46

DÉITA. 1993. *La Légende des Loa du Vodou haïtien* (Port-au-Prince: [n. p.])

DEIVE, CARLOS ESTEBAN. 1988. *Vodú y magia en Santo Domingo*, 2nd edn (Santo Domingo: Fundación Cultural Dominicana)

DELOUGHREY, ELIZABETH. 2007. *Routes and Roots: Navigating Caribbean and Pacific Island Literatures* (Honolulu: University of Hawai'i Press)

DESMANGLES, LESLIE G. 1992. *The Faces of the Gods: Vodou and Roman Catholicism in Haiti* (Chapel Hill: University of North Carolina Press)

——2010. 'The Faces of the Cosmic Gods', in *Perspectives on the Caribbean: A Reader in Culture, History, and Representation*, ed. by Philip W. Scher (Chichester: Wiley-Blackwell), pp. 185–206

——2012. 'Replacing the term "Voodoo" with "Vodou": A Proposal', *Journal of Haitian Studies*, 18(2): 26–28

DESQUIRON, LILAS. 1990. *Les Chemins de Loco-Miroir* (Paris: Stock)

DEYITA. 1989. *Esperans Dezire* (Port-au-Prince: Henri Deschamps)

DIANTEILL, ERWIN, and MARTHA SWEARINGEN. 2003. 'From Hierography to Ethnography and Back: Lydia Cabrera's Texts and the Written Tradition in Afro-Cuban Religions', *Journal of American Folklore*, 116(461): 273–92

DÍAZ-QUIÑONES, ARCADIO. 1993. *La memoria rota* (Río Piedras: Ediciones Huracán)

DIEDERICH, BERNARD, and AL BURT. 1972. *Papa Doc: Haiti and its Dictator* (Harmondsworth: Penguin)

DREWAL, MARGARET THOMPSON. 1992. *Yoruba Ritual: Performers, Play, Agency* (Bloomington: Indiana University Press)

DROOGERS, ANDRÉ. 1989. 'Syncretism: The Problem of Definition, the Definition of the Problem', in *Dialogue and Syncretism: An Interdisciplinary Approach*, ed. by Jerald D. Gort and others (Amsterdam: Rodopi), pp. 7–25

DUCHESNE WINTER, JUAN. 2015. 'Rita Indiana y sus nuevos misterios', *80grados*, 15 May 2015, <http://www.80grados.net/rita-indiana-y-sus-nuevos-misterios> [accessed 16 May 2015]

DURAND, OSWALD. 1992. *Poésies choisies: commentaires par le Dr. Pradel Pompilus* (Port-au-Prince: Éditions Christophe)

DUVALIER, FRANÇOIS. 1969. *Mémoires d'un leader du Tiers Monde: mes négociations avec le Saint-Siège ou, Une tranche d'histoire* (Paris: Librairie Hachette)

ELLIOTT, RICHARD. 2010. *Fado and the Place of Longing: Loss, Memory and the City* (Farnham: Ashgate)

ÉTONNANTS-VOYAGEURS. 2011. 'MARS, Kettly', <http://etonnants-voyageurs.com/spip.php?page=inviteshaiti&id_article=2330> [accessed 8 February 2012]

FANON, FRANTZ. 1952. *Peau noire, masques blancs* (Paris: Du Seuil)

——1961. *Les Damnés de la terre* (Paris: Maspero)

——1990. *The Wretched of the Earth*, trans. by Constance Farrington (London: Penguin Books)

FATTON, ROBERT, JR. 2002. *Haiti's Predatory Republic: The Unending Transition to Democracy* (Boulder, CO: Lynne Rienner)

FERGUSON, JAMES. 1988. *Papa Doc, Baby Doc: Haiti and the Duvaliers* (Oxford: Basil Blackwell)

FERNÁNDEZ OLMOS, MARGARITE. 1997. 'Trans-Caribbean Identity and the Fictional World of Mayra Montero', in *Sacred Possessions: Vodou, Santería, Obeah, and the Caribbean*, ed. by Margarite Fernández Olmos and Lizabeth Paravisini-Gebert (New Brunswick, NJ: Rutgers University Press), pp. 267–82

FERNÁNDEZ OLMOS, MARGARITE, and LIZABETH PARAVISINI-GEBERT. 2011. *Creole Religions of the Caribbean: An Introduction from Vodou and Santería to Obeah and Espiritismo*, 2nd edn (New York: New York University Press)

FERNÁNDEZ ROBAINA, TOMÁS. 2008. *Hablen paleros y santeros* (Havana: Editorial Ciencias Sociales)

FERRÉ, ROSARIO. 1980. 'La cocina de la escritura', in *Sitio a Eros* (Mexico City: J. Mortiz), pp. 13–33

——1986. 'The Writer's Kitchen', trans. by Diana L. Vélez, *Feminist Studies*, 12(2): 227–42

FOUCAULT, MICHEL. 1984. *Histoire de la sexualité 2: L'Usage des plaisirs* (Paris: Gallimard)

——1990. *The History of Sexuality. Volume II: Use of Pleasure*, trans. by Robert Hurley (New York: Vintage Books)

FOUCHÉ, FRANCK. 1968. *Bouqui au paradis*, in *L'Haïtien: Cahiers de Sainte-Marie*, 10 (Montreal: Éditions Sainte-Marie), pp. 99–137

——1974. *Général Baron-la-Croix ou Le Silence masqué: tragédie moderne en 2 calvaires, 28 stations et une messe en noir et rouge* (Ottawa: Leméac)

FOURCAND, JEAN M. 1964. *Catéchisme de la Révolution* ([Port-au-Prince]: Imprimerie de l'État)

FRANCIS, DONETTE. 2011. 'Novel Insights: Sex Work, Secrets and Depression in Angie Cruz's *Soledad*', in *Sex and the Citizen: Interrogating the Caribbean*, ed. by Faith Smith (Charlottesville: University of Virginia Press), pp. 53–71

FRANCO, JEAN. 1988. 'Beyond Ethnocentrism: Gender, Power, and the Third-World Intelligentsia', in *Marxism and the Interpretation of Culture*, ed. by Cary Nelson and Lawrence Grossberg (Basingstoke: Macmillan Education), pp. 503–15

FULLEDA, GERARDO. 2003. 'El teatro ritual caribeño, cauce de lo popular', in *Rito y representación: los sistemas mágico-religiosos en la cultura cubana contemporánea*, ed. by Yana Elsa Brugal and Beatriz J. Rizk (Madrid: Iberoamericana), pp. 173–80

FUMAGALLI, MARIA CRISTINA. 2015. *On the Edge: Writing the Border Between Haiti and the Dominican Republic* (Liverpool: Liverpool University Press)

GARCÍA, CRISTINA. 1992. *Dreaming in Cuban* (London: Flamingo)

——1997. *The Agüero Sisters* (London: Picador)

GARCÍA-CALDERÓN, MYRNA. 2004. 'La imaginación insubordinada: el Caribe y la cultura marginal', in *El artista caribeño como guerrero de lo imaginario*, ed. by Rita De Maeseneer and An Van Hecke (Madrid: Iberoamericana), pp. 153–63

GEGGUS, DAVID PATRICK. 2002. *Haitian Revolutionary Studies* (Bloomington: Indiana University Press)

GIRAL, SERGIO. 2013. 'La mujer en mis films. Segunda parte', *The Broken Image/La imagen rota*, 16 August 2013, <http://laimagenrota.blogspot.com/2013/08/la-mujer-en-mis-films_16.html> [accessed 25 October 2013]

GLISSANT, ÉDOUARD. 1989. *Caribbean Discourse: Selected Essays*, trans. by J. Michael Dash (Charlottesville: University Press of Virginia)

——1997. *Le Discours antillais* (Paris: Gallimard)

GONZÁLEZ, FLORA. 1998. 'De lo invisible a lo espectacular en la creación de la mulata en la cultura cubana: *Cecilia Valdés* y *María Antonia*', *Revista Iberoamericana*, 64(184–85): 543–57

GONZÁLEZ MANDRI, FLORA. 2006. *Guarding Cultural Memory: Afro-Cuban Women in Literature and the Arts* (Charlottesville: University of Virginia Press)

GONZÁLEZ PÉREZ, TOMÁS. 2003. 'La posesión (privilegio de la teatralidad)', in *Rito y representación: los sistemas mágico-religiosos en la cultura cubana contemporánea*, ed. by Yana Elsa Brugal and Beatriz J. Rizk (Madrid: Iberoamericana), pp. 199–209

GONZÁLEZ-WIPPLER, MIGENE. 2004. *Santería: The Religion* (St Paul, MN: Llewellyn Publications)

GOODWIN, SARAH WEBSTER. 1993. 'Romanticism and the Ghost of Prostitution: Freud, *Maria*, and "Alice Fell"', in *Death and Representation*, ed. by Sarah Webster Goodwin and Elisabeth Bronfen (Baltimore, MD: Johns Hopkins University Press), pp. 152–73

GORDON, AVERY F. 2008. *Ghostly Matters: Haunting and the Sociological Imagination* (Minneapolis: University of Minnesota Press)

GORDON, LEAH (dir.). 2008. *Atis Rezistans: Sculptors of the Grand Rue* (London: Haiti Support Group)

GRAY, LILA ELLEN. 2007. 'Memories of Empire, Mythologies of the Soul: Fado Performance and the Shaping of Saudade', *Ethnomusicology*, 51(1): 106–30

GREWAL, INDERPAL, and CAREN KAPLAN. 1994. 'Introduction: Transnational Feminist Practices and Questions of Postmodernity', in *Scattered Hegemonies: Postmodernity and Transnational Feminist Practices*, ed. by Inderpal Grewal and Caren Kaplan (Minneapolis: University of Minnesota Press), pp. 1–33

GROSSBERG, LAWRENCE. 1986. 'On Postmodernism and Articulation: An Interview with Stuart Hall', *Journal of Communication Inquiry*, 10: 45–60

GUERLAC, SUZANNE. 1990. '"Recognition" by a Woman!: A Reading of Bataille's *L'Erotisme*', *Yale French Studies*, 78: 90–105

HABERMAS, JÜRGEN. 1987. *The Philosophical Discourse of Modernity*, trans. by Frederick Lawrence (Cambridge: Polity Press)

HAGEDORN, KATHERINE JOHANNA. 2010. 'To Have and To Hold: Possession Performance in Afro-Cuban Regla de Ocha', in *Women and New and Africana Religions*, ed. by Lillian Ashcraft-Eason, Darnise C. Martin, and Oyeronke Olademo (Santa Barbara, CA: Praeger), pp. 145–65

HALL, STUART. 1991. *Redemption Song. Part 3: Paradise Lost*, dir. by Roger Mills (London: BBC)

HAYNES, JEFF. 1994. *Religion in Third World Politics* (Boulder, CO: Lynn Rienner Publishers)

HEATH, JULIE. 1999. 'Representing Haiti: Vodou and Nationalism in the Writings of François Duvalier and Jean-Bertrand Aristide', *Midwestern Folklore*, 25(1): 22–41

HENNESSY, ALISTAIR (ed.). 1992. *Intellectuals in the Twentieth-Century Caribbean: Volume II. Unity in Variety: the Hispanic and Francophone Caribbean* (London: Macmillan)

HERNÁNDEZ ESPINOSA, EUGENIO. 1992. *María Antonia*, in *Teatro cubano contemporáneo: antología*, ed. by Carlos Espinosa Domínguez (Madrid: Centro de Documentación Teatral; Sociedad Estatal Quinto Centenario; Fondo de Cultura Económica), pp. 941–1039

HERRERA, GEORGINA. 2004. 'Conversación con María Antonia (cuarenta años después)', in *Una pasión compartida*, ed. by Inés María Martiatu (Havana: Letras Cubanas), pp. 155–68

HOLTON, KIMBERLY DACOSTA. 2002. 'Bearing Material Witness to Musical Sound: Fado's L94 Museum Debut', *Luso-Brazilian Review*, 39(2): 107–23

HOOKS, BELL. 2004. *The Will to Change: Men, Masculinity and Love* (New York: Atria Books)

HOULBERG, MARILYN. 2005. 'Magique Marasa: The Ritual Cosmos of the Twins and Other Sacred Children', in *Fragments of Bone: Neo-African Religions in a New World*, ed. by Patrick Bellegarde-Smith (Champaign: University of Illinois Press), pp. 13–31

HU-DEHART, EVELYN. 1999. 'Race Construction and Race Relations: Chinese and Blacks in Nineteenth-Century Cuba', in *Encounters: People of Asian Descent in the Americas*, ed. by Roshini Rustomiji-Kerns (Lanham, MD: Rowman), pp. 105–12

HUMPHREY, PAUL. 2012. 'Gods, Gender and Nation: Building an Alternative Concept of Nation in Four Novels by Mayra Montero', *Journal of Haitian Studies*, 18(2): 119–34

——2014. 'Of Sound, Mind and Body: Female Sexuality and Vodou in Kettly Mars' *Fado*', *International Journal of Francophone Studies*, 17(2): 137–57

——2018. '"El manto que cubre el mar": Religion, Identity, and the Sea in Rita Indiana's *La mucama de Omicunlé*', *Sargasso*, 2016–17(1 & 2): 109–25

——2019. 'Capital Prostitution: Voices from the Shadows in Post-Earthquake Haitian Fiction', in *Capital Culture: Perspectives in Ethnic Studies II*, ed. by Cheryl Toman and Gilbert Doho (Paris: La Doxa), pp. 137–60

——forthcoming. 'Ikú, Cumachela and the Figure of Death in *María Antonia* by Eugenio Hernández Espinosa', *Bulletin of Hispanic Studies*

HURBON, LAËNNEC. 1987. *Comprendre Haïti: essai sur l'état, la nation, la culture* (Paris: Karthala)

——2001. 'Current Evolution of Relations between Religion and Politics in Haiti', in *Nation Dance: Religion, Identity, and Cultural Difference in the Caribbean*, ed. by Patrick Taylor (Bloomington: Indiana University Press), pp. 118–25

HURSTON, ZORA NEALE. 1990. *Tell My Horse: Voodoo and Life in Haiti and Jamaica* (New York: Harper and Row)

INDIANA, RITA. 2003. *La estrategia de Chochueca* (San Juan: Isla Negra Editores)

——2005. *Papi* (San Juan: Ediciones Vértigo)

——2013. *Nombres y animales* (Cáceres: Periférica)

——2015. *La mucama de Omicunlé* (Cáceres: Periférica)

——2016. *Papi*, trans. by Achy Obejas (Chicago, IL: The University of Chicago Press)

——2018. *Tentacle*, trans. by Achy Obejas (Sheffield: And Other Stories)

INDIANA, RITA, and LOS MISTERIOS. 2010. 'Da pa lo do', dir. by Engel Leonardo, <https://vimeo.com/29644615> [accessed 20 July 2016]

INSTITUTE FOR JUSTICE and DEMOCRACY IN HAITI and OTHERS. 2010. *Our Bodies Are Still Trembling: Haitian Women's Fight Against Rape*, <https://www.madre.org/sites/default/files/PDFs/1283377138_2010.07.26%20-%20HAITI%20GBV%20REPORT%20FINAL.pdf> [accessed 25 August 2017]

JAMES, CONRAD. 2009. 'Marginality, Sacrifice & Transgression: Mothers & Rebellious Women in Two Plays by Cuba's Eugenio Hernández Espinosa', in *African Theatre: Diasporas*, ed. by Christine Matzke and Osita A. Okagbue (Woodbridge: James Currey), pp. 39–51

JAMES, LESLIE R. 2000. 'Text and the Rhetoric of Change', in *Religion, Culture, and Tradition in the Caribbean*, ed. by Hemchand Gossai and Nathaniel Samuel Murrell (Basingstoke: Macmillan), pp. 143–66

JEAN-CHARLES, RÉGINE MICHELLE. 2006. 'They Never Call It Rape: Critical Reception and Representation of Sexual Violence in Marie Vieux-Chauvet's *Amour, Colère et Folie*', *Journal of Haitian Studies*, 12(2): 4–21

——2011. 'À travers l'Atlantique noire: l'imagerie de l'eau dans les textes des femmes haïtiennes', in *Écrits d'Haïti: perspectives sur la littérature haïtienne contemporaine (1986–2006)*, ed. by Nadève Ménard (Paris: Karthala), pp. 163–76

——2014. *Conflict Bodies: The Politics of Rape Representation in the Francophone Imaginary* (Columbus: Ohio State University Press)

JOHNSON, PAUL CHRISTOPHER. 2006. 'Secretism and the Apotheosis of Duvalier', *Journal of the American Academy of Religion*, 74(2): 420–45

JOSEPH, RÉGINE ISABELLE. 2007. 'Écrire sous la dictature', in Marie Vieux-Chauvet, *Amour, colère et folie: adaptation théâtrale*, ed. by José Pliya (Paris: Avant-scène theatre), pp. 145–50

KAITY, KATHI (dir.). 2011. *Seguimos: retorno de María Antonia*, <http://www.youtube.com/watch?v=Kxrhjq_Iuls> [accessed 19 August 2011]

KALISA, CHANTAL. 2009. *Violence in Francophone African and Caribbean Women's Literature* (Lincoln: University of Nebraska Press)

KAPLAN, CAREN. 1996. *Questions of Travel: Postmodern Discourses of Displacement* (Durham, NC, & London: Duke University Press)

KAUFMAN, MICHAEL. 1995. 'The Construction of Masculinity and the Triad of Men's Violence', in *Men's Lives*, ed. by Michael S. Kimmel and Michael A. Messner, 3rd edn (Needham Heights, MA: Allyn and Bacon), pp. 13–25

KLEIN, NAOMI. 2007. *The Shock Doctrine: The Rise of Disaster Capitalism* (New York: Metropolitan Books)

——2018. *The Battle for Paradise: Puerto Rico Takes on the Disaster Capitalists* (Chicago, IL: Haymarket Books)

KRISTEVA, JULIA. 1987. 'Stabat Mater', in *Tales of Love*, trans. by Leon S. Roudiez (New York: Columbia University Press), pp. 234–63

LACHATAÑERÉ, RÓMULO. 1992. *¡¡Oh, mío Yemayá!!* (Havana: Editorial de Ciencias Sociales)

——2005. *Afro-Cuban Myths: Yemayá and other Orishas*, trans. by Christine Ayorinde (Princeton, NJ: Markus Wiener)

LAFERRIÈRE, DANY. 1997. *Down Among the Dead Men*, trans by. David Homel (Vancouver: Douglas & McIntyre)

——2007. *Pays sans chapeau* (Paris: Motifs)

LAGOS-POPE, MARÍA INÉS. 1985. 'Sumisión y rebeldía: el doble o la representación de la alienación femenina en narraciones de Marta Brunet y Rosario Ferré', *Revista Iberoamericana*, 51(132–33): 731–49

LAGUERRE, MICHEL S. 1982. *Urban Life in the Caribbean: A Study of a Haitian Urban Community* (Cambridge, MA: Schenkman)

——1989. *Voodoo and Politics in Haiti* (Basingstoke: Macmillan)

——1993. *The Military and Society in Haiti* (Knoxville: University of Tennessee Press)

LAHENS, YANICK. 1994. *Tante Résia et les dieux* (Paris: L'Harmattan)

——2000. *Dans la maison du père* (Paris: Le Serpent à Plumes)

LAROCHE, MAXIMILIEN. 1984. *Trois études sur 'Folie' de Marie Chauvet* (Sainte-Foy: GRELCA)

——1998. 'Imaginaire populaire et littérature: le houngan, le zombi et le mécréant', *Notre Librairie: Revue du Livre: Afrique, Caraïbes, Océan Indien*, 133: 82–89

LARRIER, RENÉE. 2000. *Francophone Women's Writers of Africa and the Caribbean* (Gainesville: University Press of Florida)

LATORTUE, RÉGINE. 1990. 'In Search of Women's Voice: The Woman Novelist in Haiti', in *Wild Women in the Whirlwind: Afra-American Culture and the Contemporary Literary Renaissance*, ed. by Joanne M. Braxton and Andrée Nicola McLaughlin (New Brunswick, NJ: Rutgers University Press), pp. 181–94

LAWLESS, ROBERT. 2002. 'Haiti: Voodoo, Christianity, and Politics', in *Religion and Politics in the Developing World: Explosive Interactions*, ed. by Rolin G. Mainuddin (Aldershot: Ashgate), pp. 39–49

LECONTE, FRANTZ-ANTOINE. 1998. *La République* (Montreal: CIDIHCA)

LEÓN ROJAS, GLORIA MARÍA. 2014. *Haití en la memoria* (Havana: Editorial Ciencias Sociales)

LESCOT, ANNE, and LAURENCE MAGLOIRE (dirs). 2002. *Of Men and Gods (Des hommes et dieux)* (Watertown, MA: Documentary Education Resources)

LORA, ERMINIO (ed.). 2003. *Enchiridion dei concordati: due secoli di storia dei rapporti chiesa-stato* (Bologna: Centro Editoriale Dehoniano)

LORDE, AUDRE. 1984. 'Uses of the Erotic: The Erotic as Power', in *Sister Outsider: Essays & Speeches by Audre Lorde* (Freedom, CA: The Crossing Press), pp. 53–59

LUMSDEN, IAN. 1996. *Machos, Maricones, and Gays: Cuba and Homosexuality* (Philadelphia, PA: Temple University Press)

MADRE and OTHERS. 2011. *Our Bodies Are Still Trembling: Haitian Women's Fight Against Rape. One-Year Update*, <http://www.peacewomen.org/assets/file/Resources/NGO/vaw_haitianwomencontinuetofightagainstrape_madre_january2011.pdf> [accessed 25 August 2017]

MARBÁN, JORGE. 2005. 'Historia, intertextualidad y mitología afro-sino-cubana en *Como un mensajero tuyo* de Mayra Montero', *Explicación de textos literarios*, 34(1–2): 89–99

MARS, KETTLY. 1999. 'Lobo', in *Un parfum d'encens: nouvelles* (Port-au-Prince: Imprimeur II)

——2007. *Kasalé* (La Roque d'Anthéron: Vents d'ailleurs)

——2008. *Fado* (Paris: Mercure de France)

——2010A. *Saisons sauvages* (Paris: Mercure de France)

——2010B. 'Les Spectres du passé. Avec: Kettly Mars, Yanick Lahens, Evelyne Trouillot, Raoul Peck', round table at Étonnants Voyageurs Festival International du Livre et du Film, Saint-Malo, 22–24 May 2010

——2013. *Aux frontières de la soif* (Paris: Mercure)

——2014. 'Et tant pis pour la mort', in *Et tant pis pour la mort: nouvelles* (Pétion-Ville: C3 éditions)

——2015. *Savage Seasons*, trans. by Jeanine Herman (Lincoln: University of Nebraska Press)

MARTIATU, INÉS MARÍA. 1984. 'María Antonia: wa-ni-ile-re...', *Tablas*, 3: 35–44

——1992. 'Una Carmen caribeña', in *Teatro cubano contemporáneo: antología*, ed. by Carlos Espinosa Domínguez (Madrid: Centro de Documentación Teatral; Sociedad Estatal Quinto Centenario; Fondo de Cultura Económica), pp. 935–40

——2000. *El rito como representación: teatro ritual caribeño* (Havana: Ediciones Unión)

——2004A. 'Chivo que rompe tambó: Santería, género y raza en *María Antonia*', in *Una pasión compartida*, ed. by Inés María Martiatu (Havana: Letras Cubanas), pp. 32–74

——2004B. 'Reflexiones en los cuarenta años de *María Antonia*', in *Una pasión compartida*, ed. by Inés María Martiatu (Havana: Letras Cubanas), pp. 5–17

——2005. 'Prólogo', *Wanilere Teatro: selección, prólogo y notas bibliográficas de Inés María Martiatu* (Havana: Letras Cubanas), pp. 5–33

MARTIATU, INÉS MARÍA (ed.). 2009. *Bufo y nación: interpelaciones desde el presente* (Havana: Editorial Letras Cubanas)

MARTIATU TERRY, INÉS MARÍA. 1992. 'El caribe: teatro sagrado, teatro de dioses', *El Público: Revista bimestral del espectáculo*, Sept-Oct: 96–115

——1998. 'Mythological and Ritual Theatre in Cuba', trans. by Günther Berghaus, *Performance Research*, 3(3): 53–59

MARTÍNEZ-ECHAZÁBAL, LOURDES. 1994. 'The Politics of Afro-Cuban Religion in Contemporary Cuban Cinema', *Afro-Hispanic Review*, Spring: 16–22

——1997. 'Hybridity and Diasporization in the "Black Atlantic": The Case of *Chombo*', *PALARA*, 1: 117–29

MARTÍNEZ-SAN MIGUEL, YOLANDA. 2014. *Coloniality of Diasporas: Rethinking Intra-Colonial Migrations in a Pan-Caribbean Context* (New York: Palgrave Macmillan)

MARTY, ANNE. 1997. 'Note de lecture. Marie CHAUVET, *Amour, Colère et Folie*', *Notre Librairie: Haïti I*, Oct-Dec: 151–53

MATIBAG, EUGENIO. 1996. *Afro-Cuban Religious Experience: Cultural Reflections in Narrative* (Gainesville: University Press of Florida)

MAXWELL, IAN. 1998. 'Football Is Not Theatre', *About Performance*, 4: 77–84

MCALISTER, ELIZABETH A. 2006. '"The Jew" in the Haitian Imagination: Pre-Modern Anti-Judaism in the Postmodern Caribbean', in *Vodou in Haitian Life and Culture: Invisible Powers*, ed. by Claudine Michel and Patrick Bellegarde-Smith (New York: Palgrave Macmillan), pp. 79–99

——2012. 'From Slave Revolt to a Blood Pact with Satan: The Evangelical Rewriting of Haitian History', *Studies in Religion / Sciences Religieuses*, 41(2): 187–215

MÉNARD, NADÈVE. 2011. 'Kettly Mars: la sensualité au cœur de la vie', in *Écrits d'Haïti: perspectives sur la littérature haïtienne contemporaine (1986–2006)*, ed. by Nadève Ménard (Paris: Karthala), pp. 229–33

MENÉNDEZ, LÁZARA. 2002. *Rodar el coco: proceso de cambio en la santería* (Havana: Editorial de Ciencias Sociales)

——2004. 'María Antonia y su madrina: dos caras del dodecaedro', in *Una pasión compartida*, ed. by Inés María Martiatu (Havana: Letras Cubanas), pp. 75–97

MÉTRAUX, ALFRED. 1958. *Le Vaudou haïtien* (Paris: Gallimard)

——1959. *Voodoo in Haiti*, trans. by Hugo Charteris (London: Andre Deutsch)

MICHEL, CLAUDINE. 2006. 'Of Worlds Seen and Unseen: The Educational Character of Haitian Vodou', in *Haitian Vodou: Spirit, Myth, and Reality*, ed. by Patrick Bellegarde-Smith and Claudine Michel (Bloomington: Indiana University Press), pp. 32–45

——2010. 'Foreword to the 2010 Edition. Mama Lola's Triplets: Three Decades, Three Rituals, Marasa Twa', in Karen McCarthy Brown, *Mama Lola: A Vodou Priestess in Brooklyn*, 3rd edn (Berkeley: University of California Press), pp. ix–xxxi

MICHEL, CLAUDINE, PATRICK BELLEGARDE-SMITH, and MARLÈNE RACINE-TOUSSAINT. 2006. 'From the Horses' Mouths: Women's Words / Women's Worlds', in *Haitian Vodou: Spirit, Myth, and Reality*, ed. by Patrick Bellegarde-Smith and Claudine Michel (Bloomington: Indiana University Press), pp. 70–83

MILLER, IVOR. 2000. 'Religious Symbolism in Cuban Political Performance', *The Drama Review*, 44(2): 30–55

MIRANDA-RODRÍGUEZ, EDGARDO. 2018A. *Ricanstruction: Reminiscing and Rebuilding Puerto Rico* (New York: Somos Arte)

——2018B. *La Borinqueña #2* (New York: Somos Arte)

MOHAMMED, PATRICIA. 2003. 'A Symbiotic Visiting Relationship: Caribbean Feminist Historiography and Caribbean Feminist Theory', in *Confronting Power, Theorizing Gender: Interdisciplinary Perspectives in the Caribbean*, ed. by Eudine Barriteau (Kingston: University of the West Indies Press)

MOHAMMED, PATRICIA (ed.). 2002. *Gendered Realities: Essays in Caribbean Feminist Thought* (Kingston: University of the West Indies Press)

MONTERO, MAYRA. 1987. *La trenza de la hermosa luna* (Barcelona: Editorial Anagrama)

——1992. *Del rojo de su sombra* (Barcelona: Tusquets)

——1995. *Tú, la oscuridad* (Barcelona: Tusquets)

——1997. *You, Darkness*, trans. by Edith Grossman (London: Harvill)

——1998. *Como un mensajero tuyo* (Barcelona: Tusquets)

——2000. *The Messenger*, trans. by Edith Grossman (London: Harvill)

——2002. *The Red of His Shadow*, trans. by Edith Grossman (London: Harvill)

MUGGAH, ROBERT, and ATHENA KOLBE. 'Haiti: Why an Accurate Count of Civilian Deaths Matters', *Los Angeles Times*, 12 July 2011, <http://articles.latimes.com/2011/jul/12/opinion/la-oe-muggah-haiti-count-20110712> [accessed 7 November 2014]

MÜHLEISEN, SUSANNE. 1996. 'Encoding the Voice: Caribbean Women's Writing and Creole', in *Framing the Word: Gender and Genre in Caribbean Women's Writing*, ed. by Joan Anim-Addo (London: Whiting & Birch), pp. 169–84

MUNRO, MARTIN. 2014. *Writing on the Fault Line: Haitian Literature and the Earthquake of 2010* (Liverpool: Liverpool University Press)

——2015. 'Chauvet the Prophet: Writing the Future and the Future of Writing', in *Paradoxes of the Postcolonial Feminine*, ed. by Kaiama L. Glover and Alessandra Benedicty-Kokken, special issue of *Yale French Studies*, 128: 43–56

MUNRO, MARTIN (ed.). 2010. *Haiti Rising: Haitian History, Culture and the Earthquake of 2010* (Liverpool: Liverpool University Press)

MURPHY, JOSEPH. 1994. *Working the Spirit: Ceremonies of the African Diaspora* (Boston, MA: Beacon Press)

——2001. 'Yéyé Cachita: Ochún in a Cuban Mirror', in *Òṣun Across the Waters: A Yoruba Goddess in Africa and the Americas*, ed. by Joseph Murphy and Mei-Mei Sanford (Bloomington: Indiana University Press), pp. 87–101

N'ZENGOU-TAYO, MARIE-JOSÉ. 1998. 'Fanm Se Poto Mitan: Haitian Woman, the Pillar of Society', *Feminist Review*, 59: 118–42

——2010. 'The Haitian Short Story: An Overview', *Journal of Caribbean Literatures*, 6(3): 37–52

NAGEL, JOANE. 1998. 'Masculinity and Nationalism: Gender and Sexuality in the Making of Nations', *Ethnic and Racial Studies*, 21(2): 242–69

NÉRESTANT, MICIAL M. 1994. *Religions et politiques en Haïti (1804–1990)* (Paris: Karthala)

NERY, RUI VIEIRA. 2004. *Para uma história do fado* (Lisbon: Público/Corda Seca)

New York Times. 1920. 'Bomb Exploded at Caruso Performance; Six Injured in Havana Opera Panic', <http://query.nytimes.com/mem/archive-free/pdf?_r=1&res=9A04E0D9 133AE03ABC4C52DFB066838B639EDE> [accessed 14 June 2010]

OLIVER, KELLY. 2004. *Colonization of the Psychic Space: A Psychoanalytic Social Theory of Oppression* (Minneapolis: University of Minnesota Press)

ONG, WALTER J. 1982. *Orality and Literacy: The Technologizing of the Word* (London: Methuen & Co)

ORCEL, MAKENZY. 2010. *Les Immortelles* (Montreal: Mémoire d'encrier)

——2016A. *L'Ombre animale* (Paris: Zulma)

——2016B. 'Entre ombre et lumière avec Makenzy Orcel', interview with Augustin Trapenard, *Boomerang*, France Inter, 20 January 2016, <https://www.franceinter.fr/ emissions/boomerang/boomerang-20-janvier-2016> [accessed 15 August 2017]

ORIZIO, RICCARDO. 2007. *Hablando con el diablo: entrevistas con dictadores*, trans. by Bernardo Moreno Carrillo (Mexico City: Fondo de Cultura Económica)

ORNER, PETER, and EVAN LYON. 2017. *Lavil: Life, Love, and Death in Port-au-Prince* (London: Verso)

ORTIZ, FERNANDO. 1947. *Cuban Counterpoint: Tobacco and Sugar*, trans. by Harriet de Onís (New York: Alfred A. Kopf)

——1963. *Contrapunteo cubano del tabaco y el azúcar* (Havana: Consejo Nacional de Cuba)

OTERO, SOLIMAR. 2013. '*Yemayá and Ochún*: Queering the Vernacular Logics of the Waters', in *Yemoja: Gender, Sexuality, and Creativity in the Latina/o and Afro-Atlantic Diasporas*, ed. by Solimar Otero and Toyin Falola (Albany: State University of New York Press), pp. 85–112

PALMIÉ, STEPHAN. 2002. *Wizards and Scientists: Explorations in Afro-Cuban Modernity and Tradition* (Durham, NC: Duke University Press)

PARAVISINI-GEBERT, LIZABETH. 2008. *Literature of the Caribbean* (Westport, CT: Greenwood Press)

PECK, RAOUL (dir.). 2013. *Assistance mortelle* (Paris: Velvet)

PÉREZ FERNÁNDEZ, ROLANDO, and SANTIAGO RODRÍGUEZ GONZÁLEZ. 2008. 'La corneta china (*suona*) en Cuba: una contribución cultural asiática trascendente', *Afro-Hispanic Review*, 27(1): 139–60

PINO, AMADO DEL. 2003. 'María Antonia y Camila: gracia y castigo', in *Rito y representación: Los sistemas mágico-religiosos en la cultura cubana contemporánea*, ed. by Yana Elsa Brugal and Beatriz J. Rizk (Madrid: Iberoamericana), pp. 181–89

PLUCHON, PIERRE. 1987. *Vaudou, sorciers, empoisonneurs: de Saint-Domingue à Haïti* (Paris: Karthala)

POGOLOTTI, GRAZIELLA. 2004. 'El silencio de los excluidos', in *Una pasión compartida*, ed. by Inés María Martiatu (Havana: Letras Cubanas), pp. 21–31

PRESSLEY-SANON, TONI. 2013. 'One Plus One Equals Three: *Marasa* Consciousness, the *Lwa*, and Three Stories', *Research in African Literatures*, 44(3): 118–37

PRICE-MARS, JEAN. 1928. *Ainsi parla l'oncle* (Port-au-Prince: Imprimerie de Compiègne)

PURI, SHALINI. 2004. *The Caribbean Postcolonial: Social Equality, Post-nationalism, and Cultural Hybridity* (New York: Palgrave Macmillan)

QUEIROGA, PERDIGÃO (dir.). 1947. *Fado: história d'uma cantadeira* (Lisbon: Lisboa-Filme)

QUILLER-COUCH, ARTHUR THOMAS. 1901. *The Oxford Book of English Verse: 1250–1900* (Oxford: Clarendon)

QUIÑONES, TATO. 1994. *Ecorie Abakuá* (Havana: Ediciones Unión)

RAMSEY, KATE. 2011. *The Spirits and the Law: Vodou and Power in Haiti* (Chicago, IL: University of Chicago Press)

—— 2012. 'From "Voodooism" to "Vodou": Changing a US Library of Congress Subject Heading', *Journal of Haitian Studies*, 18(2): 14–25

REYES, ANGELITA. 2002. *Mothering Across Cultures: Postcolonial Representations* (Minneapolis: University of Minnesota Press)

RICH, ADRIENNE. 1977. *Of Woman Born: Motherhood as Experience and Institution* (London: Virago)

RICHMAN, KAREN. 2012. 'The Vodou State and the Protestant Nation: Haiti in the Long Twentieth Century', in *Obeah and Other Powers: The Politics of Caribbean Religion and Healing*, ed. by Diana Paton and Maarit Forde (Durham, NC: Duke University Press), pp. 268–87

RIZK, BEATRIZ J. 2001. *Posmodernismo y teatro en América Latina: teorías y prácticas en el umbral del siglo XXI* (Madrid: Iberoamericana)

ROBLES CARRASQUILLO, HUÁSCAR. 2015. *Puertos príncipes: temblemos todos* (San Juan: La secta de los perros)

RODRÍGUEZ CORONEL, ROGELIO. 1997. *Crítica al paso* (Havana: Ediciones Unión)

ROSENBERG, JUNE. 1979. *El Gagá: religión y sociedad de un culto dominicano* (Santo Domingo: Universidad Autónoma de Santo Domingo)

ROUMAIN, JACQUES. 1946. *Gouverneurs de la rosée* (Paris: Éditeurs français réunis)

SALDAÑA, EXCILIA. 1987. *Kele Kele* (Havana: Editorial Letras Cubanas)

SANTOS-FEBRES, MAYRA. 2000. *Sirena Selena*, trans. by Stephen Lytle (New York: Picador)

—— 2005. *boat people* (San Juan: Ediciones Callejón)

—— 2009. *Sirena Selena vestida de pena* (Doral: Punto de lectura)

—— 2018. *Huracanada* (San Juan: Trabalis)

SARTRE, JEAN-PAUL. 1991. 'Préface', in Frantz Fanon, *Les Damnés de la terre* (Paris: Gallimard)

SCHARFMAN, RONNIE. 1996. 'Theorizing Terror: The Discourse of Violence in Marie Chauvet's *Amour, Colère, Folie*', in *Postcolonial Subjects: Francophone Women Writers*, ed. by Mary Jean Green, Karen Gould, and Micheline Rice-Maximin (Minneapolis: University of Minnesota Press), pp. 229–45

SCHECHNER, RICHARD. 1985. *Between Theatre and Anthropology* (Philadelphia: University of Pennsylvania Press)

—— 2002. *Performance Studies: An Introduction* (London: Routledge)

SCHERER, FRANK. 2001. 'Sanfancón: Orientalism, Self-Orientalization, and "Chinese Religion" in Cuba', in *Nation Dance: Religion, Identity, and Cultural Difference in the Caribbean*, ed. by Patrick Taylor (Bloomington: Indiana University Press), pp. 153–70

SCHULLER, MARK. 2012. *Killing with Kindness: Haiti, International Aid and NGOs* (New Brunswick, NJ: Rutgers University Press)

—— 2015. '"Pa Manyen Fanm Nan Konsa": Intersectionality, Structural Violence, and Vulnerability Before and After Haiti's Earthquake', *Feminist Studies*, 41(1): 184–210

—— 2016A. *Humanitarian Aftershocks in Haiti* (New Brunswick, NJ: Rutgers University Press)

—— 2016B. 'Hurricane Matthew in Haiti: Looking Beyond the Disaster Narrative', *Common Dreams*, 5 October 2016, <http://commondreams.org/views/2016/10/05/hurricane-matthew-haiti-looking-beyond-disaster-narrative> [accessed 5 October 2016]

—— 2016C. 'The Anthropological Uses of Haiti: A *Longue Durée* Approach', in *The Haiti Exception: Anthropology and the Predicament of Narrative*, ed. by Alessandra Benedicty-Kokken and others (Liverpool: Liverpool University Press), pp. 15–32

——2017. 'Chronicling a Forgotten Disaster: Hurricane Matthew, Ten Months On', *Common Dreams*, 9 August 2017, <https://www.commondreams.org/views/2017/08/09/chronicling-forgotten-disaster-hurricane-matthew-ten-months> [accessed 14 August 2017]

SCHULLER, MARK, and PABLO MORALES (eds). 2012. *Tectonic Shifts: Haiti Since the Earthquake* (Sterling, VA: Kumarian Press)

SHAW, ROSALIND, and CHARLES STEWART. 1994. 'Introduction: Problematizing Syncretism', in *Syncretism/Anti-Syncretism: The Politics of Religious Synthesis*, ed. by Charles Stewart and Rosalind Shaw (London: Routledge), pp. 1–24

SLOAN, CYNTHIA. 2000. 'Caricature, Parody, and Dolls: How to Play at Deconstructing and (Re-)Constructing Female Identity in Rosario Ferré's *Papeles de Pandora*', *Pacific Coast Philology*, 35(1): 35–48

SMITH, KATHERINE. 2012. 'Atis Rezistans: Gede and the Art of Vagabondaj', in *Obeah and Other Powers: The Politics of Caribbean Religion and Healing*, ed. by Diana Paton and Maarit Forde (Durham, NC: Duke University Press), pp. 121–45

SOSA RODRÍGUEZ, ENRIQUE. 1982. *Los ñáñigos* (Havana: Casa de las Américas)

SPEAR, THOMAS C. 2015. 'Marie Chauvet: The Fortress Still Stands', in *Revisiting Marie Vieux Chauvet: Paradoxes of the Postcolonial Feminine*, ed. by Kaiama L. Glover and Alessandra Benedicty-Kokken, special issue of *Yale French Studies*, 128: 9–24

STERLING DUPREY, AWILDA. 2018. 'Lacks Criticality', dance performance at Temple University's 2018 *Reflection: Response Choreographic Commission*, Conwell Dance Theatre, Philadelphia, 21–22 September 2018

STINCHCOMB, DAWN. 2013. 'The Archetypes of the Immaterial Bodies of the African "Supernatural": Transience, Sexual Ambiguity and Santería in Contemporary Hispanic Novels', *Chasqui*, 42(2): 3–14

STRONGMAN, ROBERTO. 2008. 'Transcorporeality in Vodou', *Journal of Haitian Studies*, 14(2): 4–29

——2013. 'The Body of Vodou: Corporeality and the Location of Gender in Afro-Diasporic Religion', in *The Cross-Dressed Caribbean: Writing, Politics, Sexualities*, ed. by Maria Cristina Fumagalli, Bénédicte Ledent, and Roberto del Valle Alcalá (Charlottesville: University of Virginia Press), pp. 203–19

SUCENA, EDUARDO. 2002. *Lisboa, o fado e os fadistas*, 2nd edn (Lisbon: Vega)

TATE, CLAUDIA. 1983A. 'Conversation with Audre Lorde', in *Black Women Writers at Work* (Harpenden: Oldcastle Books), pp. 100–16

——1983B. 'Introduction', in *Black Women Writers at Work* (Harpenden: Oldcastle Books), pp. xv–xxvi

TAVARES, JOÃO MIGUEL, and RUI VIEIRA NERY. 2002. 'Personalidades como Amália Não Deixam Herdeiros', *Diário de Notícias*, 6 October 2002, pp. 14–15

TAYLOR, DIANA. 1994. 'Opening Remarks', in *Negotiating Performance: Gender, Sexuality, and Theatricality in Latin/o America*, ed. by Diana Taylor and Juan Villegas (Durham, NC: Duke University Press), pp. 1–16

TINHORÃO, JOSÉ RAMOS. 1994. *Fado: dança do Brasil, cantar de Lisboa* (Lisbon: Caminho)

TORRES-SAILLANT, SILVIO. 2006. *An Intellectual History of the Caribbean* (New York: Palgrave Macmillan)

TORTEL, CHRISTIAN. 2010. 'Kettly Mars, *Saisons sauvages*: "Nous avons besoin d'un changement de mentalité" (Kettly Mars)', *Cultures Sud: la revue en ligne des littératures sud*, <http://www.culturessud.com/contenu.php?id=166> [accessed 18 May 2012]

TRINH T. MINH-HA. 1989. *Woman, Native, Other: Writing Postcoloniality and Feminism* (Bloomington: Indiana University Press)

TROUILLOT, MICHEL-ROLPH. 1990. *Haiti: State Against Nation: The Origins and Legacy of Duvalierism* (New York: Monthly Review Press)

TURNER, VICTOR. 1969. 'Liminality and Communitas', in *The Ritual Process* (London: Routledge & Kegan Paul), pp. 94–130

—— 1994. 'El negro en el teatro cubano', *Cultura afrocubana*, ed. by Jorge Castellanos and Isabel Castellanos, 4 vols (Miami: Universal), IV, 195–263

ULYSSE, GINA ATHENA. 2015. *Why Haiti Needs New Narratives: A Post-Quake Chronicle* (Middletown, CT: Wesleyan University Press)

UNESCO. 1988–. *Oralidad: anuario para el rescate de la tradición oral en América Latina y el Caribe* (Havana: UNESCO)

VADILLO, ALICIA E. 2002. *Santería y vodú; sexualidad y homoerotismo: caminos que se cruzan sobre la narrativa cubana contemporánea* (Madrid: Biblioteca Nueva)

VASSEROT, CHRISTILLA. 1998. 'Mi cultura personal es un ajiaco: entrevista a Eugenio Hernández Espinosa', *Conjunto: Revista de Teatro Latinoamericano*, 109: 43–48

VEGA, ANA LYDIA. 1982. 'Encancaranublado', in *Encancaranublado y otros cuentos* (Havana: Casa de las Américas), pp. 11–17

—— 1990. 'Cloud Cover Caribbean', trans. by Mark McCaffrey, in *Her True True Name*, ed. by Pamela Mordecai and Betty Wilson (Oxford: Heinemann), pp. 105–11

VÉTÉ-CONGOLO, HANÉTHA. 2008. 'Sexual Pleasure and Eroticism in Nicole Cage-Florentiny's "Amours marines ou Erótico mar": Toward a Postmodern Writing of Women's Body and Sexuality', *Dalhousie French Studies*, 83: 127–39

—— 2010A. 'Book review: *Fado*, Kettly Mars', *The French Review*, 83(4): 913–14

—— 2010B. 'Love and Lovemaking in French Caribbean Women's Writing: Kettly Mars, Nicolas Cage-Florentiny and Suzanne Dracius', in *Caribbean Erotic: Poetry, Prose and Essays*, ed. by Opal Palmer Adisa and Donna Aza Weir-Soley (Leeds: Peepal Tree), pp. 302–23

VICTOR, GARY. 1990. *Clair de manbo* (Port-au-Prince: Henri Deschamps)

—— 2007. *Treize nouvelles vaudou* (Montreal: Mémoire d'encrier)

VICTOR, MARVIN. 2008. '"Fado" ou l'échappement de soi', *Le Nouvelliste*, <http://www.lenouvelliste.com/articleforprint.php?PubID=1&ArticleID=60390> [accessed 19 February 2012]

—— 2010. *Corps mêlés* (Paris: Gallimard)

VIEUX-CHAUVET, MARIE. 2005. *Amour, Colère et Folie* (Léchelle: Zellige)

—— 2009. *Love, Anger, Madness*, trans. by Rose-Myriam Réjouis and Val Vinokur (New York: Modern Library)

VITIELLO, JOËLLE. 2004. '"De l'autre côté de mes murs": le désir de l'engagement dans l'écriture de Yanick Lahens', in *Écrire en pays assiégé: Haïti: Writing Under Siege*, ed. by Marie-Agnès Sourieau and Kathleen M. Balutansky (Amsterdam: Rodopi), pp. 170–90

—— 2011. 'Douceurs et violences dans l'écriture de Kettly Mars', in *Écrits d'Haïti: perspectives sur la littérature haïtienne contemporaine (1986–2006)*, ed. by Nadève Ménard (Paris: Karthala), pp. 369–83

WALSH, JOHN P. 2014. 'Reading (in the) Ruins: Kettly Mars's *Saisons sauvages*', *Journal of Haitian Studies*, 20(1): 66–83

—— 2015. 'Haiti mon amour', in *Raoul Peck: Power, Politics, and the Cinematic Imagination*, ed. by Toni Pressley-Sanon and Sophie Saint-Just (Lanham, MD: Lexington Books), pp. 195–216

WEBB, BARBARA. 1992. *Myth and History in Caribbean Fiction: Alejo Carpentier, Wilson Harris, and Edouard Glissant* (Amherst: University of Massachusetts Press)

WEDEL, JOHAN. 2004. *Santería Healing: A Journey into the Afro-Cuban World of Divinities, Spirits, and Sorcery* (Gainesville: University Press of Florida)

WHITE, KRISTA. 2000. 'Espousing Ezili: Images of a Lwa, Reflections of the Haitian Woman', *Journal of Haitian Studies*, 5/6: 62–79

WILENTZ, GAY. 1992. *Binding Cultures* (Bloomington: Indiana University Press)

ZULMA. 2016. 'List May 2016', <http://www.zulma.fr/datas/pdf/pdf-ext-146zulma-list-may-2016-bdpdf.pdf> [accessed 18 August 2017]

——2017. 'List 2017', <http://www.zulma.fr/datas/pdf/pdf-ext-146zulma-list-2017-bdpdf.pdf> [accessed 18 August 2017]

INDEX

Abakuá 2, 5, 31, 35, 37, 44, 54, 66–67
Abbott, Elizabeth 107, 108, 110–11, 117, 119
agency 5, 6, 7, 24, 26, 32, 44, 48, 58, 61–62, 66,
    68–73, 88–102, 115, 131, 136, 146–49, 154–56, 164
Agwe (*also* Athagwe) 30, 84–85, 95, 119
Andrade, Orlando, *Mesyè Prezidan* 164–65
Anglade de Aguerrevere, Lucía 28
Antonin, Arnaud, *Zombi candidat à la présidence, ou Les
    Amours d'un zombi* 118
Arendt, Hannah 8, 115–16, 119, 127, 136
Aristide, Jean-Bertrand 106
Astles, Cariad 46
Ayorinde, Christine 12

babalao 16, 17, 19, 25, 47, 48, 50–53, 55, 56, 61, 152, 167
Baby Doc, *see* Duvalier, Jean-Claude
Balbuena Gutiérrez, Bárbara 46
Barnet, Miguel 17
Baron Samedi 15, 23, 108–13, 115, 117, 118, 127–28,
    135–36, 141
Baron-la-Croix 109–10, 119–20, 142
Bataille, Georges 8, 64–65, 144–47, 155
Baudrillard, Jean 8, 65, 144–47
Beauvoir, Max 114
Beauvoir, Rachel 135
Beauvoir, Simone de 96, 150
Belié Belcán 22, 30, 36, 90
Bell, Catherine 6, 47–48
Bellegarde-Smith, Patrick 97
    and Claudine Michel 37 n. 1
    and Claudine Michel and Marlène Racine-Toussaint
        24
    and Kate Ramsey 9 n. 7
Benedicty-Kokken, Alessandra 25–26, 46, 97, 123
Benítez Rojo, Antonio 2, 166
Bergan, Renée, and Mark Schuller, *Poto Mitan: Haitian
    Women, Pillars of the Global Economy* 24, 115
Bois Caïman 14, 24, 38 n. 18, 39 n. 34
bòkò 90, 117, 118, 119, 133, 139 n. 61, 155–56
Bolívar Aróstegui, Natalia 52, 54, 59–60, 141
bonanj 96, 101, 124
    gwobonanj 26
    tibonanj 26, 117, 167
Botting, Fred, and Scott Wilson 65
Boukman 13–14, 24
Brandon, George 11–12, 37 n. 1
Brazil 79, 101

Brene, José Ramón, *Santa Camila de La Habana Vieja*
    44
Bronfen, Elisabeth, and Sarah Webster Goodwin
    145–46
Brown, Karen McCarthy 22–23, 26, 84, 112, 117, 141
Burton, Richard D.E. 38 n. 11, 118
Butler, Judith 6, 26, 58
    'stylized repetition of acts' 46, 64, 69–72

Caballero, Rufo 45
Cabranes-Grant, Leo 44–45, 58, 67–68
Cabrera, Lydia 35, 54, 157 n. 25
Candomblé 29, 79
Cárdenas, Raúl de, *Los hijos de Ochún* 166, 167
Carfú 22, 71, 133, 147, 155
Carpentier, Alejo, *El reino de este mundo* 14, 24,
    103 n. 53
Castellanos, Isabel 18
Castellanos Llanos, Gabriela 26
Catholicism 3–5, 11–13, 15–20, 29, 31, 37, 83, 105,
    106–09, 111–12, 114, 119, 121, 123–28, 135,
    137 nn. 5 & 10, 138 nn. 30 & 33
Centeno, Elaine, *La piedra de Elliot* 44
Chancy, Myriam 84, 121, 154, 160
    Spirit of Haiti 166, 167
Changó 6, 17–20, 22, 26, 30, 32, 34, 44, 54–55, 56,
    59–60, 66, 72, 98, 141–43, 151–52, 167
Charles, Carolle 116, 128–29
Chauvet, Marie:
    Amour, Colère et Folie 7, 81, 106, 114, 120–21
        Amour 121–22, 123, 124, 127, 130, 136; *Colère*
        113–14, 121, 122–23, 124, 127, 130–32, 136,
        144, 146, 150, 154, 164; *Folie* 7, 106, 121,
        123–28, 130, 146, 165
    Les rapaces 123
Chen, Edith Wen-Chu 31
Chinese:
    in the Caribbean 19, 29–31, 147, 151
Clark, Mary Ann 25–26, 44, 50
Clark, VèVè 109
Coates, Carrol F. 109
Conway, Fred 112
Cooper, Carolyn 33
corporeality 6–7, 25–26, 31–32, 46–48, 76–77, 80–81,
    82–83, 85–92, 95–97, 101–02, 144, 159, 167, 168
    see also performance and corporeality
Courlander, Harold, and Rémy Bastien 112

creolization 3, 12, 16, 27–31, 37
Cros Sandoval, Mercedes 51, 59
Cuba 2–6, 12, 14–22, 24–37, 43–73, 79, 90–91, 98–99,
    100–01, 141–42, 159, 166–68
    literature from 2, 5–6, 14, 16–22, 25, 28–37, 43–73,
        90–91, 100, 132, 142–44, 147–56, 159, 164–65,
        166–67
Cuban Revolution 14, 44–45, 49–50
Curbelo Mezquida, Alberto 43, 49, 72

Dambalá 4
Danticat, Edwidge 160
    Breath, Eyes, Memory 97, 166, 167
    Create Dangerously: The Immigrant Artist at Work 160
    The Dew Breaker 166, 167
Davies, Catherine 44, 51
Dayan, Colin (also Joan) 24, 68, 120, 121, 122, 123,
    124, 127
De Ferrari, Guillermina 27–28
De Lauretis, Teresa 116
De Maeseneer, Rita 27
death 6, 8, 19, 20, 23–24, 30, 35, 47, 51–53, 59, 62,
    64, 66, 76, 96–102, 108, 117, 119, 127–28, 130–31,
    133–34, 161, 165, 168
    and gender 145–47, 149, 162
    and sexuality 8, 23, 64–73, 96, 115, 117, 141–56, 164
dehumanization 86, 123, 126–28, 131, 146, 154, 156,
    164–65, 168
Déita (also Deyita) 117
    Esperans Dezire 97
DeLoughrey, Elizabeth 4, 37
Desmangles, Leslie 9 n. 7, 12, 20, 37 n. 1, 112–13, 131
Desquiron, Lilas, Les Chemins de Loco-Miroir 97
Dessalines 106–08, 126
destructive masculinity 7–8, 105, 116–23, 127–36, 141,
    164
diaspora 2, 3, 4, 5, 166–69
Díaz-Quiñones, Arcadio 1, 166
dichotomy 77, 81, 121, 136, 145
    gendered 7–8, 28, 31–32, 37, 60–61, 64, 81–82,
        115–17, 119–20, 135–36, 145–46
    public versus private 31–32, 37, 60–61, 64, 72,
        85–86, 97, 119
    reason and insanity 77, 102, 123, 126–27, 140 n. 83
    uptown versus downtown 77, 79–80, 81, 82, 85,
        86–87, 90–92, 97, 101–02, 102 n. 16
    wife versus whore 58, 76–77, 82, 85, 87, 89–90, 97,
        101–02, 134, 149
dictatorship 7, 15, 28–29, 36, 72, 105–36, 145–46, 164
Diederich, Bernard, and Al Burt 117
divination 3, 13, 16, 25, 34, 47, 51, 53
Dominican Republic 13, 21–24, 27, 28–37, 71–72,
    90–91, 98–99, 100–01, 108, 117, 130, 133, 134, 142,
    147–48, 155, 165–66
    literature from 1, 2, 27, 37, 91, 98–99, 100–01, 165–66
Drewal, Margaret Thompson 26, 68

duality 6–7, 76–78, 79–102, 109, 116, 121–22, 125, 135,
    139 n. 71, 164, 167, 170 n. 17
Durand, Oswald, Choucoune 29, 33
Duvalier, François 7, 15–16, 23–24, 28, 72, 105–36,
    141, 145–46, 150, 165
    and divine status 107–12, 115
    Mémoires d'un leader du Tiers Monde 108, 111
Duvalier, Jean-Claude 15–16, 23–24, 29, 36, 39 n. 33,
    72, 105, 110, 114, 128, 129, 145–46, 156 n. 6

earthquake:
    in Haiti, 2010: 8, 159–60, 162–63, 168
    post-earthquake literature 76, 159–64
Elegguá 13
Elliott, Richard 80
emasculation 8, 35, 58, 65, 67–69, 116, 119, 123, 127–
    28, 135–36, 143, 146
eroticism 65
Ezili 7, 20, 21, 24, 30, 34, 36, 71, 83, 85, 95, 121–22, 167
    Dantò 1, 20–22, 76, 81, 83–86, 89–90, 94–97, 121,
        135, 141, 150, 165
    Freda 20–22, 76, 80, 81, 83–86, 88, 89–90, 94–97,
        99–100, 121, 135, 141
    Je Wouj 20–21, 121
    Mapiang 20, 83, 141

Fanon, Frantz 2, 111, 125, 127, 136
Felipe, Carlos, Réquiem por Yarini 44
Ferguson, James 108, 112, 119, 139 n. 64
Fernández Olmos, Marguerite 21, 22, 72
    and Lizabeth Paravisini-Gebert 3, 9 n. 8, 18, 37 n. 1,
        38 n. 5, 85, 117
Ferré, Rosario 76, 82
Foucault, Michel 65, 144–45
Fouché, Franck:
    Bouqui au paradis 109, 110, 138 n. 20
    Général Baron-la-Croix ou Le Silence masqué 8, 106,
        109–10, 117, 119–20, 124–25, 128, 129, 135, 142
Fourcand, Jean, Catéchisme de la Révolution 107, 108,
    109, 111
fracturing 76–78, 81, 85, 89, 93, 100–02, 121, 122, 123,
    149, 151, 154, 167
Francis, Donette 71
Franco, Jean 7, 82, 89, 94, 149
Fulleda, Gerardo 44, 66
    Chago de Guisa 44
Fumagalli, Maria Cristina 165

Gagá 2, 21–23, 29–31, 36–37, 71, 147, 155, 165
García, Cristina:
    The Agüero Sisters 166
    Dreaming in Cuban 166
García-Calderón, Myrna 13
Gede 1, 7, 22–24, 64, 108, 109–10, 112–14, 117, 119,
    135, 141–44
    Nibo 23, 32, 147

Geggus, David 13–14, 38 n. 15, 138 n. 26
gender 2, 3, 5, 9, 11, 24–27, 31–35, 40 n. 91, 49–73,
    81–85, 123, 156, 159, 168
  hierarchy, *see* hierarchy, gender
  and historiography 33–34, 169
  and nation 105, 107–28, 135–36
  roles 6, 23, 54, 64, 76–78, 82–85, 134, 150–54
Ginen 77, 79, 100–01, 102 n. 3, 133, 143, 150
Giral, Sergio 51
    María Antonia 43, 45, 49, 71
Glissant, Édouard 2, 34, 37
González Mandri, Flora 44
Goodwin, Sarah Webster 149–50, 153
    see also Bronfen, Elisabeth, and Sarah Webster Goodwin
Gordon, Avery 106
Grann Brijit 23
Gray, Lila Ellen 79, 81
Guadeloupe 30, 37
Guerlac, Suzanne 146

Habermas, Jürgen 146
Hagedorn, Katherine 51, 62
Haiti 2, 3, 5, 6–8, 13–16, 20–24, 28–36, 71–72, 76–102,
    105–36, 141–44, 146–47, 149–51, 153–56, 159–68
  literature from 6–8, 21, 29, 33, 76–102, 105–36, 142,
    144, 146, 149–51, 154–56, 159–64
Haitian Revolution 13–15, 20, 22, 24, 83, 92, 106, 136
hembrismo 53–65, 148, 152–53
Henri Christophe 107, 108
Hernández Espinosa, Eugenio 105
    María Antonia 6, 19–20, 25, 43–73, 86–87, 88, 100,
      132, 142–44, 147–56
    María de los cuchillos 45
    El masigüere 45
    Obá y Shangó 43, 60
    Ochún y las cotorras 43
    Odebí el cazador 43, 60
    Oyá Ayawá 43
    Quiquiribú Mandinga 43
Herrera, Georgina, 'Conversación con María Antonia
    (cuarenta años después)' 6, 45–46, 57, 59, 61,
    69–72, 143, 156
heterogeneity 5, 9, 28, 34, 37
hierarchy:
  gender 5–6, 8, 11, 24–27, 31–32, 33–35, 50–73, 76,
    78–96, 99–102, 105, 115–36, 149–56, 161, 169
  of power 15, 48, 77–78, 80–83, 105, 113, 121–28,
    136, 148, 155
  racial 4, 5–6, 12, 15, 124, 151, 157 n. 34
  and religion 12, 48, 50–53, 57, 61, 68–73, 136
historiography 6, 20, 31–34, 169
  and oral testimony 33–34, 43, 159–60, 162
Holton, Kimberly DaCosta 80
homogeneity 2, 4, 28, 89
hooks, bell 116
Hu-DeHart, Evelyn 30

Hurricane Maria 168
hybridity 3, 4, 6, 11, 12, 27–31, 37, 78–79, 101, 151

Ibeyi 98, 157 n. 25, 166–67
identity 3, 167
  African-descended 5, 37, 70, 79, 101, 106–07, 156, 159
  Caribbean 1–4, 9, 27–28, 37, 79, 91, 101, 156, 159,
    166–67, 168–69
  gender 2, 3, 7, 13, 37, 67–73, 76–78, 81–92, 98, 154,
    156, 159
  national 2, 4, 5, 9, 59, 105, 115, 167
  religious 2, 3, 11, 37, 89, 159, 167–69
  sexual 2, 3, 7, 37, 76–78, 82–102, 134, 154, 156, 159
Ifá 16, 18, 25, 29, 37, 47, 48, 50–53, 69
Ikú 6, 51–52, 62, 64–66, 141–44, 148, 152
Indiana, Rita:
    La estrategia de Chochueca 165
    La mucama de Omicunlé 1–2, 11, 27, 37, 91, 98–99,
      100, 142, 165–66
    and Los Misterios, 'Da pa lo do' 165
    Nombres y animales 165
    Papi 165
initiation:
  in Santería 16, 25, 37, 47, 57, 64, 74 n. 58, 143–44
  sexual 50, 63, 80, 88, 93
  in Vodou 23, 36, 80, 143–44, 167
iyanifá 16, 25

James, Conrad 50, 51–52, 59, 67
Jean-Charles, Régine Michelle 100, 101, 120, 121, 122,
    129, 130–31, 132, 150, 153, 155, 161, 164
Johnson, Paul Christopher 107, 108, 111
Joseph, Régine Isabelle 119

Kalisa, Chantal 120
Kaplan, Caren 36
Klein, Naomi 168, 170 n. 39
Kristeva, Julia 7, 8, 94, 96, 149

Laferrière, Dany:
    Pays sans chapeau 166, 167
Lagos-Pope, María Inés 82
Laguerre, Michel 8, 13, 114
Lahens, Yanick:
    Dans la maison du père 81
    Tante Résia et les dieux 81
Laroche, Maximilien 124
Larrier, Renée 122
Lasirèn 1–2, 84–85, 101
Latortue, Régine 81, 82
Leconte, Frantz-Antoine, *La République* 109–10,
    137 n. 18
Legba 126
León Rojas, Gloria María, *Haití en la memoria* 166
Lescot, Anne, and Laurence Magloire, *Of Men and
    Gods (Des hommes et dieux)* 103 n. 49

Lora, Erminio 138 n. 30
Lorde, Audre 82, 84, 90, 101
Lucumí 17, 22, 30, 39 n. 38, 51–53
Lumsden, Ian 50
Lwa 22 Os 108

machismo 19–20, 35, 53–61, 63–65, 68–73, 148–49,
    153–54, 156
Macoutes 15, 23, 28, 29, 72, 90, 105, 110, 112–15,
    117–24, 128–36, 141–42, 150, 167
madrina 10 n. 14, 16, 34, 45, 46–48, 52, 56, 57, 58,
    61–63, 65
Makandal 13–14, 24, 92, 103 n. 53
manbo 4, 16, 24, 28, 32, 36, 71, 95, 114, 118–19, 133–35,
    147, 155
marasa 77, 85–86, 123–24, 164, 165, 166–67, 170 n. 30
    twa 7, 77, 78, 96–102, 124, 164, 165
marginalization 5, 11, 13–16, 20, 30–31, 37, 45, 56–57,
    58–65, 67–73, 77, 82–83, 85–102, 106–07, 149–56,
    159, 162–64, 168
Mars, Kettly 81, 105, 130
    Fado 6–7, 21, 76–102, 140 n. 83, 142, 144, 149–51,
        154–55, 162, 164
    Aux frontières de la soif 76, 163–64
    Kasalé 76, 84, 95–96, 100
    'Lobo' 97
    Saisons sauvages 7, 106–07, 110–11, 114, 117–18, 120,
        128–32, 134–36, 142, 144, 146, 149–50, 154
    'Et tant pis pour la mort' 85
Martelly, Michel 106
Martiatu, Inés María 44, 49, 50, 53, 54, 55, 59, 64, 143
Martínez-Echazábal, Lourdes 30
Martínez-San Miguel, Yolanda 27, 37
Marty, Anne 127
masculinity 8, 18, 23, 26, 31, 55–56, 58–61, 105, 115–
    22, 127–28, 132–34, 136, 144
    violent 6, 49–56, 67–73, 136
    see also destructive masculinity
Matibag, Eugenio 9 n. 2
McAlister, Elizabeth 38 n. 18, 39 n. 34
Menéndez, Lázara 25, 56, 57, 60
mestizaje 4, 12, 27–31
Métraux, Alfred 21
Metresilí 21, 165
Michel, Claudine 12, 100, 143
    see also Bellegarde-Smith, Patrick, and Claudine
        Michel
Miranda-Rodríguez, Edgardo 168
Montero, Mayra 5, 16, 28, 31–34, 37, 43, 105, 165
    Como un mensajero tuyo 2, 17–20, 28–30, 32–34, 37,
        43, 142–43, 151, 166
    Del rojo de su sombra 2, 21–24, 28–31, 32–33, 36,
        71–72, 90–91, 100, 117, 119, 130, 133–34, 142,
        147, 155, 166
    La trenza de la hermosa luna 2, 29, 33, 36, 114

Tú, la oscuridad 2, 29–30, 34–35, 37
Morejón, Nancy 44
motherhood 7, 8, 17, 20, 24, 76–78, 82–85, 93–102,
    103 n. 58, 121, 129–30, 132, 134, 141–42, 144,
    149–52, 156, 157 n. 25, 162, 168
Mühleisen, Susanne 33
Munro, Martin 139 n. 71, 160, 162, 165
Murphy, Joseph 32
music 27, 88, 100
    fado 6, 76–77, 78–81, 87, 88, 90, 92–93, 100, 101
    in religious contexts 25, 33, 46–47, 61–62, 67–69,
        80, 161
    sacred drum 25, 35, 47, 67, 80, 161
myth 6, 11, 21, 22, 30, 31, 33–35, 36, 43, 60, 79, 108,
    109, 121

N'Zengou-Tayo, Marie-José 115, 118
nation 7, 105, 107–15, 120, 122, 125–26, 127–28,
    136
Néréstant, Micial 119

Obatalá 13
Ochún 4, 6, 12, 13, 17–20, 22, 34, 44, 46–48, 51, 55,
    56–62, 64–73, 98, 101, 141–43, 148, 150, 152–53,
    156, 167
Ogou 22, 83, 107
    Chango 22
    Feray 21–22, 32, 147
Ogún 18, 22, 61
Oliver, Kelly 82, 94
Olodumare 16
Olofi 17
Olokún 1, 17–18, 26, 27, 91, 98–99
oral history 33–35, 60, 160, 162
Orcel, Makenzy 161, 162
    Les Immortelles 162–64, 165
    L'Ombre animale 161–62, 163–64
Orisha-Oko 99
Orner, Peter, and Evan Lyon, Lavil: Life, Love, and
    Death in Port-au-Prince 160
Ortiz, Fernando 12
Orula 16, 18, 25, 48, 51, 52
Otero, Solimar 27
oungan 15, 16, 29, 31, 108, 114–15
Oyá 141–42

padrino 10 n. 14, 16, 17, 30, 34
Palo Monte 5, 37
Papa Doc, see Duvalier, François
patakí 6, 17–20, 30, 33, 34, 43–44, 50, 51, 52, 55,
    59–60, 70, 72
patriarchy 5, 6, 7, 20, 23–24, 25, 29, 31–32, 33–35,
    44, 49–53, 56–63, 65–73, 76–78, 81–88, 93–96,
    99–102, 116, 121–22, 142, 144, 147–50, 153–56,
    159, 161, 169

Peck, Raoul, *Assistance mortelle* 163, 164
performance 46–49, 62–63, 72, 148, 168
  and corporeality 25, 44, 46–49, 64, 67–73, 168
  of gender 6, 25–27, 40 n. 91, 44, 48–49, 60–62, 64–73
  and liminality 47–48, 63–65, 70–73
  of possession 6, 25–27, 46–49, 61–63, 64, 67–73, 108, 148–49
  and repetition 6, 46, 53, 63–64, 69–73
  of ritual 3, 5, 6, 44, 47–49, 65, 72
phallologocentric framework 82, 88–92, 94–96, 99, 102, 149
Pluchon, Pierre 92
poisoning 77, 90–92, 97–98, 101, 150
possession 6, 16, 17, 25–27, 32, 40 n. 91, 46–48, 57–59, 61–63, 64–65, 67–73, 108, 148–49, 152, 156
postcolonial 2, 3, 12, 27, 106, 125
power 5, 7, 26, 32, 37, 48–49, 61–63, 71–73, 78, 84, 87–90, 107, 109–11, 115–22, 125–27, 130–31, 135–36, 146–47, 155–56, 165, 168
Pressley-Sanon, Toni 97, 99
prostitution 6, 8, 54–55, 57–60, 66, 68, 72, 76, 77–78, 80–102, 134, 144, 146, 149–54, 156, 162–64, 168
Protestantism 3, 9 n. 13, 16, 31, 39 n. 34, 105, 106, 111–12, 114, 137 n. 5
Puerto Rico 4, 13, 79, 100, 164, 168
  literature from 1–2, 4, 12, 13, 14–16, 17–22, 24–37, 76, 82, 90–91, 100–01, 142, 147–48, 151, 155, 164, 166, 168
Puri, Shalini 28

Queiroga, Perdigão, *Fado: história d'uma cantadeira* 102 n. 16

race 5–6, 15, 27, 59–60, 70, 92, 168
Ramsey, Kate 9 n. 7, 15, 117
rape 6, 8, 64, 68, 77–78, 83, 86, 87, 91, 93, 94, 113–14, 121–22, 129–34, 140 n. 79, 142, 144, 146, 150, 153–56, 161, 164
resistance 160
  against hegemony 6, 8, 11, 15, 24–25, 48, 60–73, 76, 78, 82–85, 87–102, 122, 125, 156, 162, 169
  through religion 5, 6, 8, 11–16, 24, 32, 60–62, 69–73, 83–85, 89, 94–99, 101–02, 105, 113, 115, 118–20, 125, 135–36, 156, 159, 169
Rich, Adrienne 78
Richman, Karen 108, 111
Rizk, Beatriz 48
Robles Carrasquillo, Huáscar, *Puertos príncipes: temblemos todos* 164
Rodríguez Coronel, Rogelio 33
Roumain, Jacques, *Gouverneurs de la rosée* 9 n. 4, 83, 139 n. 65

sacrifice 8, 16, 36, 65–73, 119, 144, 153–56
Saint-Domingue 8, 13–14, 92

Saldaña, Excilia, *Kele Kele* 20, 43
Sanfancón 2, 18–19, 30, 151
Santa Bárbara 18–19
Santos-Febres, Mayra 13
  boat people 1–2, 37, 100
  Huracanada 168
  Sirena Selena vestida de pena 13, 16, 27, 37, 100–01
Sartre, Jean-Paul 136
Scharfman, Ronnie 119, 120–23
Schechner, Richard 6, 26, 47
Schuller, Mark 160, 162–63, 164
sea 1, 2, 13, 17, 27, 37, 79, 91, 99–101, 162
sexuality 5, 7, 8, 9, 19–20, 23–24, 32, 60–61, 64, 69–73, 76–78, 80–81, 82–102, 105, 118, 121, 129–36, 141–56, 159, 168
Shirley, James, *Death the Leveller* 149–50, 157 n. 30
Siete Ponencias Africanas 4, 12, 13
Sikán 31, 35, 54, 67
Sloan, Cynthia 76, 94
Sogbo 131, 134–35
Sosa Rodríguez, Enrique 35
state 5, 7–8, 14–16, 23, 31–32, 36, 105–07, 111–28, 136, 141, 146, 154, 163
Sterling Duprey, Awilda 168
Stinchcomb, Dawn 13
Strongman, Roberto 46, 85
subjectivity 7, 46, 64, 72, 76, 79, 81–85, 88–102
Sucena, Eduardo 81
syncretism 9 n. 11, 11, 12

Tate, Claudia 92, 98
Taylor, Diana 47
terror 8, 113, 115–36, 141, 146, 150, 164
theatre 6, 7, 26, 38 n. 24, 43–73, 106, 109–10, 119–20, 124–25, 128, 129, 135, 142–43, 148–49, 150, 151–54, 156, 168
Ti Jean Petró (*also* Ti Jan Petwo) 21
Tonton Macoutes, *see* Macoutes
Toro Belecou 21–22, 30, 34, 36
Torres-Saillant, Silvio 27
transculturation 9 n. 11, 12, 27–28
travel 36–37, 92
Trinh T. Minh-ha 7, 96, 150
Trinidad and Tobago 137 n. 5
Trouillot, Michel-Rolph 115, 119, 129
Trujillo Molina, Rafael Leónidas 108
twins 109
  see also Ibeyi, *marasa and marasa twa*

Ulysse, Gina Athena 160

Vadillo, Alicia 22, 35
Vega, Ana Lydia, 'Encancaranublado' 4, 11, 12, 37
Vété-Congolo, Hanétha 77, 85, 99
vèvè 20, 133–34, 155–56

Victor, Gary:
  Clair de manbo 118–19, 130, 133–35, 142, 155, 164
  'Nuit de chance' 118
  Zombi candidat à la présidence, ou Les Amours d'un
    zombi 118
Victor, Marvin:
  Corps mêlés 162, 165
Vieux-Chauvet, Marie, *see* Chauvet, Marie
violence 53–73, 76–78, 93, 100, 113–28, 135–36,
    140 n. 79, 144, 146–47
  political 7–8, 9, 113–36, 146, 161, 164–65
  psychological 7, 77–78, 116, 118, 122–23, 131, 134,
    136
  sexual 7–8, 9, 53, 64–69, 72–73, 77, 83–84, 86,
    94, 113–14, 121–23, 129–36, 141, 144, 150–51,
    153–56, 161, 164, 168
  see also rape
Virgin Mary 121–22, 149, 165
  of Altagracia 4
  of Caridad del Cobre 4, 12, 17, 19, 46, 59, 61

Mater Salvatoris 20, 83
Our Lady of Czestochowa 20, 83
Our Lady of Sorrows 20
of Regla 17
Vitiello, Joëlle 77, 81, 84

Walsh, John 120
Webb, Barbara 34
White, Krista 90
women:
  participation in religious contexts 5, 11, 20, 24–27,
    31–32, 35, 60–64, 68–73, 115, 169
  in society 6, 20, 49–73, 76–102, 115, 122, 134, 149–
    50, 154, 159, 161, 168–69

Yemayá 1, 6, 13, 17–20, 22, 27, 30, 32, 34, 44, 52, 84,
  98–99, 101, 141, 148, 151–52, 167

Zaka 22, 112–14
zonbi 3, 101, 117, 147

Lightning Source UK Ltd.
Milton Keynes UK
UKHW030707050619

343806UK00004B/34/P